Developing the Amazon

DEVELOPING
THE AMAZON

Emilio F. Moran

INDIANA UNIVERSITY PRESS
Bloomington

Manufactured in the United States of America

Library of Congress Cataloging in Publication Data
Moran, Emilio F.
    Developing the Amazon.
    Bibliography   p.
    Includes index.
    1. Anthropo-geography—Brazil.   2. Anthropo-
geography—Amazon Valley.   3. Agriculture—
Amazon Valley.   4. Frontier and pioneer life—
Amazon Valley.   5. Amazon Valley—Description and
travel.   I. Title.
GF532.B7M67   304.2'0981'1   80-8382
ISBN 0-253-14564-3   1 2 3 4 5 85 84 83 82 81

Contents

Figures

Tables

Preface

The Amazon, the world's largest rain forest, was opened to farmers, miners, ranchers, and other developers when the Transamazon Highway was built in 1970. This book explores the impact of some of these new activities upon the rain forest and its inhabitants, particularly the activities of homesteaders, who came on the heels of road construction crews.

The homesteading programs associated with the Transamazon Highway were predicted by some experts to be the acid test of the potential of the humid tropics for intensive agriculture. Never before had such vast capital and human resources been mobilized to create a small farm sector in tropical lowlands and planned communities to provide needed shelter and services. To the surprise of many observers, four years after its inception, the government announced that the effort had failed, and that government incentives would begin to favor large-scale developers rather than homesteaders.

I was engaged in research in one of the new farm communities along the Transamazon Highway when the policy change was announced. The government claimed that the homestead program had been too expensive, and that production had been low. Ecologists took the failure as proof that the environment could not support intensive cultivation. Political economists took it as another example of the displacement of peasants by capitalism. In an effort to evaluate the "failure" claimed by the government, and accepted by so many, I have looked into the possible relevance of environmental constraints, such as poor soils and excessive rainfall; management constraints, such as use of land, labor and capital; cultural constraints, such as knowledge of resources and personal attitudes; and social constraints, such as the absence of community organization/leadership and social class differences.

The examination of these various constraints to agricultural performance helped me establish the fact that some strategies had succeeded, and that the government's action to reduce support of homesteading may have been premature. The analysis found herein shows that among farmers there was significant variation in their ability to recognize and use resources, in managerial ability, and in overall farm productivity. In addition, these differences were found to be associated with the previous residential mobility and the work experience of the homesteaders.

The development of an agricultural sector can occur only by making adjustments to micro-level variations in habitat and socio-economic conditions. However, the highly centralized structure of the Brazilian bureaucracy is unable to process micro-level inputs, so it aggregates the results without regard for representativeness, with the consequence that differential conditions and performance are hidden from view. This study shows the need to include micro-level analyses in the planning and evaluation of projects in the Amazon. In this, the first volume to document the differential performance of homesteaders along the Transamazon Highway, I make a strong plea to stop thinking of one Amazon, but to recognize the presence of many, highly diverse Amazons.

The tendency to view the Amazon as homogeneous has profoundly affected both research and policy-making. Most of the evidence available is at the micro-level. Researchers and policy-makers alike have tended to take micro-level data to generate macro-level explanations, which gloss over variations, and which obscure differential habitat productivity and human performance. Given the absence of systematic data collecting to assure a region-wide representative sample of areas, macro-level analysis stands on shaky ground. The ambiguities that have entered into our understanding of the Amazon as a result of premature attempts to integrate micro- and macro-levels are discussed in the last chapter.

More and more researchers now acknowledge the heterogeneity of the Amazonian rain forest. Vickers (1980), Hames (1980), and Beckerman (1980) shed new light on the availability-of-protein debate by documenting variation. Fearnside (1978) did likewise in studying carrying capacity in the Transamazon. The Amazon is currently the focus, not only of major development efforts, but also of active research programs. This intense interest is reflected in the proliferation of scholarly meetings focusing on the Amazon. The first such conference, which surveyed the natural resources of the area, was held in Brazil in 1966 (Lent 1967). The seven volumes of those proceedings have become a fundamental guide to research. A second conference was held at the University of Florida in 1973 (Wagley 1974), with an emphasis on the potential impact of highways and development projects on the human populations. Two conferences at the University of Wisconsin in 1977 and 1978 focused on the impact of current activities on the aboriginal populations of the Amazon (Stark and McDonald, forthcoming). In 1979 the University of Cambridge in England hosted a conference that explored the ecological and social impact of colonization in Amazonia (Scazzocchio, forthcoming). Conferences are being planned already at Paris and at the University of Florida for the 1980–82 period. The increasing frequency with which these conferences are taking place is a simple but telling indicator of the interest in and the rapid generation of new data on the region. I wish to thank the organizers of the Florida, Wisconsin, and Cambridge conferences for inviting me to participate. The exchange of information was always stimulating, and much of it has influenced the views I have developed in this book.

The approach I have taken is best described as cultural ecological. In other words, my concern is to explain the interactions between a human population and its habitat. Unlike the majority of existing studies on Amazonian populations, which deal with communities that have traditions going back for many generations, this book deals with the first stages of new and, to some degree, artificial communities. For this reason it has become necessary to include considerable descriptive material that will alert the reader to the particularities of the setting within which the population studied operated. It has also been necessary because this book is the first one to document the settlement and performance of the homesteaders who came to the Transamazon Highway. Available accounts have dealt with general policy issues but are not based on extended fieldwork among the homesteaders (e.g., Cardoso and Müller 1977; Mahar 1979) or are brief articles in professional journals. It is my hope that colleagues Nigel Smith (Worldwatch Institute), Philip Fearnside (Institute for Amazonian Research), and others who have also done fieldwork will publish their field data on the colonization of the Transamazon Highway in extended volumes. Whenever possible I have contrasted the results of their research with those obtained in my study. Readers may wish to consult their cited works.

Field research for this book took place in three separate trips—one in 1972, another in 1973–74, and the most recent in 1976–77. The first expedition was made possible by an NIMH small grant (MH #22581–01), the second by a Social Science Research Council Fellowship and supplementary funds from the Tropical South American Program at the University of Florida. Data analysis was facilitated during 1974–75 by grants from the National Institutes of Mental Health (MH #58493–01) and the Social Science Research Council. The third field trip was made possible by a research/travel grant from the Council for the International Exchange of Scholars (Fulbright-Hays). The author thanks all these funding agencies for their assistance, but none of them should be held responsible for the views espoused herein.

My intellectual debts are owed to many who have encouraged, stimulated, critiqued, and shared their thoughts with me over the years. My interest in the Amazon was originally sparked by Prof. Charles Wagley. Over the years I have benefited from his scholarly insights into the region and his warm friendship. This book is dedicated to him in acknowledgement of his contribution to Amazonian studies in general, and to this research in particular. Profs. William Vickers, Anthony Stocks, Daniel Gross, William Denevan, Nigel Smith, Donald Sawyer, Stephen Bunker,

Charles Wood, Philip Fearnside, Tony Seeger, William Carter, Solon Kimball, Raymond Crist, and many others, whom I cannot cite due to space considerations, have helped me formulate my ideas through their collegial friendship and critical comments. Whatever is of merit in the discussions of agriculture and resource management owes a great deal to Profs. Hugh Popenoe, Victor Green, Victor Carlisle, Ítalo Claudio Falesi, Pedro Sanchez, and W. W. McPherson, who have assisted me in connecting the concerns of the social sciences to those of the agricultural sciences. I am also grateful to the many ecologists who have taught me to appreciate the exquisite complexity of the rain forest: Ariel Lugo, Sam Snedacker, Jack Ewel, Howard Odum, Joshua Dickinson III, Herbert Shubert, Carl Jordan, Ernesto Medina, Rafael Herrera, and last, but not least, Harald Sioli.

In Brazil I have had the good fortune of always finding a large and open community of friends and scholars. The respective directors of the Museu Paraense Emilio Goeldi, the Agronomy Institute (IPEAN/EMBRAPA), the Center for Amazonian Studies (NAEA), and the Anthropology Department at the Federal University of Pará, and the National Institute of Amazonian Research (INPA) gave me continuous support in my expeditions and permitted me to share my preliminary insights in technical seminars and informal discussions. I beg the forgiveness of the numerous staff members of the above institutes for not acknowledging each and every one of them by name. Their friendship and help are not forgotten. I am grateful for the welcome of the anthropology community in Brazil, in particular, Roberto da Matta, and Otavio Guilherme Velho of the National Museum at Rio de Janeiro; Roberto Cardoso de Oliveira, Gentil Martins Dias, Alcida Ramos, Kenneth Taylor, and Julio Cesar Mellatti of the University of Brasilia; Samuel Sá and Napoleão Figuereido of the Federal University of Pará; Mario Simões, Expedito Arnaud, and the late Eduardo Galvão of the Museu Goeldi in Belem. Dr. Antonio Vizeu, Vice-Rector of the Federal University of Pará, and his wife, Celia, became like father and mother to me and my wife, and we look back to their open arms as a reason for our love and optimism about the potential of the Amazon Basin.

In the course of writing this book over the past three years I have been encouraged by many people. Many of them have been acknowledged above. Profs. Ivan Karp and Dennis Conway of Indiana University helped me formulate my ideas concerning levels of analysis and have proved to be always stimulating sounding boards and friends. I also wish to thank Robert Cook, anthropology editor at Indiana University Press, for securing a superior set of reviewers, whose extensive comments led to substantial changes that greatly improved the final version of the manuscript. Rita Brown, Mary Vaughan, and Penny Shaneyfelt typed many versions of the manuscript as it took shape through the years.

Finally, I wish to acknowledge the contributions of Millicent Fleming-

Moran and the people of the Transamazon Highway. Millicent worked alongside me for the year-long research of 1973–74. Her skills as an anthropologist and as a person enriched me and all around her. She has commented on early drafts of this manuscript, with remarkable insights each time. Her master's thesis is the basis of much of Chapter 10, and her imprint may be found throughout this research. The homesteading farmers were a real surprise to me. My presence among them must have seemed slightly odd to many of them, but instead of distrust I found openness, friendship, and assistance. In return, I hope this study shows that small farmers can and do succeed despite erratic support from the government. There is much about conservation, about farming in the Amazon, about courage and hope that one can learn from these men and women who dared enter the forest to find a new life for their families. It is my hope that the government will look again towards these people, rather than towards large-scale developers alone, as appropriate managers of selected areas of the vast Amazonian forest.

Developing the Amazon

The Amazon Basin: Problems and Potential of a Vast Rain Forest

Introduction

The vast Amazon tropical forest of South America calls to mind a verdant emptiness, broken only by the sounds of beautiful birds, howling monkeys, the sleek movement of jaguars, and the presence of still "wild" Indians. In 1970 the vast uplands, commonly known as *terra firme*, were opened up by the Transamazon Highway to farmers, ranchers, miners, and other entrepreneurs.[1] Before this time, human occupation of the Amazon region was concentrated in the flood plain (*várzea*) because of the richness of the aquatic resources, its alluvial soils, and the ease of transportation. Until construction of the highway, the Amazonian terra firme (98% of the whole basin) remained virtually protected from the impact of outsiders due to the difficulty of entering it by way of the rivers. Today, however, three thousand kilometers of the Transamazon link up with the north-south Belem-Brasilia and Cuiabá-Santarém Highways (see Figure 1.1). In addition, the Perimeter Road will eventually circle along Brazil's 12,967 kilometers of Amazonian frontiers. Consciences of many people world-wide have been stirred by these events, which open the largest rain forest on earth to widespread deforestation and could have serious consequences on the world's hydrologic cycle, climate, the rich life of the largest forest on earth, and the well-being of Indians and landless peasants. This book explores the impact of some of these activities, particularly the activities of homesteaders that entered the Transamazon on the heels of road construction crews engaged in the construction of the Transamazon Highway in Brazil.

These roads, built explicitly to integrate the Amazonian region into Brazil's economy, were foreseen in the geopolitical writings of Brazilian military officers (e.g., Couto e Silva 1957). Until 1970, Brazil's intense interest in the Amazon was not manifest in effective forms of direct control. Indeed, the Amazon looked more towards Europe and North America, with whom most of its trade took place. Efforts to interna-

1

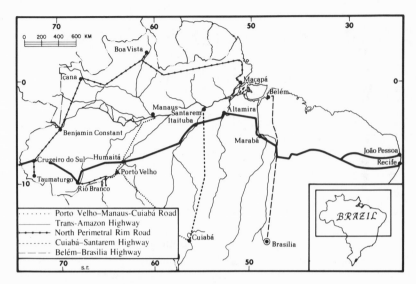

Fig. 1.1   The Amazon Region and Its Highways
Source: Wagley 1974:292
N.B. Only 200 kilometers of the North Peri-
metral Rim Road was completed by the end
of 1979, west from Macapá. A short stretch
east from Boa Vista also exists.

tionalize the Amazon in the 1940s and 1950s brought about a vigorous
reaction from Brazilian leaders and may have served as a catalyst for the
penetration of the Amazon by roads and colonization.[2] After spending
more than US$500 million in four short years in the Transamazon ven-
ture, Brazil began negotiations for a Treaty of Amazonian cooperation
with other South American nations. The treaty was signed in June 1978
and aims at promoting cooperation in the development of health services,
telecommunications, tourism, river traffic, frontier trade, and knowledge
about conservation and development of the region. The Amazon Pact
allows Brazil to become the center of gravity for an international conglom-
erate in which it holds an upper hand—because of the vastness of
Brazil's Amazonian holdings and because of its current industrial super-
iority. Brazil is years ahead of neighboring countries in the completion of
roads that penetrate into the Amazon and permit the entrance of population from anywhere in Brazil and the exit of resources to the industrial
heart of Brazil at São Paulo.[3]

There has been a serious gap between good intentions and execution;
there is more patriotic spirit than adequate knowledge in the current thrust
to conquer the Amazon and integrate it into Brazil economically and politically.[4] The gap has caused authors to predict the conversion of this

"green hell" or "counterfeit paradise" into a "red desert." The effect of these dire predictions has been to attract world-wide interest and to stimulate scientific investigation.

The Amazon Basin has become an important focus of research in the past two decades. This increased interest may be partially attributed to initiatives by South American governments in the economic development of the region and recognition by scientists that such economic activities may be premature. Fear of ecologically irreversible damage, loss of species not yet known, ethnic decimation of aboriginal peoples due to contact and disease, and conflict over the available resources in the frontier areas are among the relevant concerns of biological and social scientists in the basin.

Problems and Potential

Tropical rain forests are among the most extensive environments on the face of the earth, occupying over 700 million hectares (1 hectare=2.5 acres) world-wide. Of all the rain forests, the Amazon basin is the largest, occupying 557 million hectares—compared with 124 million hectares remaining in Asia or 82 million hectares in Africa (UNESCO 1978:22). The Brazilian Amazon includes 362 million hectares of rain forest. While it seems incomprehensible that this world-wide belt of equatorial green could ever be threatened, a number of ecologists have suggested that by the end of this century the Amazon rain forest may vanish (see Denevan 1973; Gómez-Pompa 1972). Already 20 percent of the Amazon forest has been cut and only about one-third of the African and Asian rain forests still stand (UNESCO 1978).

The biological resources of the Amazon are rich and varied. Despite its apparent homogeneity, the Amazon contains a large variety of habitats discussed in some detail in Chapter 2 and in Pires (1978) and Denevan (1976). Considerable debate exists over the fragility and/or resiliency of the Amazon (cf. Odum and Pigeon 1970; Farnworth and Golley 1974). Goodland (1980) has suggested that development activities should be deflected to the *cerrado* (central plateau) of Central Brazil, which he characterizes as robust, resilient, and familiar to Brazilians. The Amazon, on the other hand, he characterizes as fragile, intractable, and generally unfamiliar. It is unlikely that such deflection can be effective. The cerrado has been the object of much attention and occupation since the construction of Brasilia began in the 1950s. At that time ignorance of the cerrado was comparable to ignorance about the Amazon environment. Since that time efforts have been made to overcome this gap in knowledge, and a considerable literature has been generated (Briquet 1976; Ferri 1963, 1971, 1976; Goodland and Ferri 1979). A cerrado development deflection offers only a temporary solution to the need to generate more knowledge about the natural resources of the basin before undertaking developmental activities.

Until 1974 insufficient evidence was available to permit adequate evaluation of Amazonian resources along the minimal lines recommended by UNESCO (1972). When the Transamazon Highway was begun the knowledge base was fragmentary and certainly insufficient for such a mammoth undertaking. Natural resource maps at a scale of 1 to 5 million were available but too generalized to permit accurate land use planning. A major breakthrough came with the systematic survey of the Amazon carried out by Projeto Radar da Amazônia (RADAM) using sideways-looking radar. Publication of that survey began in 1974 and continues to this day.

The questions that most trouble ecological scientists about current activities are those of large-scale deforestation, the establishment of cattle ranches, and potentially irreversible desertification. The extent of deforestation is based more often on estimates and opinions than on solid data. LANDSAT images have helped, but the available figures include a large area of scrubland (cerrado) from central Brazil, and it is not possible to provide data specific to the rain forest. Research on the effects of deforestation gives cause for concern: species extinction, soil erosion and compaction, destruction of a nearly closed nutrient cycle, and climatic change to name but a few.[5] The expansion of cattle ranches from the Brazilian plateau into the rain forest is among the major causes of deforestation. Cattle ranches have enjoyed unusually favorable incentives in Brazil: interest-free loans with a two-year grace period, application of personal and corporate tax liability toward capitalization of ranches, and minimal control over speculative land sales. Economic benefit from the ranches remains undemonstrated, however, and doubts about the policies have begun to be documented (Fearnside 1979b; Hecht, forthcoming). The evidence for desertification is thin, although this may be happening in areas, like the upper Rio Negro, which are extremely poor to start with.

Not only is the future of the forests threatened, so are the lives of its original human inhabitants. Anthropologists have suggested that the reduction of the forests threatens the way of life and even the biological survival of the people who have lived there for thousands of years (Meggers 1971; Davis 1977). Amazonian development projects have begun to have negative consequences upon the aboriginal population. The decimation of Brazilian Indians in the sixteenth and seventeenth centuries (Hemming 1978) is being repeated today as isolated groups fall ill to Western diseases soon after contact is made (Baruzzi et al. 1977). This loss is devastating, not only on humanistic grounds, but also because the aboriginal population appears to have complex knowledge of micro-zones and has adjusted to local resources (Reichel-Dolmatoff 1976). Depopulation and relocation lead to loss of an expertise that may be crucial to the future of the rain forest environment and that of humans who may depend on it. A summary of the native forms of resource use is found in Chapter 3 and in Meggers (1971).

A number of observers have noted that the social impacts of development have not been absent from Amazonian projects. At least eight Indian groups are affected by mining projects. Even more are affected by the agropastoral advance of frontiersmen. The Brazilian Constitution guarantees the right of Amazonians to the land, but enforcement has been lax. Brazilian political leaders and planners like to use the phrase "the demographically empty Amazon" to justify the thrust of current efforts—thereby ignoring the more than 3 million Amazonian creoles and 150,000 Indians who live there. Once the decision was made to build the Transamazon Highway, the Indian protection service (FUNAI) and associated anthropologists were asked to produce impact assessments and policy recommendations regarding aboriginal groups likely to be affected. This move was too late to influence decisions on whether, and where, to build. The rights of Indians to the land have tended to be imprecisely defined and periodically reinterpreted—always to the Indians' detriment—an approach reminiscent of that taken in North America. Whereas the creation of a reservation for an Indian group is the subject of prolonged parliamentary debates, cattle ranches as large as 500,000 hectares are being established with fiscal incentives along the margins of the Santarém-Cuiabá Highway (Davis 1979).

Aims of This Book

This study is primarily concerned with two questions: What are the consequences of various forms of resource use? and What is the potential of the Amazon Basin for intensive agriculture as implied by the differential performance of the Transamazon homesteaders? Despite widely reported views that have seen attempts at agriculture in the Amazon Basin as failures, this analysis will show that both success and failure have taken place—and that it is possible to account for the environmental, social, and cultural factors responsible for these differences. Aboriginal, colonial and pre–1970 approaches to resource use helped shape the adaptive strategies of the Amazonian populations (cf. Moran 1974) and give us a measure against which to measure the performance of the homesteading population and evaluate Amazonian agricultural potential.

The impact of the Western world on Brazilian Indians has been documented by Hemming (1978), Wagley (1977), and Denevan (1976). The conflict between ranchers or multinationals and the rights of Indians has been documented by Davis (1977) and Cardoso and Müller (1977). The potential danger to the basin from development without adequate knowledge has been documented competently by Meggers (1971) and Goodland

and Irwin (1975). Studies of the impact of farming along the Transamazon Highway have remained buried in professional journals inaccessible even to scholars with an interest in the area. Many of those studies are cited throughout this book.[6]

This book is the first, and surely won't be the last, to document the settlement of the Transamazon Highway and to assess the performances of both farmers and government institutions. The assessment begins by taking a close look at the historical use of resources and proceeds to document the basis for the differential performance of the migrant farmers. This book discounts the usual explanation given by the Brazilian government and accepted by many observers that, in short, the failure of the farmers resulted from their lack of education, lack of technical expertise, and conservatism.[7] Rather, this study will show that unaccounted for factors such as previous managerial experience, previous residential mobility, timing of loan releases, knowledge of plant-soil associations, and use of family labor better explain differential performance and help address the question of agricultural potential.

The question of the potential of the humid tropics for intensive agriculture has engaged the interests of scholars and travelers at least since the nineteenth century. Humboldt (1942) predicted in the last century that the Amazon would be a future breadbasket, as did Alfred Russell Wallace (1895). Similar opinions have been voiced off and on since that time. On the other hand, it has been even more fashionable to dismiss the world's rain forests as desirable habitats for civilized societies (Price 1939; Meggers 1954, 1971).

The very vastness of the Amazon has been an obstacle in the development and conservation of resources. Conflicting evidence can be seen everywhere, and it is difficult at times to appreciate the fact that the various sources are referring to the same area. On the one hand we have the conservationists who see most uses of the forest as undesirable. On the other hand, agronomists, economists, and others define the problem as one of developing suitable production systems for the region. The advocacy of one type of land use (e.g., tree farming) is often taken to refer to the whole basin without reference to scale, multiple uses, alternatives, and suitability from place to place. Both the positive and the negative views have been founded on a homogeneous view of the Amazon rather than on recognition of the variability present in Amazon rain forest ecosystems. A fundamental direction in the clarification of resource management is to clarify land use potential, alternative means to use that potential, and the impact of such practices on the forest, the fauna, the human population, and the region's economic productivity.

The time is rapidly approaching when scholars will finally be able to deal with specific types of Amazonian habitats, rather than attempt to extrapolate information from highly specific studies and apply it to the whole basin. This book is a contribution towards this process of increasing our knowledge of the Amazon rain forest and its potential for human use. The conclusions of this study do not claim to apply everywhere in the Amazon. In fact, one of the thrusts of this book is to argue for and partially document the heterogeneity of the Amazon Basin. This heterogeneity or diversity means that micro-level studies are needed, but that extrapolations from such studies applied to the region as a whole may be inappropriate and, surely, premature.

Research in the Amazon shows a marked tendency through time to make greater distinctions in both geographical and cultural areas. The basin and the surrounding Brazilian and Guiana Massifs were originally treated as one, under the rubric of lowland South America, or the "Manioc Area" (cf. Wissler 1917). Later a distinction was made between the flood plain (várzea) and the uplands (terra firme). The former was able to support larger population aggregates than was the latter (cf. Steward 1939–46). This distinction has proven useful and continues as the dominant ecological distinction made in Amazonian studies. More recently, Denevan (1976) has proposed a sixfold classification based upon climate, flora, fauna, altitude, soils, and population density. Pires (1978) has proposed a sevenfold classification based primarily on botanical distinctions. This tendency towards making finer distinctions reflects the accumulation of knowledge through time and the inadequacy of grosser categories in accounting for empirical differences. The process is likely to continue as the research programs of various investigators become published and previously held assumptions are challenged. Such a tendency has been demonstrated with studies of the Central American lowland rain forests. A recent volume edited by Harrison and Turner (1978) reevaluates the views of Maya agriculture and finds that traditional approaches erred in two significant ways: that almost no variation in subsistence practices was acknowledged (long fallow swidden was commonly the only subsistence strategy mentioned) and that lowlands were considered to be environmentally uniform, so that information from any part could be extended to the entire area (Harrison and Turner 1978:157). The same simplifications are still being made about the Amazon lowland rain forest zone.

Scientific interest in the settlement of the South American lowlands has produced a rich literature over the years. Much of that literature has focused on the movement of population from the Andean highlands into the lowlands. The process is as old as colonialism. It began with the creation of trading posts from which natural resources could be controlled and exploited. Later the demand for rubber brought about even greater changes in regional population and resource use. More recently the search for cultivable land has brought people from the highlands to the lowlands. The geographical and anthropological literature has emphasized questions relative to the habitability of the rain forest, the adaptation of highland peoples to hot/humid conditions, and the infrastructural inadequacies of an isolated region. Studies had clearly shown before the construction of the Transamazon Highway that unclear land titling, seasonally impassable roads, and lack of credit and technology were fundamental obstacles to the development of the lowlands in the Western Amazon (Casagrande and Thompson 1964; Hanson 1965; Hegen 1966; Snyder 1967; Stewart 1968; Dozier 1969; Watters 1971; among others).

Studies have also shown over the years that spontaneous colonization is more cost efficient than planned colonization. In the Ecuadorian Oriente, colonization has often progressed years in advance of road construction (Bromley 1978), but economic development above the subsistence level has been hampered in these projects by elementary human and institutional malfunctioning (Crist and Nissly 1973:81; Wesche 1967). The problems faced by planned colonization are different more in degree than in kind. Planned projects suffer from lack of credit, from impassable roads, declining yields due to poor advice on soil selection, unrealistic loan repayment demands, inadequate markets to absorb produce, and naive advisors (Nelson 1973; Dozier 1969). Many of these problems surfaced again in the Transamazon Project. Planning documents gave little evidence of an awareness of past experiences and available studies.

Study Area

The Transamazon Highway cut through a variety of environmentally distinct zones, but one of them became the central focus of colonization efforts and of this study. The Altamira Integrated Colonization Project became the showcase for Brazilian efforts at occupying the Amazon in 1971. This riverine town of Altamira had a long history. It was founded in the eighteenth century by Jesuit missionaries seeking a point above the rapids where the Indians brought to the mission could have some protection from the civilian slavers. The town is located on the Xingú River, one of the major tributaries of the Amazon.

The Xingú River, the eleventh longest river in the world, runs from its source in Mato Grosso through hilly terrain until its flow is broken by a series of rapids along a Great Bend between the contemporary towns of Altamira and Vitória (see Figure 1.2). It then continues on to meet the Amazon River. Only the first 120 miles of waterway are continuously navigable (Kelly 1975:3). The Xingú is the first major right bank tributary encountered upon ascending the Amazon and was of interest to outsiders at an early time (Sternberg 1975:29).

The presence of rapids and waterfalls is not unique to the Xingú. Tributaries flowing into the Amazon from the north and south all share this

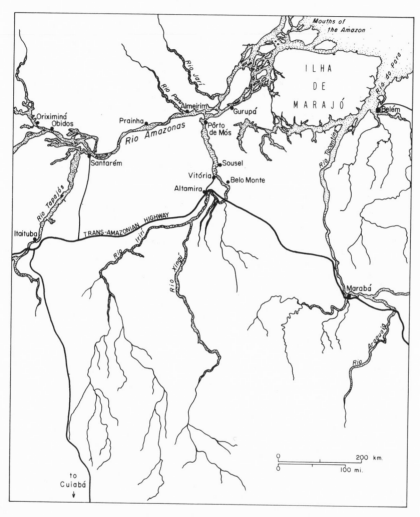

Fig. 1.2 Xingú Basin and Surroundings

characteristic as a result of the region's two major geological formations: the Guiana and the Brazilian Shields.[8] As the rivers flow toward the main channel of the Amazon they reach the borders of these granite shields and tumble downward to the lower level of the flood plain. This dividing line forms two "fall zones," characterized by dangerous and commonly impassable rapids (Rocha Penteado 1978). The tributaries rising out of these headwater areas differ in their stream loads, that is, the varying amounts of solids carried in their current. The stream load depends on the geological makeup of the headwater areas and affects the stream's optical visibility and the chemical and biological properties of the waters[9] (Sternberg 1975:13).

The Xingú is classified as a blue, or clear-water river; the transparency of the water resulting from low levels of particulate matter in the stream. This property is explained by the fact that the river rises from the Old Brazilian Shield (Sternberg 1975:30). The Xingú region, in addition to the rapids, is marked by a number of obstacles that impeded river communication. The level of the Amazon and its Xingú tributary vacillate greatly during the year, from peak heights in June and July, to shallowness in October and November at the end of the dry season. In the past, this variation meant that river transports, especially larger vessels, had to be scheduled for periods when upstream inlets and small cataracts could be crossed during flood periods (Sternberg 1975; Kelly 1975:6). This seasonal change discouraged the development of areas other than the main channel of the Amazon. In addition, goods and passengers had to be portaged from the higher elevations of the towns to navigable areas.

Many towns are located at the ridge between these uplands, perhaps near a portage point on the fall line, and the border of the flood plain, or várzea region.[10] These flood plains, most prevalent along the main Amazon channel and its confluences, are continually enriched by alluvial deposits contributed by the white-water streams. The várzeas present great differences in flora and fauna from the uplands. They serve as spawning grounds for fish and other aquatic species, and as germination areas for vegetation carried by the traveling streams (Sternberg 1975:25). These lush, often swampy areas provide great potentials for hunting, fishing, and annual crops, which have been exploited by both aboriginal and European settlers.

Successive groups established settlements at the interfluves between the lowland forests and várzea lands in order to exploit the resources of both macro-ecological zones. Until the nineteenth century, few Europeans explored the length of the Xingú, as they were intimidated by the numerous rapids. Portuguese occupation of the basin followed the navigable portions of rivers, and most of the towns were limited to 100 miles or so below the fall zones. The lower Xingú was ignored by the Portuguese in the early colonial period. In 1610 the Dutch built trading posts at its mouth, while the English established trade settlements along the Xingú in the next decade. These settlements were small, with fewer than 100 persons, and engaged in cultivation of the land as well as in trade. Their existence was short-lived, as the Portuguese defeated and captured them in 1623 (Sternberg 1975:29).

The founding of Portuguese towns along the Xingú can be traced to the creation of Indian missions (*aldéias*) by Catholic missionaries following the penetration of the river by Padre Luis Figueiro in 1637 (Kelly 1975:7). The Jesuits, and later the Capuchins, chose secluded locations, far from the centers of trade activity, in an effort to protect the Indians from Portuguese enslavement.[11] The Jesuits began their missionary work in the Amazon in 1655, and in the decades that followed, they established and administered dozens of mission villages. In an effort to keep the Indians from contact with Portuguese laymen, they established their missions in distant places. Because of their tax-exempt status, they were able to operate productive export-import operations independent of the civil authorities.[12] Achipayas, Araras, Penas, and Juruna Indians were brought together at the mission and given the rudiments of the Christian faith and Portuguese culture (Kelly 1975:7). Unlike some towns, however, few goods of economic importance were produced here at the time, and white explorers felt it unprofitable to risk the rapids for such poor returns. The Xingú Valley had marketable resources, such as Brazil nuts, sarsaparilla, cloves, and cedar (known collectively as *drogas do sertão*). Of these, sarsaparilla was the region's most important product (Coudreau 1897). But the amounts found never succeeded in luring a large Portuguese contingent. The few who came intermarried with the natives, as did some fugitive black slaves (Kelly 1975:8).

Altamira grew rapidly during the Rubber Era (1880–1920), in great part due to the Xingú's rubber baron, José Porfirio. Porfirio built a port at the beginning of the Great Bend of the Xingú and named it Vitória. From there he brought in work crews to improve the road connecting Vitória to Altamira, and still others to work the rubber stands at its end, near the village of Altamira. By 1926 the road was wide enough for automobile travel, and José Porfirio was so confident of the area's productivity that he approached Henry Ford to build a railroad along the road bed and invest in rubber plantations along the Xingú. Porfirio himself was already using the innovation of steamships to pick up rubber produced above the falls. Ford, however, was still leary of the problematic Xingú Falls and opted to establish his plantations along the more accessible rubber areas of the Tapajós River (Kelly 1975:55–57).

The twin towns of Vitória and Altamira were late in developing but grew rapidly during the productive rubber years of 1912–1925. By 1926, however, competition from the British East Indies plantations was already taking its toll, and the price of rubber began to decline (Kelly 1975:58–68). Undaunted, Porfirio continued to invest at least a portion of his wealth in developing Vitória and Altamira. In Vitória he built a trading-post warehouse and docks, and established a steamship line connecting it with Belem. He created a small sugar plantation and mill, with an accompanying distillery to process sugar cane into raw rum (*cachaça*). His plantation workers were given smaller plots and encouraged to produce corn, manioc, and other vegetables for local consumption. In Altamira a second warehouse/trading post was established to exchange rubber for

Porfirio's raw rum and other consumables. All this investment encouraged the city of Altamira to grow from a village with a handful of huts to a town of more than 100 homes, built along well-defined streets provided by José Porfirio. A church, major trading establishments, and homes of prominent citizens lined the first street facing the river front. Smaller stores and lower class citizens inhabited the more inland streets, which ran parallel to the first, a pattern that is common in traditional Amazon towns (Wagley 1953).

The town suffered economic and political decline as the price of rubber continued to fall. José Porfirio lost political office during the Brazilian revolution of 1930, and his financial empire was undermined by his competitors. Broken economically and politically, Porfirio sold a portion of his land to Altamira county, and his rights to the Vitória port to the state government of Pará.

At the close of the 1960s, Altamira was a dusty town of hardly 6,000 souls looking very much like other Amazon River towns. Its unpaved and poorly drained streets turned to bogs with the winter rains. There was no phone service, and, at that time, no electricity due to the early demise of the town's steam-powered generator. The population still lived within the city limits established in 1917, although homes with spacious lots and gardens had spread out, sometimes two to a block around this older area (Glick 1975). There was a landing strip, the old Catholic hospital manned by two doctors, small branches of the Bank of Brazil and the Bank of Amazonia (BASA), an agronomist, and two dentists (IBGE 1970). There were yet conflicts with Kayapó Indians, only twenty-five miles from town, and small game still could be seen in the open areas of town (Glick 1975). The county seat boasted eighty-two commerces of various sizes, most of them small, and there were service enterprises such as small eateries, bars, boarding houses, and drugstores (IBGE 1970). One gas station supplied the small motorized canoes, launches, and the few motorized vehicles of the area.

Five years later, in 1974, Altamira had grown to an estimated 12,000 in population (IBGE, Altamira county office). The number of commercial establishments burgeoned to 350. Phone service (one phone) linked the town to any other city in Brazil, and electricity illuminated the city nearly twenty-four hours a day. A municipal market place had been built, a new movie house established, a radio station broadcast local news, bus and truck service to Brasilia and Belem was available, a library and small bookstores had recently opened, and the airport was lengthening its runway to accommodate jet service. Only the town's streets retained their seasonally dust-choked, or mud-luscious, personality. This, too, was destined to change as new paving and drainage projects were undertaken in late 1974.

The Altamira Area

The county (*municipio*) of Altamira and its municipal seat of the same name are located at eighty meters above sea level. At the last census, the county had an average of only 0.10 persons per square kilometer (IBGE 1970), and a total population, including the urban areas, of 15,345 persons (see Table 1.1). The rural portion of this population was scat-

TABLE 1.1

POPULATION FIGURES FOR ALTAMIRA AND ALTAMIRA COUNTY

	TOTAL URBAN POPULATION	% URBAN	TOTAL RURAL POPULATION	% RURAL	TOTAL MUNICIPIO POPULATION	LAND AREA IN KM^2
1940	1,573	32.2	3,310	67.8	4,883	279,071
1950	2,625	27.9	6,790	72.1	9,415	279,071
1960	3,425	28.3	8,665	71.7	12,090	279,071
1970	5,741	37.4	9,604	62.6	15,345	153,862
1973	11,740	31.4	25,675	68.6	37,415	153,862

SOURCE: IBGE office in Altamira

tered over an area of 153,862 square kilometers. Most of these rural dwellers subsisted on their production from shifting cultivation along the streams and rivers, and gained small cash incomes from the sale of wild game, prized pelts, Brazil nuts, and small volumes of agricultural produce. Population growth in the municipio had been steady since the 1940s, despite reapportionment of the county in 1962 (see Table 1.1).

The port of Vitória, forty-seven kilometers from Altamira, connects Altamira to the Xingú River and the outside world (see Figure 1.2). The head of the longshoremen's union told me that before the time of the Transamazon Highway, Altamira was largely self-sufficient in basic food items, and even exported rice, coffee, and beans to Belem. With the coming of the highway, however, the population grew too fast, and production of certain items lagged behind demand. As a result, food imports have now become necessary. Because some of the larger purchases of food are made by upper- and middle-class administrators, luxury food items such as canned foods, imported liquor, and high-quality staples such as long-grain rice (*agulha*) are now brought in from as far as Rio Grande do Sul. It is possible that much of the current surplus of basic staples in Altamira may be leaving by other transport means. Wholesalers indicated that rice bought from farm settlers is sent by truck to Goiás, where better prices can be obtained than if it is shipped to Belem.

Altamira changed with the coming of the highway. An economic boom occurred during the time that the town was occupied by road construction companies. Since their leaving, the town has been stabilizing itself at a higher level of development. There are more people, more businesses, more services, more banks, more cars, and better communication with the outside than ever before. At the same time, many of the merchants who came to get rich have left unrewarded. Some of the older businessmen in town attribute this to overspecialization. "In the interior, one must sell everything," is a local theme repeated time and again. This piece of local wisdom can be seen at work with the rapid turnover of those stores which sold only clothes, fabric, or car parts. The older businesses earned a share of the boom business while it lasted, but after it was over they had managed, not only to retain their old customers, but had attracted many of the immigrants as well, because nearly all necessities could be obtained in one stop at their establishments, and credit was extended to regular customers.

As might be expected, prices in the frontier area of Altamira are high, but they are generally lower than in isolated riverine towns such as Gurupá and São Félix do Xingú. Nevertheless, rates of inflation for basic necessities were two to three times those found in major Brazilian urban centers—72 percent in 1974. Some items considered as basic necessities of life were even higher—sugar up 150 percent and coffee 90 percent in one year. Local agricultural produce either remained unchanged or went down in price, in contrast to extra-regional produce and manufactured items.

The boom situation is, therefore, not as exploitative as that found in traditional towns, where a small number of commercial patrons and maverick river traders (*regatões*) regulate prices at will. Competition is fierce in Altamira, and this acts as a restraint on inflationary prices. Between 1972 and 1974, businessmen, both old and new, agreed that weekly profits had been halved by the exit of cash-laden construction crews. All the wholesalers were new merchants who had come from the center-south. Three gas stations, three banks, six drugstores, eight hotels, six restaurants, and twenty-eight bars, including prostitutes, provided services. The number of professionals had expanded to six doctors, five dentists, two lawyers, one engineer, and two agronomists. This number did not include technical advisors nor recent arrivals associated with the highway project. Registered motor vehicles numbered 610 and were evenly divided between truck and passenger cars (IBGE 1972). The boom had indeed brought many changes to the town of Altamira.

Planned Communities

While Altamira was the hub of colonization activity, it was never intended as the final home for either the colonists or the administrators. Rather, an impressive modular approach to colonization was designed for the area. Part of this modular scheme involved the creation of planned communities at set intervals to serve the farmers. The highway was designed to use traditional towns like Altamira as supply centers for the *agrovilas*, *agropolis*, and *ruropolis*, planned communities specially developed for the Transamazon (see Figure 1.3). An agrovila is a planned

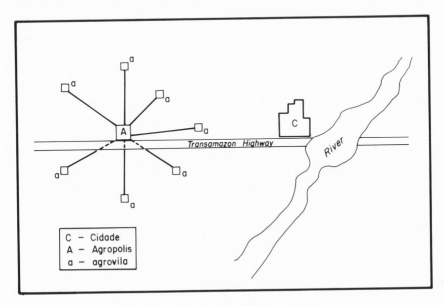

Fig. 1.3 Colonization Settlement Pattern

village for approximately forty-eight to sixty colonist families, built either along the highway or on side roads. Ideally, the agrovila would be located along the main highway at ten-kilometer intervals, and at midpoint along the fifteen- to twenty-kilometer side roads. Agrovilas provide basic services, such as primary education, minor first aid, and, in some cases, a treated water source.

An agropolis corresponds to a planned settlement for approximately 300 families, including both colonists and government administrators. Each agropolis serves a maximum of twenty-two agrovilas with marketing, storage, and service facilities. Electricity, government administrative offices, large warehouses, restaurants, sawmills, and other small industries add to the benefits of such a center.

Even more elaborate is the ruropolis, a planned city of over 1,000 families to serve as a "development pole." Rural industries, motels, and larger facilities for technical and economic matters are concentrated in a ruropolis. A ruropolis acts like an agropolis in the modular arrangement, servicing a number of agropolis in their radius of influence. One currently exists at the crossroads of the Transamazon and Cuiabá-Santarém Highways (see Figure 1.1).

At the time of this study, three project areas of planned settlement existed in the areas of Altamira, Marabá, and Itaituba. Altamira became the largest of these owing to the high rates of malaria in Marabá and the subsequent discovery of poor soils in the area of Itaituba (IPEAN 1974).

Each agrovila was located either on the main highway, or 15 to 20 kilometers down along a side road penetrating to interior sections of lots. The 20-kilometer small-farming area along the highway was divided into rectangular lots with areas of 10,000 square meters each (100 hectares). The division of lots into these neat units preceded any surveying or investigation of the physical environment with a view to deciding its optimum use. Figure 1.4 represents the standardized pattern which was

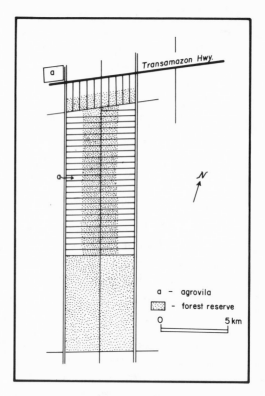

Fig. 1.4 Arrangement of Lots
along the Transamazon
Highway and Side Roads

used throughout the Altamira Project. One-half of each rectangular lot was supposed to be left as an uncleared forest. In this way, a forested strip of 2.5 kilometers in width would remain as a small forest reserve.[13] Side roads (*travessões*) would link the farms to the main highway.

The modular scheme for settlement was developed by government planners in Brasilia (Camargo 1973), and competitions were held to develop an architectural design for tropical climate (Hasek 1971). The winning design incorporated slanted multilevel roofs for sun and rain protection, verandas, and walls ventilated by jalousies, low interior partitions, and open slat-work. The construction and settlement layout embodied many philosophical aspects of the project as well.

The nucleated settlements were to facilitate the dispensing of services and administrative functions of settlers in a ten-twenty kilometer radius. Agrovilas were U-shaped with all communal buildings, such as schools, meeting halls, health posts, storage, and water facilities in the center. Fostering a sense of community among immigrants from many states was an explicit goal of project designers. Even a nondenominational hall was provided for communal meetings and religious services. More importantly, in the settlements, all pioneers were conceived of as equal, and planners wrote of a semi-utopian emergence of a "new Brazilian society." Such equality was reflected most strongly, not only in the public buildings, but in the rigid uniformity of the colonist homes. All the houses were designed to be the same in size, layout, and color. The other interesting facet of early agrovila design is that no building was designated as an administrative office. The goals of the planners precluded the election of local officials and thus political factions in the new communities. Administrative functions were to be centered, ultimately, in the larger settlements, the agropolis and ruropolis. The colonists would refer to various agropolis offices for credit processing, sale of crops, technical advice, major health problems, and farming supplies. An INCRA mayor would link each agrovila to the broader bureaucratic network.

Studying a Planned Amazonian Community

It is traditional in anthropology to choose a small community in which to intensively research the internal workings of a society and its culture. The choice of a single Transamazon planned village, which we will call Vila Roxa from here on, was based not solely on this traditional concern, but also on the difficulty posed by transportation during the long wet season and the need for precise farming data in a twelve-month cycle. Residing in the nucleated settlement of Vila Roxa allowed us day-to-day contact with a large group of colonists who had come to this small farm sector of the Transamazon Project. The representativeness of Vila Roxa was established by use of a scalogram to rate twenty-one communities. This included nine agrovilas along the highway, six agrovilas on side roads, three agropolis, one ruropolis, two traditional river towns, and two cities. They were rated on a 100-point scale from most to least socioeconomically developed, using material features as indicators of such development (cf. Doughty et al. 1966).

Through both personal knowledge and the interviewing of a group of community residents to stimulate mutual correction on public information, the presence of items and institutions was noted. The maximum score was achievable only by Belem, the largest urban center in the Amazon. The schedule was fine-tuned to deal with the highway communities but was flexible enough to be applied in two traditional riverine county seats for the purpose of contrast. Vila Roxa rated forty-two points, which placed it at nearly the midpoint position in the scale of complexity. Figure 1.5 illustrates the variability present. For the communities on the Transamazon Highway, the advantage of being along the main artery is evident in the scores. Side road communities have much less access to services and facilities. Some of these agrovilas are experiencing depopulation as the migrants move permanently to their plots. The schedule used may be found in Moran (1975, 1976a).

Through the intercession of the director of IPEAN, a house was granted us in Vila Roxa by the director of INCRA at Altamira. The house had been vacant for six months and was located at a high point from which a large portion of the village was visible. Field notes were kept by myself and my wife, Millicent Fleming-Moran, who also carried on research on complementary aspects of social organization and health (Fleming-Moran 1975; Fleming-Moran and Moran 1978).

Informal open-ended interviewing constituted a significant portion of our activity in the first months of research. During this rainy period we concentrated on gathering the history of the settlement and the past and present experiences of numerous families. We were fortunate that our house was located next to the only front-room store in Vila Roxa. The store also served as a main gathering place in the village. Social groupings and economic activity could be easily observed from our vantage point. We chose not to hire colonists to work for us as servants, cooks, or messengers. While we certainly were outsiders, the lack of familiar status symbols confused our neighbors at first but was gradually appreciated by the colonists who saw in it a desire "to feel the colonization experience." We walked to the fields with the farmers, rather than ride to them in motor vehicles. We ate *farinha puba*, coarse Amazonian manioc flour, rather than fine southern style flour. We lacked our own kerosene refrigerator. We used work clothes rather than fashionable clothes or shoewear. These differences prevented our being automatically classified as upperclass government employees, despite our economic independence from farming and regular interaction with civil servants.

Once having established rapport as neighbors, we had ample time to explain why we were in the community, and more formal research was undertaken. Data on cropping techniques, agricultural inputs and out-

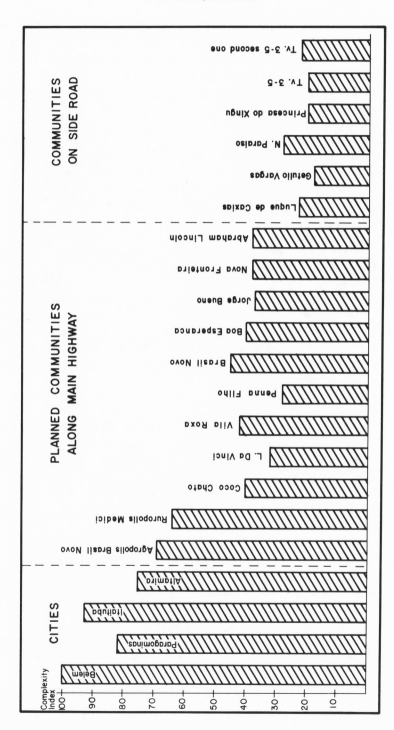

Fig. 1.5 Scale of Community Development in Twenty-one Amazonian Communities

puts, soil sampling, credit, and economic exchanges were collected, and the pretesting of a farm management survey schedule began. Collections of secondary-succession plants and medicinal herbs were also made. Their identification was made by Dr. Paulo Calvacante of the Museu Goeldi in Belem. Maps were obtained from the topography division of INCRA, and photographs were taken to document social and technical activities.

An extensive farm management survey was developed based on a Food and Agriculture Organization Manual (Yang 1965). Added to this essentially economic survey were questions regarding child-raising, health and nutritional status, education, and migration history. Two sample populations were used. First, a 50 percent sample of Vila Roxa households was collected and represents the existing factions of Catholics and Protestants, and the areas of origin of the farmers (N=25). Then, as a way of checking the representativeness of Vila Roxa residents, vis-á-vis the situation of other farmers in the Transamazon, interviews were made at other points along the highway and transecting side roads covering an area of 900 square kilometers. In the latter, I used a stratified random sample of households based on the proportion of settlers from each area of origin (N=101).

In the summer we were joined by a group of graduate students from the University of Florida's Tropical South American Fellowship Program. Some stayed in Altamira (Lynn Bushman, Arlene Kelly, and Curtis Glick), and others in two traditional Amazon riverine towns (Brian Burkhalter and Darrell Miller), and still others resided with us in Vila Roxa (Maria del Carmen Arrue and Susan Poats). While my wife and I administered the Vila Roxa survey, the larger sample required more interviews, and the summer students helped administer the farm management survey. Two Brazilian students (José Américo Boução Viana and Lourdes Rodrigues) also aided in this effort as part of a cooperative arrangement made with the Federal University of Pará in Belem. Several of these students also collected data on topics of individual interest. Several theses resulted, which, in the aggregate, enriched our understanding of the region (Arrue 1976; Burkhalter 1975; Glick 1975; Kelly 1975; Miller 1975; Poats 1975).

The area covered was 108 kilometers along the main highway from 18 kilometers east of Altamira to kilometer 90 west of the city, and as deep as 20 kilometers on various side roads. In interviewing, an attempt was made to include farmers under all possible conditions: living in agrovilas along the highway, in agrovilas far into side roads, in individual homesteads along the highway and the side roads, near Altamira and far from it. Such a variety of situations aimed both at exploring the possible relationship of location to success, and at representing all types of possible situations in which farmers found themselves.

Frequently, I took along soil research equipment in order to collect soil samples in the areas cultivated by Vila Roxa farmers (N=240). An Eyelkamp bi-partite soil auger for complete profiles, a Hoffer soil sampler tube for fertility cores, a Hellige-Truog soil reaction (pH) testing kit, and a soil thermometer were regularly taken to the field. A spring balance and a metric measuring tape were also carried to verify weights and measures given. In these cases, I remained all day with a farmer so as to verify the answers provided in the survey and explore other aspects of farm management. The formal interview was carried on both before, and, more commonly, after the farmstead had been observed, soils collected, and other activities (e.g., observation of threshing or cutting rice) observed. These lengthier management studies, carried out by field measurements, testing, observation, as well as formal interviewing, gave added assurance that the farmers were knowledgeable, reasonably accurate in their figures, and frank. In the surveys outside Vila Roxa, doubt was cast on farmers' responses to hunting activities. Since there was a general prohibition on such hunting, they may have feared answering openly. But a more accurate picture of these activities could be obtained in Vila Roxa, where farmers knew us well and such knowledge was commonly exchanged. In Chapter 7 I have relied heavily on the data collected by a colleague, Nigel Smith, who devoted considerable attention to the hunting practices and yields of colonists (1976a; 1976b; 1976c).

Migration histories were obtained informally, as well as by formal interview. A map of Brazil hung on the wall of our house, covered with a plastic sheet. When local families came to visit, they took delight in using crayons to mark the various places where they had lived and recalled how life was in each of these places. In general, this provided a good outline of their life histories.[14] Such questions were also included in our farm management schedules and asked of those who had not given us such data already.

To a large extent, research activities had to keep balance with what was happening in the community. Thus, when the men were home during the rainy season, we obtained data which is best gotten through memory-recall. Such data, when the farmers are working in the field, tend to get short treatment. While they are in the field, we stayed out of the way and observed, did time-and-motion measurements, mapped crop distribution in fields, weighed harvested crops, and kept notes on storage methods and other behaviors. Interviews were held, not only with the colonists themselves, but also with a wide variety of INCRA personnel, medical professionals, agronomists, bureaucrats, and scientists.

Organization of the Book

Any assessment of the agricultural performance and agricultural potential of a region must, perforce, begin with a delineation of the physical environment. In Chapter 2 the complex diversity of the rain forest ecosystem is discussed, gradually focusing on the habitat diversity present. Even within the micro-ecological zone of Altamira, it will become evident why broad generalization about the rain forest flies in the face of the evident heterogeneity therein.

Chapter 3 explores the approaches to resource use of aboriginal peoples, and Chapter 4 the changes brought about by colonialism and an export-oriented economy. Chapters 5 and 6 explore the migration of populations and the efforts at getting the agricultural sector out of its stagnant condition—a result of extractive activities. Chapters 7 through 10 examine the use of resources by the Transamazon homesteaders, their interaction with each other and the government, and their health and nutritional status. The last chapter examines the implications of the earlier chapters. Of particular significance is the discussion of the relevance of micro-ecological analysis in overcoming the tendency to generalize, and an acknowledgement of its limitations. Whereas most books touch upon macro-level (e.g., national) issues and anthropologists and micro-sociologists also include a discussion of a local community (e.g., micro-level), these analytical levels are rarely articulated, and are analytically problematic. In Chapter 11 I have attempted to show how insights derived from various levels provide a distinctive view of human adaptations in the Amazon, and how policies built upon either macro- or micro-levels of analysis will overlook fundamental considerations for the human use of resources. It is my hope that this tentative effort will be improved upon in the years ahead and help address the complex problems of managing an ecosystem as diverse as the Amazon.

Tropical Rain Forest Ecosystems

2

Tropical rain forests form an equatorial green belt around the globe. Tropical forests differ from most other ecosystems in their high plant biomass, in the concentration of nutrients in the plant biomass, and in their rapid rates of nutrient cycling (UNESCO 1978:283). Both plants and animals are profoundly affected by the region's climatic characteristics: warm temperatures, high humidity, high levels of rainfall year round, and lack of a marked seasonality in most areas.[1] The climatic regime, the paleoecological record, and human activities through time have brought about significant habitat differences from area to area in the Amazon Basin. These differences are just as important to an understanding of the ecosystem as are the generally shared characteristics. In this chapter the discussion begins with the general characteristics of the ecosystem and continues with an increased specification of the habitats in order to suggest the relevance of local ecological variation to Amazonian studies.

The paleogeography and paleoclimatology of the Amazon Basin is scarcely known. Pollen analyses are available only for a site in Rondonia. The rest are all from the Andean zone. Evidence of drying periods has been deduced from geomorphological and biogeographical data (Haffer 1969; Bigarella and Andrade 1965). Recent palynological data strongly supports the former existence of savanna areas where tropical forest now stands (Van der Hammen 1972). However, much research is needed in the Amazon itself and including a whole range of current habitats before such region-wide deductions can be accepted to apply throughout the basin (cf. UNESCO 1978:71–80).

Tropical forests are important components of the global hydrologic cycle. Much of the absorbed solar radiation captured by the forest enters the atmosphere by way of the process of evapotranspiration. By this process water is vaporized, and it should be noted that the humid tropics[2] contribute 58 percent of the earth's total water vapor available—an important figure in the world's water balance. Because precipitation in the humid tropics is three times the global average, the land surfaces channel

23

a remarkable volume of water along huge tropical river networks, the largest of which is the Amazon's. Twenty percent of the world's potable water each year enters the ocean from the mouth of the Amazon and five percent from the Congo and Orinoco Basins combined (UNESCO 1978:48). The impact of deforestation is likely to have its most immediate impact upon the water cycle.

Rainfall variation in space and time is greater in the humid tropics than in temperate climates, although it is not as great as in the dry tropics. Considerable variation, too, has been noted in total solar insolation and net radiation, both of which accent the variability of rainfall (UNESCO 1978:43). Unpredictable periods of water deficiency occur in the humid tropics, in part resulting from the excellent percolation of some tropical soils in response to the high level of precipitation during wet months. High levels of solar radiation may also be responsible for seasonal deficiencies in water supply to plants.

Monthly temperature means in rain forests are relatively constant, but daily temperatures can vary by as much as 9°C inside the forest and as much as 15°C in open areas. Rainfall commonly exceeds 2,000 millimeters annually, with none of the months receiving less than 50 millimeters. Plants respond in dry months in a manner that resembles the response to cold of temperate zone plants: shedding leaves, becoming dormant, and closing their stomata (Sanchez and Buol 1975). Humidity hovers between 75 and 100 percent year round. The area receives 2.5 times more solar radiation than the poles, but atmospheric circulation carries away most of this excess heat (Steila 1976:152). The year-round sunshine, humid conditions, and warm temperatures provide an ideal climate for life forms.

Total rain forest biomass ranges between 200 and 400 tons per hectare, although the number of studies is insufficient to permit region-wide extrapolations.[3] The distribution of the biomass among the parts of the forest is relatively constant in the available studies: 75 percent consists of trunk and branches, 15 to 20 percent of roots, 4 to 6 percent of leaves, and 1 to 2 percent of litter (Sanchez et al. 1972:47). The trend of rain forests to accumulate a large proportion of the nutrients in the living biomass (Herrera 1979) may make the system more susceptible to man-induced changes than are systems wherein a greater proportion of the total nutrient pool is stored in the soil (Klinge 1978). Despite this potential fragility, rain forests accumulate nutrients at a remarkably fast rate. Studies indicate that rain forests are capable of attaining 90 percent of maximum biomass within eight to ten years after forest clearing (Sanchez 1976:351). Most of the nutrients are accumulated steadily, following a linear function (Bartholomew et al. 1953). Temperate forests, by contrast, take 50 to 100 years to reach maximum biomass (Farnworth and Golley 1974:76).

The aggressive colonization of open areas by rain forest species is remarkable. Leaves attain 94 percent of maximum biomass within two years after forest clearing (Sanchez et al. 1972:48). The notion of rain forests as "fragile ecosystems," which has become a common phrase, is an imperfect and somewhat misleading figure of speech. In experiments carried out by the U.S. Atomic Energy Commission in a rain forest of Puerto Rico, the vegetation proved to be surprisingly able to withstand levels of gamma radiation which devastated pine forests in North America (Odum and Pigeon 1970:1–257). The reason for this resiliency of tropical forests may lie in their diversity of species and their intense competition for light (UNESCO 1978:216) and nutrients.[4]

Most of the nutrients stored in the soil medium under rain forests are found in the top thirty centimeters. Studies have also shown that 65 to 80 percent of the vegetation's root system is found within that topsoil layer (Greenland and Kowal 1960; Jordan and Uhl 1978; Stark and Spratt 1977). The high gross productivity of rain forests is dependent on the contribution made by the vegetation to the nutrient pool. Each year 10 to 20 percent of total biomass dies off and drops to the ground in the form of litterfall. The nutrient composition of the litter is similar to that of the forest, except for a higher nitrogen concentration. Once the litter falls to the ground, it is rapidly decomposed and mineralized. Approximately half of the dry matter is mineralized within the first eight to ten weeks (Sanchez et al. 1972:49). Despite the high levels of rainfall, there is no appreciable loss of nutrients due to leaching. Research in the Brazilian Amazon found the presence of tree-feeding rootlets at a depth of only two to fifteen centimeters associated with mycorrhiza (root fungi) by means of which the trees were directly connected with the litter layer.[5] The trees can thus exploit the fungi to obtain their inorganic nutrients directly from the litter, instead of having to wait to have them become part of the soil layer itself. Stark (1969) estimated that 5.4 $g/m^2/day$ were mineralized, a figure that approached the gross primary production of the forest of 6.0 $g/m^2/$ day.

As a result of recent research in the nutrient-poor Rio Negro Basin in southern Venezuela, it is now recognized that the structure and function of rain forests on nutrient-rich soils (e.g., alfisols and inceptisols) is fundamentally different from that on nutrient-poor soils (e.g., oxisols and podzols). Forests in impoverished areas act like gigantic filters that capture nutrients in rainfall and prevent nutrients from escaping once they enter the system. Forests on nutrient-poor soils have a thick above-ground root mat on top of the mineral soil. This root mat layer acts as the major filter that prevents nutrients from being lost (Jordan et al. 1979). Other nutrient-conserving mechanisms are: the synthesis of alkaloids and polyphenols to reduce herbivory; sclerophylly (thick, leathery leaves); movement of nitrogen, phosphorus, and potassium to the twig before leaf shedding; algae/mosses/lichens/bacteria filtering of rain water nutrients (Herrera et al. 1978). The net effect is to reduce losses of nutrients in the system and to increase the efficiency of capturing nutrients entering the system. Nutrient-rich environments appear to dispense with conservative ecological adaptations like thick root mats, extreme forms of chemical protection against herbivory, and reduction of nutrients lost by leaf fall. Instead, nutrients are able to enter the mineral soil or are cycled through the more significant herbivore population supported by this less protective type of rain forest. However, integrated ecosystem research in eutrophic rain forests is sadly lacking. Despite the differences in nutrient-conserving mechanisms, net primary productivity, secondary successional rates, and other structural and functional characteristics remain fundamentally alike in both types.

Whether in nutrient-rich or in nutrient-poor soils, the rain forest vegetation feeds on itself in what must be one of the most efficient closed nutrient cycles on earth. The vigor of secondary succession is aided by the fact that only 40 to 50 percent of the total biomass normally is part of this cycling—mainly leaves, limbs, and roots. In addition, 20 percent of the total nutrient uptake is derived from the subsoil (Sanchez et al. 1972:50), although this figure may be lower in nutrient-poor areas.

Variability in Tropical Soils

Perhaps the most misunderstood aspect of the humid tropical environment is the presence of "laterite" in the soils.[6] Among soil scientists the term laterite is being abandoned due to its lack of clarity in the literature. The term *plinthite* has replaced it—to refer to the iron-rich, humus-poor soil material which irreversibly hardens after repeated wetting and drying once exposed to atmospheric oxygen.

It has been recently estimated that "laterite" occurs in only 7 percent of the tropical world (Sanchez and Buol 1975) and probably in less than 2 percent of the Amazon (Wambecke 1978:235). Laterite should not be seen as a non-resource, however. In Thailand the people recognize plinthite deposits. They pour soil into large blocks before it hardens and use it in construction. Some of the most ancient Thai temples are made from "laterite."

Tropical soils are said to be old, leached, acidic, lacking in horizons, poor in nutrients, and able to be cultivated for only a couple of years (Meggers 1971; Gourou 1953). Recent agronomic research, however, is showing that soils under tropical rain forests tend to be very much like those in the forested areas of the nonglaciated temperate zone. Where the parent materials are acidic, the soils closely correspond to those of the southeastern United States and southeast China, both areas now under highly productive intensive cultivation. These soils all share problems of low cation retention, high acidity, and high exchangeable aluminum content. Where soils are derived from basic rocks, they are frequently neutral in reaction (Sanchez and Buol 1975).

Three major soil types predominate in the humid tropics: oxisols, alfisols, and ultisols. The most extensive are the oxisols, characterized by an oxic horizon (that is, consisting of hydrated oxides of iron and/or aluminum). When the conditions that create the oxic horizon are accompanied by a fluctuating water table, plinthite develops. Alfisols and ultisols are soils with a subsurface clay horizon found in humid areas, but they are less weathered than oxisols and commonly result from weathering of basic rocks. Other soils occur as well throughout the region in varied dispersion.

In temperate regions, low winter temperatures greatly reduce biological activity for soil formation, while in the 78 percent of the tropics that has a pronounced dry season of at least ninety days, the lack of moisture has a similar effect toward organic matter accumulation. A comparison made between soils of the United States and soils in Brazil and Zaïre led to the conclusion that differences in organic matter content were agronomically and statistically insignificant between these areas. The average organic matter in the top one meter of southeastern United States soils was 1.11 percent, while it was 1.05 percent for those of Zaïre and Brazil. In general, organic matter content was higher in the tropical soils than in those of the United States in areas with comparable temperature and rainfall regimes.

Floral Diversity

The most conspicuous feature of tropical rain forests is the large number of tree species and the presence of few individuals of a species in a given area.[7] Although the flora of rain forests is still relatively unknown, the clear trend has been to increase earlier estimates of species diversity. The flora of the Amazon is the least known, although it appears to be, in species diversity, second only to the flora of Malaysia (UNESCO 1978: 93).[8] Species diversity in the humid tropics has been explained in terms of (a) genetic drift (Federov 1966); (b) variety of niches (Richards (1969); (c) predator pressure on seeds and seedlings (Janzen 1970); and (d) climatic fluctuations (Prance 1978). Research on species diversity suggests that sample plot size is a significant factor in predicting species diversity. Whereas samples in 1-hectare plots yielded 60 to 79 species in the Amazon, the number of species is more than 90 in 1.5 hectares,

173 with 2 hectares, and continues to increase (Cain and Castro 1959: 60). Studies are too limited in number to predict at what plot size the diversity of species identified levels off. Jordan (1979) found a marked and continuous increase in species number when sampling sites within a few kilometers of each other in the Venezuelan Amazon. Regional extrapolations are of doubtful reliability because of this diversity factor.

The tree stratum can reach a height of ninety meters, but such instances are rare. Some ecologists hold that three stories are recognizable in the forest,[9] but these layers may reflect simply stages in succession brought about by forest openings (Uhl 1980; Pires 1978). The number of available forest profiles, however, is still too low and not sufficiently representative (UNESCO 1978:114). It would be misleading to draw conclusions about the presence or absence of strata from the evidence of one or a few profiles.

In the rain forest the trunks of the trees are usually slender and have thin barks. The crowns begin high up and are relatively small as a result of crowding. It is difficult to judge the age of the trees since annual rings are not present. Much of the vegetation lacks deep roots and the trees achieve support by developing plank buttresses which reach as high as nine meters up the tree. The presence of these buttresses has led to the nearly universal use among indigenous peoples of platforms in order to cut the giant trees above the planks. It should be noted that the Amazon rain forest contains fewer large trees and fewer buttressed trees than the forests of Africa. The understory is less dense in the Amazon but is richer in palm species than is that of Africa.

Forest types vary depending on moisture regime, altitude, and soil factors. The differences resulting from these factors produce very different types of rain forests. For example, montane rain forests differ from lowland forests in the following ways: there is a reduction in tree height; there are reduced buttresses in trees; trees have crooked trunks; leaves are smaller; there are fewer lianas; biomass is lower; annual productivity is lower; understory species like mosses, lichens, and epiphytes are more significant (Whitmore 1975). Floral, faunal, and human interactions differ as the result of these differences in the tree strata. Comparable differences could be noted for each of the forest types mentioned above.

Both growth and flowering are periodic, but fairly independent of any particular season since external conditions are relatively constant. In some tree species leaf fall occurs before the new leaves begin to form, and a tree may even be bare for a short period. Individuals of the same species may bloom at different times, or the branches of the same tree species may bloom at different times. These are all manifestations of an autonomous periodicity which is not bound to a twelve-month cycle. This means that a rain forest has no definite flowering season, but that there is always a variety of trees in bloom.[10] Such autonomy presents a particular problem for tropical animals and humans, who depend on forest resources for survival. Nomadic habits are resorted to by humans and other animals in order to take advantage of this continuous but dispersed resource base.

In the rain forest, plants have evolved effective ways to repel and control the herbivore population. Numbers of animals may be restricted through alternate seasons of fruit abundance and shortage. In the latter, mass starvation may occur (Leigh, Jr. 1975:82). Other trees reproduce by means of large, hard nuts. The hard endocarp protects the nuts from predators, but the mesocarp tend to be rewarding, and some species of animals function as dispersal agents for it (Smith 1974b). Animals play important roles in processes such as pollination, fruiting, flowering, litter decomposition, consumption of green plants, and in mineral cycling (Fittkau and Klinge 1973). Animal consumption of plant tissue, and consequent excretion of feces, represents a short cut in nutrient cycling.

Faunal Diversity

The richness of speciation is as true for animals as it is for plants. The increase in richness and diversity from the higher latitudes towards the equatorial regions is well documented for many of the larger taxa (UNESCO 1978:161). Numerous archaic types of both animals and plants survive in the numerous niches of the rain forest. Many scientists feel that the rate of evolution in the rain forest is particularly high and that many of the species presently occupying northern temperate environments evolved in tropical environments[11] (Bates 1960:109–10).

Animals represent a small fraction of the ecosystem's total biomass and are largely unobtrusive. A much larger proportion of animals live in the upper layers of vegetation than in temperate forests. Thirty-one of fifty-nine species of mammals in Guyana are arboreal, five are amphibious, and only twenty-three are ground dwellers. The larger predators are ground dwellers and it comes as no surprise to find that much of the ground animal life is nocturnal. Some Amazonian native species represent the largest animals in the world for their taxonomic group: harpy eagle (*Harpia harpyja*), the largest rodent capybara (*Hydrochoerus hydrochoeris*), the giant otter (*Ptenoura brasiliensis*), the anaconda snake (*Eunectes murinus*), the giant river turtle (*Podocnemis expansa*), and the giant fresh-water fish (*Arapaima gigas*). These giants rely on aquatic plants and animals for most of their food.

Fittkau and Klinge (1973) calculated that the living plant biomass was 900 metric tons per hectare while that of terra firme animals was only 0.2 tons per hectare. A number of biogeographers and ecologists have indicated that the low net productivity of the rain forest biome provides little food for forest animals and that their biomass per unit area is quite small. While this argument is sound, it does not take into account the large area utilized by most indigenous populations as well as the lack of adequate quantitative data. Eisenberg and Thorington (1973) estimated 4,431 kg/km^2 of nonvolant terrestrial mammals, of which 72.3 percent is entirely arboreal. The hunting territory of a group varies with its population size and settlement pattern. In a quantitative study of hunting among the Siona-Secoya in Ecuador, Vickers (1976) estimated that the population harvested 9.8 percent of the potential 337,000 kg of animal biomass of interest to hunters—not an insignificant amount of meat for a population of 132 persons.

Tropical rain forest fauna undergoes changes in population size and structure as a result of seasonal changes in precipitation (Brown and Sexton 1973), food availability (Janzen 1967), and weather periodicity. On the whole, however, animal populations in a complex biome exhibit greater longevity, have fewer offspring, and are more sedentary than are their counterparts in temperate regions (McArthur and Wilson 1967). Part of the stability of tropical forest animal populations results from the intense inter- and intra-specific competition characteristic of a complex ecosystem. Animals appear to partition resources in such a way that minimal niche overlap occurs (Moreau 1948), a situation that favors the development of interstitial, sequential, specialist, and hypercontingent species represented by few individuals (Colwell 1973). Predator-prey interactions are not well understood, but mutualism has been extensively researched. Because of the abundance of insects and their impact on plants, mutualistic bonds are frequent between plants and insects, particularly in pollination processes.

Some mammals adopt a more or less uniform distribution of individuals, each defending a home range; others pursue a continuous nomadism over a wider area in search of fruiting trees. These two strategies are not necessarily exclusive. Most nonarboreal rain forest mammals are solitary and have a dispersed form of social organization. Among arboreal rain forest mammals two major trends are also discernible: small troops scatter over the habitat range of the species, or, in a more fluid type of social organization, the age/sex groups join and separate according to prevalent food distribution.

In sum, then, the tropical rain forest habitat is diverse in variety of plant and animal species, and diverse per unit of space as compared to other habitats. This diversity reflects the complex ecosystem linkages, high levels of productivity, and its recuperative powers when disturbed by nature or by human intervention.

Human Adaptability to Rain Forest Ecosystems

There is no evidence that genetic adaptations are significant for the adaptability of human populations to humid tropical conditions. More common in the humid tropics are acclimatory (reversible physiological changes) and behavioral/cultural adjustments.

Behavioral and cultural adjustments take similar forms throughout the humid tropics: settlements are located on a rise of ground near a water source; houses are characterized by either open design to enhance daytime cooling or by designs aimed at the conservation of heat for nighttime protection from chill (Moran 1979a:278–79); there is minimal use of clothing to minimize the body's heat load (Ladell 1964:650–51); daily tasks are adjusted to the pattern of solar insolation; settlers rely on swidden agriculture, hunting, fishing, and gathering for subsistence; there is maintenance of low population densities and regular movement over a relatively large territory—facilitated by warfare, village fissioning, or witchcraft accusations (Rappaport 1968; Chagnon 1968; Meggers 1971; Vayda 1968; Vickers 1976).

Humans have developed similar settlement patterns to cope with the previously described characteristics. Near major rivers or on the coast, settlements tend to be large because of the concentration of food sources. In forested areas, away from rivers, seasonal nomadic hunting and gathering are more common with the cycle of dispersal timed to the availability of certain forest resources and the cycle of reunion timed to the increased difficulty of movement during the rainy season. Carneiro (1970a) explains these two subsistence strategies as environmentally determined. Hunting and horticulture do not differ significantly in energetic efficiency or productivity. The choice is rooted, according to Carneiro, on location. Most of the data surveyed, however, suggest that hunting is not energetically efficient when compared to horticulture, even in relatively rich areas (Rappaport 1968; Vickers 1976; Smith 1976a; Eder 1977; Ross 1978).

The physiological mechanisms of human adjustment to humid heat are still not well understood. Most of the research on physiological adjustments is from Africa (Ladell 1964), and only one study is available from South America (Baker 1966). The main biological adaptation of indigenous peoples is the combination of cutaneous vasodilation and a ready onset of sweating (Ladell 1964:626). On the other hand, because of the high humidity, there is a fairly low limit to the cooling possible from evaporation. Physiologists have noted that tropical people "move more efficiently" and do not allow themselves to get overheated (Ladell 1964:652). Most tropical peoples avoid heavy work after thermal midday (14:00 hours) and stay under the shade engaged in relatively unstrenuous activity. Sweat rates cross-culturally do not lead to any conclusive claim of adaptativeness by tropical native peoples (Lowenstein 1973:294). At moderate levels of activity, tropical peoples sweat less, have slightly lower body temperatures, and their heart rates increase less with rises in body temperatures than do unacclimatized temperate people. This may be associated with the low salt intake of tropical populations, which is dictated by appetite, custom, and availability. Nontropical peoples, during acclimatization, overadapt to heat with uneconomical high sweat rates, steep increases in heart rate, and rise in body temperature. This leads to fatigue, dehydration, and serious salt losses.

Other biological adaptations of value to rain forest dwellers are a relative reduction of mass with respect to surface area (cf. Newman 1975; Ladell 1964:647; Baker 1966:296); highly tannable skin; insensible sweat evaporation, which insures maximum evaporation with a minimum loss of electrolytes (Lowenstein 1968; Ladell 1964:652); and reduced heart rates at moderate levels of activity (Hanna and Baker 1974). A study that compared Shipibo Indians with acclimatized mestizo workers in South America found that, while neither group was seriously stressed by heat and radiation loads during moderate exercise, the situation changed when the level of activity was increased (Hanna and Baker 1974). Lowenstein concluded that tropical indigenous populations do not show any remarkable adaptations to heat stress, but rather enjoy comfortable lives in humid heat due to a prevalence of moderate levels of activity and sensible low-sodium diets (1968:394).

Amazonian Rain Forest Ecosystems

The previous discussion has emphasized the shared characteristics of rain forests, rather than their many differences. The anthropological literature dealing with South America has relied heavily on the classification used in the *Handbook of South American Indians* (Steward 1939–46). In that research collection most of the peoples of the Amazon fell into the "tropical forest culture" type, a classification resulting from the cultural area approach dominant in anthropology during the 1930s. This typology treated the Amazon as a broad habitat type, across which homogeneous populations could move, transferring their knowledge and systems of production with ease and familiarity. Thus, the Amazon peoples were said to be characterized by small settlement size, low population densities, frequent movement of settlements, local political autonomy, and warfare/witchcraft complexes. In other words, one habitat type resulted in one set of shared social and cultural characteristics.

This level of generality was reduced somewhat when scholars began to make use of the distinction between the upland (terra firme) and the flood plain (várzea) habitats (Sioli 1951; Wagley 1953; Denevan 1966a;

Lathrap 1970; Meggers 1971). Unlike the homogeneous descriptions of the tropical forest and its culture, this distinction helped make it clear that populations along the flood plain had achieved higher population densities, larger and relatively permanent settlements, and control over neighboring groups than did terra firme groups. This put them in a classificatory position close to that of the Circum-Caribbean cultures described in the *Handbook* and characteristic of the northern Andes, northern South America, and portions of Central America and the Caribbean. However, the limited number of flood plain populations that survived after contact with Europeans allowed very few comparisons. Most anthropologists have concentrated on the populations of the terra firme habitat, with their classical tropical forest culture characteristics. Explanations as to the presence, absence, development, or devolution of these characteristics have tended to focus on single-factor explanations emphasizing soil deficiencies (Meggers 1971); inadequate protein resources (Lathrap 1968; Gross 1975); weed invasion (Carneiro 1974); and political atomization (Chagnon 1968).[12]

It is only recently that attention is being given to the heterogeneity of the Amazon and the presence of many more habitats than were previously recognized. Denevan (1976:208) has correctly noted that the traditional ecological division of the Amazon into flood plain and upland is inadequate. He shows that historically populations of the Amazon differed greatly in density as a response to the diverse resource base (see Table 2.1). Minimally, Denevan identifies seven types of habitat. The *coast*

TABLE 2.1

POPULATION ESTIMATES OF AMAZON NATIVE PEOPLES
PER HABITAT TYPES

HABITAT	AREA IN KILOMETERS	ESTIMATED DENSITY PER KM^2 IN 1492	ESTIMATED TOTAL POPULATION IN 1492
Flood plain	102,814	14.6	1,501,084
Coastal	105,000	9.5	997,500
Upland forest	1,472,800	0.8	1,211,000
Lowland forest*	5,037,886	0.2	1,007,577
Central savannas	2,178,000	0.5	1,089,000
Northern savannas	395,000	1.3	513,500
Lowland savannas	180,000	2.0	350,000

* Both wet and moist forest, as well as Rio Negro caatingas, are included. These are areas about which the demographic history is quite obscure.
SOURCE: Adapted from Denevan 1976:230

probably offered the earliest habitat, as evidenced by the Marajó sites at the mouth of the Amazon (Meggers and Evans 1957). The *flood plain* formed a natural extension of the coastal adaptations—both characterized by rich aquatic resources and high agricultural productivity resulting from the silt-enriched soils on the levees (Meggers 1971). Archeological studies indicate that relatively dense settlements were located here. *Lowland savannas* are semiaquatic, periodically inundated zones with poor soil resources. Nevertheless, they were cultivated by use of ridges, drainage ditches, and raised platforms (Denevan 1966a). A transitional form characterized by white sand and podzolic soils, nutrient conservation mechanisms, and which are criss-crossed by black-water rivers are the *caatinga* forests or scrub forests of the upper Rio Negro (Herrera et al. 1978). These are the classic areas known as "rivers of hunger" due to their low biotic productivity.

The *upland forests (montaña)* should be distinguished from lowland forests. The distinction has been suggested only in the past decade. Upland areas begin at about 700 meters or a mean annual temperature of 24° C. The cooler temperatures and the gently sloping land provide a less leached soil environment for agriculture, but the amount of game is highly variable. In areas where conditions are very wet or very dry, game other than birds may be nearly impossible to find (Denevan 1976:220). Fishing is poor due to a lack of major streams and the absence of lagoons comparable to those in the flood plain and lowland savannas. Given the poverty of the game, tribal groups are small and seminomadic.

The *lowland interfluvial forest* is not uniform. Making up close to 85 percent of Amazonia, it includes a wide range of habitats which remain to be precisely characterized. Rainfall varies between 40 and 80 inches and elevations vary between sea level and 600 meters. Eastern areas of the lowland forest are lower in rainfall than western parts; this leads to the distinction between dry, moist, and wet tropical forests (Tosi 1960; Denevan 1976). Soils are generally highly weathered, but sizable areas of medium to high fertility, perhaps comprising as much as 10 to 20 percent of the basin, are present in dispersed form (Wambeke 1978). The potential of this vast habitat remains largely unexplored.

A portion of the Amazon Basin is *upland savanna (campos de terra firme)*, covering areas in Central Brazil and the Guianas. Soils are leached and there is a prolonged dry season. Some native populations were nomadic hunter/gatherers, although most practice agriculture in the adjacent gallery forests (Maybury-Lewis 1967).

The variation that has been noted in Amazonian habitats so far only begins to give an idea that the Amazon Basin is more differentiated than most writings would have us believe. To date we lack a systematic comparison of these habitats according to standard measures such as density, productivity, species diversity, soil/plant associations. Indeed, it is highly questionable whether Amazonian aggregate figures tell us anything about the potential of the region for any particular purpose. Since the bulk of this study deals with the populations that came to inhabit the Altamira area in the Xingú Basin, it is important that the specific environmental features of the area be indicated so that the constraints and opportunities of this area be evaluated.

The Physical Environment of the Altamira Area

The land to which the Transamazon pioneers came is variously referred to as "the tropical rain forest," "jungle," or more accurately "tropical moist forest" (Holdridge 1967:17). The climate of Altamira is classified as *Aw* according to Köppen's system, that is, it has a tropical climate with monthly temperatures always above 18° C and a marked dry season (Falesi 1972). The topographic relief is highly variable with steep slopes not at all uncommon. Many of the relief features are likely inherited from alternating wet and dry climatic cycles, which are reported to have affected Amazonia in the Quaternary (Meggers 1975; Haffer 1969). Geomorphological indicators of a drier climate, such as pediments, lateritic plateaus, and stone lines have been observed by some investigators (Smith 1976a: 68). However, Whitten (1979:241) has questioned whether the climatic change affected the whole Amazon Basin. It has been suggested that the change may have involved a change from wet to moist and moist to drier forests (Whitten 1979).

Data on climate for most of the Amazon Basin is based on sporadic readings of macroclimatic factors. Microclimatic and energy/moisture balances based on long-term data sets are not available. Until such data is collected and studied, the full impact of climatic variability on systems of production cannot be assessed. What we have in the colonization zone of Altamira is based on a thirty-five year period and is of uncertain reliability. Mean monthly temperatures vary by less than 2° C year round in the Altamira area, with 26° C as the annual mean (see Figure 2.1). However, temperatures can reach 36° C in the shade and fall to 16° C the same day at nightfall (Smith 1976a:34). The greatest fluctuations seem to occur primarily in the months of July and August when clear skies facilitate the movement of long-wave radiation across the land surface and its exit at night. The daily variation is less during the rainy season due to cloudiness and the moderating effect of the almost daily rainfall from November through April. Cloudiness may be the most significant single factor in mean temperature variations across the Amazon Basin.

But no matter what month, daily temperature variations are greater than monthly averages. This daily cycle of temperatures plays a role in the scheduling of agricultural work. During my 1973–74 fieldwork in Vila Roxa, most colonists native to the Amazon began work around 06:30

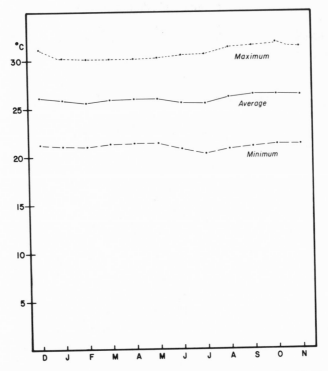

Fig. 2.1   Mean Temperatures at Altamira (1931–1967)
Source: Falesi 1972:9

hours and stopped work by 11:00 hours. Between 11:00 and 15:00 to 16:00 hours they would go home, rest in the shade, and carry out moderate types of activities such as sharpening tools, feeding livestock, and visiting neighbors. This is the hottest time of day and when humidity levels go above the already high mean of 85 percent. Cooling is difficult during strenuous work since humidity hovers between 86 and 90 percent from March through October, the months of most intense work effort. In the course of strenuous work such as forest clearing and cutting, for instance, four men consumed an average of a gallon of water in a half day of work. Work is resumed between 15:00 and 16:00 hours. Not all colonists, however, scheduled their work as well. Most colonists in Vila Roxa did not even leave their homes until about 08:00 hours, and by the time they reached the fields the sun was hot and work burdensome.

The volume and relative constancy of precipitation in the humid tropics can blind one to the significant patterns of variation. Altamira has a marked dry season of four months, during which time rainfall is below 60 millimeters per month. The mean annual precipitation is 1,705 millimeters, although variability from year to year can be great (see Figure

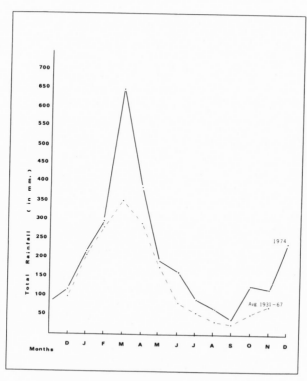

Fig. 2.2 Altamira Rainfall
Sources: Falesi 1972; Moran,
field notes, 1973–74

2.2). Annual potential evapotranspiration is 1,595 millimeters. Variation is not only seasonal (dry and wet seasons) but also daily. Smith noted that 33 percent of the rainfall at Marabá in February 1974 came down in a twenty-four hour period (1976a:39). In Altamira, I noted that in March 1974 there were twenty-four consecutive rainy days, in which 522 millimeters of rain fell—an amount greater than any monthly total and 30 percent of the annual mean. There were only two rainless days on that month. Downpours during these beginning months of the rainy season are the most important factor in annual soil erosion, since most crops have not yet grown sufficiently to provide effective soil cover. Fearnside (1978: 58) has also noted the considerable differences between daily and even monthly rainfall totals from kilometer-to-kilometer.

For the sake of contrast, one can compare the Altamira ecosystem with that of the upper Rio Negro near San Carlos. Whereas annual temperature averages 26° C in both sites, rainfall is twice as high (3,500 millimeters) at San Carlos with all months receiving in excess of 100 millimeters of rainfall. The absence of a marked dry season affects the biotic and abiotic components of the Rio Negro ecosystem. Over time the soils have become deeply weathered and extremely poor in available nutrients and in exchange capacity. While both forests are diverse in number of species, the Rio Negro area is lower in height, and has a lower basal area per hectare (Uhl 1980). The lower biomass (Jordan and Uhl 1978) and the lack of a marked dry season prevent the beneficial effects of traditional slash-and-burn agricultural methods from being achieved, even for an initial cropping period. The nutrient-conserving mechanisms of the oligotrophic Rio Negro ecosystem were summarized earlier in the chapter. In the Altamira area I did not observe the deep root mat above ground characteristic of such systems.

The seasonal pattern of rainfall distribution influences the pattern of hunting-gathering activities as well as agricultural operations. Pursuit of large bands of white-lipped peccaries (*Tayassu pecari*) is frequent during the rainy season. This is a period of fruit abundance and peccaries actively seek out the fruits—even within close proximity to settlements. In addition, the size of the bands increases, making the hunt all the more attractive. Except for this single type of hunting, however, the pattern of nocturnal downpours and the wet conditions of the litter make the hunting of most game less rewarding than it is in the dry season. Gathering during the rainy season is also worthwhile since major fruits consumed by Amazon populations become available: cupuaçú (*Theobroma grandiflora*), frutão (*Pouteria pariry*), and Brazil nuts (*Bertholetia excelsis*).

When the Transamazon Highway was built, it cut through a variety of types of upland forest, such as mature upland forest and vine forest (*mata de cipó*). It is the latter which is common in the area studied near Altamira. The appearance of vine forest there is not correlated with any particular soil type or topographical feature (Pires 1978). The canopy ranges between ten and twenty-five meters. Considerable variation in forest density occurs between sample plots, and species diversity is high. No reduction in vine forest hunting yields was noted by Smith (1976a:49). Caboclos tended to prefer these areas of forest because the thinner undergrowth provided a cleaner field after the burn due to the large mass of kindling and fewer large trees to cut.

The colonization areas between Marabá, Altamira, and Itaituba are characterized by a generally undulating topography. The area between the Tocantins (Marabá) and the Xingú (Altamira) traverses an area of Pre-Cambrian granitic shields, while the area between the Xingú and the Tapajós Rivers (Itaituba) is characterized by Carboniferous limestones and sandstones, and Devonian sand and siltstones. The Pre-Cambrian shield dominant in the Marabá-Altamira colonization stretch has weathered to form red and yellow ultisols (i.e., podzolic soils) of relatively low natural fertility. By contrast, the basic igneous parent material in the Altamira area and 250 kilometers west in the direction of Itaituba has formed an alfisol of medium to high fertility. Moreover, the parent materials, which are relatively close to the surface, continue to release nutrients that are capturable by some deep rooted plants. This should not be taken, however, as an implication that the soils in this zone are homogeneous. The mosaiclike pattern I have suggested is found in Altamira as well.

The major soil types in the Altamira area are oxisols (latosols), ultisols (podzolics), and alfisols (*terra roxa estruturada*). Oxisols account for an estimated 46 percent of the soils within the Transamazon transect; they are well structured but are low in nutrients, pH, and exchange capacity. Ultisols account for 38 percent of the soils and are characterized by excellent drainage and variable fertility. Alfisols are restricted to about 8 percent of the area cut by the highway, but their superior qualities make them particularly important. Alfisols are of medium to high fertility, characterized by near-neutral pH, high exchange capacity, low aluminum levels, and excellent structure. Smaller areas of spodozols and vertisols are also found in the Altamira area (Falesi 1972; IPEAN 1974; Smith 1976a:69–72). Smith (1976a:93) found in three communities along the Transamazon Highway that base saturation was much higher in the alfisols under forest than in oxisols and ultisols. Cation exchange capacity, on the other hand, was low in all three soils—ranging from a mean of 19.67 me/100 grams in alfisols to 7.36 me/100 grams in ultisols. Burning played an important role in increasing the base saturation of all soils, although the rise was more pronounced in the less fertile oxisols and ultisols. This positive change in base status is primarily due to the increase in calcium and magnesium after the burn.

The Altamira soils cut by the highway are among the best nonalluvial soils found in the Amazon. Nevertheless, they are inferior to the volcanic soils studied by Popenoe (1960) in the Polochic Valley of Central America. Organic matter levels are far lower in Altamira, but the levels are more constant than in that Guatemalan area. The average nitrogen content in Altamira soils I sampled was 0.20 percent, considerably below the 1.13 percent reported by Popenoe (1960:82–83). The Transamazon project, therefore, was not limited by the absence of relatively fertile soils for agriculture.

In short, the Altamira ecosystem differs from other Amazonian rain forest ecosystems in a number of ways. Whereas low fertility oxisols comparable to those found throughout most of the basin are the most frequently encountered soils, the Altamira area also has significant patches of medium to high fertility soils. This situation is similar, for example, for Rondonia (Furley 1979). It may or may not be the case elsewhere. Only further research in other sites will clarify the nature of soil patchiness in the Amazon Basin. The Altamira and Rondonia areas suggest that just as critical as soil fertility is the ability of human populations to identify the available good soils and to manage them for agriculture.

The vine forests of Altamira have higher biomass, higher basal area per hectare, and greater height than do the oligotrophic forests of the upper Rio Negro. They are, however, lower in these values than are the upland forests of the Central Amazon near Manaus (Fittkau and Klinge 1973). But the author noted patches of forest comparable to those in Manaus in the Altamira area. These forest patches may have been associated with the poorer podzols and oxisols found in the area, whereas the vine forest may have been associated with the alfisols and ultisols. The soil identification criteria of the Amazonian population would suggest this association (see Chapter 7).

Some scholars have suggested that the Altamira area is atypical of the Amazon. This judgment is based on the obvious presence of medium to high fertility soils which contrast markedly with the more commonly found low fertility oxisols and podzols. However, as I have tried to point out, the Altamira area is also dominated by these poorer soils, but the areal extent of the better soils suggests that if proper identification is made, the poorer soils could be protected from deforestation and the better soils managed for crop production. The Altamira area is actually "typical" in that soil patchiness characterizes it, and a variety of forest types with differential biological productivity may be found within the micro-region.

The simplistic notion that flood plains have high potential whereas terra firme does not is problematic. The flood plains of Rondonia, for example, are not fertile since they are associated with acid alluvium or with low humus, aluminum-affected gleys, acid sands, or concretionary lateritic soils, and are of little value for agriculture (Furley 1979:6). In addition, the more fertile flood plains present numerous problems to managers who are unable to mobilize sizable amounts of capital and technology (Falesi 1974). The terra firme includes a large variety of habitats which remain generally uncharacterized. Within a short walking distance from Vila Roxa in Altamira one could find fertile alfisols, easily managed but less fertile ultisols and oxisols, small patches of infertile sandy podzols, and a few alluvial areas. One might also expect forest structure and function, biomass productivity, nutrient cycling, resilience to deforestation, and other ecological features to vary from patch to patch (cf. UNESCO 1978:134).

The potential of the Amazon rain forest for human populations is highly variable and will require a great deal of research in which precise data on environmental parameters is collected and related to management strategies. Given the diversity of the forest that has been noted, it is useful to look towards the aboriginal population for insight into the use of Amazonian resources. Since Amazonian autochthonous populations are characterized by village-level organization, they are very likely to be sensitive to micro-level ecological variation. That is the subject of the next chapter.

Aboriginal Use of Amazonian Resources

3

The Adjustments of Tropical
Forest Societies

Most anthropologists and ecologists have come to accept the culture and technology of tropical forest aborigines as the optimal approach to the management of the Amazonian tropical rain forest (Meggers 1971; Goodland and Irwin 1975, to name two leading spokesmen). It is not difficult to see why such a view has become generalized. Studies of tropical forest populations have usually noted the extensive knowledge of wild plants, the remarkable familiarity with animal behavior, and the varied use of resources of these populations. Certainly, when compared with the failures so often documented in the literature (e.g., Price 1939; Bates 1952; Fosberg 1973; Nelson 1973) for efforts of temperate zone peoples, the knowledge of the tropical forest inhabitants seemed both awesome and accurate. And indeed, their knowledge is the product of accumulated observation and dependence on the wild resources available in the forest and the rivers. That knowledge, however, may not be easy to extrapolate due to the variety of habitats and the equally varied solutions devised to manage resources.

The cultural knowledge of tropical forest populations is worth studying because herein lies the potential for discovering approaches to resource use in Amazonia, which may provide sustained yields through time without causing severe environmental destruction. In this chapter an examination of this native approach to resource use is surveyed with an eye to establishing both the productivity and the limitations of their approaches to resource use. The reader is reminded that most studies of tropical forest populations are based on contemporary populations whose way of life may have been severely disrupted by the arrival of Europeans in 1492. It is clear from early accounts that riverine groups were larger and more complex at that time than are those observable at present (Lathrap 1968).

Indeed, the depopulation of the native American population was a major demographic disaster, the nature of which has occupied historical demographers for some time (cf. Hemming 1978; Denevan 1976; Dobyns

41

1966; Steward and Faron 1959; Rosenblat 1954). What is even sadder is that this process is repeated on a small scale each year, as isolated tropical forest groups come into contact with outsiders and decimation follows. In this century alone, at least eighty-seven Indian groups have become extinct (Ribeiro 1970:238). According to Bourne (1978:233) 45 percent of the Parakana died in the first months after the Transamazon cut through their traditional territory, and Price (1977:605) has documented a reduction of two-thirds in the Nambiquara population of Mato Grosso in the last ten years due to the invasion of cattle ranches. Epidemic disease appears to be the major causative factor in this depopulation. As many observers have noted, the death of these peoples is a profound loss on many counts. The native peoples of the Amazon represent part of that rich variety of human societies and cultures which enriches our understanding of human possibilities. Decimation and relocation of groups in reservations set aside to provide a temporary haven provide a measure of relief, but in such locational change there must surely be great loss of cultural knowledge about the environment. The very diversity of the tropical forest militates against the ability of a population to transfer their ethnoscientific knowledge from place to place (Moran, 1979d). Perhaps more important than any specific knowledge may be the attitude towards the forest of most aboriginal populations—one characterized by respect and a recognition of the need to balance human demands with the capacity of the environment to supply them.

It should be noted that most native Amazonians lived in small communities, within which a broad spectrum of practices appears to have regulated population growth and distribution. Low population densities were maintained by practices that included warfare, female infanticide, and village fissioning. The regulation of population appears to be most closely related to the need to maintain the integrity and productivity of a hunting way of life. Ross (1978) has shown that the length of hunting trips is directly related to the size of settlements, and Lathrap (1968) noted a decade earlier than he that tropical forest dwellers were distributed in accordance with the availability of protein sources.

The ease and frequency of village fissioning in Amazonian tribes is striking. Carneiro (1961) believes that villages rarely had a chance to reach carrying capacity, but split up well before the point of overshooting resources was ever reached. As population increased, stresses and strains increased, and the lack of internal political controls and weak chieftainship failed to discourage a village faction from splitting off (Carneiro 1974: 78). Nor are there any ecological deterrents to splitting off from a parent community. Suitable unoccupied land is easily found, and the vast network of streams and rivers facilitate travel except in cases where hostile populations may have interfered with free river traffic. In other words, in the absence of both internal and external deterrents, tropical forest tribes followed the path of least resistance and sought avoidance of the natural stresses that come with increased population density.[1] The situation is quite different in Asia and Africa. Clarke (1966) notes that with increased population in New Guinea there is a shift from extensive to intensive shifting cultivation, with shortening of fallows, lower productivity per unit of land and per unit of labor, but higher total production as a function of higher labor inputs and more intensive methods. Boserup (1965) notes a similar relationship between increased population and the intensification of agriculture in Africa. But as with the New Guinean case, the situation in Africa was one of limited land availability. Lacking this constraint, populations will opt for extensive and labor efficient agricultural methods, with high productivity maintained by periodic relocation and dispersion.

Ethnographers have noted time and again the practices of female infanticide, abortion, long periods of sexual abstinence after childbirth, warfare, and a strong male fear of too frequent sexual contact with women. Indeed, the "population policies" of native Amazonians span the range from unrestricted expansion to highly controlled reproduction (Wagley 1969). Among some populations, intercourse between husband and wife was forbidden from the onset of pregnancy until the child was weaned— often between the age of three to five. Sexual continence was sometimes required prior to ceremonies, raids, and hunting. The number of these prohibitions varied a great deal and may have been related to other forms of population control (Meggers 1974:104). All these practices had the net effect of controlling the size of aboriginal Amazonian populations.[2]

Harris has recently argued that the chronic warfare of Amazonian village societies adapts them to the low environmental potential of the area. He bases his conclusions chiefly on the Yanomamo, one of the largest aboriginal groups in lowland South America. While women contribute the bulk of the calories among the Yanomamo, "recurring intergroup combat places a premium upon rearing males rather than female infants" (Harris 1974b:75). Thus, they practice female infanticide because the more numerous the adult males, the more likely the group is to hold on to its territory and, when needed, increase it. By reducing the number of females, the reproductive potential of the population is reduced and the competition for scarce females leads to competition between males. War, in itself, does not significantly control population, although in aboriginal groups continuous feuding may have played a major role in population control (Livingstone 1968:8).[3]

The ecological role of aggressive, or agonistic, behavior has not been adequately demonstrated, and King (1973:133) suggests that the problem lies in the difficulty of controlling relevant variables under "natural conditions." It is fairly certain, however, that the larger the settlements, the greater the resource area required and the more frequently warfare may have appeared as a strategy of resource control. Access to resources, warfare, and the productivity of hunting are intimately associated in aboriginal use of Amazonian resources.

The Earliest Amazonian Populations

It is estimated that the hunters who entered South America from North America around 20,000 B.P. followed the now extinct large mammals down the Andean Cordillera (Meggers 1972; Myers 1973). Only at around 10,000 B.P. is there archeological evidence of human penetration into the edge between the forest and the savannas of Central Brazil (cited in Carneiro 1970a) and entry into the upper Amazon at about 4,000 B.P. (Lathrap 1970:45). The groups exploiting the then rich megafauna would have had little reason to enter the humid tropics where the terrestrial mammal biomass per unit area was probably but a fraction of that in the Andean zone at the time (Clark 1976).

Accurate data on human habitation at the mouth of the Amazon dates to around 3,000 B.P. (PRONAPA 1970; Meggers and Evans 1957). Settlements consisted of a single longhouse sheltering approximately forty people. This typical pattern of small settlements gives way around A.D. 500 to larger human concentrations with houses located along the river bank in linear form, suggesting an increasingly riverine orientation. A similar upward shift in population size and a riverine focus has been noted in the Upper Amazon near the Napo River (Evans and Meggers 1968). The explanation for this sudden growth in complexity has been attributed by Evans and Meggers to immigration from the northern Andes. An alternative explanation has been offered by Lathrap (1970). According to Lathrap, large communities already existed in the Upper Amazon around 400 B.C. and continued into the historic period. While one cannot be certain that these Upper Amazon communities were not ultimately products of immigration, a great deal of additional archeological research is necessary before postulating that the development of large riverine settlements was not endogenous (Myers 1973).

It has not been well established whether or not the earliest inhabitants of the Amazon, as elsewhere, were hunter/gatherers. Lathrap (1970) suggests that the origins of tropical forest inhabitants should be sought in lake basins with extensive alluvial fill. A tradition of exploitation of aquatic resources held an advantage comparable to that of the shellfish collectors of the northwestern coast of South America and the southern coast of Brazil. The majority of the Amazonian populations appear to have concentrated along the major streams and developed relatively large aggregates and complex forms of social and political organization. The productivity of these aquatic areas was, in part, responsible for the leap of population noted in the archeological record. But all aboriginal populations of the

Amazon, in varying degrees, relied also upon hunting for some of their protein needs. As we will see in the sections that follow, the degree of dependence on hunting was a function of proximity to major riverine resources, cultural prescriptions as regards forest resources, and of the size reached by settlements. The integrity of a hunting way of life, however, is enhanced by maintaining a relatively small size in settlements.

Hunting and Gathering in a Diverse Environment

Amazonian Indians rely on a hunting technology to exploit the tropical forest resources. The specifics of hunting reflect local habitat characteristics, periodicity, seasonality, and previous patterns of exploitation in a given territory. The technology of hunting in the tropical rain forest consisted primarily of the use of bow and arrow, lances, and blowguns. Hunting has been a male-dominated occupation, and observers have noted that it is viewed as a half-work, half-sport activity (Vickers 1976:96).

The use of blowguns with poisoned tipped darts is a delicate art and allows hunters to shoot repeatedly without scaring the prey, thereby increasing the chances of a multiple kill (Bates 1962). They are used primarily against the arboreal fauna. Blowgun darts are often dipped in poison to increase the projectile's effectiveness. The poison is fashioned of several ingredients, although *curare* (*Strychnos toxifera*) is often one of them. Researchers have also noted the use of poisons derived from *Ocgodia ternstroemiifolia* and *Naucleopsis mellobarretoi* (Gottlieb and Mors 1978). The blowgun is effective against animals up to the size of peccaries and within a range of about twenty-five meters (Vickers 1976:96). Native peoples may have given up their blowguns in exchange for firearms, not so much for their hunting effectiveness, but in response to the advantage they provide in warfare (Ross 1978).

Lances are primarily aimed at the larger land mammals, and hunting with them usually involves open pursuit of animals. Tapirs, boars, and other group animals are pursued by several hunters, who foresee in a good kill a chance of several days off from hunting. A tapir weighs up to 250 kilograms and can provide meat for several days. Many studies, however, indicate that the efficiency of hunting large game is inferior, especially in areas occupied for several years (Vickers 1976; Ross 1978). Whenever the bow and arrow are used, they preempt the use of the blowgun, since the bow and arrow is useful in both hunting and fishing.

Aboriginal populations also relied on traps (Vickers 1976; Ryden 1950; Ruddle 1970). Deadfall traps are used chiefly to catch agoutis, armadillos, and rodents. Tension traps can be effectively used to catch ground-dwelling birds. Pitfall traps are used also; these consist of shallow holes with sharp bamboo points that are then covered with leaves.

Just as the Amazon is diverse, it is clear that animal biomass is highly variable from area to area. These differences reflect both the net productivity of the forest and the hunting pressure in the area. A forest area near Manaus had a total dry weight plant biomass of 585 tons per hectare (Klinge and Rodrigues 1968), while Jordan (1971) has measured it as low as 228 tons in an area of nutrient-poor tropical forest in the upper Rio Negro. The protected forest of Barro Colorado had an estimated animal biomass of 4,400 to 5,300 kilograms per square kilometer (Eisenberg and Thorington 1973:152), while an unprotected area in the Brazilian Amazon had only 2,100 kilograms per square kilometer (Fittkau and Klinge 1973).[4]

Hunters must rely, not only on an appropriate hunting technology, but also on intimate knowledge of the forest and the animals.[5] Forest hunters are capable of imitating the calls and sounds of most animals they hunt, as well as of recognizing their telltale footsteps. Knowledge of the animals' diet is particularly useful to hunters in the tropical rain forest. As hunters move through the forest, they note what trees are flowering or fruiting where and use that knowledge in their next hunting expedition. Since trees of a given species do not flower simultaneously, hunters must maintain constant attention to these details, and wide-ranging movement over a hunting territory may be necessary to find trees in a period that makes them attract game.

Yields from hunting are extremely variable (cf. Gross et al. 1979; Chagnon and Hames 1979; Lizot 1979; Hames 1979; Vickers 1976; Ross 1978). Lathrap (1968), Carneiro (1970a:243), and Gross (1975) suggest that the productivity of hunting limits the size and permanence of settlements in the Amazon. Such a single factor explanation has been questioned recently (Beckerman 1979; Chagnon and Hames 1979, Vickers 1976). Vickers (1975, 1976) shows that while, indeed, animal biomass is considerably inferior to the plant biomass, the yield is still significant. The problems of obtaining protein reside more in its dispersed nature and the behavioral habits of the animals than in its absolute amount. The amount of game obtained is surprisingly large in both new and old settlements. Most of the statements concerning the lack of meat among native South Americans is based, not on personal observation and careful data gathering of game hunted and eaten, but on the acceptance of the natives' point of view. Indeed, among tropical forest peoples, "hunger for meat" appears to be either a constant concern or a periodic lack (cf. Holmberg 1969; Siskind 1973). But that ethnoecological concern may not be based on a real and constant dietary lack. Fortunately, the heated debates over the availability of protein in the rain forest has attracted many researchers in the past few years and more precise studies have begun to appear (Vickers 1976; Smith 1976a; Hames 1979; Sponsel n.d., among others).

Among the Siona-Secoya inhabiting an upland forest area of Ecuador, even the least successful hunter managed a mean of 13.08 kilograms of butchered meat per hunt—with an average for all hunters of 21.35 kilograms. This translated into 80.7 grams of protein per person per day, an amount well above protein needs. Even in an area inhabited for thirty-two years continuously, the mean kill was 5.67 kilograms per hunt per hunter. Chagnon and Hames (1979) show that the Yanomamo and the Yecuana obtain a more than sufficient amount of animal protein. They argue that Gross (1975) underestimated protein intakes because he did not normalize the data to account for age and sex variables. The mean consumption per adult was 88 grams of protein per day, an amount higher than in many contemporary urban societies. These protein intakes from hunting are possible only because of low population densities and would quickly fall with population growth. Of course, even if the hunters are successful, given the nocturnal habits of much of the game, the high canopy habits of most of the birds and monkeys, and the aggressiveness of the peccaries, it is not surprising to see a great deal of cultural attention given to hunter/ animal relations.

Of all the subsistence activities, hunting is the least secure of them all. The uncertainty associated with hunting is reduced in numerous aboriginal societies by elaborate symbolic systems that reflect culturally sanctioned adjustments of populations to resources. These adjustments take the form of prohibitions. Some tribes taboo the eating of some or all game animals during puberty (Lévi-Strauss 1948; Metráux 1948), menstruation (Nimuendajú 1948a), pregnancy (Nimuendajú 1948a), and postpartum (Metráux 1948; Nimuendajú 1948a, 1948b). Mura fathers may not hunt until their offspring can walk (Nimuendajú 1948c), a practice that may encourage conservation, intensify social exchange, and create close bonds between father and child. Ipurina fathers must refrain from eating tapir or peccary meat for a year after their child is born (Metráux 1948). Ross (1978) has argued that these taboos reflect ecological adaptations to the differential productivity of some species.

Belief in game spirits is very widespread throughout the rainforest (Zerries 1954), and concepts of supernatural protectors of the animals serve to create a respectful attitude between the hunter and his game.[6] The Mundurucu, for example, believe that a hunter can lose his soul if he kills an animal for any purpose other than the need for meat (Murphy 1958:14–17), and the Yukpa believe that the master of birds, *yorsäthe*, devours the hunter who kills more birds than he needs (Wilbert 1974:38).

Restrictions on hunting are balanced by prescribed reciprocity. The practice is widely documented among native groups (Nimuendajú 1952; Maybury-Lewis 1956; Leacock 1964; Frikel 1968; Carneiro 1970b). Such reciprocity, however, is quick to break down after contact with a cash economy and a more individualized pattern of economic production. Other controls such as warfare, sexual restrictions, and infanticide also decline rapidly in these circumstances. The net result is a rapid decline in yield per hunt and available protein per capita, and an increased dependence on extra-regional inputs for subsistence.

One case documented recently is particularly enlightening. According to Reichel-Dolmatoff (1971), the Tukano of the Vaupés River see human society and the fauna of their habitat as sharing the same pool of reproductive energy. The fertility of both men and animals has a fixed limit, rather than being an infinite or unrestricted resource. It is important for them, therefore, to seek an equilibrium in human sexual activity in order to allow the animals of the forest to reproduce and, in turn, serve as nourishment for the human population. Cultural rules place strict controls over the recognized tendency of people to exploit the environment to the limits of their technological capacity.

Within this system of controls, sexual repression of the hunter plays a major role. Since this repression could have highly undesirable psychological effects,[7] the Tukano have filled the relationship between hunter and prey with erotic content. The hunter dreams and hallucinates about sexual contact with the animals, which he fertilizes so they multiply for his benefit. At times, the animals ravish the hunter in dreams. The hunt is part courtship and part sexual act, filled with care, respect, and ritual. The verb "to hunt," for example, is *vai-mera gametarari*, which literally means "to make love to the animals." The practice of courtship behavior manifests the idea of sexually attracting the game so it can be killed, and the kill has a strong element of sexual domination. Before and after the hunt, the hunter abstains from sexual contact. None of the women in the long house (*maloca*) must be menstruating, nor should he allow erotic dreams before a hunt. Such a system, in fact, limits both the sexual activity of the hunter and the frequency of hunting. A child is gradually indoctrinated into this complex set of beliefs, and before puberty the child already knows that he should never mock a dead animal or treat them carelessly, and that not all of the animals can be hunted, but only some of them, and only under stringent conditions. Noncompliance leads to fear of death, since the spirits of the animals can lure them away from familiar terrain and kill them.

The Tukano believe in small families. Families with six or seven children are criticized as resembling "a family of dogs." There is cultural hostility towards these incontinent families since their lack of sexual abstinence robs the animals of their energy for reproduction, while at the same time the families demand more meat to feed the added children. The animals are believed to grow jealous and refuse to serve as prey— an idea which reflects the experience of lower hunting yields under conditions of population growth. Worldviews such as those of the Tukano operate well under aboriginal conditions but are quickly disrupted by contact with outside groups. This is particularly the case if the cultural contact is associated with the spread of diseases to which the population has not built immunities (cf. Wagley 1969).

In addition to the cosmologically based practices found among the Tukano, ethnographic evidence notes a wide range of cultural practices which permitted native groups to use wild sources of animal protein without bringing about its rapid depletion. Perhaps most important of all is reliance on animals other than large mammals.[8]

Arthropods (i.e., insects) constitute the bulk of the animal biomass in the Amazon rain forest (Fittkau and Klinge 1973) and are consumed widely by the native population (Carvalho 1951; Baldus 1970; Taylor 1974). Arthropods are an excellent source of high quality protein, at least as good on a per weight basis as is the meat of domestic animals. Ruddle notes that the Yukpa regularly consumed twenty-two genera of insects (1973). Chagnon writes that the Yanomamo ate caterpillars, beetle larvae, ants, and spiders (1968:30–32). Tribes in the upland forests of the Vaupés (Bruzzi 1962:221–22; Reichel-Dolmatoff 1976), the lowland forest in the Xingú (Carvalho 1951), and in the upland savannas of Mato Grosso (Oberg 1953) have also engaged in entomophagy. The Amazonian arthropod biomass is overwhelmingly higher than mammalian, avian, reptilian or amphibian biomass.

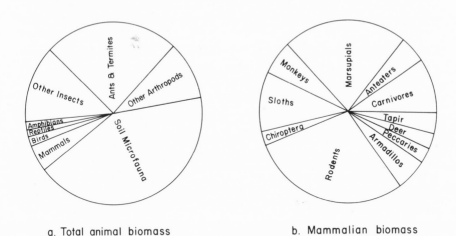

a. Total animal biomass   b. Mammalian biomass

Fig. 3.1 Composition of the Fauna in a Central Amazon
Rain Forest
Source: Adapted from Fittkau and Klinge 1973

Birds, rodents, and marsupials offer a relatively more abundant biomass resource than larger taxa such as peccary, tapir, and brocket deer. Among some Amerindian groups, birds are important in the diet. Among the Achuara, birds were the most reliable game (Ross 1978). The Maraca crop ninety-one species of birds belonging to twenty-eight families (Ruddle 1970). Vickers (1976) has also noted their use in the diet.[9] Birds appear to be important in providing diversity rather than being a major contributor to the diet. More important are the numerous rodents of the Amazon. Rodents made up about a third of the mammalian fauna studied by Fittkau and Klinge (1973). Not only are they relatively abundant in the forest, but they seem to thrive near planted clearings. This makes "garden hunting" both possible and economic for the hunter. Linares (1976) has noted that hunting in the vicinity of planted gardens may have partially eliminated seasonality and scheduling problems and served as a substitute for animal domestication. The Guaymi and the Cuna of Panama, in particular, seem to have effectively used garden hunting. Unlike the energy-costly diurnal hunting of large game, hunting of rodents, like agouti and paca, is chiefly a nocturnal, waiting affair. Hunters lie in wait while slung in their hammocks up in a tree, or wait sitting on a platform built for the purpose.

In addition to a preference for smaller game, natives hunt a large territory. The northern Kayapó of the upper Xingú River and the Xikrin of the Itacaiunas River conduct trips lasting from several days to over a month (Dreyfus 1963; Caron 1971). Game taken on such trips is preserved by smoking and sun drying. Hunting treks are combined with seasonal movement undertaken to exploit wild fruit resources.

Gathering forest products is subject, too, to the peculiar periodicities and seasonality of the tropical forest. During the dry season, forest populations engage in concentrated gathering efforts because of the availability of game and greater ease of traveling. Forest plant products make important contributions to the diet and involve work by men, women, and children. While hunting, the men do not overlook the presence of plant resources and may collect or consume them on the spot. A wide variety of products is gathered, but major contributors, by volume, are few in number.

It is difficult to generalize about gathering given the opportunistic nature of the activity and the lack of nutritional studies that include such foods in their assessments. The ability to exploit such resources is dependent upon the cultural identification of these foods as edible, and on a certain degree of mobility. While it is doubtful that wild plants provide the bulk of the calories on a year-round basis, they provide an important supplement to the diet and sustain the trekking population while on the move. The absence of rituals associated with the collection of wild plants suggests the relative ease and certainty of their obtainment. Honey is collected with relish among most native groups, and fruits and nuts are major contributors to the diet during treks.

For at least 3,000 years now, the majority of Amazonian native peoples have combined hunting and gathering in the forest with fishing and agriculture. The advantages of inhabiting riverine areas such as the flood plain, the lowland savanna, and the lowland forests are numerous. Not only is the fish fauna rich and easily procured by means as simple as the bow and arrow, traps, and fish stupefiers (piscicides), but some of the larger mammals in the forest and many birds come to eat the vegetation growing along the banks, thereby becoming prey to the hunter/fisherman. In addition, the river is the most convenient way to travel through the immensity of the rain forest habitat.

Fishing and Farming in a Diverse Environment

Fishing and farming have long gone together in the flood plain, the coast, and the lowland forests of the Amazon. Population densities have been traditionally low in the Amazon Basin as a whole, where 0.6 to 1.0 persons per square kilometer are still common over wide regions. Densities are higher in the African (seven to ten persons/km²) and Asian rain forests (over twenty persons/km²). Note should be taken, however, that the low figures for the Amazon are based on region-wide estimates, which do not reflect realistic densities possible in rich habitats such as the Amazonian flood plain. Denevan estimates that in the flood plain regions population probably averaged twenty-eight persons per square kilometer before 1492 (Denevan 1976:218), while it was probably around 1.2 in the aquatically and agriculturally poorer upland forests.[10]

What was it about the riverine and coastal habitats that permitted such relatively high population densities? The flood plain zone is an area of variable width, of low elevation (under 300 meters), covered by meandering rivers with considerable overflow basins. The rivers are always changing course and creating a complex network of lakes, swamps, and islands. Recent estimates place the extent of the Amazonian flood plain at 2 percent of the basin, but the flood plain may have supported a population equal in size to the rest of the basin. The rivers fluctuate with the changing seasons and reach up the river banks, making such areas rich for plant growth through silt deposition. Traditionally, the population plants fast-growing annual crops as the water level goes down with the dry season.

Not all flooded areas are equally enriched by the rise and fall of the Amazon rivers. The rivers emerging from the ancient Guiana and Brazilian Massifs, usually called "clear-water" rivers, carry less silt and provide a minimal benefit to the soils they flood. "Black-water" rivers arise from the Amazonian plain. While the water also has a low content of suspended silt, its black color is due to the humic substances washed out of the forests through which it flows. They lack dissolved mineral salts and are acidic in pH (Janzen 1975). On the other hand, the rivers coming from the geologically young Andes, known as "white-water" rivers, carry greater amounts of silt from basic rocks (Sioli 1951).

Large, sedentary settlements are possible also in selected lowland interfluvial forests (Smith 1976a:282). Smith found in twenty-three archeological sites visited on terra firme a number of shared characteristics: all were located within 500 meters of a perennial stream, all were located on relatively flat ground, and all concentrated their population in small clearings of 0.5 to 5.0 hectares. Proximity to streams facilitated transportation, bathing, cleaning up, and fishing. Compact, flat settlements helped reduce erosion and facilitated social interaction. Houses (*malocas*) were communal, made of sturdy palm-thatch and poles. The malocas have a high roof design that reduces heat radiation and enhances cooling. The constant upkeep of fires inside discourages the presence of black flies and other insects (Smith 1976a:305).

Smith has noted that many of the sites are located on *terra roxa* or *terra preta* (Smith 1976a:283). The former is a medium to high fertility soil (usually an alfisol), while the latter is a humus-rich, anthropogenic soil sought out for swidden plots. While the soils in lowland savanna are not as desirable, the richness of game in this semiaquatic area also permitted relatively dense settlement (Denevan 1966). For four to eight months these areas are inundated by overflowing rivers. In the Llanos de Mojos in northeastern Bolivia the native population raised platforms to provide high ground for crops, some as large as 25 by 300 meters (Denevan 1966b).

This fish species richness in rivers cutting through lowland regions has only begun to be carefully studied. Junk (1975:109) notes that 1,300 to 2,000 species have been identified in the Amazon rivers, and that yearly harvests of 633,000 metric tons are theoretically possible on a sustained basis. Such potential has never been realized, and the harvests of aboriginal peoples are miniscule by comparison with this maximum theoretical figure.

Unlike hunting, which as we have seen is surrounded with ritual and taboo due to its insecurity, fishing is relatively free of restrictions due to the abundance of the resource relative to aboriginal capacity for its exploitation.[11] In addition, among aboriginal peoples fishing is not restricted to men as is the case with hunting.

Before the adoption of the hook-and-line, tropical forest populations used a variety of harpoons, bow and arrow, traps, and "poisons" to capture fish. The use of the bow and arrow in fishing is widely practiced in tropical areas. It is usually practiced early in the day and involves standing in the canoe or near the river bank and waiting for a fish to pass underneath. Spears and harpoons are used against larger prey, such as *pirarucu* (*Arapaima gigas*), cayman, and manatee. These techniques are not generalized, but represent specific techniques applicable in particular times and places to catch specific species of fish (Vickers 1976:105).

Fishing with poisons can be practiced only in small streams and requires a large group effort.[12] The plants used as poisons are wild but, because of their importance, have become semi-domesticates. A barrier must be built in the stream to prevent the fish from escaping, and the plants usually have to be beaten so as to release the substance. The fish are stupefied, their breathing impaired by the substance, and they float to the surface where they are caught. These communal fishing efforts usually occur during the dry season.

The fishing of Amazon river turtles (*Podocnemis* spp.) and the collecting of their eggs were important subsistence activities until relatively recent times. The early Portuguese explorers made note of the large numbers of turtles kept in pens by riverine populations. The turtles provide an abundant high quality source of animal protein, while the eggs are tasty— whether raw, boiled, or smoked.

The largest of these turtles, *Podocnemis expansa*, weighs around 100 pounds and can lay about 150 eggs yearly. The trouble is that they are relatively easy to capture during the egg-laying period, when they invade nesting areas along the Amazon. Traditionally, Orinoco and Amazon River tribes collected thousands of turtles during this short period of dry season exposure.[13] They also probed the sand with sticks looking for the eggs—which were smoked and dried on babricots (Smith 1974a:86). The turtles were used to stock aquatic corrals, which were turned to during the wet season, when fish are difficult to find in the now muddied waters and when piscicides are impractical due to the increased volume of water (Smith 1977). The Conibo of the upper Amazon developed special bows and arrows for shooting *Podocnemis*, while the Paumari and the Mura swam underwater to grab the aquatically elusive turtles.

Vickers (1976:124) estimated the energetic efficiency of fishing at 2.99 to 1, while that of hunting was 9.33 to 1 in a new village settlement, but dropped to a ratio of 2.48 to 1 in a long-occupied site. Game depletion is a problem of greater immediacy than is fish depletion in aboriginal situations. As a result, populations probably preferred riverine locations to those inland, where hunting would have to be relied on to supply the bulk of the protein. The productivity of fishing is a function of location. In one study villagers on or near a large river obtained over 2 kilograms per person per fishing trip, while those in smaller streams ranged between 0.39 and 1.10 kilograms per fishing trip. The chronic state of warfare/raiding in tropical rain forest regions before contact, and since then, has been explained by some as a result of a constant effort to control riverine sites where subsistence efforts, particularly protein obtention, were more rewarding.

Agriculture in the lowland and upland forested areas of the Amazon followed a pattern emphasizing root crops and the technique known as slash-and-burn, swidden, or shifting cultivation found across all tropical rain forests. Shifting cultivation can be defined as an agricultural system in which fields are cropped for fewer years than they are allowed to remain fallow. In this system an area of land is cut, allowed to dry for a few months, and is then burnt. Burning has been shown to kill parasites, insects, fungi, nematodes, and pathogenic bacteria. Weeds are destroyed and anaerobic nitrogen-fixing bacteria increase their activity. The heating of the soil during the burn leads to increased fertility due to the increased rate of nitrification (Nye and Greenland 1960:72). This allows more of the nitrogen to become available to plants for a period after the burn. The availability of nitrogen, phosphorus, and potassium—the three major macronutrients for plant growth—is increased by turning the vegetation into a nutrient-rich ash layer. The ash layer is not only fertilizer, but it also raises the pH of acid tropical soils. Rodents and other plant predators are driven out by the fire, thereby giving the young crops a better chance at maturing.[14]

The practice of slash-and-burn agriculture, originally seen as destructive, is now seen as ecologically sound within certain limits.[15] The type of swiddening known as "long fallow" is the most protective and least likely to lead to irreversible damage. This is the approach most commonly taken by Amazonian aborigines. In this approach, cultivation of a field lasts only two to three years, and the length of fallow is relatively long (twenty years not uncommon). Fields are widely scattered and small in size. Regeneration of forest is rapid due to proximity of seeds. In other areas of the tropics with higher population densities, fallows are shorter and tree species in the succession may be managed for certain needs of the group. In pioneer areas the forest may be converted to rangeland due to unfamiliarity with appropriate management of the swidden cycle.

In the Amazon, as in other rain forest areas, some populations use intercropping as part of their swidden strategy. This means that plants having different heights, nutrient demands, and leaf exposure to the sun exist side by side. This multistoried arrangement provides good soil protection from both solar radiation and the erosive force of precipitation. Moreover, they intercept more light per unit of land than monocropped fields. It is diverse in numbers of species, generalized in purpose, and provides the soil with the needed protection from the intense action of sun and rain. It is also effective in preserving natural biological controls, that is, avoiding concentration of food sources for arthropod pests, providing intense shade that discourages the colonization of sun-loving weeds, and providing a higher net yield per unit of land than can monocrop systems (IRRI 1973). The polycultural swidden is more common in Southeast Asia, where short fallow strategies are used. In the Amazon, fields may be 80 to 95 percent planted in manioc, and production problems are solved more often by long fallow rather than by imitation of the forest (Denevan, personal communication).

Swidden systems assume that the land will be periodically left fallow. Reasons for abandonment include weed invasion with every growing season, decline in the available nutrient pool, pest infestation, and consequent decline in yields. Crucial to the long-term productivity of swidden systems is the existence of mechanisms that encourage abandonment of fields at regular intervals so that forest can take over. Terra firme populations appear to have shifted more often due to game depletion than in response to the perception of decreased yields. In the flood plain the reason for shifting areas may have been weed invasion.

Manioc and bananas are often planted first because they start slower than crops like maize or rice, and the latter also requires more nutrients. Manioc is a most reliable crop—the chief staple of most rain forest people in the Amazon, occupying up to 90 percent of cultivated fields. Its cultivation is not demanding, but when processing technology includes the production of manioc into flour, cakes, and other consumables, it is demanding of labor. Manioc is universally associated with women among Amazonian aborigines. Women manage the crop and are responsible for the processing. Manioc is ready to be harvested after six months, but can stay in the ground up to two years, during which time it continues to grow. Women harvest the manioc as they need it. Vickers estimated that the efficiency of horticulture among the Siona-Secoya was 52.1:1.[16] This figure is close to that for the Kuikuru of Brazil (i.e., 56.5:1) reported by Carneiro (1957:170) but considerably higher than estimates of Rappaport (1968) among the Tsembaga of New Guinea, Nietschmann (1973) among the Miskito of Central America, or Carter (1969) among the Kekchi of Guatemala. The greater horticultural efficiency may be directly attributable to the Kuikuru and the Siona-Secoya emphases on manioc cultivation, and their relatively minor labor inputs in the form of fencing, terracing, piling and burning, and weeding.

The location of outlying gardens is dependent on the suitability of soils in the proximity of the village and other factors. Each population uses different criteria in the classification and selection of suitable soils for agriculture. The Siona-Secoya use color and texture in their classification of soils. While they never go out to look for land, they know their territory well, and on hunting and gathering trips they make note of the potential of different areas. They frequently relocate their settlements on old habitation sites (Vickers 1976:63). Whenever possible they clear land near the river since it is easier to transport the produce by canoe than by netted bag strung over the forehead—which is the common means of carrying produce over land. Thus soil quality considerations may take secondary importance to the labor requirements of transportation.

Most ethnographers who have noted criteria for choosing village sites in Amazonia rarely mention soils for agriculture as an important consideration. Rather, availability of white clay for rituals, game availability, protection from enemy raids, and proximity to a major river predominate as criteria for village selection. I have argued elsewhere (Moran, 1979) that the mobility required to maintain the productivity of hunting was the prime consideration of native Amazonians, and that such mobility reduced the accuracy of agronomic knowledge. Farming expertise (meaning input/ output ratios and total production achieved) thrives, not on mobility, but on sedentarization.

Diversification as a Resource Use Strategy

While it would be naive to suggest that all Amazon native peoples were in balance with nature before 1492, the evidence presented in this chapter suggests that a wide spectrum of subsistence practices were applied to resource use. Because they lacked access to extra-regional subsidies, Amazon populations developed site-specific solutions that reflected the characteristic diversity of Amazon ecosystems. Native peoples adjusted to the limitations of each zone; exploited, whenever possible, areas at the edge between habitats; and maintained strategies that adjusted resource use to resource availability in highly localized micro-environments. The many disagreements over, for example, the availability of protein in Amazonia may be resolved as the micro-ecological distinctiveness of various habitats studied is acknowledged. The same will be even truer of micro-ecological studies of farming systems.

One of the important consequences of the introduction of a monetary economy into the Amazon is the gradual erosion of the traditional strategies of diversified resource use. Hunting of a wide variety of game animals for subsistence gives way to hunting animals prized for their skins in trading posts (Smith 1976c). In the process, the meat of the animals is misused or left unused as a protein source. Smith (1974a) and Mittermeier (1975) have dramatically shown the devastating effect of the Portuguese demand for turtle oil on the giant river turtle, now near extinction. The demand for alligator skins also led to the wholesale slaughter of these animals; because of the scale of operations only the skins were used, the rest was wasted. Native horticulturalists abandoned their swidden plots when the potential for wealth from tapping rubber or collecting Brazil nuts became alluring. Murphy and Murphy (1974) have shown that rubber tapping and desire for trade goods led to the dispersion of the Mundurucu into single households, to a neglect of agriculture, and to debt/dependency on rubber traders. A comparable development has been studied in relation to the Brazil nut trade (Laraia and da Matta 1967).

Hemming (1978), Wagley (1977), and Denevan (1976) have documented the devastating impact of post-Columbian contact on the aboriginal populations. The forest, however, has been more resilient to human efforts to subdue it. Wave after wave of immigrants to the Amazon have had to adopt local patterns of resource use, or they have left, defeated. The question must be raised whether an ecosystem as diverse and resilient as the Amazon Basin is best managed by site-specific diversity—as exemplified by aboriginal resource use—or whether the attempts at simplification introduced since 1492 are appropriate and productive. In the following chapter I briefly examine the historical evolution of resource use in the Amazon Basin in an attempt to answer this query.

The Impact of Colonialism and an Extractive Economy

4

The arrival of the Portuguese on the Brazilian coast in 1500 initiated major and devastating changes in the Amazon Basin. While the impact of Post-Columbian contact was most severely felt along the Brazilian coast and the flood plain, the diseases brought by the Europeans initiated a process of decimation that, coupled with warfare, made its mark deep in the Amazon interior. The Portuguese sought to establish a plantation society in the Amazon just as they had done in the Northeast coast. Such a society needed a continuous supply of slaves to maintain its viability, so expeditions were organized yearly to scour the Amazon interior for Indian slaves. However, their penetration was limited by regional characteristics and the relatively meager results they derived from efforts at establishing plantations.

The resources identified by the Portuguese did not offer the wealth of the mythical El Dorado. A few aromatic plants and the oil from river turtles were all that the explorers deemed useful. A combination of low revenues for the Crown and unfamiliarity with the vast Amazon interior kept the Amazon realm neglected by the Crown and thinly settled by the colonists. Since the settlers had come after a stay in the sugar-producing state of Pernambuco, their only goal was to plant sugar plantation-style and to rely on Indian slaves for labor. This led to a chronic state of warfare between the Portuguese and the Indians. The plantations were unable to succeed, therefore, due to the difficulty of finding a labor force and because of the discovery of lucrative forest products such as clove and cocoa (Sweet 1974:57). Except along the main channel, few Portuguese settlements were able to establish a permanent hold in the Amazon.

Colonial use of resources was characterized by the simultaneous presence of an extractive sector oriented to the gathering of forest products and an agricultural sector favoring cash crops rather than subsistence production. This pattern, which started during the colonial period (1500–1822), lasted well into the national period (1822–present), making the Amazon region dependent on regions located at great distances from the scattered population inhabiting the Amazon while, at the same time, failing

58

to generate any internal development.[1] Throughout the period, the production of cash crops was based on large land grants (*sesmarias*) controlled by Europeans—with cocoa as the predominant product (Alden 1974). The Indian villages were producers of subsistence crops—but output figures were close to the minimum needs of the population (Anderson 1976: 58). Surplus agricultural production of staple crops and capital formation were not encouraged in these subsistence operations. The result was an economy dominated by extractivism and export crops, with subsistence agricultural production being a weak appendage. This structure continued into the post-1850 period.

Agriculture in an Extractive Economy

Efforts at creating a viable agricultural sector in the Amazon were hampered by the emphasis placed on extractivism. During most of the colonial period, Indian males living in missions or in Portuguese-controlled settlements were sent on annual expeditions to gather forest products. The most consistent source of forest wealth was cocoa, and its production was significant enough to inhibit further efforts to establish cocoa plantations. Between 1756 and 1822 cocoa contributed between 40 and 82 percent annually to the export receipts from Pará (Alden 1974:55–56). None of the early efforts to produce sugar or to domesticate cocoa for export were significantly productive. To the Portuguese, the only worthwhile agriculture was production of cash crops for export. Therefore, through neglect, the agricultural export sector stagnated. This left the natives and mixed bloods to pursue subsistence in small agricultural plots according to aboriginal methods. Despite the disruptions brought about by the annual expeditions, the subsistence agricultural sector was able to feed the Amazon population—except during periods of high immigration.[2]

In order to keep the Indians brought into the missions from being captured by laymen, the Jesuits created communities which were capable both of self-sufficiency and of export capacity. Settlements concentrated on the major southern tributaries: the Tocantins, the Xingú, and the Tapajós Rivers. Most of the towns created by the missionaries have continued to exist to this day, as they have combined commercial control over whole watersheds, ease of communication to and from the main river channel, and healthful locations on a high promontory. Those that did not persist were short-lived due to their poor locations in flooded areas, the presence of unhealthy stagnant waters in the vicinities, and/or rapid misuse of local resources.

Daily life in the Jesuit missions followed the routine recommended by Padre Antonio Vieira in 1600. Each mission was expected to be self-supporting and to sell its surplus in Belem to buy tools and other goods needed by the mission (Hemming 1978:412). As long as the mission was distant from white settlements, it worked well in protecting the Indians from disease and slavery. But the Portuguese established themselves close enough to the large missions to assure themselves of Indian labor. If a mission village was within range of a Portuguese settlement, the settlers could demand a portion of the Indians' labor.

Subsistence agriculture in the mission villages consisted of manioc cultivation, with areas also dedicated to rice, corn, beans, fruit trees, tobacco, and sugar cane. Tobacco and sugar, both of which do well in some areas of the Amazon, were grown strictly for local use, since competition with the thriving economy of the Bahia area was discouraged by the authorities. Sugar cane was primarily converted to cachaça (raw-distilled rum). Coffee was moderately successful and was exported. On Marajó Island, the Jesuits had ranches with a total of 300,000 head of cattle. They exported oxen and steers and trained Indians to be excellent cowhands (Hemming 1978: 449). There was, however, very little incentive at the missions to produce food surpluses. Many missions grew and wove cotton into the cloth that became the standard currency of payment to Indian workers. Most Indians initially would have rather done without the cloth, but accepted it because it was the only form of payment received.

The conflict over rights to the Indians' labor grew so bitter between the Portuguese and the Jesuits that a compromise reached in 1686 resulted in a net loss for the Indians. The Jesuits yielded many of their villages to other missionaries. The mission Indians thereafter had to work for nearby settlers six months each year, instead of the four months required before. Indian slavery was reintroduced with its necessary yearly expeditions, in which enslaving Indians was no less important than gathering forest products. This opened the doors to legal and illegal trafficking in Indians. As the years dragged on, the will of the Jesuits to fight off their compatriots declined (Hemming 1978:423). With the rise to power of Pombal in Portugal, the Jesuits saw their hands tied first, and later their religious order abolished. Instead of freedom, the Indians were confined to directorate villages created by Pombal—villages existing for the expressed purpose of providing labor for the Portuguese settlers.

These civilian-run Indian villages also did not encourage surplus staple crop production. In the directorate villages, the directors charged the tithe and, in addition, a host of deductions were made that could not have had any other effect but to discourage the farming population. The desire for high profits led administrators at each level to levy increasingly burdensome taxes on the farming population: the tithe, the Captain's Fifth, the Treasurer's Share, and the Director's Sixth, for a total deduction of 32 percent of production (Anderson 1976:142). The tithe charged was based on projected production, and cases have been recorded in which the tithe was actually higher than the farm production for that year. Inadequate storage facilities often resulted in a high percentage of loss after harvest.

Most of the land in government-controlled directorate villages was in communal fields (*roça comum*) planted in export crops. Small, private plots of about one hectare were assigned to each Indian family for subsistence, although this production, too, was subject to the tithe (Anderson 1976:221). Even the small plots, however, could not be highly productive, because the male Indians were sent off in expeditions lasting no less than six months during the crucial period of land preparation—a task that had always been done by the men.

Productivity in the colonial Indian villages was low because health conditions were so dismal. Practically all villages lacked medical personnel, and the decimation by disease that has been so impressively documented by Hemming (1978) kept the villages under continual threat of extinction. The traditional native healers (*pajés*) continued to function, but they were virtually helpless against smallpox, measles, yellow fever, malaria, and the other new ailments introduced by Europeans.

Patterns of Resource Use: Extractivism

Collection of forest and river products was the principal economic activity of the Portuguese during the colonial period (Anderson 1976:5). Little effort was spent on the development of agriculture, because yields had not impressed colonial governors, whose main task was to generate Crown revenues. Agriculture in the Indian villages was geared at subsistence production—a task left mainly to the women. Most of the males were required by the government to travel for a good portion of the year in extractive expeditions deep into the interior. Especially after 1757, with the expulsion of the Jesuits, emphasis was completely diverted into collecting expeditions capable of producing revenue for the Crown.

Resources in the Amazon are not evenly distributed. The colonial period population exploited macro-regions in accordance with the abundance of particular resources identified in each area. The Xingú, Furos, and Tapajós River basins were primarily exploited for forest products. Marajó Island and the estuaries contributed the bulk of the riverine products—mainly turtle and fish. The Tocantins, Guajará, and coastal areas provided most of the agricultural products for export—both because of their proximity to the mouth of the Amazon and the major town and because of their relatively good soils. Most of the area exploited was in flood plain areas, which were enriched by yearly siltation (Anderson 1976:35).

The Xingú area yielded a number of important forest products. In addition to the economically dominant "clove" and sarsaparilla, Brazil nuts

(*Bertholletia excelsa*), andiroba oil (*Carapa guyanensis*), copaiba oil (*Copahifera officinalis*), wood from the giant *sumaúma* (*Ceiba pentandra*), and an assortment of forest fruits and game meats were extracted. Sarsaparilla comes from a small tree of the *Labiadas* family used to make medicinal teas and restoratives. Initially, only the berries were collected. But the constant demand for it coupled with the dwindling supply within reasonable distances made collectors exploit the root as well. Since taking the root involved killing the tree, the species became increasingly hard to find (Anderson 1976:14). "Clove" was the aromatic bark of the tree *Dicypellium cariophyllatum* which has a scent similar to that of the real clove. If care was not taken to leave enough bark on the tree, it died from girdling, so it too suffered from over-collecting. As with sarsaparilla, each year the collectors had to travel farther to harvest clove. The length of time expeditions occupied contributed to the neglect of agriculture (Anderson 1976:15–16).

Even more notorious than the exploitation of the forest was the exploitation of giant river turtles. The turtles had been a source of meat protein, cooking fat, and shell for containers and decorations. Turtle eggs could be safely stored for lengthy periods when fishing was unprofitable for the native peoples along the main channel of the Amazon. The Portuguese did not find as many uses for this animal, but were primarily interested in its fat and oil. Naturalists traveling in the Amazon noted that most of the meat was thrown into the water for the "benefit" of the buzzards, alligators, and piranha (Anderson 1976:17). Even more damaging than the exploitation of the adult turtles was the wholesale collection of the eggs. As with the turtles themselves, the protein value of the eggs was discarded, while the oil was extracted from the eggs. Estimates suggest that over 1.5 million eggs were destroyed in some years. There is no indication in historical records that the settlers or the administrators imagined the possibility that this rich resource would one day be exhausted (Anderson 1976:17).

During the colonial period the pattern of credit indebtedness became solidly established. Because the exploitation of widely scattered forest products was a seasonal affair, trade with the outside required long-term credit. Moreover, the absence of collateral meant that credit losses were covered by charging excessive prices for shoddy goods. Nevertheless, the lure of possible wealth from the extraction of forest products attracted colonists away from farming and into an unending search for aromatic plants. The Crown, instead of discouraging this economic orientation, actually encouraged it by instituting a licensing structure that became rife with corruption (Sweet 1974:59). To add to the cost of the expeditions, once Indians were deep into the forest interior they were able to run away from enslavement with relative ease. This made the task of outfitting expeditions a continuous, expensive, and ever-discouraging task for the colonials. Just when one might have expected the small Amazon communities to give up on extractivism, however, a new find or increased market demand for forest products would encourage the inhabitants to again abandon their efforts at agriculture. This was particularly the case when the market for rubber began in the mid-nineteenth century.

Rubber Boom: Heyday of Extractivism

Rubber was of no commercial interest to the Portuguese when they first saw the native population use it. In addition to being used for balls in games, Amazonian natives had been observed pouring it over their feet as protection against wetness. Throughout the colonial period, natural rubber remained a largely unexploited forest resource. Priestley discovered its usefulness in erasing pencil marks on paper in 1770, but this relatively esoteric use did not create significant demand for the product (Collier 1968:42). Later, the French found it useful for certain kinds of surgical tubing, and the Scots found ways to make waterproof capes from it (Kelly 1975:9). But until the first half of the nineteenth century, the usefulness of rubber was limited by its lack of resistance to temperature extremes. Rubberized articles melted in hot weather and cracked in cold weather. Only in 1839, with the discovery of vulcanization, did rubber become useful in cold, temperate areas of Europe and North America. Soon thereafter the craze for bicycles, and later for wheeled vehicles of other sorts, created a sudden demand for natural rubber.

The Amazon was the world's chief source of crude rubber during the mid-nineteenth century. The basic economic structure that developed to meet this demand for rubber was not new but, rather, continued the traditional system of extraction inherited from the colonial period. River traders (*regatões*) who had earlier bartered manufactured and subsistence goods for *drogas do sertão*, turtles, and pelts of wild animals turned their attention to the profits to be gained from rubber and advised the scattered population they traded with to turn their attention to rubber collecting if they wished a continued supply of goods. As the demand for rubber rose beginning in the 1850s, so did the single-mindedness of the river traders. Their success in tapping this sudden source of wealth is evident from Figure 4.1 (Anderson 1976:61). Such were the riches in some areas of a basin that the mobile river traders in numerous cases became stationary, as they managed their rubber domains from trading posts at the confluence of several tributaries, to which the collectors brought their coagulated latex.

Merchants in the major port cities, like Belem and Manaus, sent traders replete with goods along the fluvial network. Prices were high even when accounting for transportation costs and spoilage. Trade involved mono-

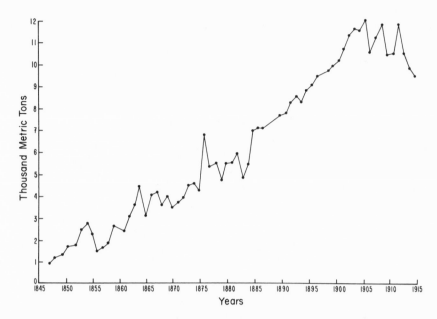

Fig. 4.1   Rubber Exports from Belem, Pará (1847–1915)
Source: Adapted from Anderson 1976:61

polistic control over parts of the river network. Most rubber gatherers and farmers were under obligation to buy goods from the trader who outfitted them for work, or who provided loans and credit at his store. Given the demand to gather as much rubber as possible and the isolation of most families, there was no opportunity to compare prices. In turn, the prices paid the gatherer for his product were relatively low—even when figuring overhead and defaults. But the trader seldom got rich. He was, in turn, in debt to the river trader and his urban boss, so the whole economy of the Amazon Basin was controlled from two points (i.e., Belem and Manaus). Their hold on supplies was so complete that they were able to keep all other Amazon towns from developing special services for their adjacent regions.

Extractivism in the Xingú Basin

While most of the rubber production for the rubber boom came from the region of the upper Amazon, the Xingú Basin rubber trade shared in this sudden prosperity. In the Xingú, most of the rubber barons were concentrated below the fall zone, around the county seat of Souzel (see Figure 1.2). This short expanse along the navigable waters produced less rubber than did some of the famous areas in the western Amazon. Nonetheless, competition among the barons was brisk, and several vied for political power in the Xingú. One mid-century patron, by the name of José Leocadio Souza, relocated the county seat across the river to an area which he then controlled. The local Capuchin priests helped to provide a land route around the falls. Leocadio's competitors Raimundo José de Souza Gaioso[3] and Agrario Cavalcante improved this trail several times when they discovered rich virgin rubber stands laying on the Irirí tributary. Of these two, Cavalcante finally gained control of the Great Bend area and passed on his land and the nearly completed road to his nephew and heir, José Porfírio de Miranda Júnior (Kelly 1975:35–38).[4]

The growth of the Xingú towns of Souzel and Altamira reflect the important role rubber barons generally played in building the Amazon area. The pattern repeated itself throughout the region, and Altamira was no exception. Rubber barons penetrated into areas far from civilization, recruited some 30,000 Northeastern workers in the late nineteenth century (Vergolino e Silva 1971), and established trading posts which formed the only contact with the outside world for most of the rubber collectors. It is a story filled with tales of human suffering. Collectors entered the Amazon with a sizeable debt, since both their trip and their tools were charged to their account with the rubber trader. It was rarely possible for a rubber collector to pay off his debt to the local rubber trader. Supplies were expensive, and it was not unusual for the trader to cheat on weights. As mentioned, out of this debt-credit relationship emerged an intimate, but exploitative, patron-client bond, which characterizes rural Brazilian life. Profits were great only for the exporter (*aviador*) in the extractive economy of the Rubber Era, and the Xingú area was no exception.

Many rubber barons, like José Porfírio, came to the Xingú from the Northeast of Brazil, and had brought with them the system of economic and social controls familiar in Northeast plantations (cf. Johnson 1971). By establishing a tradepost (*barracão*), which bought all the rubber collected by the worker (*seringueiro*), this trader controlled not only the price of rubber, but also the type of goods sold in his store and the credit to be extended to each client. He guaranteed the production and exclusive rights to the rubber through the force of hired gunmen (*capangas*), who regularly patrolled the rivulets to make sure that the collectors sold only to the tradepost and not to maverick traders. Exclusive sale to the patron was also ensured by the collectors' constant debts at the trading post.

The extractive economy created a chain of dependency that took control over how to use resources out of the hands of the local population. It also meant that the distant managers were unaware of, or insensitive to, the reasons for declining productivity. Although the absence of quantitative data on the credit system hampers definitive conclusions, the prevalent system of credit (*aviamento*) encouraged indebtedness and sustained the extractive economy. Because everyone was perpetually in debt to the next person up in the economic structure, even minor fluctuations in the world market price for the product could mean bankruptcy all the way down to the local trading post (Santos 1968; Wagley 1953).

Long-term regional development was not considered by the rubber barons and the government officials who benefitted from the windfall revenues. As Schneider and Schneider (1976) have suggested, "broker capitalists" benefit primarily from speculation in commodities and have little investment tied to the area. Health and educational facilities did not improve significantly outside of Belem and Manaus—where the elites resided. There were no efforts to plant rubber trees in homogeneous stands to lower costs so they could improve their market competitiveness with the Malayan plantations. No money was spent on agricultural research—a serious fault in human judgment, since at the same time, the creation of land grant colleges in the U.S. was laying a solid basis for agriculture, even in inferior soils such as those of the southeastern United States. When the rubber revenues dropped off in 1920, there was nothing else built into the Amazonian economy to pick up the slack. The area stagnated, part of the population left, and the rest settled down to a subsistence inferior in quality to that of the native peoples who had earlier inhabited the areas.

Since the arrival of Europeans, extractive economic exploitation has been a common experience throughout the tropics. The Amazon and the Altamira region of the Xingú Basin chosen for study here present no exceptions. The consolidation and missionization of Indians into *aldeias* was but a first step in forming towns that were dependent on river transportation and trade of natural resources for imported goods. The history of the Amazon reflects not only the dependence on an extractive economy, but also the consequences of such a situation. The river towns are dependent upon outside demand for an extractable resource, and are subject to boom/bust cycles of growth and decline. They are also dependent upon the power of their strongest entrepreneur, who dictates economic relationships, level of community development, and the social and political life of the town. His interests, in effect, governed even religious aspects of local life. Communities like Altamira remained isolated and undeveloped because of their lack of control over the production process and the inability or unwillingness of regional entrepreneurs to invest their windfall profits in internal development.

This system reflects the general situation in most of colonial Brazil. But unlike the agriculturally based society found elsewhere in Brazil, the Amazon region had little to fall back on during the "bust" periods. Its entrepreneurs left, there were few social services to sustain the population, and there was little communication between the isolated towns. In other words, there was little to spur internal development until the next demand for an export product appeared. The region's isolation, not only from other areas of the country, but even within its own sparse population, made growth and development a distant dream.

Migration to the Amazon

5

Economic growth and development seemed closer to reality, when in 1970 the Brazilian president committed substantial resources to a spearhead effort across the Amazon region. This chapter examines the transition from a traditional extractive economy controlled by a few river traders to what appeared to be a more open economic system created by the federal commitment to develop the Amazon. This process can be best examined by looking at the two major forces behind the change: the process of migration into the Xingú Basin and the development of a small farming sector fueled by government investments.

Colonization between 1850 and 1920

Since 1850, governing authorities have been involved in the promotion of Amazonian colonization.[1] One of the solutions invoked to resolve the lack of an agricultural labor force in the Amazon was to encourage European migration. To most Luso-Brazilians, who were yet attached to Portugal, the European was a superior individual characterized by industriousness, advanced notions of agriculture and a solid sense of citizenship—an opinion not surprising during the heyday of racial determinism.[2] To the chagrin of the government authorities, only a few of the Europeans who made their way to the Amazon proved to be farmers. Reports at the turn of the century discuss the presence of foreign "colonists" who refused to leave the city of Belem and to begin farm work in the interior (Anderson 1976:199).

Conditions provided by the government were shockingly inadequate, despite rosy promises made in European advertisements. One colony received twenty-one Azorean families, who upon looking at their future home refused to get off the train, and returned to Belem. The houses lacked roofs, the village space was incompletely cleared, and the secondary growth had already begun to take over everywhere (Anderson 1976:207).

68

The majority of the European migrants ended up in Belem and a few other cities and engaged in trade rather than in agriculture.

Just as the authorities were beginning to question their hope in the benefits of European migration, the simultaneous expansion in demand for rubber in the world market and the devastating drought of 1877 in Northeast Brazil brought a sudden on-rush of population into the Amazon region, seeking relief from disaster and lured by the possibility of enrichment.[3] For a while planners hoped that the Northeasterners fleeing from what turned out to be the worst recorded drought in Brazilian history, would settle in colonies and farm the land. But most migrants went on to the rubber fields, encouraged by the recruiters who had attracted them to the Amazon. While some government officials decried the effect of rubber exploitation on agriculture, their dependence on rubber export revenues prevented them from taking any positive steps in favor of agriculture. Efforts did not go beyond setting aside land for colonies and placing people on them. These colonies were rarely provided with the infrastructure required to encourage agricultural development (Anderson 1976:78). The rate of immigration was so high, and the health facilities so inadequate, that half of the recorded deaths in Belem in 1878 were of Northeast refugees who died chiefly from fevers, smallpox and dysentery while waiting to go to the interior (Anderson 1976:201). The promises made to those who would settle in farm colonies were seldom kept: food and medicines were never provided, subsidies until the first harvest were never paid, and no contact was maintained between the colonies and the government officials after the colonists left Belem.

The period between 1880 and 1930 was characterized by a lack of policy continuity regarding colonization.[4] Programs were created and ended with a dispatch that was all the more confusing because of the slowness of communication in the Amazon. Colonists could not be sure from one day to the next about the status of their community, whether promised aid would be delivered, or whether their marketable produce would be transported.[5] Nor were they allowed any voice in the policy-making process. Those colonists that survived learned the bitter lesson of government neglect, the priority assigned to extractive products in the market, and that the government bureaucrats did not understand the farming way of life. Europeans and Northeasterners alike learned that to survive it was necessary to be self-sufficient, to be diversified in the exploitation of resources, and to be distrustful of the promises of government officials—lessons learned by the Amazonian backwoodsman, or *caboclo*, long before (Wagley 1952; Moran 1974). Perhaps the most important factor of all was the incongruity of promoting agriculture during a boom period in the extraction of a forest product—rubber. Devolution, rather than development, was the result of efforts during this period. Coffee production dropped, as did the production of rum and manioc flour (Anderson 1976:65). Beans, cotton, rice, and other products remained stable, but the increased demand from the larger population meant that production was inadequate, and much had to be imported.

The Period 1920–1960

Following the end of the Rubber Era bonanza, interest in the Amazon declined. Brazil's coffee boom made Brazil's southern region the focus of economic interest. During this period what had been Amazon boom towns declined in population and settled into a marginalized position, wherein a trickle of products of economic interest were bartered for even more insignificant amounts of manufactured goods. The classic study of one such community is Wagley's (1953). The economy of the interior communities continued to be dominated by the cities of Belem and Manaus and by the system of aviamento established during the previous century.

During the period 1920 to 1960 the Brazilian economy moved from one based on agriculture to one increasingly industrial in overall orientation. This trend became all the clearer during the 1960s. Much of this evolution was centered in southern Brazil. During the 1940s, the rich lands of the state of Paraná were occupied by coffee planters guided by private colonization enterprises (Margolis 1973), and in the 1950s the migratory movement reached Goiás with a production system based on extensive ranching. A minor flow of population into the Amazon motivated by the Japanese capture of the Malaysian rubber plantations concurrent with another Northeastern drought episode took place during World War II.

Following the rubber market crash of the 1920s, Henry Ford was granted extensive concessions in the Tapajós Basin. He began the so-called Fordlandia in 1926 in order to compete with the high prices charged by the British and Dutch monopoly in the East Indies. Fordlandia included 10,000 square kilometers and some 800,000 rubber trees arranged within close proximity. Other capital-intensive investments in the area included a port for ocean-going vessels, a sawmill to utilize local lumber for buildings, and extensive medical and housing facilities (Wagley 1953:89).

However, the rubber tree plantation was short-lived. In 1932 the trees were infested with a fungal leaf disease called *Dothidella ulei*. Ford exchanged one quarter of his land grant for a new plantation at Belterra, further up river on the Tapajós. The move, plus attempts to graft disease-resistant trees eventually succeeded in saving the trees. However, the need to resort to grafting made such production economically indefensible, and Ford returned his plantations to the Brazilian government shortly after World War II (Sioli 1973:331). It was not, however, only the fungus that was problematic. Throughout the existence of the plantations Ford had difficulty securing labor due to the low wages he paid (Wagley 1953: 90).

Of greater long-term importance to the Amazon than Henry Ford's effort is the 1940 "march to the West" speech of President Getúlio Vargas. In that speech the President pointed to the Amazon and its untapped natural resources. No investments took place during the war, but the government cooperated in the war effort by mobilizing Northeast laborers and sending them to the Amazon to gather rubber. Unlike the previous efforts, in which there was an almost total lack of health services provided to the migrating population, this time the services of the Serviço Especial de Saúde Pública (SESP) were called forth, and throughout the war, and since then, these health officers have plied the waters of the Amazon providing medical services and education in towns throughout the region.

While the 1940s were not years of brisk economic activity, certain regional improvements were made. The Brazilian Public Health Service helped stabilize the health situation in the area. Malaria and yellow fever, in particular, were brought under control by the use of DDT, educational materials, and distribution of antimalarial medications (Wagley 1974:290). New federal territories, such as Acre and Roraima, were established and organized, and Amazonian government units benefited from the inflow of federal funds beginning in 1946. Such funds made possible the construction of municipal buildings, schools, central markets, small sawmills, slaughterhouses, port facilities, and roads. In towns like Altamira, the Catholic Church also promoted the building of schools and hospitals.

Many Northeasterners came to the Amazon during World War II and stayed on, in small river towns or scattered along riverbanks, carrying on a subsistence pattern adopted from the resident caboclos. During their work as rubber gatherers, the incoming population learned from an earlier generation of caboclos about the forest, its resources, and the crops that produce well with a minimum of care. This was important, because throughout the period a relatively minor demand for certain products such as alligator skins or jaguar pelts made exploitation of these animals only somewhat profitable.

Survival of the isolated population in the Amazon Valley was contingent upon their exploitation of a wide array of resources: now rubber, then Brazil nuts, *timbó, andiroba*, natural oils, some hunting or fishing, and agriculture. The disadvantageous terms of trade and the uncertainty of supplies from Belem caused Amazon towns to experience periodic scarcities of basic staples such as manioc flour, kerosene, and beans (Wagley 1953), but through such a mixed economy the population remained relatively self-sufficient except when high prices for extractive products led to neglect of diversification.

The trade in spotted cat skins (i.e., jaguar and ocelot) was particularly active during the 1960s, when an average of 15,000 jaguars and 80,000 ocelots were killed annually. Prices paid to hunters during the period fluctuated around US$130 for a top quality jaguar pelt and US$40 for an ocelot (Smith 1976b). A decade earlier trade in alligator skins had dominated.

In 1953 the Brazilian national assembly created the Superintendência do Plano de Valorização da Amazônia (SPVEA) to deal with these problems. In addition to receiving 3 percent of federal tax funds, SPVEA also had recourse to 3 percent of state and municipal tax funds from the area known as *Amazonia Legal.*[6] SPVEA received few of these earmarked funds, as most of them were diverted to regions of greater interest to the legislators—chiefly in the industrial South. To a large extent the high rates of inflation and the ballooning costs of building the new capital at Brasilia during the 1950s appear to have been the chief motives behind the diversion of funds (SPVEA 1960; SUDAM 1976). While its main function was socio-economic planning for regional development, lack of funds and late release of available funds made planning and execution difficult, if not impossible (SPVEA 1960:49), and the very legislation that created SPVEA tied the hands of the agency. A restriction that limited staffing expenditures to 8 percent of the budget kept the agency permanently understaffed. During the peak period of SPVEA activity the ten regional offices had only a total of thirty-four college-level functionaries, most of whom lacked training in technical fields (Cavalcanti 1967:46; SPVEA 1960:108). In addition to these handicaps, conflicts between political, economic, and bureaucratic goals interfered with the progression of plans from design to implementation stages.

Final approval of SPVEA's five-year plan was in the hands of the national Congress, a body less committed to Amazonian development than was President Vargas. The first plan failed to get approval in 1955, and SPVEA was, in effect, divested of its planning functions. The agency was permitted to serve merely as a pass-through agency for the Federal funds that reached it. Despite these difficult conditions, the agency did not lose sight of its purpose and gave financial support to research efforts in the region, such as those of the FAO/UNESCO surveys on forestry resources of the basin (1972) and the creation of the National Institute of Amazonian Research (INPA), dedicated to the study of Amazonian ecology. A substantial effort was also made to expand the work in the study of Amazonian populations, both prehistoric and contemporary, at the Museu Goeldi in Belem. An active research program based here has, over the years, added much to our knowledge.[7] SPVEA also established a small farming project near Belem, the Núcleo Colonial do Guamá, in 1955. Perhaps the most notable contribution of the agency was to spur the construction of a highway linking Belem with the new capital city of Brasilia through an area of virgin forest. The road was formally opened in 1965 and permitted overland access between the Amazon's chief city and the heartland of the country (Valverde and Vergolino 1967:321). Despite the pessimistic criticisms of the road, over 2 million people migrated along its path within a few years and developed a stable cattle industry. Its economic value was sufficient to justify paving it by 1973.

Incentives to Amazonian Development

The 1964 military take-over in Brazil led to a number of changes in the Amazon's position within the nation. The regime of Castelo Branco called for an "Operation Amazonia," which acted swiftly to abolish SPVEA under charges of misuse of funds and technical incompetence. In its place the new regime created in 1966 a new Amazon Development Agency (SUDAM) and made it a part of the Ministry of Interior. The old Credit Bank of the Amazon was reorganized as the Banco da Amazônia (BASA) to serve as the financial arm of the development agency. In addition, a duty-free port (SUFRAMA) was created in Manaus to stimulate industrial development in the region by reducing the high import tariffs in effect elsewhere in Brazil. The free port was associated with fiscal incentives for private investments in the Amazon, such as the possibility of allocating up to 50 percent of annual federal taxes into SUDAM/BASA-approved industries and agropastoral concerns. The first SUDAM development plan (1967–71) encouraged private investment in agricultural, livestock, industrial, and forestry resource development (SUDAM 1976). The second plan (1972–74) generated by President Medici's plan of national integration (PIN) gave priority to road building and small farmer colonization. However, the areas of SUDAM/BASA involvement remained focused on the promotion of region-wide investment in ranches and industries. The third plan (1975–1979) returned to a policy of openly favoring regional development through large-scale enterprises. As of 1976, 335 investment projects had been approved in the agricultural sector (mostly in cattle ranches), 171 in the industrial sector, and 22 for services and infrastructure (Kleinpenning 1978:9).

SUDAM is a faithful heir to SPVEA. Thus far, it shows the same tendency to foster projects located in or near Belem and Manaus, the two major urban centers; favor capital intensive projects which affect a minimum of the region's population; and to produce products mainly for export to the industrial south (Kleinpenning 1978: 10–11; Visão 1976:77). For example, numerous cattle projects have been approved for northern Mato Grosso and southern Pará. These projects are large—with an average size per project of 23,465 hectares. Cattle ranching in such projects is not intensive, but extensive, due to the cheap value of land. In terms of employment, such extensive cattle ranching projects provide only 2.3 jobs per 1,000 hectares (Kleinpenning 1978:11–12).

SUFRAMA is the most important aspect of the federal legislation providing fiscal incentives in the Amazon. It creates a free trade zone in the western Amazon in order to stimulate the formation of an industrial, commercial, and agricultural center in the region's interior. SUFRAMA has been relatively more successful than SUDAM in allocating resources to agriculture and forestry projects in the interior, and to industry within the city's confines. The industrial park in Manaus includes 138 projects representing industries that can take advantage of the tax exemptions and make profits through a favorable weight to value ratio, as in textiles, electronics, and luxury goods (Kleinpenning 1978:6). Almost 50 percent of total investment and employment is concentrated in textiles and electronics (see Table 5.1). Manaus' free port has brought a rapid increase in the

TABLE 5.1

INDUSTRIAL PROJECTS APPROVED BY STATE
OF AMAZONAS AND SUFRAMA, 1968–1974
(Constant 1975 Prices)

SECTOR	NO. OF FIRMS	TOTAL INVESTMENT (CR$ MILLIONS)	%	EMPLOYMENT NUMBER	%
Textiles	5	830.1	24.7	3,883	17.6
Electronics	21	740.1	22.0	6,628	30.0
Metallurgy	8	288.9	8.6	1,628	7.8
Chemicals	6	264.7	7.9	687	3.1
Wood products	12	238.0	7.1	2,140	9,7
Transport equipment	6	135.0	4.0	1,150	5.2
Food products	7	80.1	2.4	1,053	4.8
Apparel	4	53.6	1.6	696	3.2
Perfumes: soaps	1	48.5	1.4	77	0.4
Beverages	4	44.6	1.3	373	1.7
Miscellaneous*	32	634.2	19.0	3,769	17.1
Total	106	3,357.8	100.0	22,084	100.0

* Includes such product lines as: jewelry, toys, watches, optical equipment, and glassware.
SOURCE: Calculated from data provided by SUFRAMA, in Mahar 1976a:362.

city's population and improved local employment opportunities. However, certain negative effects can be noted. Few of the benefits have extended beyond the city's limits, and the majority of the items sold are fully-manufactured consumer items from southern Brazil (Mahar 1976b:162). This has resulted in an unfavorable trade balance with all regions of Brazil. In fact, the inflow is mainly of manufactured goods from the south, and the outflow is of raw materials such as rubber and jute in exchange (Kleinpenning 1978:7). It has been argued that SUFRAMA has succeeded as an urban development policy, but failed as a regional policy (Mahar 1976b:173).

To sum up, then, regional development bureaucracies undertook a strategy that was not significantly different from colonial use of resources. Emphasis was placed on extensive landholdings, projects having low labor requirements, on urban development in the two entrepots (i.e., nodal cities), and on the production of a limited number of products for export. Such a strategy failed to encourage any significant in-migration, and may have even served to further depopulate the interior of Amazonia by attracting its rural peoples to Belem and Manaus. The attempt to promote migration into the interior came from a presidential fiat.

The New Commitment to Amazon Economic Integration

In 1970 Brazilian President Emílio G. Médici ordered a major thrust into the Amazon under the aegis of the Program of National Integration (PIN). Its aim was said to be to integrate the largely unexploited resources of the Amazon Basin into the strategy of national economic development. The program got off to a dramatic start with the construction of the Transamazon Highway, linking the Northeast with the Peruvian frontier and with the nation's capital. Associated with road construction, the government set out to promote the migration of peoples from throughout the country to land plots parceled out for smallholder agriculture. Ten kilometers were allotted for smallholder agriculture on each side of the highway, and an ambitious scheme of inputs was devised with a view to promoting the productivity of the agricultural sector.

Brazilian spokesmen claimed that the primary motive of Amazon development was social. In the words of President Médici, "to give men without land a land without men." Others have suggested that "it is hard to see how the transfer of several hundred thousand, (or) even two to three million, people from the northeast into Amazonia can possibly make any more than a dent in the problem of poverty" (Wagley 1974:6). In fact, the settlement of families has proceeded at a much slower pace than originally forecasted. Less than 6,000 families have been settled in four years, rather than the 100,000 families forecasted by the government in 1971.

The sudden interest in developing the Amazon in the 1970s went far beyond a concern for the landless masses. Brazil's all-out effort to develop the Amazon is primarily based on economic and geopolitical considerations (Tambs 1974). The existence of spectacular deposits of mineral wealth discovered with the help of sideways-looking radar[8] (Goodland and Irwin (1975:13); the presence of reasonably good lands for agriculture in some areas (Falesi 1972); the potential of some forested areas, with an estimated yield of 178 cubic meters of lumber per hectare (SUDAM 1974:11); and a long-standing geopolitical fear of encroachment by covetous foreigners (Reis 1968), all lent impetus to the Highway Project and its associated projects. Contini (1976:125) has argued that the project aimed also at promoting the legitimation of the military regime by undertaking a program of social benefit on a grand scale.

This development of the Amazon is being promoted in three different areas: industrialized exploitation of natural resources, large-scale cattle ranching, and small-farm colonization. First, efforts are being made to attract large private corporate enterprises to invest heavily in the area. Large land concessions have been granted to both Brazilian and foreign business groups. U.S. Steel, Bethlehem Steel, Georgia Pacific, Alcoa, King Ranch, and Swift-Armour were among the first United States companies to take advantage of the opportunities available in the region. Over fifty international companies are involved in mineral exploration alone (Davis and Mathews, 1976:25). European companies such as Holland's Bruynseel and Germany's Volkswagen have acquired large areas for wood exploration. Southern Brazilian companies are also investing heavily in cattle ranching and expanding from current holdings in southern Pará, Mato Grosso, and Goiás. Well over two-thirds of the projects approved by SUDAM, for example, deal in livestock (cattle) production (SUDAM, 1972). This expansion into a new area follows Brazil's tradition of expanding the agricultural frontier to keep up with growth in demand for agricultural products.[9]

While agricultural production grew more rapidly than population in the 1950s and 60s, there was no significant increase in yields per hectare. What had been done was to increase the area under cultivation by opening up frontier areas (USDA, 1970:XV). Even though current Brazilian plans aim at integration of the isolated Amazon with the rest of the nation, it is questionable whether or not the policies are any different from earlier ones which emphasized export of natural resources to the disadvantage of renewable resource development, in particular, agricultural development.

The large cattle raising and industrial operations encouraged by SUDAM are just getting underway, and studies are not yet available (cf. Hecht, forthcoming). In some cases this is due to the secrecy practiced in projects such as that of millionaire E. Ludwig in the Jarí Basin. In others it is simply due to the lack of activity in the projects.[10] In several areas of the flood plain, I was told by local representatives of multinational firms that the price of wood had not yet reached a price that justified the investments required to exploit these forests. On the other hand, the third area of development, small farm colonization, got underway in 1971 and provided an excellent study setting. Over 5,000 families have come to three separate colonization projects and are adjusting to a new physical and social environment. Unlike many development schemes in Latin America and elsewhere, this one proceeded with an unusual degree of central planning and a wealth of inputs.

Small Farmer Colonization in the 1970s

Aside from the publicized social goals for the colonization efforts, there were also agricultural assumptions built into the settlement scheme. Preliminary soil studies had shown that the Transamazon would cut across some good farming soils in the region of Altamira (IPEAN 1967). It was thus projected that the small farm sector would specialize in food crops and serve as a "bread basket" project.[11] The plan was to have the colonists plant "national" staples such as beans, corn, and rice in the first three years to provide food for their own use and for export to the south (Ministério da Agricultura 1972a). The allocation of land planted in rice to soybean production in southern Brazil created a demand for new areas to produce rice and prevent a serious food deficit (Théry 1979). Each year colonists would plant more of their land in permanent crops such as coffee, sugar, guaraná, cocoa, and black pepper. Again, as so many times in the past, the governmental emphasis was on producing goods primarily for outside the region rather than creating a sustained-yield system (Janzen 1975).

Small farm colonization was centered in three traditional river towns linked by the Transamazon Highway: Marabá, on the Tocantins river, Altamira on the Xingú, and Itaituba on the Tapajós. In each town, agencies of the National Institute of Colonization and Agrarian Reform (INCRA) were set up to regularize the occupation of the land.[12] The agency was charged with choosing the colonists, bringing them to the Amazon, processing them on arrival, assigning them lots and house sites, surveying the agricultural areas, and guaranteeing that their land rights would be protected. Their corps were made up of agronomists, topographers, pilots, doctors, extension workers, social workers, and administrators.

The INCRA personnel in Altamira, as in Marabá and Itaituba, was essentially responsible for settling colonists chosen by regional INCRA offices located in major cities around the country. The colonization effort was to emphasize the settlement of landless farmers from the Northeast (75 percent) (Ministério da Agricultura 1972a, 1972b). The other 25 percent, interestingly enough, was programmed to come from the "progressive" South, whose farmers were to serve for a "demonstration effect" to the industrious, but "technologically backward" Northeasterners (Ministério da Agricultura 1972a:23). This is one of the many biases and assumptions built into the blueprints of colonization resulting from regional stereotypes rather than actual fact.[13] Even more curious than the use of stereotypes was the lack of mention of the recently opened frontier of the Central-West and of the "demographically empty" Amazon itself.

Other assumptions also colored the selection criteria used for choosing colonists. Many variables were worked into a candidate's application, several of which simply reflected family size. Preference was given to applicants between the ages of twenty-five and forty-five who were married and had large families. According to the plan, the labor potential of each man, woman, and child over twelve in the household was weighed and used to compute the family labor force.[14] It was assumed that a minimum force of 2.5 workers was needed to preclude the need for hired labor on each farm. How this figure was determined is not clearly understood. Obviously large families easily scored over the minimum points necessary for selection, so that families with many children, almost regardless of age, were given precedence over families with few, all else being equal (Kleinpenning 1975:117).

It was also assumed that extensive agricultural experience should be a prime requirement. This information was elicited by simply asking how many years of agricultural employment an individual had, rather than by pursuing a careful employment history to identify the kind of experience acquired over the years. The system allowed former cattle ranchers, share-croppers, ranch hands, and even bakers and druggists, to be selected.[15] In some selection headquarters, a "farm knowledge" exam was given. One ex-soldier I met told me he went to the library, read a book on farming, and passed the test. He was one of the first to be selected, although he later failed completely as a farmer.

Years of schooling were also considered in the selection process, but this item was not sufficiently weighed in order to bring more educated colonists to the area. Moreover, selection records were inaccurate and often contained errors. For example, a functionally literate farmer might be recorded as illiterate simply because he had not completed formal primary education. This and other selection criteria were not always vigorously or uniformly applied. As will be seen, they also were not appropriate in selecting those with the best capabilities to farm the Amazon.

Promoting Transamazon Colonization

The job of moving any sizeable group to the Amazon is a complex problem. Early in the project, the government recognized that the Amazon region was much feared and mythologized, and that most earlier migrants had gone only under drought duress. The Northeasterner in particular had built up an apprehension toward migration to the area. The tales of the rubber gatherers who survived debt slavery in the Amazon and re-turned to their native land gave the Amazon more than its share of color-ful facts and fiction. With available lands elsewhere, such as in the Center-West, the rural poor would not likely migrate to the Amazon Basin on their own. Therefore, an impressive package of benefits was offered to families willing to leave the relatively tame environments of the Northeast,

Center-West, and South, and brave the last great frontier on earth. Brazil set out to complete these Herculean tasks of road building and colonization in record time. By September 1972 the first half of the highway had been cut as far as Itaituba on the Tapajós River at an estimated cost of Cr$213 million (US$35 million). Real costs turned out to be close to three times this figure. While estimated costs per kilometer were Cr$134,856, real costs were actually Cr$375,970 (US$53,710). Table 5.2 summarizes the estimated and real costs of road construction. The second half of the highway was completed in 1976.

Interest in moving to the Amazon was stirred among the landless in Brazil through both the media and personal contact. Agronomists and extension agents approached whomever the technicians thought would be good candidates in their areas. Prospective candidates traveled to cities where selection quotas were still open. Protestant church leaders used their pulpits to make the congregation members aware of the opportunities to "seek a promised land." Letters from the first pioneers to those back home encouraged many to apply who otherwise might never have come.

An attractive package of benefits was also offered to the farmers. One hundred hectares of virgin land along a federal highway were given, complete with boundaries and titles supported by the Federal Colonization Agency (INCRA). All colonists were guaranteed financing by the Bank of Brazil, according to the size of the area cleared and planted in the subsidized crops of rice, corn, and beans. Household subsidies, in the form of a six-month minimum salary were paid by the Colonization Agency to each family head to help tide the family over until the first crops were up. This payment was unlike welfare, in that each colonist was expected to pay back these initial salaries and food subsidies within three years. In 1971 the colonists received Cr$204 per month (US$35) plus food subsidies, but these food subsidies were cut out after the first six months and the salary was then increased to Cr$308 (US$50), and extended over a period of eight months. All salaries and foodstuffs were equally apportioned, regardless of the number of members in each family. In the early stages, wages for work on local projects, such as building the agrovilas and other public buildings, were also provided.

Government-built houses on the individual lots, schools, medical facilities, tools, household items, technical aid, and transportation of farm produce were also promised the colonists. Primary schools of similar construction were built in the agrovilas, and teachers were enticed by a "hardship" bonus to come and teach there. Secondary and vocational schooling was available in the larger planned settlements and in the towns of Altamira, Marabá, and Itaituba. A first aid post was built in each planned village, often manned by nurse's aides. Doctors were expected to pay visits each week. A minimal area of cleared land on each lot and a pass-

TABLE 5.2
REAL AND ESTIMATED COSTS OF TRANSAMAZON HIGHWAY CONSTRUCTION

COMPANY AWARDED CONTRACT	FROM-TO	KILOMETERS	DAYS	ESTIMATED (IN 1,000 CRUZEIROS)	REAL (IN 1,000 CRUZEIROS)
Constructora Mendes Júnior	Estreito-Marabá	280	1,000	38,000	82,000**
S.A. Paulista	Marabá-Jatobal-Rio Repartimento	270	817	43,000	119,859
Constructora Mendes Júnior	Rio Repartimento-Altamira	342	817	43,793	115,487
Consorcio Transcon-Humberto Santana*	Marabá-Rio Repartimento Altamira Lot 3	Consultant	548	2,200	3,982
Queiroz Galvão S.A.	Altamira-54 W. 4 S.	256	1,000	38,000	82,000**
Louis Berger Eng. Ltda.	Altamira-54 W. 4 S.	Consultant	760	2,200	5,202
Empresa Industrial Técnica, S.A.	54 W. 4 S.-Itaituba	230	1,000	45,861	117,500**
Constructora Rabello S.A.	Itaituba-Jacareacanga	300	565	28,868	171,443
Camargo Corrêa S.A.	Jacareacanga-Rio Aripuaná	406	504	57,211	140,429
Companhia Constructora Parapanema	Rio Aripuaná-Humaitá	350	566	29,107	74,783
Totals		2,434	7,577	328,240***	912,685***

* This company defaulted on its contract and its task was taken up by Mendes Júnior S.A.
** In these three cases the added cost is partially explained by the post-contract request for construction of a military post at an average cost of Cr$32,000,000 for each one. Inflation undoubtedly added to the cost.
*** Estimated cost per kilometer was Cr$134,856. Real costs were actually Cr$375,970 (US$53,710) per kilometer.
SOURCE: Contracts Office, Departamento Nacional de Estradas de Rodagem, Rio de Janeiro, 1974

able side road for crop transport was to be available to each farmer. News media proclaimed the fertility of the soil and the high yields of experimental crops—promises reminiscent of the advertisements used to attract Europeans to both North and South America in the late nineteenth century.

Those who wished to settle in the Amazon as colonists had to present themselves at local colonization agency offices and fill out application forms. Numerous papers had to be sought for all members of the family: identity cards (*carteira de identidade*), voter's registrations, a workers' certificate (*carteira de trabalho*), statements of good character from the county police, and health certificates. Most prospective farmers were advised to leave the bulk of their tools and household items behind. Some farmers reported being told that "they would find their houses completely equipped with furniture, agricultural tools, pots and pans, and any necessary household goods." Though some colonists were doubtful and brought what they could fit inside suitcases, the majority gave their few material possessions to friends and relatives. The transportation costs of each family to the area was covered by INCRA, but food, lodging, and other in-transit expenses were borne by the colonists. Their poultry and pigs were sold in order to buy the clothes and suitcases needed for the journey and to cover expenses in passage.

The migratory flows followed a limited number of paths (see Figure 5.1). Surprisingly, the most important flow was rural-rural migration within the Amazonian state of Pará, accounting for 36 percent of the total migration. Next in significance was the flow of Northeasterners. While the proportion of Southern migrants (23 percent) was close to the predicted figure of 25 percent, life histories I collected demonstrated that 80 percent of these were Northeasterners who had left their area of origin in the 1940s and 1950s, and gone south then in search of better economic opportunities (see Figure 5.1). Most of them moved often once in the South, because by this time the coffee frontier of Paraná was well occupied, and most of these southern-bound migrants had arrived too late to buy cheap land, so found work only as wage laborers on coffee plantations. With the opening up of the Amazon frontier, they undertook one more migration. In addition, 11 percent came from the Central-West region.

Of the three colonization projects along the Transamazon Highway, the Altamira Project became the one of central importance.[16] Not only did it settle the greatest number of immigrants (see Table 5.3) but it also brought the most sizeable contingent of government services.

The colonists of Altamira were not the only newcomers to the area. Second only to INCRA colonists were the extension agents of ACAR-Pará (*Associação Brasileira de Crédito e Assistencia Rural do Pará*), established in Altamira since 1968. While some of them were agronomists, the majority had only a short course in extension education (*curso técnico*)

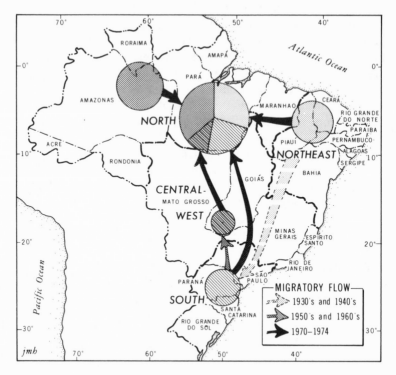

Fig. 5.1 Migratory Movements (1930–1974)

of about three months. They were charged with supervising the labor of
the farmers, facilitating the colonist's bank loans, giving technical aid in
modernizing farm practices, and making seed varieties available to co-
operating farmers. A contingent of female social workers from ACAR-
Pará were expected to give classes in hygiene, cooking, and vegetable
garden preparation to the women in farm communities. INCRA, IPEAN
(*Instituto de Pesquisa e Experimentação Agropecuária do Norte*), and
DEMA (*Departamento do Ministério de Agricultura*) also had personnel
present in the area to advise farmers in addition to the extension service.
IPEAN agronomists were engaged in various agricultural experiments.
These were carried out at the experimental station near the settlement
chosen for this study (see next section) and in sample plots in different
soil types as far away as eighty kilometers from their base. To do this,
the station had a staff of five full-time agronomists, several others who did
internships throughout the year, and a host of helpers from the vicinity.

The Public Health Service (SESP) and the Malaria Control Service
(SUCAM) served the migrants. SESP took over the São Rafael Catholic
Hospital of Altamira and increased its bed capacity and the number of its
personnel and services. It trained nurse's aides for servicing the medical

TABLE 5.3

COLONIZATION RATE ALONG THE TRANSAMAZON HIGHWAY (1972–1974)

DATE	ALTAMIRA FAMILIES SETTLED	MARABA FAMILIES SETTLED	ITAITUBA FAMILIES SETTLED	TOTAL FAMILIES SETTLED
June 1972	—	80	—	—
Oct. 1972	1,843	—	—	—
Nov. 1972	2,381	—	—	—
Dec. 1972	2,501	642	560	3,703
March 1973	2,488	—	—	—
June 1973	2,550	643	—	—
Sept. 1973	3,052	863	—	—
Dec. 1973	2,987	911	973	4,871
March 1974	3,022	1,068	—	—
June 1974	3,036	1,373	—	—
Dec. 1974*	3,095	1,422	1,200	5,717

* Estimated population of INCRA colonists in December 1974 is 34,300 (av. family size=6).
Estimated Transamazon population including squatters and migrant workers is 45,600.
SOURCE: INCRA Brasília, Marabá, and Altamira
          Smith 1976a:24

posts in the agrovilas, and was responsible for operating mobile medical care units that visited these communities on a periodic basis. SUCAM, active in controlling mosquitoes, saw its sphere of operation expanded in 1971, since road-building dammed up a large number of small streams which provided fertile breeding grounds for mosquito larvae. The agency diagnosed potential malaria cases, gave antimalarial medication, and provided vaccines against measles, typhoid, paratyphoid, and yellow fever. The expansion of malaria from the river banks to the terra firme is yet on the increase.

The food agency, COBAL (*Companhia Brasileira de Alimentos*), held the responsibility to store the produce of colonists in the area. Part of this produce was sold in COBAL supermarkets, but most of the available stock consisted of processed and canned foods from southern Brazil. Though it was supposed to ease the burden of pioneers through lower prices, its stocks often lacked items of prime necessity.

In education, the Ministry of Education (MEC) and the State Department of Education (SEDUC) were very active in the Altamira area. To encourage teachers to accept "hardship" posts in the Transamazon, the State Department of Education paid an added salary bonus. Nevertheless, the number of teachers who came from outside the project area was small. A major portion of the primary school teachers consisted of young females who came to the area with their pioneering parents, spouses, or relatives.

SESI (*Serviço Social da Industria*) was active in running a vocational school, a technical and handicraft center, a sports program, and other recreational facilities in Altamira. Teaching positions in the secondary schools are available in Altamira and the agropolis.

The Bank of Brazil (*Banco do Brasil*) and the Bank of the Amazon (BASA) were also encouraged by the government to finance the agricultural projects in the region. BASA mainly finances cattle operations of established *fazendeiros*. The Bank of Brazil, because of its role as the "national bank," has been given the injunction to provide loans at 7 percent to incoming pioneer farmers. Because of favorable markets and cultural preference in the South, financing is made available for planting rice, corn, and beans only. Loans amount to US$50 per hectare for the above crops. Manioc and other root crops, even if cultivated on a commercial scale, are not encouraged through bank financing.

The legacy of colonialism and extractivism has been a difficult one to break away from. The colonization efforts since 1850 have been marred by the lure of wealth from the exploitation of forest products such as rubber, pelts, and lumber. Also problematic have been the lack of clarity of titles to land, and the lack of adequate provision for credit, transportation, and storage facilities. Despite efforts to reverse this tradition since 1940, evidence points to the persistence of an extractive strategy of resource use: extension of credit to cattle ranches by SUDAM and BASA because of a high return per unit of investment; maintenance of an unfavorable balance of trade between the Free Port of Manaus (SUFRAMA) and its trading partners; a high rate of capitalization and low labor demand for most of the projects approved by the Amazon Development Agency (SUDAM); concentration of facilities in the two major cities of Belem and Manaus, continuing a tradition of control over the resources of the interior that separated markets from the producing areas by distances that put producers at a disadvantage vis-à-vis the traders. These conditions all amply demonstrate a persisting extractive system. The question remains, then, whether the small farmer colonization projects will be limited by the constraints of the past or whether new ones will emerge.

Policies devised by the 1970 development planners had a comprehensiveness unusual for most government-directed land development schemes. Roads were built with great speed. Whole villages were constructed in a matter of days. Farmers and civil servants were mobilized with the speed associated with a national emergency and the enthusiasm of a crusade. In the next chapter, the characteristics of human settlements are examined with a view to understanding the spatial factors involved with settlement.

Types of Settlements and
Types of Migrants

6

Vila Roxa lies midway between the traditional town of Altamira and the planned agropolis, Brasil Novo. Vila Roxa is situated on a relatively high knoll[1] that dips sharply in the middle to form a small "valley." It derives its fictitious name from its bright red clay soils—soils similar to "Georgia clay" in the United States. The large area in the middle is cleared of its original vegetation, and some portions are now planted in castor beans, black pepper, and a few papaya trees. In a number of communities, especially those situated away from the main artery of the Transamazon Highway, the forest cover in this central area has not been cleared, and vegetation annually encroaches closer to the houses. In Vila Roxa, the forest now lies at a distance, and the mayor and his fellow inhabitants feel that theirs is the most attractive agrovila in the area.

Like other planned villages along the main highway, Vila Roxa has forty-eight standardized houses, which are occupied by pioneer families and one resident nurse's aide. The houses in Vila Roxa are always full, and the mayor is kept busy juggling requests for housing from new settlers. While ideally other agrovilas should be located halfway down each transecting side road, there is one side road near Vila Roxa where the terrain and the poor soil forced the abandonment of the project. The colonists in this section are allowed to live in Vila Roxa, despite distances to lots of up to twenty kilometers, until further arrangements can be made. The mayor and the nurse's aide in Vila Roxa cater to the needs of four other side-road villages. INCRA mayors and nurse's aides reside only in the agrovilas along the highway. I was able to occupy one of the homes due to a farmer's preference to stay on his land.

In the village there is a primary school, a medical post, a water tower, a small warehouse, the mayor's office, and a colonist-owned front-room store. The U-shaped settlement looks out to the highway (see Figure 6.1). Three colonists' houses along the road have been included in the "community," since they functionally belong to Vila Roxa due to the physical

85

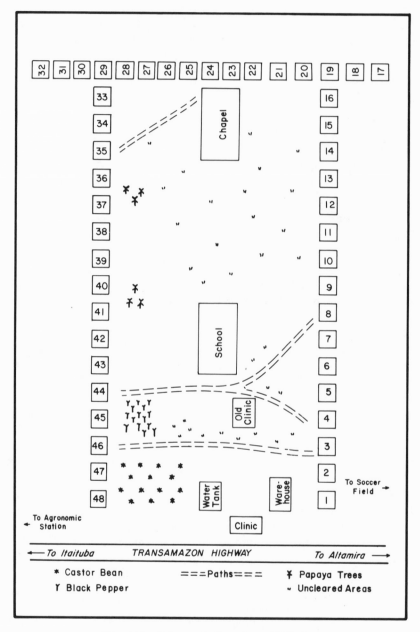

Fig. 6.1 Schematic Drawing of Vila Roxa

and social closeness between these families and the village. The dynamic processes of social life for the village are discussed in Chapter 9.

At first glance, the agrovila presents a picture of total conformity. Each agrovila house is divided into five rooms: a front porch, a living room, a dining room, two bedrooms, and a kitchen. While ideally all government-built houses are to be kept free of any unauthorized additions, this rule went unenforced in the side-road agrovilas. Here wattle-and-daub kitchens, thatch laundry areas, and animal pens next to the houses have appeared. Even in Vila Roxa, residents are slowly beginning to construct such out-buildings behind their houses, despite the fact that the community serves as a showplace to visiting dignitaries. Like buildings in Brasilia, these structures are yielding to the requirements of the population.

When hammocks are used in the homes, any room may be used for sleeping, since the hammocks can be rolled up each morning and hung on a wall hook. Only where people sleep in beds can the bedrooms be easily defined. A small bathing or storage area is located next to the kitchen. An outhouse, twenty-five meters behind the house, is also provided. Like the house, it is a clapboard structure with a roof of corrugated composite material (*brasilit*). The houses are well ventilated and relatively free of insects. Roaches, spiders, flies, and mosquitoes are present, but do not seem to constitute the serious health threat that they do in other agrovilas. This is not the case, however, with rats (*Rattus rattus*), which are abundant, bothersome, and a potential health hazard. Scorpions and snakes have rarely been seen near the houses, and no one recalls having been bitten by either around their homes.[2]

Vila Roxa houses are raised off the ground by stilts, their height depending on the inclination of the ground's surface. The area underneath the house is used as a playground by the children, a storage place for wood and tools, and sometimes as a chicken coop. While some 92 percent of the families own chickens, few chickens are kept penned during the day; rather, they are allowed to glean their existence from the meager table scraps and peelings thrown away by the housewives. Pigs, on the other hand, were prohibited for a while by the nurse's aide. Gradually they are being brought in from the distant lots, because of the difficulty of feeding them regularly. There is also the danger of losing them to untrustworthy neighbors or jungle "cats"—ocelots, jaguars, and other predators.

Around the houses, people plant fruit trees, vegetable gardens, manioc and other tuber plants, flowers, and medicinal herbs. During the first years, some colonists were reluctant to start gardens, since they intended some-day to settle on their own lots. There is an ambivalent feeling towards living in the agrovila. Most farmers understood the government to have "promised" a house on each individual lot, where the majority of colonists would prefer to be. Even the value of services such as the school and the health posts have "declined" according to the colonists, and no longer act as sufficient incentives to stay. Since the houses are government built and not yet paid for, the colonists are reluctant to invest the time and fencing materials required for a garden in a house "which isn't theirs."

Each person has a right to a back yard of eighty by twenty meters, but few had cleared such an area when we first arrived at the village in October 1973. By the time we left in October 1974, only eight families were making use of this area for gardening.

An "interdenominational" church was constructed in Vila Roxa, as in other agrovilas, to serve the purposes of religious worship and community meetings. However, this building is mainly used by the Roman Catholics. A visiting Presbyterian minister uses the interdenominational church for community services, and the Catholic priest was heard to encourage Catholic children to attend the one-week Bible course taught by a young Presbyterian lady. "Historical" Protestant churches such as the Presbyterian (Willems 1967) have more ecumenical dealings with Catholics than do the more aggressive and fundamentalist Pentecostal denominations, three of which are represented in the community. Each Pentecostal sect has a resident pastor, in whose home services are commonly held. The interdenominational building is referred to, therefore, as the (Catholic) "Church," by all the colonists.

A small two-room medical post is staffed by a resident nurse's aide from the Public Health Service (SESP). Such aides are usually young local women who receive a short training course in first aid. A Volkswagen micro-bus comes weekly with a physician to take care of the more serious problems and take blood, urine, and feces samples to Altamira for analysis. A new medical post was under construction which will primarily serve as a two-bed maternity ward attended by a midwife, serving expectant mothers awaiting an ambulance into town. A SESP ambulance driver also lives in Vila Roxa.

No one in Vila Roxa owns his own motor vehicle, but a colonist who lives near the village owns a pickup truck. This vehicle is mainly used to supply his front-room store, but also transports many expectant mothers to the hospital in Altamira. Only seven out of fifty-one households had a horse or mule. Private micro-buses travel up and down the highway and serve as the public transportation system. For the twenty-three-kilometer trip to either Altamira or Brasil Novo the charge in 1973 was Cr$5 (US $.70) per person each way. The price doubled in 1974 after the oil crisis began. The buses start their runs at about 6:00 A.M. and end at about 6:00 P.M., when the last leave Altamira for Brasil Novo where most of the micro-bus owners live. A couple of other micro-buses reach agrovilas further up the highway, but this service is available only every two to three days, and at very high cost. Regular bus service is available during the summer months at lower cost, but there are only two runs daily.

The population of Vila Roxa was made up of 331 persons. Selection criteria used by the government is reflected in the population structure (see Figure 6.2). The population is young: almost 70 percent are under the age of twenty, and only 2.4 percent are over the age of fifty. Large

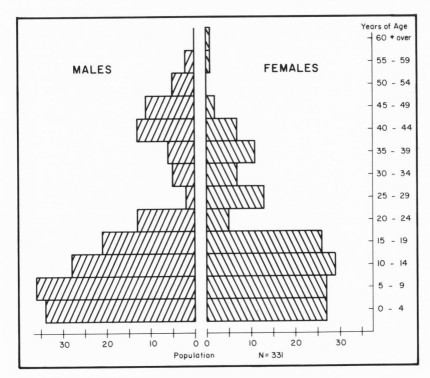

Fig. 6.2 Vila Roxa Age/Sex Pyramid
* Mean size of household is 6.22
Source: Moran, field notes, 1973–74

families were favored in the selection, consequently most farmers were concentrated in the forty- to forty-nine-year-old groups. The mean household size was similar to that for the whole colonization population (Contini 1976:159). Adult females are younger, reflecting a preference among the male population for spouses seven to nine years younger than themselves. Since nearly 55 percent of the population is under the age of fifteen, this large dependent population places costly demands on the 28 percent who produce and distribute food in the village.

Village inhabitants came from all areas of Brazil (see Table 6.1), including eleven different states that represented North, Northeast, South, and Center-West regions. These proportions, however, are not representative of the regional composition of Transamazon immigrants in general. Figure 5.1 and Table 5.3 summarized region-wide migration data. Most Amazonians chose to live on the land rather than in agrovilas, while a disproportionate number of southerners chose agrovilas as residences. Most of the Vila Roxa colonists have been in the Altamira region as long as the colonization project has existed, and have experienced both the con-

TABLE 6.1
STATE AND REGION OF ORIGIN OF VILA ROXA RESIDENTS

REGION	STATE	NUMBER OF HOUSEHOLDS	PERCENTAGE OF POPULATION
Northeast (32%)	Bahia	1	2%
	Ceará	2	4%
	Paraíba	1	2%
	Pernambuco	1	2%
	Piauí	1	2%
	Rio Grande do Norte	10	20%
North (14%)	Maranhão	1	2%
	Pará	6	12%
Center-West (16%)	Minas Gerais	7	14%
	Goiás	1	2%
South (38%)	Paraná	19	38%
		50	100%

fusion of the early days and the more stable present. The farmers are located in an area which offers a variety of economic options, such as their own agricultural work, wage labor at the experimental station, market dealings in either Altamira or "New Brazil," and various economic interactions with the Amazonian population.

Types of Migrants

Many efforts have been made in the social sciences to order and explain the social and cultural differences among members of complex societies. A useful heuristic device has been the use of typologies (Redfield 1941; Steward 1956; Wagley 1968). Such models of social structure have been helpful in ordering the variety present in any human community.[3] The typology developed here was not used during fieldwork. The colonists and the government bureaucracies used a region of origin system of classification. In fact, the government expected this to be a major index of expected success or failure. However, region of origin did not prove to be a useful distinguishing feature in assessing farm performance. In Chapter 8 I demonstrate the inappropriateness of region of origin as a predictive criterion of farming success.

The migration histories of the colonist population turned out to be one of the most significant indexes of their success or failure in farm production (see Figure 6.3). While government selection criteria emphasized

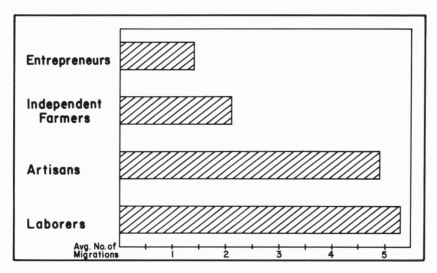

Fig. 6.3   Number of Previous Migrations among the
Four Types of Farmers

region of origin, education, and years of agricultural experience as indicative of their prospects, the more telling features of the settlers were quite different. Whether the farmer had owned or been employed as a foreman on a farm, frequency of previous migration, urban experience, and the possession of durable goods were accurate distinctive features among colonists (see Table 6.2). I have argued elsewhere (Moran 1979c) that these distinctive features are a function of Brazil's agrarian history and may be used elsewhere as criteria in colonist selection to reduce project costs, and improve prospects of migrants in colonization areas to attain the goals of increased incomes within a short time schedule.

The Transamazon colonists can first be divided into two major groupings: brokers and clients. Brokers are those persons who, through their own managerial skills, generate their own capital and reinvest a major portion back into their enterprises. The clients are persons who depend on the brokers or on outside institutions to provide a steady flow of cash in order to survive. Most of their capital resources go for consumption items rather than for farm investment.

TABLE 6.2
DIAGNOSTIC FEATURES OF FARMER TYPOLOGY

	BROKERS		CLIENTS	
Owners or managers	yes		no	
Frequently migrated	no		yes	
	ENTREPRENEURS	INDEPENDENT FARMERS	ARTISAN-FARMERS	LABORER-FARMERS
Urban experience	yes	no	yes	no
Owned many durable goods	yes	no	yes	no

Brokers are more geographically stable than are clients. They have often owned land or durable goods such as trucks or machinery. A certain managerial expertise has come from learning about the resources of an area and investing heavily in their use. In contrast, clients are basically a labor force; they go where there is a demand for their labor. Their constant mobility has kept them from acquiring the managerial acumen necessary to run their own commercial or agricultural enterprise. Basically, then, we have distinguished between colonists who are *rural managers* and those who are *rural proletarians*. In Vila Roxa there were roughly twenty brokers, and thirty residents who could be classified as client types.

These two major groupings are too broad to be operationally useful. If one is adequately to account for the performance of farmers in the Transamazon, a more precise typology must be employed. Thus, within each of the two broad categories, two subtypes may be defined. Brokers can be subdivided into entrepreneurs and independent farmers; clients into artisan-farmers and laborer-farmers.

The category of clients is essentially made up of two types of rural proletarians. First are the *laborer-farmers* who come from largely rural, sharecropping, or migrant labor backgrounds. These people are characterized by a high degree of mobility and possess few durable goods. Figure 6.3 compares the number of previous migrations among the various types of farmers. Laborer-farmers are persons who have customarily worked for others. They have had many years in low-skilled agricultural work, but little experience in farm management, and have repeatedly failed to do well economically. They traditionally have been tied to the landowner-patrons by symbiotic bonds which have provided them with security, yet effectively kept them in their low economic position. Comfort has been found in the personal treatment from boss or patron (*patrão*), since he has often been tied to the laborers' families through fictive kin ties (*compadrio*).[4] When crops failed, it was always reassuring to know that the patron would not fail to provide a minimum subsistence. The patron gained by this arrangement by paying low wages, expecting hard work, and charging high prices in the fazenda-run store, where credit was available to laborers.

Other studies indicate that this type of laborer-farmer is less frequently found in spontaneous colonization situations (Nelson 1973:73). This can probably be explained by the lack of personal initiative on the part of those bred in the paternalistic environment of the fazenda (Nelson 1973: 288). Because such laborers repay their patron in farm produce and deal with the local store on a debit-credit basis, they have little free cash of their own to spend on luxury consumer goods, much less durable goods. It also means that they may lack the skill of counting and familiarity with money management.

The second subgroup of clients, the *artisan-farmers*, are also characterized by a high degree of mobility (see Figure 6.3). A major difference between them and the laborer-farmers is that the artisan-farmers' urban experiences have permitted some of them to acquire either craft skills or better education, both of which qualify them for better-paying jobs. While their various skills might be considered second-rate in most urban areas, and could not have provided them with a substantial income, such skills are in great demand in a rural area undergoing rapid development.

So it is that, in the Transamazon, artisans seek and find well-paying jobs with government agencies as carpenters, stonemasons, construction foremen, and professional chauffeurs. Inasmuch as these artisans come to depend on these jobs for their livelihood, rather than relying on farm production or managerial talents, they should be considered clients rather than brokers. They use this situation to their advantage and overcome the problem of deficient farming experience by hiring others to work for them. This is a highly effective adaptation, particularly for urban persons coming into an unfamiliar rural area. By working for high wages, artisans can afford to hire others, who are more accustomed to rigorous agricultural labor, to prepare their land. Whenever artisans are free, they learn from their workers about farming, and over time may eventually gain enough experience to become competent farmers. In the meantime, a minimal amount of their income is being invested in farm equipment and livestock. Instead, their urban tastes for expensive food, clothing, and household goods take a sizable portion of their salaries.

In the broker category, we also find two major groups, which I will call entrepreneurs and independent farmers. *Independent farmers* are a group of largely rural persons who have previously been the owners of small landholdings (*minifundios*) or managers of landed estates. Unlike those in the client category, they have lived in the same place for most of their lives (see Figure 6.3). They bear some similarity to European-type mixed farmers, but are by no means identical (Wagley 1968:126). The European independent farmer operates a self-sufficient agricultural enterprise that integrates cattle with crops. Alfalfa and oats are planted to feed the cattle, the manure is collected and used to fertilize crops, and butter and cheese are made from the milk. Other crops are planted to supply household needs, and efficient cottage processing, including canning and preserving, stores away supplies after the harvest (Gates 1960:244–67). Such a system never was transplanted to Brazil, except among the relatively small southern population of German and Dutch descent. Sioli (1973:330–34) has indicated that such a system has worked well in the Brazilian Amazon's Zona Bragantina, an area colonized by some of these Germanic descendants.

The independent farmers of the Transamazon are in some ways like the European farmer, in that they do emphasize self-sufficiency. They plant a wide variety of crops for both home use and market sale. They are different, in that they do not generally use animals for plowing, as in Europe or Southern Brazil. However, when cattle are present, their milk is processed into curdled milk (*coalhada*) and fresh homemade cheese (*requeijão*). Some of these dairy products are sold. Manure is not usually collected for fertilizer, except among German-descended independent farmers in the area sixty kilometers west of Vila Roxa. While canning and preserving are not practiced, other cottage industries more adapted to the tropical environment are utilized. Broadly speaking, the strategies of the Transamazon independent farmers and the European farmer are similar, although their specific practices may differ. This is more a function of adaptation to particular environments than a difference in kind. Since most of their needs have been met through a variety of farm produce, the cash profits made from their agricultural production are returned to the farm in the form of livestock purchases, payment for new clearings, replacement of farm equipment, and purchases of some consumer goods. The independent farmers and their families supply most of the labor used in farming and cottage activities. Therefore, with relatively few farm capital expenditures and constant reinvestment of many of the profits in the farm itself, independent farmers show increasingly greater production.

The second group of brokers, the *entrepreneurs*, is one of limited membership. The Altamira region abounded with adventurous entrepreneurs, but most of these were in the town's commercial sector, rather than the farm sector. Any new area needs such a group to organize people and resources so as to create a profitable flow of goods, services, and capital.

Active rural entrepreneurs in the Vila Roxa area, like the independent farmers, were characterized by previous land ownership or farm administration experience, and by a low degree of previous migration. Having comparatively high capital assets on arrival, however, gave them a competitive advantage. While the majority of colonists indicated that they arrived with very little money, entrepreneur types had an average of US$500 on arrival. This small, but nevertheless significant, amount of capital allowed them to proceed quickly with land preparation and other capital-generating activities, without having to depend on the release of government subsidized loans. Local dry goods stores were established, and vehicles were acquired to provide major sources of income for these entrepreneurs.

The management expertise of these people brought rapid results. Besides the general stores and motor vehicles, these individuals now own cattle and have large areas in pasture. While their managerial skills were first developed in rural areas, from the beginning they had to deal with urban environments and the workings of financial institutions. These dealings have given them a facility in dealing with banks, bureaucracies, and client types. The entrepreneurs serve as middlemen in both economic and social transactions in the Transamazon area.[5]

Like the independent farmers, the entrepreneurs generate a great deal of capital through the sale of goods. While the independent farmers' income principally comes from the sale of agricultural production and home processed items, that of the entrepreneurs is generated through their stores, transport services, and the sale of cattle and other livestock. Both reinvest in these enterprises. Since the entrepreneurs work with much greater capital, they can afford to hire more workers, extend small amounts of credit, take on larger bank debts, and indulge in more consumer goods. Thus the entrepreneurs, rather than the independent farmers, are more likely to emulate the classic patronage behavior so frequently seen in Brazil.

Each of the aforementioned categories include persons native to the Amazon region. This needs to be explicitly mentioned, since the colonization scheme neglected to take the local people into consideration. The caboclo population, however, proved to be an important source of information to newcomers, particularly when it came to uses of the forest resources. Therefore, in the following discussion, when differences exist between caboclos and newcomers in their use of physical, social, and institutional opportunities, they will be noted. This additional variable, that is, local vis-à-vis non-local, may serve to elucidate certain aspects of both colonization planning and human adaptation to local environments. In the chapters that follow, the typology will be used as a heuristic device in describing and analyzing the subsistence and commercial practices of farmers in the Vila Roxa area.[6]

How did the various colonist types, for instance, choose their lots? How did they use the caboclos' knowledge about the soils in the area? Laziness, neglect, and ignorance of agriculture; interest in hunting jaguars to sell their prized skins; and heavy drinking were said to be attributes of the caboclos. It is the first two "characteristics" which perhaps explain why few newcomers sought the caboclo for advice. An important government administrator in the Altamira area even suggested to me that caboclos did not know much about agriculture because their "primary" interests were hunting and rubber gathering. Though happy that the highway would bring them transportation at long last, the caboclos on their part were wary of both the government and the newcomers. They stayed to themselves and preferred to live on their land rather than in the planned villages built by the government. Their preference, therefore, went against the nationalistic "melting pot" gregariousness encouraged by the government. How the various groups of homesteaders used the local forest resources is considered in the next chapter.

The Use of Forest Resources
in the Transamazon

7

Probably no single aspect of the contemporary human activities in the Amazon is of greater interest to scientists in industrialized countries than what is happening to the rain forest. Botanists predict that within one or two generations the Amazon rain forest, the world's largest, will no longer exist if current rates of deforestation continue. This chapter assesses the knowledge and use of forest resources by the colonist population that migrated to the Transamazon area of Altamira in the Xingú Basin. The analysis of this interaction is particularly important, because it was the first interaction between settlers and the new environment. How the colonists perceived the environment, what resources they recognized, how they set out to use them, and what they were effectively able to exploit are among the questions raised in Altamira, which are relevant to a human ecological study. The answers to these questions bear relevance also in understanding how colonists set out to convert the forest into agricultural land—the topic of the next chapter. It is important that an assessment be made of the part that small farmers play in the destruction of rain forests. While they are often blamed for causing deforestation, evidence from the Amazon and elsewhere suggests that the major damage is done by large-scale logging, ranching, and mining concerns (Massing 1979; UNESCO 1978:317–550; Davis 1977; Farnworth and Golley 1974).

The need to adjust to the physical environment of a rain forest, to the social life of a planned village, and to the social institutions of a complex urban-industrial society resulted in a variety of coping strategies among the colonists. Each of these environments will be discussed separately, as they provide distinct resources and posed particular problems to the population. The ways in which these resources are used will provide us with a view of the evolution of resource utilization by the population.

The Transamazon settlements offer a particularly good laboratory for the study of social and cultural adjustments to environmental conditions. As seen earlier, in addition to the newest immigrants, who displayed a wide variety of strategies reflecting past adjustments to other ecological and economic conditions, in this area we also have a population of residents who have evolved a set of adaptative strategies to deal specifically with the Amazon environment. Unlike traditional and relatively homogenous populations such as those studied by Nietschmann in Nicaragua (1973), and Rappaport (1968) and Waddell (1972) in New Guinea, the Transamazon immigrants lacked a singular or generally accepted set of cultural responses to its social and physical environment.[1] This variation makes this investigation particularly interesting, since it permits the study of the processes of change in the perception and use of resources. Immigrants from everywhere in Brazil brought to this new area a version of the cultural blueprint that once fitted their region of origin.[2] Since Frederick Jackson Turner presented his theory of the role of the frontier in shaping national character (1920), it has been common practice to view frontiers as places that facilitate technological innovation and the development of new social institutions. While such a process may indeed occur over a very long time frame, I have argued elsewhere (1975) that such change occurs not because of the "freedom of the frontier," as Turner argued, but as a result of the repeated failure of technologies and social institutions brought to the frontier from areas of origin.

Wagley has noted that in addition to a national culture Brazil is characterized by regional subcultures which reflect specific adjustments to the physical and social features of the major geo-economic regions (1948: 457–64). While all Brazilians share in a national culture to one degree or another, the older Amazonian culture (i.e., caboclo) developed as a particular response to the Amazonian forest-riverine environment (Wagley 1952; Moran 1974). The caboclo population relies on a set of strategies adapted to both the diverse physical environment of the tropical rain forest and to the traditional social and economic isolation of a region with precarious transportation facilities.

Ethnoecology of the Newcomers and the Caboclos

Resources are not an absolute reality. They are largely a matter of perception (Sternberg 1973:260–61). Not only must resources be recognized before they can be used, but an adequate strategy for harnessing them must be developed that allows the system to be efficiently operational. Unless this is done, the resource can only be used once. In terms of long-term survival, this is an inadequate solution to human adaptation (Odum 1969).

In analyzing the use of resources, I am interested in assessing the accuracy of the native conceptions of the environment (ethnoecology) in relation to the data collected by standard ecological methods. Because of the heterogeneous nature of the colonist population, no single set of native categories applicable to a domain is present. Rather, the results reflect the differences between Amazonian caboclos and recent immigrants.

Most colonists who came to farm the Transamazon land recognized neither the resources of the forest nor the alternative ways of exploiting them. Their first impulse was to clear the forest and push it as far back as possible. This is evident especially around the houses, where not a blade of grass or natural vegetation was allowed to grow. The vegetable gardens that were planted by some began three or more meters away from the dwelling, and some people feared having even these plants near the house. They had visions of snakes, scorpions, spiders, and other disagreeable forest dwellers lurking among the plants. Consequently, they did not distinguish between types of forest vegetation, nor was this vegetation properly related to soil properties. The forest fruits or game animals were also not recognized or appreciated, with perhaps the exception of brocket deer.

In contrast, the Amazonian caboclo population was familiar with the physical environment. The culture of the Amazonian caboclo developed during the colonial period and represents an adaptive system to prevalent Amazonian ecological and micro-economic conditions (Moran 1974). The resources of the forest are utilized by caboclos in ways which closely replicate aboriginal adaptations. Hunting and gathering provide protein, mineral, and vitamin food sources, while a fail-safe horticulture based on manioc provides for them the bulk of needed calories. Crops are planted in small horticultural patches prepared by slash-and-burn methods. The relative isolation of the area has led to a system of near self-sufficiency, which has been linked periodically to a cash economy.[3] The pattern of self-sufficiency was not followed in the towns, which served as commercial centers. It is the historical trend of extractivism that largely explains the caboclo's "neglect" of horticulture. Rubber, Brazil nuts, pelts, and wood brought good prices, while surplus agricultural production brought less profit and were harder to market. In the traditional Amazon town of Itá, for example, most of the food consumed by the population was and is imported, because most of the families have concentrated on extractive activities rather than farming (Wagley 1953:71–72).

The Amazonian caboclo is a generally disparaged human type. The truth is that no one wants to be a caboclo. Use of the term usually implies low education, laziness, drunkenness, and poor nutritional and hygiene habits. "Nor is a caboclo to be readily trusted," according to common belief. It is not surprising, then, to see little mention of the caboclo population in the colonization blueprints. As noted, their schemes were aimed at bringing "land-hungry Northeasterners," who in turn would hopefully be influenced by the "technologically innovative" Southerners, to the "demographically empty" Amazon. The caboclo was never considered in the plans, except in brief asides which pointed out that the way of life of traditional Amazon communities was not modern and, therefore, doomed (*Jornal da Transamazonica* 1972:2; Santos 1968:30).

The Transamazon caboclos came from nearby tributaries, Amazonian gold mining areas, or came as pioneer families when Altamira county made lands available a generation ago. The opening of municipio lands in the 1950s attracted caboclos to the vicinity of Altamira. In these pre-highway years, their activities differed little from those of caboclos elsewhere (Moran 1974). They penetrated to their lands in the traditional way, by way of streams, to the municipio lands west of Altamira and north towards Cachoeirinha. There they built thatched homes near the water's edge and began to cultivate small patches of land using slash-and-burn methods. Produce was carried on their backs to the quarters of a local entrepreneur. From there the sacks of produce were taken to Altamira on rented mules.

These Pará caboclos had largely come from a riverine environment where they planted small inter-cropped roças, and fished or hunted for their protein. They processed manioc into flour (*farinha puba*) and tobacco into cured ropes to earn cash in the nearby town. Most of their needs were supplied by the forest or cultivated land, with the exception of salt, liquor, sugar, metal tools, and kerosene. Cooking fat was supplied by pork lard or by processing *babaçú* palm oil. Spices were home grown, and baskets, brooms, and other nonmetal utensils were home processed. Vines were used as a rope equivalent, tree bark provided the material for basket making, palm leaves provided roofing material, some vines provided potable water for those who cleared the forest, dried straw was used to make brooms, and wild herbs provided medicine. River fish once provided the most abundant protein source in their riverine homes.

Caboclo colonists continue to fish and hunt. They averaged thirty-six kilograms of game and four kilograms of fish per month in Vila Roxa during 1974. Although the small streams that cut through colonists' lots do not carry the larger fish species (Honda 1972; Veríssimo 1970), the use of a simple hook-and-line is rewarded with catches of *traíra* (*Hoplias malabaricus*). Caboclos have not forgotten the use of fishing spears and a type of fish trap, the *cacurí*, but no caboclo colonist has been reported to use these methods in the study area. They do not use *timbó*, a general name given to a wide variety of poisonous vines which can stupefy fish in a dammed up stream. The use of such vines is illegal and goes on surreptitiously if it occurs at all. Catches of fish in Vila Roxa are on occasion distributed to friends and neighbors. Fish is neither sold nor used medicinally. Rather, it is used largely for family consumption.[4] Much more important in terms of time expended and the resulting quantity of protein is the hunting of wild game.

Before the highway came, wild game was much more prevalent. Caboclos recall killing large tapirs (*Tapirus terrestris*) a few meters from their huts. Now, the situation is different. While hunting is not widespread among the colonists in general, their use of the forest for agriculture has driven the game further back into the untouched areas. Tapir is difficult to come by, as is other large game. More rewarding are the returns from hunting white-lipped peccary (*Tayassu pecari*) and white-collared peccary (*Tayassu tacaju*).

Caboclos are conservation minded when it comes to hunting. Caboclos in the Vila Roxa area say that there are lucky days for the hunter (*dias do caçador*) and lucky days for the game (*dias da caça*). Tuesday, Friday, and Saturday are lucky days for the hunter, while Sunday and Monday are lucky days for the animals. On the latter days, hunting is not rewarding and is generally avoided. Wednesday and Thursday are ambiguous. Even on days when luck is supposed to be on his side, the hunter can come home empty handed. On such occasions he may become concerned and begin to investigate the possibility that he is *empanemado* (i.e., having bad luck). *Panema* is bad luck related to hunting/fishing (Galvão 1951). It can be caught by the touch of a menstruating woman on the hunter's gun or fishing equipment; through not sharing game with needy neighbors or kinfolk (leading to *desconfiança*); through mutilation or abandonment of the carcass of hunted game; and through permitting a pregnant non-kin to eat his game. Fear for the loss of his protein sources seems to be at the root of caboclo beliefs in panema (Wagley 1953:81; Moran 1974:148). Once diagnosed, the caboclo begins a set of culturally prescribed ritual to be rid of panema (Wagley 1953:79–80; Galvão 1951).[5]

The belief in "lucky days," and the social and legal restrictions which prohibit and discourage the sale of meat and animal pelts tends to diminish the amount of hunting which takes place.[6] Thus, game is not hunted for profit by Transamazon caboclos, but only for their own personal consumption and sharing with neighbors. Newcomers, on the other hand, hunt any day, do not believe in bad luck, and in a number of cases sell game meat to supplement their incomes.

Most hunting goes on during the late evening and at night. This avoids the lengthy and tiring chase of game that is customary with daytime hunting. The only exception to this rule is the hunting of diurnally active peccary (*porcos do mato*). Since these travel in bands of twenty or more, the prospect of an exciting and high-yielding chase engages a number of men on a single hunt. Otherwise, hunters leave their agricultural pursuits in the late afternoon and walk to a "waiting point," or *espera*, by the time dusk has fallen. A waiting point is usually located near flowering or fruit-bearing vegetation known to be attractive to game (Moran 1975, 1977, 1979b). The hunters tie up their hammocks about three meters above the ground and await for the arrival of game. They wear dark or colorless clothes to avoid detection by the game, and conversation is practically absent. All await to hear the distinct footsteps of various nocturnal animals. When an animal is under their hammock or eating the tree's flowers or fruits, it is blinded by a flashlight and shot. On rare occasions, a hunter will pass up a chance to kill, say a "*paca*" (*Agouti paca*), because his wife asked him to bring home a deer (*Mazama americana*). Shooting the first available animal is, however, the norm rather than the exception.

After three years of intensive settlement, hunting in the region near Vila Roxa yields mainly small game: *paca* (*Agouti paca*), *cutia* (*Dasyprocta prymnolopha*), armadillos[7] (*Dasypus novemcinctus*), and deer (*Mazama americana*). Generally, only caboclos will unhesitantly eat monkey although newcomers have been known to eat it in times of need.[8] There are numerous other culturally acceptable mammals in the forest, such as birds, but they are rarely hunted.[9]

Some newcomer colonists sell game meat. Hunting game for profit is associated with those farmers whose strategies emphasize wage labor over work on their own land. These hunters-for-profit hunt an average of twenty-two kilograms of wild meat per month, and are approaching the rate of thirty-six kilograms per month obtained for consumption and distribution to friends and relatives by the native caboclos. The price of game meat is one-third the price of beef or pork (Cr$6 versus Cr$18). It therefore makes an important addition to the diet of all and a modest contribution to the income of some newcomers.

Game provides an important contribution to the diet of all farmers. In three agrovila farm communities Smith (1976a: 171–177) found that total yields were around 3,000 kilograms for a twelve-month period. Yields, however, fluctuated a great deal within the twelve-month cycle (see Figure 7.1). These yields are not representative of the potential productivity of

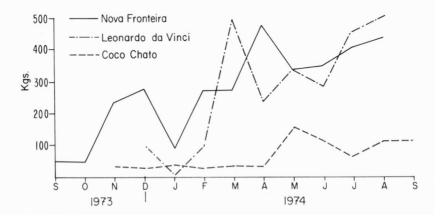

Fig. 7.1 Game Hunted per Month in Three Agrovilas
Source: Smith 1976a:178

the forest. No more than five farmers hunted regularly in any one community, and they restricted their aim to "culturally acceptable" animals—thereby leaving out monkeys, insects, sloths, porcupines, and other animals making up the bulk of the animal biomass. Rabbit (*Sylvilagus brasiliensis*) is hunted only by gauchos from Rio Grande do Sul. Its meat is considered "slippery" (*lisa*) by all others and, therefore, undesirable as food. Capybara (*Hydrochoerus hydrochoeris*), the largest rodent on the earth, can be hunted near streams, but it is only rarely found in the Altamira area. Other animals not commonly used either are the *porco de espinho* or *ouriço* (either *Coendou prehenselis* or *Proechimys guyannensis*), anteaters (*Myrmecophaga tridactyla* and *Tamandua tetradactyla*), and sloths (*Bradypus infuscatus marmoratus* and *Choloepus didactylus*).

While conservation myths such as belief in "mothers of the animals" are not active except among the caboclo population in this area, it is reassuring to know that food preferences per se exercise a restraining force on hunting (see Table 7.1). In cases of all illness and the states of pregnancy, post-partum and lactation, game meats are not consumed because they are considered to be dangerous (*remoso*). Chapter 10 discusses how foods are used to manage health status. Indirectly, this acts to lessen hunting intensity and makes game available for a longer period of time as a source of meat protein.[10]

Most of the hunters are caboclos who are familiar with the forest and its resources. Most newcomers hunt opportunistically as they travel through paths to their planted fields. Thus the newcomers seldom obtain any game other than small and familiar animals like armadillo, paca, and agouti. Their yields are but a fraction (about seven kilograms per month) of that of regular hunters (about thirty-six kilograms per month).

In a fifteen-year old community the hunters were less successful than in the newer agrovilas. Compare Coco Chato with the other two in Figure 7.1. They were able to obtain only small game near the edge of their fields and had reduced their hunting range from 6.0 kilometers to 2.0 kilometers (Smith 1976a:174–76). The reduction in range reflects their adjustment to the diseconomies of hunting in a disturbed forest. "Whereas a hunter requires an average of only 9 days to track and kill 104 kg of game in relatively undisturbed forest, he must spend some 26 days and range over 1560 ha. to crop the same quantity of game in the highly modified vegetation" (Smith 1976a:182). This depletion is all the more rapid due to the restricted variety of animals hunted by most farmers. This hunting strategy contrasts significantly with that of Amazonian aborigines (see Chapter 3). Although cultural taboos on hunting are found in autochthonous populations, a greater range of game is harvested.

The use of wild plants also differs between caboclos and the new settlers.[11] The latter use only the fruit of the *cupuaçú* (*Theobroma grandi-*

TABLE 7.1
FOLK CLASSIFICATION OF MEATS

VERY STRONG (muito reimosa)	STRONG (reimosa)	CLEAN/MILD (limpa)
Tapir (anta) (*Tapirus terrestris*)	White-lipped peccary (porcão) (*Tayassu pecari*)	Brocket deer (veado) (*Mazama americana*)
Collared peccary (caitetú) (*Tayassu tajacu*)	White paca (paca branca) (*Agouti paca*)	Wild fowl** (various)
Nine-banded armadillo (tatú verdadeiro) (*Dasypus novemcinctus*)	White agouti (cutia branca) (*Dasyprocta* spp.)	Chicken (galinha)*
Tortoise (jabutí) (*Geochelone* sp.)	Common opossum (mucura) (*Didelphis marsupialis*)	Beef (gado)*
Howler monkey (guariba) (*Aluoatta* spp.)	Rabbit (coelho) (*Sylvilagus brasiliensis*)	
Red agouti (cutia vermelha) (*Dasyprocta* spp.)	Monkeys (macaco) Cebidae (several genera)	
Red paca (paca vermelha) (*Agouti paca*)	Wild cats (gato, onça) (*Felis* spp.)	
	Domestic pig (porco)*	
	Muscovy duck (pato)** (*Cairina moschata*)**	

* Indicates domestic animal
** Occurs both as a wild and domestic species
SOURCE: Modified from Smith 1976a:180 and Fleming-Moran 1975:82–84

florum), *cacao do mato* (*Theobroma* spp.), and Brazil nuts (*Bertholletia excelsa*). Even more so than game, wild plants are viewed as dangerous and unknown. Fruits in general tend to be considered "acid" and are especially avoided during disease and periods of weakness. This is true even for caboclos. When they are healthy, however, the caboclos use a variety of seasonally available forest fruits. Caboclos use the fruits of the *açaí* (*Euterpe oleracea*), *bacaba* (*Oenocarpus bacaba*), *babaçú* (*Orbignya martiana*), *sapucaia* (*Lecythis usitata*), *piquí* (*Caryocar* spp.), *cupuaçú* (*Theobroma grandiflorum*), *taperebá* (*Spondias lutea*), cacao (*Theobroma cacao*), and Brazil nuts (*Bertholletia excelsa*). Table 7.2 lists the most important fruits available and used in the Marabá-Altamira-Itaituba highway transect (Moran 1975; Smith 1976a).

More often than not, consumption of wild fruits demands a certain degree of processing. Table 7.2 details processing required. The pulp is commonly mashed and mixed with water and sugar to make a juice (*vinho*). Children rarely wait for this juice and generally consume the fruits in their natural state. Some of the exotic fruits are unusually rich sources of vitamins. Though few have been adequately analyzed, those which have, if eaten, would tend to combat the "vitamin deficiencies" frequently discussed in the literature (Castro 1967:51–52). Most nutrition surveys fail to account for wild fruit consumption, because people forget to mention them in household food consumption surveys. They are often not classified as "food." For example, *taperebá* and *cupuaçú* provide a richer source of vitamin C than does pineapple; Brazil nuts are rich in the amino acid methionine,[12] *açaí* is rich in vitamin A, and *pupunha* (*Guilielma gasipaes*), *buriti* (*Mauritia vinifera*), and *tucumã* are three times richer in vitamin A than are carrots.[13]

Ethnoagronomy: Soil Selection in a Forested Environment

The colonization plan did not foresee that 36 percent of the homesteading population would be made up of local Amazonian settlers. Many, but not all, were already in the Altamira region. These persons had lived either as townspeople in Altamira, or along river banks engaged in swidden agriculture. Due to the limited marketing opportunities available, their economic choices were chiefly geared at subsistence, and their lifestyle by necessity became one of independent solitude. On arrival, the colonization administrator in Altamira contacted some of the local caboclos and asked them to show him the areas of good soil. Willingly, the caboclos pointed out the areas of farmable soil as well as those that would present agricultural difficulties. The small farm belt involved some of the most fertile soils in the Amazonian terra firme (Falesi 1972:192), but it also cut through infertile white sands and leached ultisols, whose location was

TABLE 7.2

Wild Fruits and Nuts Utilized by Colonists along the Maraba-Altamira-Itaituba Stretch of the Transamazon*

Name	Availability	Part(s) eaten	Preparation/consumption
Babaçú (*Orbygnia speciosa*)	Year-round	Nuts	Nuts eaten raw, also grated and pounded to extract oil for cooking purposes
Açaí (*Euterpe oleracea*)	June–December	Fruits and heart	Mesocarp mixed with sugar and water for drinking, or mixed with manioc flour and water for eating
Tucumã (*Astrocaryum vulgare*)	August–January	Fruits and heart	Fruits eaten raw, fed to pigs, or mixed with sugar and water for drinking
Najá (*Maximilliana regia*)	August–February	Fruits	Eaten raw and fed to pigs
Bacaba (*Oenocarpus distichus*)	September–December	Fruits	Mesocarp mixed with sugar and water for drinking, or mixed with manioc flour and water for eating
Frutão (*Pouteria pariry*)	December–March	Fruits	Pulpy yellow mesocarp eaten raw, mixed with sugar for dessert, or mixed with sugar and water for drinking
Cajá (*Spondias lutea*)	March–May	Drupes	Bitter-sweet mesocarp eaten raw, or mixed with sugar and water for drinking
Uxi (*Endopleura uchi*)	November–March	Drupes	Oily mesocarp eaten with sugar and manioc flour

NAME	AVAILABILITY	PART(S) EATEN	PREPARATION/CONSUMPTION
Cupuaçú (*Theobroma grandiflorum*)	December–March	Fruits	Mesocarp eaten raw, or mixed with grated Brazil nuts and eaten, also mixed with sugar and water for drinking
Cacau bravo (*Theobroma speciosum*)	December–January	Fruits	Mesocarp eaten raw, also mixed with sugar and water for drinking
Castanha do Pará (*Bertholletia excelsa*)	December–March	Nuts	Eaten raw, grated and mixed with tortoise soup, cupuaçú, condensed milk, also used in making cakes
Genipapo (*Genipa americana*)	January–February	Fruits	Fruits mixed with water and sugar for drinking
Piquí (*Caryocar villosum*)	December–January	Drupes	Oily mesocarp cooked, then mixed with manioc flour for eating

* Only the most commonly eaten fruits and nuts that could be identified with the aid of Cavalcante (1972, 1974), Le Cointe (1947), and Mors and Rizzini (1966) are included. Note the predominance of fruiting during the early part of the rainy season (December–March).
SOURCE: Modified from Smith (1976a:167–68)

not evident in preliminary soil maps. However, the colonization timetable established in faraway Brasilia pressured the local administrator to abandon such soil selectivity and forced him to make *all* the lots available to whomever was willing to assume their ownership.

Apart from this one incident of consultation with local caboclos, they have been largely ignored by government agents. Other problems have arisen as well. The caboclos who had begun to farm the county-leased lands years earlier tended to build their homes along isolated streams far from the path of the oncoming highway. Their farms were often overlooked by the surveyors who marked out the uniform rectangular lots of the colonization project. The pace of colonization was simply too rapid to check the records. Land titles had been vague, and boundaries had been set by natural markers such as streams, rather than by neat topographic lines that had previously been granted by the county to the caboclos.[14]

Many of the older tenants of these lands lost their cleared lands to newcomers, and inherited 100 hectares of virgin forest. Serious conflicts emerged at times, and were resolved in ways that left both sides unhappy with the outcome. The loser was commonly the caboclo, especially in the first year of colonization. The administrators had been instructed that the purpose of the project was to settle Northeasterners. Local inhabitants tended to lose out, given the requirements of putting Northeasterners on the land. That more Amazonian caboclos were claiming land than Northeasterners was not realized by local colonization administrators. Only as a result of the data gathered by Moran (1975) and Smith (1976a) was this fact finally accepted.

The earliest pioneers who arrived at Altamira were natives of Rio Grande do Norte, and local Amazon caboclos. They bore the brunt of early difficulties, but also the advantages of being among the first to settle in. Many of these men, however, had come without their families to first establish their homes and farms. These first settlers were allowed to choose their homes in the agrovila, and some managed to establish farms in the first year. They also received several benefits from INCRA, such as distribution of food, tools available at cost, and free furniture and poultry. Such benefits were later cut from the program.

These early colonists worked on public projects for a few months until their houses were ready, and then began to work on their chosen lots. Those who came later were taken in the back of trucks to some point along the highway and told to choose their lots. While some complained that lots had been assigned by "lottery," the majority were allowed to select the sites for their lots.

Caboclos from Pará chose lots according to criteria important to them. These included proximity to the main highway and the type of forest vegetation that they found. According to caboclos, the best land for

TABLE 7.3
Species of Forest Vegetation Used by Caboclos
to Select Agricultural Land

Local term	Scientific name
Pau d'arco or ipé (yellow variety)	*Tabebuia serratifolia*
Pau d'arco or ipé (purple variety)	*Tabebuia vilaceae*
Faveira	*Piptadenia* spp.
Mororó	*Bauhinia* spp.
Maxarimbé	*Emmotum* spp.
Pinheiro preto	Unidentified
Babaçú	*Orbignya martiana*
Açaí	*Euterpe oleracea*

agricultural purposes would be indicated by certain species of vegetation growing on it (see Table 7.3). Such vegetation was described as being made up of trees of small diameters (*paus finos*), or liana forest (*cipoal*). Most of the caboclos interviewed indicated that they had noticed their chosen land years before, while hunting in the forest. The fact that they were the first there does not mean they preempted all the good soils, leaving only weaker ones for the new settlers. However, the soil samples analyzed from those areas indicate that their criteria were very accurate (see Table 7.4). Good organic matter content, low exchangeable aluminum levels, pH of 6.0 or better, and adequate potassium and phosphorus content were among the qualities present in their soils.[15] Figure 7.2 illustrates the fertility of the soils by plotting macro-nutrients and limiting factors such as pH and aluminum. The size of the hexagon visualizes the fertility of the soil. Compare the fertility of soils chosen by caboclos with those chosen by outsiders (Figure 7.2).

Newcomers, on the other hand, were confused by the lush vegetation. They recognized few tree species at all. The government agents who assisted in lot assignments were not very helpful either. Road construction and settlement had proceeded too quickly, and analysis of the various soils had lagged behind. A preliminary discussion of the soils was available only in 1972 (Falesi 1972) and only included soil samples from along the main highway artery, not along the side roads, where most of the lots were being distributed. The arriving settlers were faced with two options: either they had to choose according to criteria that they knew, or they had to ask a caboclo.

Many opted for the first choice, and the use of non-Amazonian criteria

TABLE 7.4
FIRST-YEAR CABOCLO SOILS

	pH	P (PPM)	K	CA+MG	SUM OF EXCHANGEABLE BASES	EXCHANGEABLE ALUMINUM	EFFECTIVE CEC	C (%)	N (%)	O.M. (%)	C/N RATIO	SOIL COLOR (WET)
					(IN MILLIEQUIVALENTS PER 100 GRAMS)							
	6.0	48	.18	8.9	9.08	Traces	9.08	2.31	0.22	3.97	11	10 YR 4/2.5
	5.6	3	.12	7.6	7.72	Traces	7.72	1.78	0.22	3.06	8	10 YR 3/2.5
	7.1	26	.09	4.8	4.89	Traces	4.89	1.02	0.10	1.76	10	10 YR 2/2
Average	6.2	25.7	.13	7.1	7.23	Traces	7.23	1.70	.18	2.93	10	
Range	5.6–7.1	3–48	.09–.18	4.8–8.9	4.89–9.08		4.89–9.08	1.02–2.31	.10–.22	1.76–3.97	8–11	

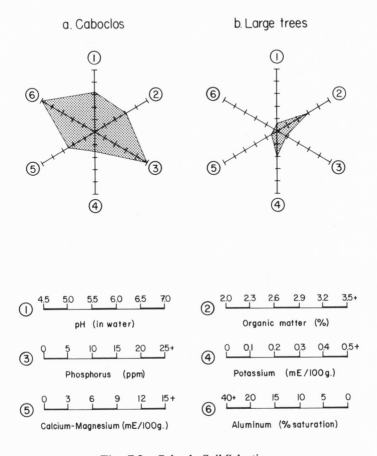

Fig. 7.2 Caboclo Soil Selection

to select good farm land led to disappointing results. One such criterion was, "the bigger the trees, the better the soil." Choosing trees with large diameters and height (*paus grossos*) meant that, in the Altamira region, they chose forests with the species listed in Table 7.5. These are the larger buttressed trees whose shallow roots seek nourishment from the fallen leaves and broken limbs. Soils under this type of vegetation and litterfall proved to be poor, and even first year crop yields were disappointing.

Another criterion the newcomers often used was particle composition of the soil. These colonists felt that the heavier and stickier the clay, the more preferable it was. While some good soils fall in this category, some of these heavy clays would be among the first to create drainage problems,

TABLE 7.5

FOREST VEGETATION INDICATIVE OF POOR AGRICULTURAL SOILS

LOCAL NAME	SCIENTIFIC NAME
Acapú	*Vouacapoua americana*
Jarana	*Holopyxidium jarana*
Sumaúma	*Ceiba pentandra*
Melancieira	*Alexa grandiflora*
Sapucaia	*Lecythis paraensis*
Piquí	*Caryocar microcarpum*
Cajú-Açú	*Anacardium giganteum*
Massaranduba	*Manilkara huberi* (or *Mimusops huberi*)

and suffer from compaction after forest clearing and cropping. Figure 7.2 visualizes the fertility of soils chosen by criteria other than the caboclos'.

Not all colonists, however, followed these unsuitable criteria for choosing their lots. Some asked the caboclos what to look for. Even in their first encounter with the new environment, some of the colonists behaved differently from others. Some colonists chose on the basis of friendship. These turned out to be client types who demonstrated a high degree of dependence on others. Whole pockets of clients grouped along isolated and seasonally-impassable sections of side roads were created in this manner. Normally they chose poor soils. While the government offered to move some of them to better areas, they refused to give up the improvements they had made in their plots unless the debts incurred were cancelled.

Brokers on the other hand, sought the advice of their caboclo neighbors. Like the caboclos, they chose lots near the main highway artery and with superior soils. Given the difficulties of keeping transportation linkages operative during the long rainy season, the locational factor is just as important as is the soil fertility factor in net income terms. In a few cases of farmers who chose superior soils, but at fifteen to twenty kilometers from the main highway, the net incomes were barely distinguishable from those who chose poor soils. The higher production could not be taken to market without accessible transportation. Figure 7.3 maps out the locations of caboclos, brokers, and clients in the proximity of agrovila Vila Roxa. The clustering of these groups reflects their use of similar criteria in choice of location and bore significantly on their farm performance.

Fig. 7.3 Soils and Settlement near Vila Roxa

Agriculture in the Transamazon

8

Slash-and-Burn Agriculture

As in other parts of the tropical world, slash-and-burn agriculture has been the most common method of land preparation in Brazil.[1] Until a decade ago this method was considered primitive and ecologically detrimental (Rocha Penteado 1967:11–12; Gourou 1966). Today, however, even ecology institutes turn to this oldest of techniques to prepare fields for agroecological experiments.

It is a common misconception that slash-and-burn methods are always practiced by primitive farmers on inferior soils. Popenoe's study in Central America (1960) found tropical soils under slash-and-burn cultivation that had high levels of organic matter, low bulk density, high exchange capacities, and high potassium content. These favorable soil qualities are not usually associated with such a method of farming. The study also called attention to the great variability of tropical soils. Sanchez and Buol (1975:598) indicate that tropical soils are comparable to temperate soils in both quality and range of variation. Both high and low base status soils exist in the tropics, as they do in the temperate areas.

Just as tropical soils have proven to be more varied than previously thought, so the ideas surrounding the slash-and-burn method have undergone equal revision in recent years. Slash-and-burn agriculture is emerging in the literature, not only as an effective agronomic practice for tropical regions, but also one based on sound economic considerations. In a number of experiments carried out in Brazil, burned areas produced 30 percent more than those which were cleared mechanically and cultivated with a plow (Baldanzi 1959). Burning kills parasites, insects, fungi, nematodes, and pathogenic bacteria. Weeds are destroyed and anaerobic nitrogen-fixing bacteria, such as *Clostridium* spp., increase their action (Baldanzi 1959). Anaerobic bacteria, however, are not comparable to aerobic bacteria such as *Azotobacter* and *Beijerinkia*. The latter are far more important nitrogen-fixers. The ashes from burning decrease soil acidity, and this aids the nitrification process. Burning also aids the flocculation of col-

114

loids, which, as Sioli (1973) points out, are sorely lacking in many tropical soils under natural conditions. These favorable results associated with slash-and-burn in Brazil were confirmed in the Peruvian Amazon. Sanchez et al. (1974) found that yields using traditional slash-and-burn methods were 50 to 60 percent higher than yields from bulldozer-cleared areas. Lower mechanized yields found in the Sanchez et al. study were attributed to reduced infiltration resulting from soil compaction, the lack of nutrients from the ash layer, and the loss of the humic horizon by bulldozer scraping.

Equally relevant data on the effects of slash-and-burn agriculture was reported in Africa by Nye and Greenland (1960). When the forest is cleared and the vegetation burnt, all nutrients, except nitrogen and sulphur, are deposited as ash. While nitrogen and sulphur are lost as gases, the

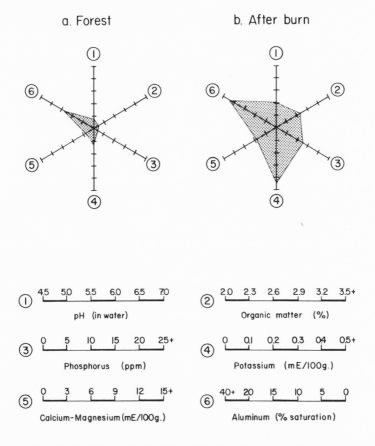

Fig. 8.1   Change in Soil Fertility Resulting from Burning
Source: Moran, soil survey, 1973–74

other elements are washed into the soil with the advent of the rainy season. Heating of the soil leads to increased fertility, largely due to the change in the state of nitrogen mineralization (Nye and Greenland 1960: 72). While the loss of nitrogen, sulphur, and carbon[2] is regrettable, increased fertility and improved conditions for plant growth are not.

The fertility of the soils found in the Vila Roxa area was significantly increased by burning (see the hexagonal area composed of major fertility criteria in Figure 8.1, a. and b.). With burning there is a marked increase in soil pH towards a less acidic condition (see Figure 8.2). This also means that effective cation-exchange capacity is increased (Buckman and Brady 1969:96). This effectively increases the availability of nutrients to plants and is compounded by a significant increase in the total amounts of phosphorus, potassium, calcium, magnesium, and carbon. Nitrogen, how-

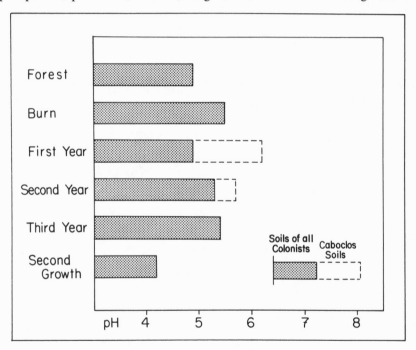

Fig. 8.2 Changes in pH in Various Stages of Utilization
Source: Moran, soil survey, 1973–74

ever, is not significantly affected, nor is there a dramatic increase in organic matter in comparison to the changes in the other soil constituents. The increase in soil pH is closely related to a reduction in exchangeable aluminum (see Figure 8.3). This lowers the ever-present danger of aluminum toxicity in tropical soils (Popenoe 1960:100).

In addition, burning eradicates seeds and vegetative material, which can lead to a large crop of weeds. Animals and insect pests are also

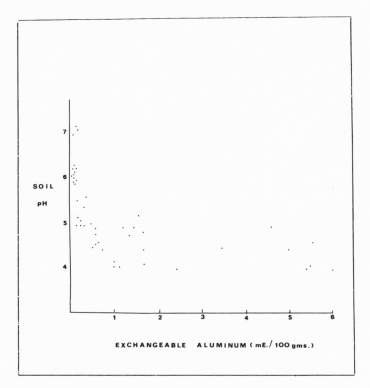

Fig. 8.3 Relationship between Soil pH and Exchangeable Aluminum
Source: Moran, soil survey, 1973–74

destroyed or temporarily driven out by the fire. These particularly beneficial results affect yields. Weed invasion limits crop production, not only
by its natural competition for soil nutrients, but through the accompanying
increase in the rodent population. During the early stages of weed invasion, rodent populations undergo accelerated growth. The damage caused
by rodents to young plants can be very severe (Popenoe 1960:59–62).

In economic terms burning is also good business. Rodrigues Lima
(1956) estimated the cost of machine clearing in a várzea area of the
Brazilian Amazon at over Cr$12,574 (US$1,825) per hectare. The same
area could be cleared by machete and hand axe at a cost of Cr$690 (US
$100).[3] The only advantage of the bulldozer is that it accomplishes the
clearing of one hectare in six days, as compared to forty-eight man-days
for the manual method.[4] However, by employing more workers, the work
could be done by manpower in less time (Rodrigues Lima 1956:59–69).
In the Yurimaguas region of Peru, a team of North Carolina State University agronomists came to a similar conclusion. Depending on the ma-

chinery used, mechanical clearing costs varied between US$106 and US $212 per hectare, while manual clearing was only US$53 per hectare (Sanchez et al. 1974).

For populations with low capital resources and low levels of affordable technology, slash-and-burn agriculture is a land preparation technique that is based on sound agronomic and economic judgments (Sanchez and Buol 1975:601). Slash-and-burn techniques are usually associated with shifting cultivation as a system. While Transamazon farmers utilize slash-and-burn techniques of land preparation, they do not seem to be going in the direction of shifting fields, although they have been noted to clear new fields each year. Rather, the land is kept in permanent production through pasture development or the establishment of permanent tree crops. The consequences of this approach will require long-term monitoring in order to establish whether or not it results in sustainable yields.

Land Preparation: Measuring the Fields

In Vila Roxa, once a colonist has chosen his lot, his first field needs to be laid out. The area is measured carefully to fulfill both credit requirements and the production needs of the farm household. Areas facing the road are cleared first, and each year the new fields move further back in the rectangular 100-hectare landholding. The common basis of measurement is the *tarefa*, or "task," although most farmers are also familiar with the term "hectare."[5] The measurement of this area varies with the size of a man's hands and arms. The stick used to plot a field, a *braça*, is cut to the size of an arm's-breadth, or ten *palmos* in length. The size of a palmo will vary from farmer to farmer; however, most men's hand palms were close to 22 centimeters. The average braça is 2.2 meters. The Transamazon tarefa is an area slightly smaller than an acre.

At the edge of the prospective field, a long wooden sighting stick or small sapling is placed in the ground, and a "flag" such as a shirt or palm frond is placed at the top. The area around the marker is next cleared of vegetation. Then, using a braça as his measuring stick, the farmer starts out from the marker, moving in a straight line, and makes a trail (*picada*) with his machete. As he clears the path, he lays the stick on the ground and aligns it with the flagged marker. If the field is meant to be, say 12 tarefas (3.63 hectares), the farmer moves forward down one side of the future field for 100 braças (220 meters). At this point, he places another upright marker in the ground, clears the area around it to improve visibility, and turns at a right angle. He then marks off another 75 braças. A fourth marker is placed, and the last 75 braças (165 meters) are cut through to the original starting point. The work is slow, because it is difficult to keep the markers in sight and maintain a straight line. The farmer must constantly check his braças' alignment with the flagged markers.

It is almost inevitable that in the course of marking his field, a farmer will run into a large tree that he cannot chop down with his machete. When this occurs, the common procedure is to avoid it, yet not lose one's place in the lined measurement. A few feet away from the tree, the farmer measures a braça towards the inside of the field, then measures a braça forward, and then a braça back to the original line of measurement (see Figure 8.4). In this manner he is back in a straight line, and the tree serves as a new point of alignment instead of the marker. If visibility is not good, he may clear some of the vegetation around the large tree. The time it

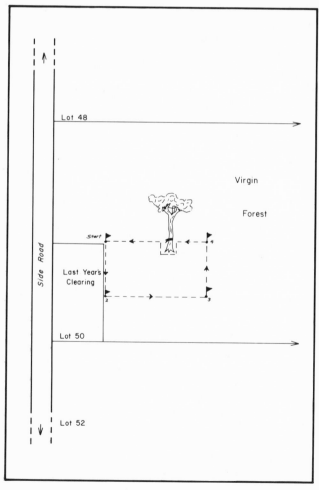

Fig. 8.4   Field Measuring Diagram
Source: Moran, field notes, 1973–74

takes to carry out field measurements varies with the worker, but most farmers in the Transamazon could do a twelve-tarefa field (3.63 hectares) as described above in one to two man-days.

Land Preparation: Underclearing

The process of underclearing, or *broca*, is basically done in the same way by all colonists. Amazon caboclos, however, demonstrate a greater ease in using tools and achieve a more even mat of cut vegetation than do newcomers. While caboclos and Northeasterners tend to use the machete (*terçado*), the Southerners, more often than not, use a *foice*, a type of long-handled scythe. The work follows a sort of circular pattern, which is executed by a single worker or a pair working in tandem. First, facing the virgin forest, the men clear their way around one side of an obstacle— usually a large tree with attached vines or a group of small trees to be felled. They work around to the back of this chosen obstacle. Then, facing the cleared area, they fell the remaining light material so that it falls from the uncut area back into the clearing (see Figure 8.5). Thus they

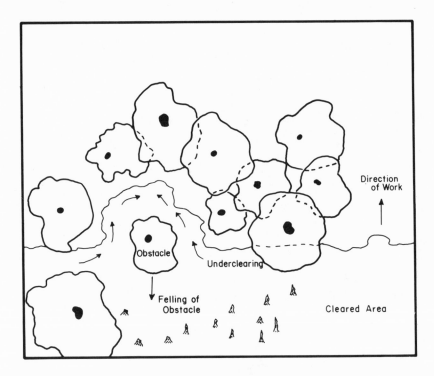

Fig. 8.5   Process of Underclearing
Source: Moran, field notes, 1973–74

prevent brush from falling on top of them and keep the next uncleared area free of fallen brush. No worker observed was hit by falling vegetation, unless a number of laborers worked too closely together. Accidents among the non-local population were far more frequent than they were among caboclos (see Chapter 10).

The usual cutting pattern for light to medium growth is to use short two-foot chops close to the ground, which leave four-inch stumps protruding from the ground. While the non-Amazonian colonists allow whole trees to fall into the clearing, caboclos have a somewhat specialized technique that minimizes the risk of falling brush. As the tall trees or a group of entangled vines begin to topple, caboclos use slower but longer strokes (about six feet) to cut the plant in sections as it falls, thereby shortening its falling distance and cutting it in smaller pieces. The worker stands to one side of the large plant as he cuts the root. Then the sideways blows of the machete, plus the initial cut of the tree away from the worker, keep the plant from falling in his direction, or the upper branches of the tree from falling on his or any of the other workers' heads. When the task is expertly done, the tree or bush falls almost in exactly the same spot in which it stood. Younger workers are slow in chopping the vegetation in sections as it falls. If a number of young workers work in a line, the number of warning shouts are indicative of unperfected technique. This suggests that it takes several years for a farmer to reach a level of proficiency in underclearing work.

The cutting of interwoven vines also calls for a slightly different technique, especially if the vines are thick. First, the vines are cut through at about arm's height, leaving intact whatever is attached to the ground. Then, cutting downwards on the lower section, the worker uses one or two strokes to whittle it down to the ground, and does this for all the vines in the bunch. Finally, he goes back to cut the hanging tendrils up above head height and leaves the rest dangling from the tree. With this method, more than one person can work on a dense bunch of vines until it is time for the final step of clearing the upper tendrils, when only one can work. By using this technique, a solid base of the vine is kept steady while the lower sections are cut; this would be harder to do if the vines were first cut through at ground level—long vines would be left swinging, and the worker would have to chop at a moving object.

While all colonists use these three techniques to one degree or another, the caboclos are smoother and more efficient in their work. Normally the work of underclearing is not a hazardous task. However, great discomfort can be caused by a razor-sharp plant called *capim cortante*, or *tiririca*, and biting *tachi* ants. Underclearing begins in June or July, and ends by August. The labor input varies with the type of forest, the size of the clearing, and the farmer himself. The number of man-days needed to clear one hectare ranged from one to seventeen among the Vila Roxa colonists studied. Wagley (1953:68) reports that among the Itá caboclos under-clearing took approximately fifteen man-days per hectare.

The underbrush is left to dry for one or two months before the larger trees are felled. Those who quickly finish either of these jobs on their lots earn wages by helping others. An alternative strategy is to clear for others and then catch up on one's own work later. The latter, however, is a risky approach that most prefer to avoid, since many men have waited too long to clear their fields before the coming of the winter rains.

Land Preparation: Tree Felling and Burning

Large tree felling, called the *derruba*, takes place between August and September after the underbrush has dried to form a crisp tinderlike material. Most persons follow a traditional method, which directs a large tree to fall on top of the smaller ones that have been partially cut but not toppled. If the area has large buttressed trees, this calls for the use of a movable scaffold, or *jiráu*, which is carried from one tree to another. It is saved also for later use in hunting, as an alternative to stringing up one's hammock in the trees to wait for game. Labor input in tree felling can be high if the forest includes numerous hardwood species. Farmers who choose the more fertile liana forests have a much easier task of tree felling, but a harder job of underclearing. As with underclearing, variation in labor input ranges from one to seventeen man-days per hectare for tree felling.

A number of colonists own powersaws and use them in their own work and to cut trees for others. In most cases of such service, the owner tends to operate his own machine, as the bank financing for the saw requires that he take a course to learn how to run it.[6] If a powersaw belongs to one man but is run by someone else, the overall charge tends to be higher, Cr$100 per hectare. The use of powersaws not only does the job more quickly but also alleviates the task of building scaffolds, as the saw can cut through any part of the tree with relative ease. This is the only modern technological innovation utilized by the Transamazon farmers. In general, however, tree felling involves the use of a single-edged steel axe and much back-breaking work. After the trees are felled, some farmers gather them into piles or cut them into smaller sections to ensure a better burn. This, however, entails a much higher input of energy, which many farmers are unwilling to provide. Ideally, the large trees will dry for one to two months before the process of burning the brush begins.

Burning takes place between late October and December, depending on the weather. One waits as long as possible to assure maximum dryness and the hottest burn. Without a weather service, the difficulty in timing the burning can be well imagined. From early October, conversations turn to the weather, and the slightest cloudiness is watched with concern. A light rain becomes a major topic of discussion for days. September is the month of lowest rainfall, but it is between October and November that a great number of rainless days occur in conjunction with a decrease in the number of days of consecutive rain. It is worth remarking that even in the dry season it still rains on occasion (see Figure 8.6). This makes it

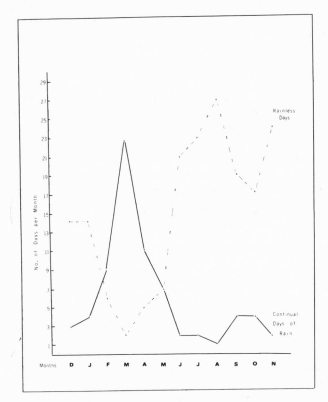

Fig. 8.6 Pattern of Rainless Days and Continuous Days of Rain (1973–1974)
Source: Moran, field notes, 1973–74

difficult to determine when the threshold for the heavy rains has been reached. Important, too, in this calculation is the lack of experience among the newcomers. By 1974, most farmers had begun to discuss the weather with local caboclos, but little interchange had occurred in the previous two years.

The beneficial effects of burning on soil properties and fertility have already been discussed. The burning technique varies a great deal among the colonists, but it usually involves a number of persons who simultaneously circle the cleared area with a homemade torch or burning stick. Some kerosene has been spread at the edge of the field to aid in the spread of the fire. At least five to six days without any rain whatsoever are preferred before attempting to burn. Noon to 2:00 P.M. is a preferred time for burning, since at that time the sun is at its hottest, and the wind is at a minimum. Some colonists use the wind to their benefit if they and their neighbors have cleared several contiguous fields; the fires are started at the edge of one field and carried by the wind across the others. During burning there is little need for a firebreak, as the green virgin forest does not burn readily at all (cf. Carter 1969:57).

The quality of the underclearing to a large extent determines the quality of the burn. Lands with liana forest burn better than those with large buttressed trees, since light, dense underbrush, if properly dried, provides a great amount of kindling for a very hot fire. Large trees hardly burn unless they are sawed into small sections. If the vegetation burns well, a good ash layer remains. If, however, much vegetation remains barely charred and in large pieces (*sapecado*), a further labor-intensive step is called for, the *coivara*.

The coivara is dirty work. The charred vegetation is chopped and put into small piles that are then burned individually with the aid of costly kerosene. In the process the labor input may be higher than all the previous steps put together: some farmers estimate that it takes up to sixty man-days per hectare. If this step is needed, the farmer usually chooses only a portion of his cleared field to reburn and lets the rest go to weed. The coivara work may not be completed before the first rains come; the nutrient pool will be small and uneven; the soil will be more acid; and the pests and weeds will be back even before the first year's crops are harvested. Lower yields and more work is the price that is paid for a bad burn.

Changes in Soils with Cropping

With cropping and the leaching action of rainfall and sun, the soil pH of Vila Roxa farms slowly begins to return to a more acidic state, and carbon and organic matter levels gradually drop. There is also a very slight decrease in nitrogen. Levels and availability of calcium, magnesium, and potassium increase after burning, but they, too, over time return to levels found in climax forest. Potassium levels gained by burning hold up well after two cropping seasons (see Appendix for complete soil analyses and changes in fertility through time). The declining fertility which follows burning is illustrated in the hexagonal drawings in Figure 8.7. A further decline in fertility occurs during fallow and is related to nutrient uptake by the successional forest vegetation.

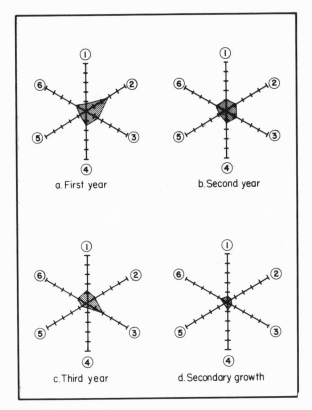

Fig. 8.7 Changes in Fertility after Burning. Refer to Fig. 8.1 for legend.
Source: Moran, soil survey,
1973–74

Very little erosion was noted in Vila Roxa farms during the fieldwork
period, despite the rolling terrain. This is probably due to the excellent
structure of the soils themselves—especially the oxisols and alfisols. In
areas with slopes of fifteen degrees or steeper, with poor ground cover,
soil erosion could become a serious limiting factor. Smith noted an annual
loss of up to two centimeters of topsoil in such areas—an amount equivalent to 100 tons per hectare per year. This loss is particularly damaging,
since the cation exchange capacity in the ten to fifty centimeter zone is
significantly lower than in the top ten centimeters (Smith 1976a:111).
Even after torrential storms, it was but a short period before the water had
percolated through and was carried off by the complex system of streams.
The relatively little weeding done by farmers also helped break the impact of the rain and sun. These minor changes shown in the soils that
are utilized by the caboclos in Vila Roxa are indicative of the high initial

pool of available nutrients, the good structure of the soils, and an agricultural management system that provides good soil cover.

Total exchange capacity does not provide an accurate picture of the actual field situation of acid tropical soils. Coleman et al. (1959) and Popenoe (1960:91) contend that the amount of permanent change, that is, the *effective* cation exchange capacity (CEC) provides a more realistic basis for assessing the fertility status of soils in the tropics than CEC. In the Transamazon, soils sampled had a mean effective cation exchange capacity of 3.68, which increased to 5.44 with burning. During cropping it declined slowly to 1.7 after three years of continuous agricultural usage. The decline in overall fertility, base saturation, and CEC are not severe enough to force the colonists to shift fields after two years of cropping. These results were confirmed by Smith (1976a:94–98) in his research in three other agrovila communities. Other factors, therefore, must be sought in explaining the avoidance of keeping fields in continuous cereal production. As we will argue later, the system of credit obtention and agronomic problems in the cultivation of cereals are primarily responsible

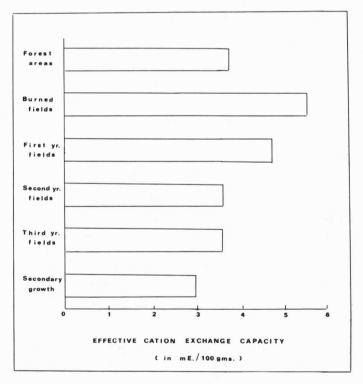

Fig. 8.8   Changes in Effective Cation Exchange Capacity
Source: Moran, soil survey, 1973–74

for the practice of clearing new land each year.[7] Effective CEC in abandoned fields covered with secondary growth is still lower, but full recovery to forest nutrient levels takes place in slightly over seven years. Figure 8.8 illustrates the changes in effective CEC.

Soil fertility on the colonists' lots is generally low, except on those which were chosen according to vegetation criteria given by local caboclos. Such soils are exceptionally good (see Figure 7.2) and compare favorably with newly burnt fields even after one cropping season (compare with Figure 8.7). Intensive agriculture is not so much limited by inherent soil infertility in the region, but by the accuracy of selection criteria.[8] While most soils in the region probably fall into the low fertility category (see Figure 8.7), sizable areas of high fertility soils exist, and local caboclos were able to identify them.

In areas with low fertility, pastures that combine grasses and legumes may be more appropriate than food crops, according to some scholars (Mott and Popenoe 1975:46). Pasture soil samples taken in Altamira indicated that calcium and magnesium levels increased after two years in pasture land from the levels present in forest.[9] Over time, one would also expect an increase in organic matter due to root biomass turnover. The most limiting soil factor to quality pastures, and to agricultural production in the region, seems to be phosphorus. Burning is the only means to cheaply increase the phosphorus levels. Figure 8.9 illustrates the benefits of burning and the changes in phosphorus levels with cropping.

Planting Sequences

Colonists' decisions as to what to plant are based on the farmer's past experience, the yields obtained by neighbors, information about crops and prices, and evaluation of needs. The influence of the extension service on land use has been minimal (see discussion in the next chapter). The most crucial decision is that between cereal crops that mature all at once and root crops whose production is available year round. Relevant, too, is the investment in foods used for medicinal purposes (cf. Fleming-Moran 1975). Table 8.1 provides a comprehensive view of the plants cultivated.

In late November and early December new fields are planted in rice (*Oriza sativa*) and corn (*Zea mays*). Rice is usually planted on well-drained slopes, while corn is planted on the low areas, which usually have less surface rock than do the weathered slopes. If the soil is poor and/or the field is poorly burned the farmers immediately plant the area in manioc (*Manihot esculenta*) which is usually a second-year field cultigen. It is important for better weed and pest control to have the seeds and cuttings in the ground before the rainy season gets underway. There is also evi-

TABLE 8.1

PLANTS CULTIVATED BY TRANSAMAZON FARMERS

LOCAL NAME	SCIENTIFIC NAME	USES*	ENGLISH NAME
Abacaxí	*Ananas comosus*	Food	Pineapple
Abóbora	*Cucurbita* spp.	Food	Pumpkin squash
Alface	*Lactuca sativa*	Food	Lettuce
Alfazema	*Ambrosia* spp.	Medicine	Lavender (?)
Alfavaca	*Ocimum basilicum*	Medicine	Basil
Algodão	*Gossypium arboreum*	Medicine	Cotton
		Other	
Araruta	*Maranta arundinacea*	Food	Arrowroot
Arroz	*Oryza sativa*	Food	Rice
Arruda	*Ruta graveolens*	Medicine	Rue
Banana	*Musa* spp.	Food	Banana
Batata de purga	*Convolvulus operculatus*	Medicine	Bindweed or jalap
Batata doce	*Ipomoea batatas*	Food	Sweet potato
Berengela	*Solanum melongena*	Food	Eggplant
Caatinga de mulata	*Leonotis neptaefolia*	Medicine	(?)
Cacau	*Theobroma cacao*	Food	Cacao

Local Name	Scientific Name	Uses*	English Name
Cajueiro	*Anacardium occidentalis*	Food Medicine	Cashew
Cana	*Saccharum officinarum*	Food	Sugar cane
Capim santo	*Cybopogon nardus*	Medicine	Lemon grass
Cará	*Dioscorea* spp.	Food	Yam
Carurú	*Amaranthus oleraceae*	Food	Caruru
Cebolinha	*Allium cepa*	Food Medicine	Green onion
Coco	*Cocus nucifera*	Food	Coconut
Coentro	*Coriandrum sativum*	Food	Young coriander
Couve	*Brassica oleracea*	Food	Cabbage relative
Erva doce	*Pimpinella anisum*	Medicine	Anise
Fava	*Vicia faba*	Food	Broadbean
Feijão andú	*Canjanus indicus*	Food	Pigeonpea
Feijão comum	*Phaseolus vulgaris*	Food	Cowpea or black-eyed pea
Fumo	*Nicotiana tabacum*	Medicine Other	Tobacco
Gergilim	*Sesamum indicum*	Food	Sesame
Gingibre	*Zingiber officinalis*	Medicine	Ginger

TABLE 8.1 (Continued)

LOCAL NAME	SCIENTIFIC NAME	USES*	ENGLISH NAME
Goiaba	Psidium guayava	Food Medicine	Guava
Graviola	Anona cherimolia	Food	Guanábana (Spanish)
Hortelã	Mentha spp.	Medicine	Mint
Inhame	Dioscorea spp.	Food	Yam
Jaca	Antocarpus integrifolia	Food	Jackfruit
Jiló	Solanum gilo	Food	(?)
Jurubeba	Solanum paniculatum	Food	(?)
Laranja	Citrus aurantium	Food	Orange
Limão	Citrus limonum	Food	Lime
Macaxeira	Manihot esculenta	Food	Sweet manioc
Mamão	Carica papaya	Food	Papaya
Mamona	Ricinus communis	Food Medicine	Castor bean
Mandioca	Manihot esculenta	Food	Bitter manioc
Mangericão	Ocimum minimum	Medicine	(?)
Mangerona	Origanum majoranum	Medicine	Wild marjoram
Maracujá	Passiflora edulis	Food	Passion fruit
Maravilha	Mirabilis spp. (?)	Medicine	(?)
Mastruz	Chenopodium anthelminthicum	Medicine	Wormseed
Maxixe	Cucumis anguria	Food	(?)
Melancia	Citrollus vulgaris	Food	Watermelon

LOCAL NAME	SCIENTIFIC NAME	USES*	ENGLISH NAME
Milho	*Zea mays*	Food	Corn
Mostarda	*Sinapis chinensis*	Medicine	Mustard
Ortemisa	*Anthemis nobilis*	Medicine	Camomile daisy
Pião roxo	*Jatropha curcus*	Medicine	(?)
		Other	
Picão	*Bidens dentata*	Medicine	(?)
Pimenta malagueta	*Capsicum frutescens*	Food	Red pepper
Pimenta do reino	*Piper nigrum*	Food	Black pepper
Pimenta de xero	(?)	Food	Yellow pepper
Pimentão	*Capsicum anuum*	Food	Bell pepper
Poejo	*Mentha pulegium*	Medicine	Pennyroyal
Quiabo	*Hibiscus esculentus*	Food	Okra
Rosa branca	*Rosa alba*	Medicine	Rose
Repolho	*Brassica oleracea*	Food	Cabbage
Sabougueiro	*Sambucus nigrum*	Medicine	Black elder
Taioba	*Xanthosoma* spp.	Food	Yautia
Tangerina	*Citrus nobilis*	Food	Tangerine
Tomate	*Lycopersicon esculentum*	Food	Tomato
Transagem	*Plantago major*	Medicine	(?)
Vassourinha	*Scoparia dulcis*	Medicine	Broom
Xurú	*Sechium edule*	Food	Chayote

* The various medicinal uses of the plants herein indicated are studied by Fleming-Moran (1975).

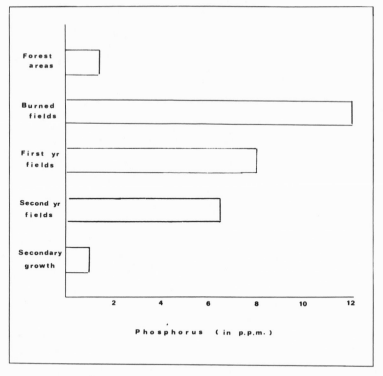

Fig. 8.9   Changes in Soil Phosphorus
Source: Moran, soil survey, 1973–74

dence that a nitrate pulse, which lasts about two weeks, follows the start of the rains (Nye and Greenland 1960:110–11). During this period nitrification is rapid, and the availability of plant absorbable nitrogen is at a peak. Crop yields are likely to be considerably higher if the farmer has acted swiftly to give his crops the advantage of this growth-stimulating nitrogen.

Beans, the third major crop, are planted only after the heavy rains have ceased and the "dry" season is underway. This occurs sometime between May and June (see Table 8.2). Each set of seeds is planted at the base of the now dry corn plant. After a small February-March harvest of fresh corn, the top of the stalk forms a sturdy support for the growing beans. Both are left in the ground and are harvested in their dried forms several months later. Not only does planting in May allow the beans to benefit from the support of the corn plant, it also protects the bean seeds from excessive rainfall, which can rot the seed. In 1972–73 farmers who planted early in April were dismayed to find that few of the seeds had germinated.

The bean varieties that are encouraged by the federal agencies include several varieties of *Phaseolus vulgaris*, such as red beans (*canário*), black beans (*rico*, EEP 23), and small cream-colored beans (*jalo*, *cristal*). In

TABLE 8.2

SCHEDULE OF AGRICULTURAL TASKS

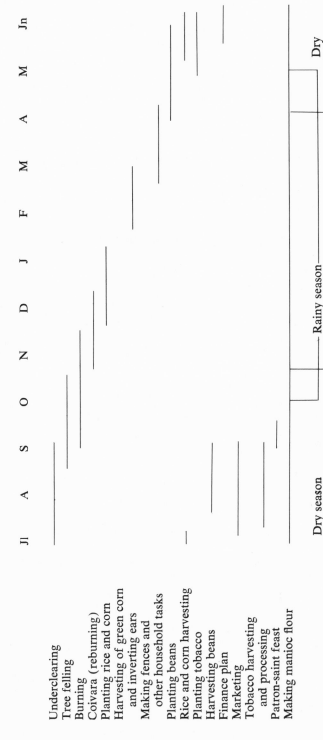

a study by BASA (1971:45), it was determined that the *Phaseolus* varieties, especially the black bean, had better market possibilities than other varieties. Therefore, farmers received bank financing to plant them. Cowpeas (*Vigna sinensis*), on the other hand, were not financed. Cowpeas have been planted successfully in the Amazon and Northeast because of their ability to produce good yields in low fertility, acidic soils. They have a relatively low cultural and market value in southern Brazil.

Planting of rice, corn, and beans is done manually, usually using a simple mechanical device introduced by the colonization agency. This is a hand-operated planter or dibbler, called a *matraca*. The seed container is filled at the top, the point of the chute stuck into the ground, and five to six grains are released when the two-handled tool is clicked together. In this method, twenty to thirty kilograms of rice seed are used to plant one hectare. No one was observed to use a dibble stick, so common in other areas of the tropics and among autochthonous Amazonians.

Manual planting depends on tools such as a machete or a *sacho*. The latter is a curved-handled spade, about forty centimeters in length, which is traditionally used by rice farmers from the state of Maranhão. The method of planting with a blade or sacho involves more bending than does use of the matraca, since the farmer must slide the instrument in at an angle, lift a clod of dirt, and manually throw in a handful of seed. The clod falls to cover the seed when the blade is removed. In the manual planting of rice, one often needs ten more kilograms of seed per hectare, because the number of grains is not mechanically controlled. With the machine planting of corn, twenty-two kilograms of seed are used per hectare. Machine planting of beans uses forty to fifty kilograms per hectare.

Manioc and bananas (*Musa sapientum*), two crops which provide a dense low canopy, are also planted about the same time as rice and corn. These crops are generally planted on "last year's field," as they demand less fertile soil. In general the time of planting of these crops is not as critical as is that of rice, corn, and beans. The spacing and acreage of all these crops will depend on the amount of land which is cleared of burned debris, the amount of wage labor available for planting, and, of course, the farmer's experience. On comparable fields, rice bunches are planted 30 to 38 centimeters apart. Between corn stalks, the distance is increased to 65 to 100 centimeters, which allows for the growth of the bean. Manioc is planted 85 to 130 centimeters apart, although the field appears to be much more densely planted, since the varieties used in this area tend to branch and spread. Therefore manioc provides better soil protection than either rice or corn, as it makes a canopy over the soil and shields it from the leaching action of rain.

Some of these major crops are intercropped with other products. Corn is associated with beans. Bananas may shade cacao (*Theobroma cacao*), or be planted with tall thin papaya trees (*Carica papaya*) and low growing pineapples (*Ananas sativus*). Manioc may be associated with bananas and pasture grasses. Sweet manioc varieties are planted near the house, together with fruit trees, vegetables, and herbs. Lastly, open fields of rice may be sown simultaneously if the farmer feels the soil is too poor to support another year of production. On the other hand, he may simply be planning to invest in cattle and will have a ready-made pasture soon after the rice is harvested. In this system grass takes over immediately to cover the soil. Other farmers may plant grass after crops of manioc and bananas have been planted. The grass seed is sown by the broadcasting method (*botar capim*). The seed may simply be collected manually from a neighbor's lot, bought for cash from other farmers, or purchased from local supply houses or the experimental station. Most commonly a variety such as *colonião*, or guinea grass (*Panicum maximum*), is used.

Farmers living on their land plant a great variety of edible plants near their houses. Sugar cane and flowers are planted between the front of the house and the access to the road to beautify the approach to the dwelling. Behind the house are found papaya, collard greens, green peppers, hot peppers, bananas, okra, *carurú* (*Amaranthus oleraceae*), guava, tomatoes, and sweet manioc. Spices, seedlings, and medicinal plants are also grown near the house, preferably on raised platforms to protect the plants from ants and chickens. Further away, citrus, jackfruit, pineapple, cashew, squashes, sweet potato, *taioba* (*Xanthosoma* spp.), *inhame* (*Dioscorea* spp.), mango, tamarind, bitter manioc, and sesame are also grown. However, none of the above cultigens are far from the house, and so provide great variation in the household diet.

After planting rice and corn, the heavy rains begin, giving farmers a period of relative rest and inactivity (see Table 8.2). The men stay at home a great deal and are reluctant even to visit others, since the thick clay mud would be tracked into neighbors' homes. Very little weeding of the fields occurs during the rainy season, even on those fields which had bad burns and, consequently, vigorous weed invasion.[10] Several fields had vines and weedy shrubs thirty-five to forty-five centimeters in height within a month of the burn. In general, the type of secondary successional vegetation that predominates depends on the soil type and the amount of time following the burn (Smith 1976a:53–54). The attitudes of many farmers about weeds were stoical, "nothing can hold back that bush (*mato*), there is nothing one can do (*não tem jeito*)." Indeed, the frequent invasion of fire ants (*Solenopsis* spp.) and thorny solanaceous shrubs such as *jurubeba* (*Solanum cyananthum* and *S. toxicaria*), or those having irritating leaves (*S. asperum*), discourage weeding. As a result, weeds compete with crops and are probably responsible for low rice yields. When weeding was done, only the tallest weeds were lobbed off with a machete as the farmer walked through his field.[11] Such neglect in the rainy season is partially explained by the infestation of tiny gnats, or black flies (*Simulium* spp., see discussion of this insect in Chapter 10).

By the end of the rains, the farmers have their busiest season. The rice must be harvested, the beans planted, arrangements made to transport the produce to market, and a plan for next year's financing must be worked out with the extension agents. There is even a celebration of the Feast of St. John at this time. Coordinating all of the above is no easy task, especially since the end of the rains also signals the peak season for malaria. Many farmers have to contend with high fevers and the debilitating side effects from this disease.

Harvesting and Marketing

Rice is the first crop to be gathered in the harvesting cycle. When it is harvested by hand, using a sickle or kitchen knife, it is cut thirty to fifty centimeters from the ground. If, however, the rice is machine-threshed, the grain heads, or *cachos*, are cut off at a height of 1.30 to 1.65 meters, so as to leave less straw for the machine to sift. Cutting the rice in cachos involves more labor, and may require fifteen to eighteen man-days to harvest one hectare. Harvesting the meter-long rice stalks for hand threshing requires only six to nine man-days per hectare to cut and pile. Rice cutting could be faster, but the practice of intercropping with grass slows the process, since by the time of the rice harvest, pasture grass surrounds the rice. At other times, farmers also plant manioc and bananas after the rice comes up so as to minimize the exposure of the fields and get optimum production in a single season.

Setting up a hand-threshing unit takes about three workers a period of some three hours, or approximately one man-day. An area for threshing is selected near a large fallen log in the middle of a rice field, and the ground about the log is cleared of stumps that may not have burned. Then four holes, two on either side of the log, are dug with a *cavadeira*, or post-hole digger, to about two feet in depth. The posts are placed in the ground and packed with the remaining dirt. Old burlap sacks are then used to make an open three-sided box, and each of the panels is strengthened by cross supports tied to the posts with vines (*cipó*). The rice is then beaten against the log, and falls to the burlap-covered ground. In the process of beating, flying grains are caught by the three-sided shield, and are diverted to the pile in front of the thresher.

Machine threshing is a much swifter operation, but is not cheap in money or labor terms. First, it takes about four times as long to cut the rice in small cachos as it does to cut the whole stalk. Second, one has to wait for a day when the thresher will be available, arrange for the gasoline, and hire more people. To run the thresher efficiently takes a minimum of five people: one or two to feed the rice into the machine, one to operate it, one to keep the chaff exit clear, and usually two young workers to keep sacking the rice as it comes out. The farmer is expected to pay Cr$2 per finished sack of rice for the use of the machine, and to feed the government-employed operator during the day. The speed of the thresher depends on many factors. The machine has to be in good working order, the workers have to set up an efficient feeding operation, and the amount of chaff the machine handles should be minimal. Such operations vary from a low of 35 to a high of 130 sacks threshed in a full work day. Obviously, it is hard to generalize; however, except in cases where a farmer needs to get a very large crop to market before it spoils, hand threshing seems to serve just as well as or better than machine threshing.

Rice yields vary a great deal. In 1972–73, a selected seed from the Northeastern state of Pernambuco was introduced to the farmers by the colonization agency. The seed was not well adapted to the area: germination levels were low; the rice was underdeveloped. While other seed types such as *canela de ferro*, "IAC 1246," and "101" were useful in the area and available to the farmers, the colonists felt obliged to use INCRA-promoted rice. The yields of the poor seed were extremely low. As rice was the best producing commodity and was used to pay bank and INCRA debts, the farmers were greatly distressed. Fortunately the rice seed used the following year produced good yields, despite the fact that a sizable number of the fields had not burned well during the clearing process.

At the current time the greatest problems of the rice production involve competition with weeds, especially *Eleusine indica*, *Digitaria horizontalis*, *Emilia coccinea*, and *Althernanthera ficoilea* (IPEAN 1973a). Also two diseases affected the crops, *bruzone* (*Piricularia oryzea*) and *Helminthosporium oryzea.* The average rice yields in 1973–74 were 597 kilograms per hectare; they were 534 kilograms per hectare in 1972–73, and 1,053 kilograms per hectare in 1971–72. The low yields of 72–73 were due to a bad seed, and those of 73–74 due to poor burns caused by early rains. Smith (1976a) also noted losses to bird predators, especially blueheaded parrots, or *curicas* (*Pionus menstruus*); blue-black grassquits, or *chupão* (*Volatinia jacarina*); yellow-bellied seedeaters (*Sporophila nigricolis*); and shiny cowbirds (*Molothrus bonariensis*). The impact of avian predators is likely to increase as grass species become increasingly abundant.[12]

A main problem with the rice crop in the Transamazon is the difficulty of marketing it. Except for farmers who have lots along the main highway and the few good side roads, most of the colonists have difficulty in getting the sacked rice out to market. Sometimes it is carried by mule one or two sacks at a time, which is a slow and expensive process. If the farmer has to borrow a mule, he has to give his neighbor one sack of rice out of every four taken to the main highway.

Rice storage is also a problem. Some production is lost when colonists cannot get the sacks to the main highway and try to store them in makeshift shelters on their lots. Here the stores are subject to rat and pest infestation, while high humidity causes molding. This also lowers the market value of the unshelled rice, since humidity causes rice to break and shatter during milling. If a colonist manages to get his rice as far as Vila Roxa, he rarely stores the rice in the communal warehouse (*silo*), for that warehouse has neither security nor adequate accounting procedures. Instead, he stores the unmilled rice in his home, where it is again subject to losses from the rat population. It seems the rats are even more attracted by unshelled rice than by the milled, household variety.

Rice is generally marketed through COBAL-CIBRAZEM, especially if the person has a debt to pay to the Bank of Brazil. In this system, the farmer's debt is deducted from the total value of his production, and the person is reasonably assured of continuing good credit. Prices paid by COBAL-CIBRAZEM, however, are considerably lower than those paid by the private entrepreneurs of Altamira and the Vila Roxa area. The latter usually retrieve the produce from the farmer's lot, give him the sacks for his rice, and pay him cash on the spot. This frees the farmer from paying Cr$4 for each burlap sack, and from the transportation costs of nearly Cr$10 per sack to take the produce into town. In 1973–74 COBAL-CIBRAZEM paid Cr$53 per sixty-kilogram sack of rice, as did the Altamira dealers. However, discounting the cost of transport and bags, the net price was actually Cr$39 per sack if sold to CIBRAZEM. The local brokers near Vila Roxa paid Cr$50 per sack, picked up the production from the farmer's land, but did not always provide the burlap bags. Others supply the sacks to guarantee a commitment of the harvest. Except for those who feel obliged by the federal institutions to sell to CIBRAZEM, by 1974 most producers were opting for the better prices and services of the private sector.

In marked contrast to rice, manioc presents few growing season problems: weeds do not impair harvesting, the tubers can be converted to an easily storable flour anytime from six months to two years after planting, and the yields are higher even in nutrient poor soils than are rice yields in the best of soils (Moran 1976b). Although mosaic virus and bacterial wilt (*Xanthomonas manihoti*) affect manioc, only leaf-cutter ants (*Atta* spp.) significantly affect production in the Brazilian Amazon (Albuquerque 1973). Most of the manioc crop is converted to farinha. A majority of farmers adopted the preference for Amazonia farinha puba over the *farinha sêca* (grated manioc flour) manufactured in the South and Northeast of Brazil. Puba is made by placing the tubers in a stream or tank for two to three days. The water-softened roots are peeled at the stream and taken to a press, where most of the water is squeezed out. The pulp is then pressed through a sieve to remove the fibers, and then stirred over a griddle until dry. Most caboclos prefer to mix puba with some sêca.

Grated manioc is squeezed to obtain *tucupí*, a tasty sauce used in Amazonian cuisine, and *goma*, high-quality tapioca starch.

About 3 kilograms of tubers yield about 1 kilogram of flour. On oxisols and ultisols, yields from manioc were on average 20,000 kilograms per hectare, or 6,500 kilograms of flour (Smith 1976a, 1977). This amount compares favorably even with the best yields obtainable for rice anywhere. Yields are considerably higher in alfisols. In the marketplace, a sack of manioc flour sold for at least twice the price brought by a sack of unhusked rice. Thus, while one hectare of rice yielded an income of US$217, the same area in manioc yielded US$1,091. While the inputs of labor are higher in processing manioc into flour, the lack of seasonality in manioc harvesting allows a family to process it year round without hiring additional labor, and to obtain a flow of capital coming in year round, rather than relying on just the once-a-year "bonanza" following the rice harvest, when prices tend to be depressed due to the oversupply in local markets (Moran 1976a). Throughout the Amazon in traditional riverine communities, manioc is the predominant crop found in fields—occupying as much as 94 percent of the planted area.

Corn makes up the second most important crop in terms of the number of sacks that are sold in the Altamira market. However, its market value, Cr$30 per sack, is less than that given for rice, beans, or manioc. Relatively little corn actually reaches the Altamira market, for the colonists generally use the small amount that is produced above home consumption needs to supplement chicken feed. The yields are affected by the lizard *lagarta militar* (*Spodoptera frugiperda*), by fungus *Puccinea polysora*, and by spotting caused by *Helminthosporium tursicum*. Ants (*Atta* spp.), rats (*Rattus rattus*), and native rodents (*Agouti paca* and *Dasyprocta*) also plunder the cobs.

Green or fresh corn on the cob is used during the months of February and March. It is roasted over coals as *milho assado*, or processed into corn puddings and a form similar to the Mexican *tamal*.[13] The rest of the corn is left to dry on the stalks and is harvested with the beans in August or September. The corn yields have been extremely low; they were roughly 400 kilograms per hectare in 1972–74. Smith (1976a:141) reports 953 kilograms in alfisols between 1972 and 1974. In the few cases where two crops of corn are planted in a single year, one in December, and a second in June—a common practice in Mesoamerica (Reina 1967)—the total yields are increased. However, the quality of the ears in Altamira has been unimpressive, despite the use of hybrids such as "Azteca" and "Central-Mex." The corn generally grows to a height of 2.5 meters, and normally produces one ear per stalk.

This meager production of dried corn is generally used by the farmers for poultry feed or as corn meal. The corn meal is either ground at a small local mill or processed manually with a mortar and pestle. If a farmer has a small surplus of dried corn, he will sell a few sacks to his neighbor. Rarely is the corn production ever used to pay off bank debts by selling it to CIBRAZEM. Stored maize is often attacked by a variety of beetles (especially *Sitophilus zeamais*), moulds, and other pests.[14] Only one in five Vila Roxa farmers had enough corn beyond family needs to sell in the market in 1973.

Beans, like corn, are not sold in the market as often as is rice. In fact, no farmer in Vila Roxa sold beans in Altamira during 1973. The bean production that year was so low that most families gained only 174 kilograms from the whole bean harvest.[15] In the majority of cases this amount did not even meet the needs of family consumption, and the families had to buy extra supplies in Altamira. Only one farmer had a small surplus of beans, and he sold it to neighbors.

One of the principal reasons for this low production is the damage caused by a fungus growth (*Thanatephorus cucumeris*). The farmers refer to this as the *queima*, since the leaves take on a burned appearance.[16] The types of beans which are most affected by this fungus are the *Phaseolus* varieties mentioned earlier. These are widely planted by farmers, in part because they were promoted by the bank, but they are also preferred by the settlers. The cowpea (*Vigna sinensis*), however, is more resistant to spore growth, as is shown by its widespread use throughout the Amazon. Young bean sprouts are a favorite food of rabbits (*Sylvilagus brasiliensis*), who exercise a negative influence on the crop. Beetles (especially *Callosobruchus maculatus* and *Zabrotes subfaciatus*) attack the beans while in storage, boring through as much as 95 percent of the stored crop within the first six months.

While the *Phaseolus* varieties can be successfully grown during a long, dry summer period, they quickly succumb to the fungus if summer rains appear. Given the unpredictability of summer rainfall, it would seem that current *Phaseolus* varieties will continually be threatened in the Amazonian environment. However, the native cowpea, or *feijão da corda*, could provide a more secure and consistent bean production, which would be important as an added source of protein. Cowpeas are also already adapted to the low base status soils found in most of the area (Sanchez and Buol 1975:602).[17] The combined average yield of *Phaseolus* bean varieties at Vila Roxa is about 144 kilograms per hectare, in 1973. If one includes all the farmers who lose their bean crops, the average is lowered to 88 kilograms per hectare.

More permanent crops produce well enough in the region, but a variety of problems has prevented their assumption of a key role in the agricultural economy. Bananas and plantains are productive, but much of those crops spoil due to saturated local markets and inadequate systems of transportation for export to urban areas or for industrial processing. Black pepper has done well in some areas of the Amazon, but damages from the fungal disease *Fusarium solani piperi* require constant spraying. Cacao is being introduced into the colonization area, but seeds were late in arriving and little direction was given to those inexperienced with its cultivation. In the past, cultivation of cacao has suffered from the fungus disease *Marasmius perniciosus*. The lack of enthusiasm for these cash crop alternatives to annual crops may have influenced the Geisel administration and agricultural analysts in Brasilia to conclude that small farmers were unproductive, and that Amazon development had to be turned over to large operators who would invest in setting up export-oriented plantations and ranches.

Aside from the factors of climate, seed variation, and natural decimation by pests—all of which may affect colonists equally—the levels of production of crops seem to be related to the background of each of the four groups of colonists. Their migratory histories, the inputs of family labor, and their area of origin are all aspects which have an effect on farm management and production.

The fewer the number of previous migrations, the better the yields of a farmer tend to be in the Transamazon (see Moran 1979c for a comprehensive discussion). As indicated earlier, entrepreneurs and independent small farmers are both characterized by low rates of migration. Entrepreneurs in the Transamazon generally tend towards cattle ranching and pasture development. Independent farmers emerge as the group with the highest total farm production (Cr$8,798 per year), as well as the greatest output of corn, beans, and rice per unit of cultivated land (804 kilograms per hectare). This suggests that agriculturalists who migrate infrequently tend to achieve more farming success than those who keep moving. Many independent farmers previously owned their own land or worked in decision-making positions, such as that of foreman. Perhaps the long periods spent in such positions resulted in the accumulation of farm management experience which is now evident in their Transamazon productivity. Independent farmers in the Transamazon tend to clear relatively small areas of land that could be managed easily (2.56 hectares per year).

A partial explanation of the independent farmer's better production seems to be that these individuals often use family members as a source of farm labor. This influences their total farm income in that, unlike the other three groups, few funds are expended for hired labor. Seven out of nine independent farmers have at least one full-time family member engaged in farm work, usually a young male or spouse. The farmer and his grown sons do the heavy tasks of underclearing and tree felling. The wife and younger children are in charge of meal preparations, care of livestock, vegetable gardening, and field tasks such as planting and harvesting. While the family of the laborer-farmer group also helps in farm work, their contribution was found to be sporadic rather than regular and continual. In fact, it is rare to find anyone other than the family head and hired laborers working at the lots of the other three groups. One hears frequent complaints that it is hard to get a full day's work out of hired men; from this it may be inferred that the independent farmer can elicit more labor from his own family members, with no need for cash outlay, than other farmers could from hired labor.

Among the independent farmers, the total farm income was also related to whether the farmer was caboclo or a newcomer. Better use of the land and its resources by caboclos is evident when a larger, more representative sample is used (N=101). In the 101 farm management surveys obtained in the region, caboclos had nearly twice the productivity per hectare than did outsiders. For 1973–74, the value of corn, rice, and bean production of these local people was Cr$808 per hectare, while it was only Cr$494 per hectare for newcomers. The highest yields in the Vila Roxa sample were obtained by an independent farmer who was native to the area. His rice yields were 1,440 kilograms per hectare, and bean yields 1,520 kilograms per hectare. This is far above yields obtained by other members of the independent farmer group, and may reflect his more judicious choice of good soil, his knowledge of the peculiarities of Amazon weather, and his knowledge of the plant and animal resources of the area. Such knowledge lowers one's cash outlay for food items, and consequently leads to higher net income.

Lastly, the caboclo independent farmers cultivate their fields intensively, not only with food crops for home use, but also with cash crops. Even before the rice and corn have been harvested, other crops such as manioc, bananas, various root crops, and tobacco are planted by caboclos. This keeps the land both in constant production and continuously protected. Production of farm items other than rice, corn, and beans also points to the caboclos' preferences for diversification. In addition, the sale of manioc flour and long coils of cured tobacco brings extra cash for caboclo families. One-third of a hectare solidly planted in tobacco can earn a family up to Cr$6,000. These intensified farming methods also involve smaller amounts of land. In 1973–74 the average area cleared by caboclos was 6.3 hectares, in contrast to 8.0 hectares for outsiders. For 1973–74 caboclos in a stratified random sample taken along the Transamazon (N=101) averaged Cr$3,370 per household from the production of manioc flour and home-cured tobacco, and the sale of milk, eggs, pigs, and chickens. Outsiders averaged only Cr$1,968 per household.

Other independent farmers have been acquiring familiarity with caboclo strategies, including the use of wild game and wild fruits to supplement their diets and lower expenses. Since their arrival, all independent farmers in Vila Roxa have learned the vegetation criteria for choosing good agricultural land. Presumably, they will use this knowledge in future land management practices. The making of coarse, Amazonian manioc flour has been adopted by half of the Vila Roxa independent farmers and a few of the artisans and laborers. While their investment in cattle is still small, all independent farmers raise poultry and swine for both marketing and home consumption.

The presence of a caboclo population in the area is beneficial. Their familiarity with the physical environment facilitates the dissemination of such agricultural knowledge among newcomers, particularly among the independent farmer and laborer-farmer groups. Artisan-farmers and entrepreneurs, both working at a higher level of income and using nonfarm skills to obtain income, are less affected by the caboclo knowledge of the area, although they do not escape its influence.

Pastures and Cattle

Transamazon farmers can do little to control crop pests and diseases once they become established. Insecticides and herbicides are beyond their means, and little is known of the required doses that effectively control local species. The Transamazon experimental station near Vila Roxa has begun treatments, but normal doses have at times failed to control the local weed invaders. It is perhaps this, more than anything else, that makes Transamazon farmers look to pasture development as the solution to their pest and weed problems. Such problems do not end with the formation of a pasture. Weed invasion is the most serious obstacle to quality pastures (Fearnside 1979a). "Successful" farmers tend to invest their profits in cattle rather than in cropping technology. This "demonstration effect" supports the smaller farmer's conception that "cereals do not give results," and that to have a successful future one must establish pasture. This general conception may be correct. Soils for twelve years under *Panicum maximum* in Pará have shown satisfactory nutrient stability (see Figure 8.10). Organic matter levels stabilize and even increase due to the rapid turnover of the root system. The pH is stable over time, as are the levels of exchangeable bases (Serrão, personal communication, 1975; Falesi 1976).

The two major pasture grasses that have been established in the Transamazon are *colonião* (*Panicum maximum*) and *elefante* (*Pennisetum purpureum*). Experimental work is proceeding with *jaraguá* (*Hyparrhenia rufa*), *gordura* (*Melinis minutiflora*), *canarana* (*Echinochloa pyramidalis*), and *kudzú tropical* (*Pueraria* spp.). A problem is that most Transamazon farmers have a simplistic idea of what it takes to establish a high quality pasture. In their minds, all one needs to do is broadcast the seed and then encourage dense growth by periodic burning. Burning helps control weeds, fertilizes the grass, and ensures a lusher growth. But a look at most pastures in the area indicates that secondary or weed growth is a

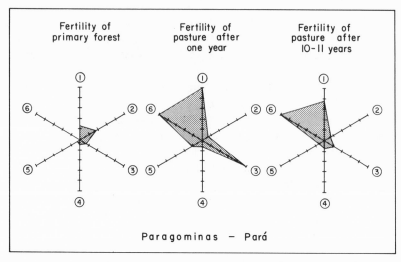

Fig. 8.10   Changes in Soil Fertility in an Area Converted
to Pasture in the Amazon. Refer to Fig. 8.1
for legend.
Sources: Falesi 1976; Alvim 1978

severe problem. Thus, cattle productivity is likely to be low given current management practices.[18] Smith (1976a:149) estimated that a colonist might be able to produce 1,760 kilograms of beef per year from forty hectares and receive US$1,056 from the sale. This is very low, and compares unfavorably with cereal or manioc cropping. However, as land is cleared and game becomes more difficult to obtain, small ranches may become important suppliers of protein to the farming population. Increased demand would increase prices and make such operations increasingly profitable.

Cattle in the Transamazon are bought from either the State Department of Agriculture (SAGRI) or from other ranchers in the region. One local farmer goes as far as Santarém to buy cattle from Lower Amazon region ranchers. The cattle are mainly for beef production, although a certain amount of dairying goes on as well. Most of the beef cattle are a mixture of Indian Brahma and creole stocks. This combination is locally referred to as *Gir* cattle, and technically should represent a mixture of one-half to three-quarters Brahma blood. A few farmers have *Holandesas*, a mixed Holstein breed, for dairying purposes, but these are very rare. Cattle are largely managed and owned by persons with previous cattle experience, such as *vaqueiros* (cowboys) from the Northeast and ranchers from the Central-West states. While most Northeastern sharecroppers have neither the capital nor the experience to handle cattle, the Northeastern cowboys have a profitable arrangement with their bosses. Normally, every fourth calf born is theirs, and they get paid a regular wage in addition.[19] If the boss has good cattle, and the droughts do not strike, in a number of years cowboys can afford to sell some of their cattle and buy land to start their own operations.

In 1974 an increasing number of small ranch owners were coming from other areas of Brazil to the Transamazon. They are still coming to buy land (400 hectares and up) in the small farm belt, and hope to establish cattle ranches. Because they are bringing superior financial resources, it is possible that these persons will succeed in productive pasture development. Previous owners came with capital and got started right away. Ranchers usually employ persons from the same area of origin "who know cattle."

Independent small farmers have started owning cattle, because they established areas in pasture quickly and, when ranchers came, they put their cattle out to graze on independent farmers' lands. The common arrangement in these situations is that either every other calf born belongs to the pasture owner—a far more profitable arrangement than that between cowboy and boss—or rent is paid at a rate of Cr$40 per tarefa per month (US$20 per hectare per month). While this arrangement is short-lived, a number of farmers have acquired three or four calves or added income without having to spend any personal capital. These few calves provide milk and curdled milk for the family. Some of the milk is sold locally, so keeping such a small number of cattle does not tax the resources of small farmers. A herd larger than ten head, however, requires a substantial investment in barbed wire, fence posts, and a much larger area to keep free of secondary successional species. In conjunction with cattle herding, the local agronomists have identified a number of plants that can harm cattle if allowed to invade the pasture.[20]

In the short period since the Transamazon Project began, there has not been time for the final direction of cattle ranching and pasture development to be definitively established. Only a handful of farmers have had the time and capital resources to establish sizable pastures and purchase needed cattle. The majority have tried to seed pastures as a means of controlling weeds and to raise the value of their land.[21] Nevertheless, those who have built herds of thirty to fifty cattle use farming only as a means of clearing new land. A crop is planted to take advantage of the optimum soil conditions, but pasture seed is sown along with cereals. Those who succeed in clearing their 100 hectares will request more land, or buy neighbors' land. Some of the more recent arrivals have bought three to five lots of 100 hectares each. They will be needing more land if they meet with success. The pattern that seems to be emerging in the area is for the side-by-side existence of medium or small ranches with small independent farmers growing crops. Large-scale cattle ranching is more common in southern Pará.[22] Both of these groups, in turn, hire the artisans and laborers for specific skilled and unskilled tasks. Examples of mixed farming occur, but they are somewhat rare. They seem to be more common among farmers of German extraction found along the highway strip between kilometer 80 and 110 (Altamira-Itaituba).

Having discussed some of the general agricultural and ranching practices in the Transamazon, it is necessary to point out that such practices are not homogeneous. While most farmers follow the practices outlined above, the four types of farmers tend to operate their farms in various ways, due to differential backgrounds, capital available, and location. Some of these differences have been discussed earlier. Others will be considered in the final section of this chapter.

Selection Criteria and Agricultural Performance

Numerous assumptions based on widely held beliefs and biases were incorporated into the blueprints of Transamazon colonization. Among these were the relation between region of origin and likelihood of success, the necessity of education for pioneer progress, and the importance of previous agricultural experience. Such assumptions were set up as major criteria for the selection of colonists. First, and perhaps most pervasive, was the belief in regional differentials as affecting agricultural productivity. I have examined these criteria in another publication (Moran 1979c), wherein readers will find extensive tabular data, which is the basis for the discussion below. I have omitted the complex tables here due to cost considerations and because they are available in the article cited above. According to stereotype, rural Northeasterners were landless peasants with a low level of technological skill, a low level of education, and a tendency for shiftless wandering. Nearly the only positive thing that popular stereotypes had to say about the Northeasterners was that they were hard working and long suffering. The nonindigenous Amazon population (caboclo) was not part of the colonization plans, since it was believed that they were illiterate, lazy, and preferred to hunt wild game rather than farm the land. In contrast, Southerners were incorporated into the colonization plan under the assumption that they would serve in a "demonstration effect." That is, they would teach, by example, the more advanced agricultural methods used in southern Brazil (Ministerio da Agricultura 1972a:203). The government projected the colonist population to be made up of 75 percent Northeasterners and 25 percent Southerners. Such population predictions, however, have fallen wide from their mark: 34 percent came from the Amazon region, 30 percent from the Northeast, 23 percent from the South, and 13 percent from the Center-West (INCRA Sec. de Planejamento 6 February 1975).

By "Southerners" the government usually implied either the *gaúchos* of Rio Grande do Sul and Santa Catarina or the aggressive *paulistas* of

São Paulo. The gaúchos, often of German descent, have an agricultural tradition that is appreciated by urban Brazilians. Their farms are attractive to the eye and rich in ethnic details. All German immigrants, however, are not good farmers, Willems, a noted student of German immigrants in Brazil, feels that Germans are among both the best and the worst of farmers in Brazil (1975, personal communication). While a sizable group of highly successful *gaúchos* are found in kilometers 80 to 110 of the Altamira-Itaituba stretch of the Transamazon, they are only 4 percent of the colonists, and their success may largely be related to the fact that they have the best soils to be found in the Brazilian Amazon. Paulistas represent only 2 percent of the population in the major colonization project.

The bulk of "Southerners" are, in fact, ex-Northeasterners who went to Paraná and São Paulo as young men and women looking for economic opportunity. A few found it and stayed, the rest sought a new haven and found the Transamazon offer attractive. The Southerners' successes have not been dramatic. A few Southerners, just like a few Northeasterners, Northerners, and Central-Western farmers, have thrived and are becoming leaders in their communities. For example, the president of an incipient cooperative is from the southern state of Rio Grande do Sul. His vice-president is a Northeasterner. But the Southern colonists are no better, and no worse, than those of other regions. They are hard working, but demonstrate a propensity to overextend themselves. They often clear areas too large to manage adequately (eight to fifteen hectares per year), or they over-emphasize cash cropping to the neglect of a diversified subsistence garden. Translated into economic terms, the Southerners are more deeply in debt than others, and are more likely to adopt the ways of Northerners and Northeasterners than vice versa.

It was assumed by government planners that the agricultural performance of the colonists would follow the stereotypical behaviors of the various regions. While the Southerners may fulfill the expectation that they are hard workers because they have cleared a good bit more acreage each year than the average farmer, this is most probably a function of the sizeable bank loans which they received (about US$1,000). On the average, Southerners apply for and receive the largest loans of any of the regional groups.

Regarding the use of modern farm technology, hardly any of the colonists use fertilizers, insecticides, or herbicides. The only important technological innovation in Transamazon farming is the use of powersaws to clear the forest. It is the local Amazonian population which first made use of this device, rather than the stereotypically "innovative" Southerners. The caboclos, in fact, own 41 percent of all the powersaws in the area. It would seem, then, that the Southerners are not applying their credit to the improvement of farm technology, and even their increasing productivity does not suggest that the Southerners are greatly superior farmers. While the Southerners' productivity per hectare has steadily increased from Cr$356 to Cr$687 (between 1972 and 1974), they are not alone in this feat. Northerners and Central-West farmers have also improved each year.

On the other hand, the "lazy" Northerners, who supposedly preferred jaguar hunting to farming, are impressive in their agricultural performance. They have adopted new clearing technology that came with the highway. They have had the highest yields per hectare of any region, and have earned consistently higher wages than persons from other regions. Their income from the sale of crops and other farm produce (for example, eggs, milk, manioc flour, tobacco, meat) is over twice that of Northeasterners, and over a thousand cruzeiros above that of Southerners and Central-Westerners. Due to their relative lack of cattle, their total liquid assets are the lowest of any regional group. Also operative in this low level of liquid assets is the relatively low debt owed by Northerners to the Bank of Brazil. Unlike some other regional groups, Northerners apply for and receive moderately sized loans. Only the farmers from the Central-West region have a lower rate of debt than do the Northerners. The Central-West farmers are relative newcomers to the Transamazon and have been fortunate to bring a good deal of capital with them. Therefore, they do not need to rely as much on loans to work the land. Having a ready supply of cash also helps to explain why the Central-West farmers use far more wage laborers on their farms, an average of 3.8 persons on a full-time basis. They can then afford to catch up in their production in a relatively short period of time.

The Central-West farmers form the smallest group of farmers. Their numbers are slowly growing, but the Central-West Region, a frontier in itself, has only a small number of persons to "export." Their economic performance has not been impressive to date, but this is due to their relatively late arrival, and their emphasis on cattle and pasture development rather than food crops. Their gross income has been low, and their other earnings are not worthy of note. Their financial strength is indicated by their low debt to the Bank (US$500 per farm), their high liquid assets (US$1,500 per farm), and their employment of numerous wage laborers (mean of 3.8 workers per farm) in clearing forest and preparing pasture. Without exception they all plan to develop cattle ranches in the Amazon.

It seems clear that the Northeasterners, Northerners, and Central-Westerners are not technologically inferior to the Southerners. If anything, they have shown some signs of superior performance. In showing that the Northern and Northeastern populations are not impeding the agricultural production of the Transamazon, we do not wish to infer that the Southerners are doing so. Southerners have averaged over thirty hectares cleared in three years, a feat well worth mentioning. Only the Northerners come close to this rate, with twenty-two hectares cleared in the same period. Income from production of the three major crops is highest among Southerners, but this cannot obscure the fact that the Southerners have lower yields per hectare than do their Northern neighbors (i.e., Cr$687 vis-à-vis Cr$807 for the Northerners).

What the Northerners lack in gross income from major crops they have made up in earnings from wages and other farm activities. Gross income for Northerners was Cr$13,600 per household in 1973–74. On the other hand, Southerners earned only Cr$11,691, despite higher bank loans, more cattle (see Moran 1975, 1976a), and more liquid assets. Northeasterners had the lowest gross income per household (Cr$7,331), followed closely by the Central-West farmers (Cr$7,349). Lest we conclude that Northerners are "the best farmers," it is important to weigh all the above assets and liabilities for the regional groups involved.

Another indicator of agricultural success would be the production of cattle. While this is not strictly a "farming" pursuit, it nevertheless can be used to illustrate the variety of managerial skills among the colonists. Secondly, the colonists themselves view cattle ranching as preferable to or more prestigious than farming. All aspire someday to own cattle.

Thirty-nine percent of the cattle in the Transamazon are owned by Northeasterners. In addition, the Northeastern owners have more cattle per capita than owners from the other regional groups (38.5 apiece). There is, however, a great maldistribution of cattle among the Northeastern group, as only 7 percent of the Northeastern colonists are cattle owners. All these owners have had previous experience with cattle raising in their region of origin, either as vaqueiros or fazendeiros.

The widest distribution of cattle ownership is found among the Southerners, who control one-third of the cattle in the area. These small herds (8.1 head per owner) are maintained principally by gaúchos who have come from the European tradition of mixed farming. While some of the herd are utilized for meat, the gaúchos make a greater use of a broad range of dairy products produced by the cattle.

The Central-West farmers, although new to the area, already rank second in the number of cattle per owner (20.5 each). As was mentioned previously, the Central-West colonists intend to reestablish cattle fazendas in this new area. The Northerners, on the other hand, represent the second lowest number of owners per region, and the least number of cattle per owner. This is to be expected. Unlike the Southern gaúchos, the Northeastern vaqueiros, and the Central-Western fazendeiros, the caboclo farmer has not had much of a cattle raising tradition.[23]

What emerges from this discussion is that the evidence does not point to any cultural advantage on the part of Southerners in all areas of farm management. Their yields per hectare are low, they incur heavy debts, they do not compare favorably in the use of the available technology, and they have lower gross income than, for example, persons from the North region. Nor does the evidence show the Northeasterner as an inferior farmer.

What is perhaps most evident and characteristic of Northeastern farmers is the wide disparities among them. Some are excellent independent farmers and entrepreneurs, while others come close to living up to popular stereotypes. For instance, the disparities are noted in terms of the ownership of powersaws. One in five persons from the Northeast has one, and it is the use of this tool which supplies much of the wages earned by the Northeasterners. In all, there is no justifiable evidence to accept "region of origin" stereotypes as a factor in predicting the bottlenecks to agricultural development in the Transamazon.

How long a man has worked in the agricultural sector had been considered by planners as an important criterion in choosing potentially successful settlers. The evidence also fails to support the relevancy of this factor. While colonists with no agricultural experience whatsoever performed below the norm in the first two seasons, by the third year they had a crop production that compared favorably with that of farmers who had six to fifteen years of previous experience. What the largely urban farmers lacked in agricultural production in the first years they made up in superior wages. The average income from major crops from 1971 to 1974 illustrates that having only one to five years of experience was no less a handicap than having six to fifteen, or even over twenty-one years of previous farm experience.

If we make a brief graph of the gross income for 1973–74, it can be seen that there is little basis for claiming that urban persons, or those with less agricultural experience, are less likely to adapt to agricultural work requirements or be less productive than are more experienced colonists (see Figure 8.11). As a matter of fact, in a number of ways, persons with largely urban experiences provide several skills that otherwise would be lacking in a frontier area. Part of the reason for the relatively high gross income of persons with zero to five years of farming experience is that, while they seek wage labor, they pay other workers to till their fields. This, in effect, gives them time to learn about farming and eases their adaptation to the hard work of tilling the land. Some individuals with far more farming experience are not doing as well, because they insist on doing things according to customs which are not always adapted to the requirements of the Amazon Region.

Strategies in the Use of Resources

With the coming of the highway, government funds poured into the Transamazon area in the form of minimum salaries, credit, jobs, and access to larger markets. The caboclos have not wholly changed their subsistence mode, but have adapted it to these changing conditions. They first began by increasing the amount of acreage cleared and planted each

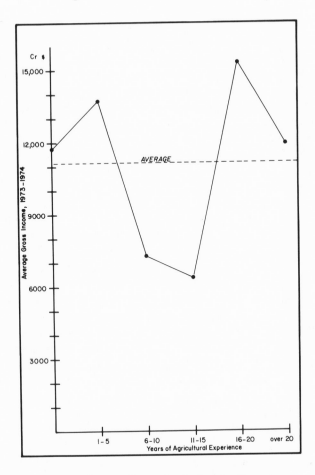

Fig. 8.11 Previous Agricultural Experience and Gross Income (1973–
1974)
Source: Moran, field notes,
1973–74

year to meet the expanded local market for foodstuffs. They and the other
independent farmers plant this acreage not solely in rice, corn, and beans,
but diversify their farm produce. For instance, while others await their
income from highly seasonal cash crops, independent farmers have a
steady year-round production of manioc flour to supply their own needs
as well as to supply the local market demands. Independent farmers, in
other words, have become the main suppliers of basic consumption items
such as manioc flour, tobacco, eggs, pork, meat, and lard.

Independent farmers supply their fresh produce for the entrepreneurs'
general stores, and they sell to individual neighbors as well. In addition,

wives and children of independent farmers work, producing farm surplus for sale rather than leaving the home to earn wages. "Cottage industries" such as the making of manioc flour and the curing of tobacco involve the participation of both child and adult in a process that is productive as well as a means of socializing. Bank credit is used to acquire liquid assets that will help increase farm income, such as buying larger griddles for toasting manioc flour, cattle, horses, and powersaws. The exchange of labor among independent farmers is rare. As Nietschmann (1973:133) and Hammel (1969:111) have noted, whenever a community joins a cash economy, wages must be paid even to kinsmen, since credit and cash are available to everyone.

Entrepreneurs in the Transamazon use a combination of farm production, the general store, and transportation services to cope with their new situation. Seldom is their strategy solely based on agriculture. Their main goal is to plant cash crops the first year in order to pay back outstanding bank loans, and eventually buy cattle and/or fencing to get their cattle ranch underway. In the meantime, while most of their farm work is done by paid laborers, entrepreneurs are busy transporting people and produce, and operating stores in local villages and along the highway.

The entrepreneur's wife tends either to have a salaried job of her own or to mind the general store. She is in charge of keeping the books which record the shop's inventory and credit accounts. Unlike the household of the independent farmer family, which often works together, the entrepreneur family rarely does so. The one exception is perhaps on Sunday, when both the husband and wife are home, and the man may have to take his turn at attending customers and credit seekers.

Entrepreneurs vary in degree of managerial talent, but most showed sensitivity to seasonal fluctuations in demand. They are busy during the weeks preceding the harvest season attempting to convince the farmers to sell their whole harvest to them at a low price in exchange for cash in advance. This is often successful since the farmers tend to be low on cash just preceding the harvest—a situation especially found among the laborer-farmer group. The entrepreneur often resells the produce at a better price in Altamira or holds on to it for a few months until the market is less flooded and the prices are rising. This was effectively done by a number of entrepreneurs in the area studied. For example, while beans sold for Cr$100 per sack at harvest time, the price skyrocketed to Cr$200 per sack in four to five months. Some who could store their purchased supply of beans were able to sell them and buy as much as thirty head of cattle from the transaction.

Other farmers often ask the entrepreneurs for informal credit. Although the latter try to discourage borrowing, credit is often provided and is an effective ally in the entrepreneur's control over local agricultural production. If a farmer has a long-standing debt at his store, it is common practice for the entrepreneur to drive out to the debtor's land and buy off his harvest at the lowest price, or carry off some of the farmer's poultry or swine as payment for the debt. The debtor is usually thankful that his debt has been cleared by the forceful creditor. However, in strictly economic terms, the farmer has suffered a net capital loss. His only consolation is that he has personalized credit available whenever he lacks the cash resources to pay for needed goods or services elsewhere.

Both the independent farmers and the entrepreneurs serve as brokers to the two other groups in our typology. Entrepreneurs provide credit and services of various kinds. Independent farmers have become providers of basic food items, of information about the land, and of wages when seasonal labor is required. Both artisans and laborers are clients to the above groups. Their survival is dependent on the success of these brokers, who provide a market for both skilled and unskilled work.

Artisan-farmers and laborer-farmers spend a considerable portion of their time earning wages outside their farms. Yields tended to be lower among those who spend considerable time in salaried labor. Independent farmers, by dedicating themselves to farm work, obtain the highest farm incomes in the region (US$1,400 per household). Artisans draw most of their income from skilled jobs (US$2,900 per household) and employ other workers to cultivate their land for them.

A sizable portion of pioneers belong to the laborer-farmer category. Accustomed to sharecropping and/or wage labor arrangements, the management of a one-hundred-hectare farmstead has brought them landowner status but no expertise. Laborer-farmers seek credit from the bank to carry out ambitious cash cropping schemes, though such schemes often are beyond their management capacity, or the limitations of the local transportation facilities.

The areas cleared by laborer-farmers are often too large for their capital resources, which generally consist solely of what the bank can provide in loans (US$55 per hectare). Since such credit seldom is provided "on time," and they have few savings to fall back on, they are unable to carry out the operations of underclearing, tree felling, and burning in accordance with the climatic schedule. Many attempt to augment their cash income by doing odd jobs or manual labor. They have come to depend on the independent farmers, the entrepreneurs, and the local agencies for such jobs. However, as they do not have the skills of an artisan-farmer, they earn little for their labor (US$700 per household per year). To help out, their wives also perform low-skill jobs such as washing clothes for neighbors, gardening, and selling eggs. While none of these jobs are very lucrative, laborers' wives nevertheless tend to make a bigger contribution to the total household income than do the other wives in the community.

The laborer-farmer's emphasis on cash crops often leads to the neglect of basic subsistence crops and forest resources for the needs of family consumption. Household gardens are rarely planted in their agrovila homes, because they are never quite sure when they will move again. Laborer-farmers often indicate that they are "too busy" farming to hunt and fish. As a result, the laborer family's diets are generally poor, and sometimes lack animal protein sources. With their meager cash incomes and insufficient food production for family needs, the laborer-farmers often need to buy much of their foodstuff and ask for credit as well. They often have outstanding debts not only with the local entrepreneurs, but also with the stores in town. The farm production of many laborer-farmers has been insufficient to pay off their bank loans, and some have been cut off from future credit. The net income of Vila Roxa laborer-farmers was estimated to be negative (US$–160 per household). Farmers often sell their lots back to the bank to cover the loan, and become full-time wage earners for others in the area.

The farmer "types" discussed vary greatly in their farm management strategies. The independent farmers produce most of their foodstuffs, fish for their protein, and produce household tools and items of prime necessity for sale to neighbors. Entrepreneurs provide transportation services, operate stores with basic inventories, run small cattle concerns, and serve as spokesmen for others with government officials. Their agricultural goals aim at quick returns on cash cropping and subsequent pasture development. Laborer-farmers try to carry out the government directions as they understand them. They plant relatively large areas in the three cash crops, and neglect such subsistence activities as hunting, fishing, and horticulture. Meanwhile, they rely on bank loans to pay for the food needs of their large families.

Independent farmers began with a relatively low amount of capital (US $105 per household) (see Table 8.3), but in three years they have set up a profitable farm production unit through judicious use of bank loans, family labor, and farm diversification. Their accumulated small assets, in the form of animals and farm equipment, is particularly notable (US $1,390 per household) (see Table 8.3). This increase in liquid assets, by them as well as by entrepreneurs (US$8,000 per household), reflects both a commitment to the farm as a main generator of income, and successful management. Entrepreneurs have accumulated heavy bank debts in their acquisition of cattle. However, such debts could be easily paid off through sale of their other assets.

The low liquid assets of artisans (US$55 per household), despite relatively high initial capital (US$290 per household) and high net incomes (US$2,100 per household), reflect their relative noncommitment to the farm (Table 8.3). Very little of their income, credit, or initial capital has been invested in farm equipment or livestock. The artisan strategy emphasizes salaried labor by one or more of the family members (US$3,100 per household per year). This group has not achieved the higher yields

TABLE 8.3
ECONOMIC STATUS OF VILA ROXA FARMERS

	ENTREPRENEURS	INDEPENDENT FARMERS	ARTISAN-FARMERS	LABORER-FARMERS
Beginning capital	4,000	678	1,700	140
Average debt to bank and INCRA	37,740	12,498	6,462	5,247
Salaried income per year	48,000	5,603	18,269	4,500
Farm income per year	5,000	8,798	3,752	2,666
Gross income per year	53,000	14,401	22,021	7,166
Expenses	24,000	8,100	9,190	8,072
Net income per year	29,000	6,301	12,831	–902
Liquid assets accumulated	50,500	8,000	370	440

Based on a 50% sample of Vila Roxa households (N=25). See Chapter 1 for discussion of sampling procedure used. Figures are in cruzeiros, 1 CR = US $0.14.

in the area, but their possession of money has freed them from the deleterious delays in credit to which laborer-farmers have been subjected. During 1972–74 laborers had heavy bank and INCRA debts but low yields per hectare; artisans had low debts but high salaries that gave them "medium" yields; independent farmers had fairly high debts to bank and INCRA, but they devoted less time to salaried labor and obtained high yields per hectare.

The physical environment, whether natural or man controlled, offers a varied set of alternative economic strategies. Its use varies according to the householder's management background and his growing familiarity with the physical resources. Agriculture which uses restricted or large areas, extensive cattle pasture, and intensively cultivated gardens may exist singly or as multiple strategies. Any combination of these can be used effectively to make a living in this tropical environment, especially when supplemented with utilization of seasonal forest resources. Table 8.4 summarizes the distinctive features that separate the various types of farmers in the region. Brokers are distinguished from clients by their high yields in rice, corn, and beans, and by their ownership of cattle. Within the

TABLE 8.4
DISTINCTIVE FEATURES OF FARMER TYPES

CATEGORY	BROKERS		CLIENTS	
High yielding 3 crops	YES		NO	
Owns cattle	YES		NO	

SUB-CATEGORY	ENTRE-PRENEUR	INDEPENDENT FARMER	ARTISANS	LABORERS
High initial capital	Yes	No	Yes	No
High salary per capita	No	No	Yes	No
Stores	Yes	No	No	No
Powersaws	No	Yes	No	No
Cottage industries	No	Yes	No	No
Hunts for food	No	Yes	No	Yes
Gathers wild plants	No	Yes	No	Yes
Subsistence garden	No	Yes	No	No

broker class, the differences between entrepreneurs and independent farmers are the high initial capital and stores of the former vis-à-vis the cottage industry, and the self-sufficient subsistence activities of the latter. The only features which differentiate artisans from laborers are the high initial capital and the high salaried income per capita of the artisans. Laborers have begun to acquire a hunting-and-gathering strategy and may start diversified horticulture in the near future, but they are unlikely to achieve proficiency in cottage industries or high yields in major crops for some time. The majority of the laborers will likely sell their land and become wage laborers, or will begin anew in another frontier (Velho 1976; Cardoso and Müller 1977).

It should be pointed out that this static typology fails to suggest the real life processes of economic decision-making. As I have suggested earlier, this static view of society is a result of the synchronic character of community-level field research. A dynamic view is possible only by either repeated visits over a prolonged period of time or by a regional-level analysis that can include a range of communities at different points along an evolutionary scale. It is possible to suggest, for example, that artisan-farmers may develop into entrepreneurs or return to urban areas. It is almost certain that laborer-farmers will mostly evolve into wage laborers, although a few may become independent farmers. A few independent farmers may become entrepreneurs, while some may become wage earners—the latter due mainly to misfortunes of weather or the market.

Human beings do not develop their strategies in isolation, but rather they engage in a set of interactional activities which lead to the exchange of information. In many cases, such information relates to the particular adjustments each one has made to cope with his own situation. From such exchanges come decisions, either individual or collective, as to which strategies have yielded the best results in the physical and socio-institutional environment. Over time, such information becomes widely shared, until a certain degree of consensus is reached and produces what we may call a communal adaptive strategy (Bennett 1972:239). In the next chapter I examine the social field of the Transamazon farmers.

Social and Institutional Life

9

Just as they evolved strategies to make use of unfamiliar physical resources, the Transamazon farmers developed ways to cope with the social and institutional environment. In some ways, their "social strategies" reflected the adaptations to available resources, and to resources with which they were familiar in their areas of origin. I will attempt, in surveying personal relations, group activities, attitudes, and other details of social life, to present an inductive analysis that will shed light upon the processes by which individuals are united, groups are formed, community is created, and conflict emerges from social interaction (cf. Arensberg and Kimball 1968). Such conflict is normal in human societies due to the conflicting goals of individuals and groups (Cancian 1976). These conflicting goals are commonly expressed, not in open rifts, but in ambiguity in cultural conventions wherein the roles of actors express the relative balance of power in particular interactive contexts. Leach (1954) earlier noted this manipulation of ambiguous symbols and statuses by individuals striving for higher rank in highland Burma. Particularly in complex, stratified societies, these conflicts are the forces that help explain stability and change, and the evolution and reproduction of social systems (cf. Cancian 1976:246; Fleming-Moran and Moran 1978).[1]

Such a view of society is quite distinct from Radcliffe-Brown's concept of social structure as a "concrete reality" (1940), which holds that social structure is visible to a social scientist. The approach taken here holds that social structure is an abstraction derived from a sample of social happenings.

Rather than present an "average" Transamazon farmer, my analysis of the social structure of an incipient community will emphasize the interactive process out of which eventually emerged a set of structural relations based upon the relative economic strength of households. While the "reality" of this social structure is relevant only to the local community, which is the subject of the local level of analysis, the processes of social interaction may be equivalent across a large segment of other Amazon local

158

communities and even in regions as distinct socially and culturally from Vila Roxa as villages in northern Ghana (Mendonça 1979). These similarities in the structure of social relations result from similarities in (a) the status positions of the actors, (b) the structure of economic relations, and (c) the customary process of association and interaction between members of a social class. These structural relations only become manifest at the cross-cultural or biome level. At the local level of analysis, what we have are forms of social organization reflecting local social contexts (Fortes 1970:32). The structural context of such action results from a different level of analysis.

Unlike the "traditional communities" commonly studied by anthropologists, Vila Roxa is a new community which is still seeking to develop a structure of leadership, rules of cooperation, status positions, and other details of social organization that can better serve the needs of the community members. The community is also one, however, which shares in Brazilian culture and is heir to Brazil's historical experience (Wagley 1971). Arensberg and Kimball have noted that *time* is a necessary requirement for all human groups to develop systems of relations which give stability and meaning to human life. On the formal level this is accomplished through schools, churches, clubs, and organizations. More informally, this is achieved through neighborliness, mutual interests, and cooperation (1965:138–39). The fact that the local community is new, but that the regional *entrepôt* of Altamira has a long history, makes the setting an ideal place in which to observe the processes which take place in the earliest stages of community organization, how communities create network linkages with other communities, and which elements have primacy in the formation of a social system.

Farmers and Civil Servants: Status and Behavior

Vila Roxa received its first residents in late 1971. Many of these families have since moved out to their lots or to other nearby agrovilas closer to their homesteads. Most of the current inhabitants of Vila Roxa moved in sometime between 1972 and 1973. As discussed in earlier chapters, the village is made up of families which come from eleven different states, representing all major regions of Brazil (see Table 6.1), and this heterogeneity was consciously included in the colonization plans as a way of preventing "stifling traditionalisms" from hampering the progress of the new communities (Camargo 1973:8). The emphasis of this section is on the farmers' interaction with government civil servants.

The government provided for outside agents to organize and stimulate "community development" in the agrovila. Along with the farmers came agricultural technicians, bureaucrats, extension agents, and social workers.

These government employees were settled either in the town of Altamira or in Brasil Novo, the larger planned settlement that concentrated government services and personnel. Even while living physically and socially apart from the farmers, they were designated as "official leaders" of the various planned communities.

Although the colonization scheme explicitly envisioned a nearly egalitarian society, real differences in education, social level, and work experience between farmers and government employees surfaced from the very beginning. These differences were expressed in settlement layout, and in behavioral and economic ways. For example, the headquarters of government agents in Brasil Novo manifest spatially the delineation of social distance. The homes of government administrators, technicians, and office employees are all physically separated. The top administrators are located at the rear of the settlement, away from the dusty highway and the bustle of the shopping center and warehouses. They live in impressively spacious, wood-paneled brick houses with elaborately tiered roofs for ventilation, and white picket fences. The technicians, who have an equal educational level[2] but fewer years of bureaucratic experience, are on a lower pay scale. Their relative lack of influence is socially marked, again by housing. While constructed of many of the same materials, their houses are smaller and more closely spaced.

Next in line from the technicians are the office workers, who also have their own residential sector. They are located near the busy shopping and industrial area to the center of the planned town. While the houses are small like colonists' and lack the brick facing, they still have stained wood paneling and better roofs.

Both administrators and bureaucrats attend a well-equipped social club on their side of town. This social club attracts most of the government employees in the evenings for social intercourse. The bar is open daily. The farmers' social club exists on the other side of town at the furthest point possible from the government social club and is opened only for occasional parties. Hard liquor is never sold at the colonists' club; it is at the administrators' club. The colonists' club, like their houses, is built of simple clapboard construction.

Almost all of the government employees identify themselves to the colonists as *dotores*, or persons with college-level education. However, many of the extension agents have had only a brief course, which required a junior high school (*ginasial*) education. Others have taken what is called the *curso técnico*, a senior high–level program which substitutes for the more classical program (*científico*). The curso técnico allows a person to enter into civil service jobs in rural areas and is an acceptable background if he or she plans to enter a school of agronomy. The Transamazon farmers are aware of these differences and scoff that "everyone around

TABLE 9.1
MONTHLY SALARIES PAID TO GOVERNMENT EMPLOYEES*

IPEAN Agrónomo	Cr$3,500 to 5,000	(US$500–715)
INCRA Técnico	Cr$3,200 to 3,800	(US$457–543)
ACAR Técnico	Cr$3,000 to 3,500	(US$430–500)
Social workers	Cr$2,000 to 3,000	(US$285–430)
Village mayor	Cr$2,000 to 2,800	(US$285–400)
Certified teacher	Cr$800 to 1,000	(US$114–143)
Non-certified teacher	Cr$300 to 450	(US$43–64)
School maid	Cr$150 to 240	(US$21–34)
MINERVA Teacher	Cr$100	(US$14)

* Salary given includes the hardship bonus (gratificação).
SOURCE: Moran, field interviews, 1973–74

here is a *dotor*." This is especially the case when the "dotor" is young and inexperienced in day-to-day rural problems.

Salaries are relatively high among government employees (see Table 9.1). To recruit an adequate number of civil servants (*funcionários*), the government adds a "hardship" bonus (*gratificação*) to normal salary scales that is sometimes equal to or higher than the actual salary. Such relatively high salaries are an important input into the local economy. Most expenditures from these salaries are largely for consumption items—mainly clothing, food, and drink.

Upper class status is expressed not only by salary level, educational background, and house type, but also by certain mannerisms and dress. As in the rest of Brazil, lower class persons treat their social superiors with extreme deference (Hutchinson 1957; Harris 1956; Margolis 1973: 193). By waiting wordlessly outside the door hoping to be recognized, or being hesitant and laconic in speech, most colonists present themselves in a clearly subservient position to the administrator. The administrator, in turn, is sharp and confident, and speaks to the farmer in a staccato manner. Seldom is their intercourse a dialogue; rather, it is a monologue with the government employee giving advice to the farmer in a patronizing manner—and rarely are social amenities observed in giving instructions to the colonist. The farmer leaves these meetings not really understanding his obligations and feeling that the civil servants are either useless fixtures of the federal government, or actively seeking to undo the good intentions of the federal government.

The civil servants are also well marked from the farmers by their use of casual, but fashionable and expensive, clothing. Imported blue jeans, halter tops, polyester slacks, high heeled fashion shoes, or designer sandals are worn universally, although such clothing is impractical for the mud, insects, and humid heat of a frontier area. Most social workers and technicians are so encumbered by such outfits that their service functions are actually impaired. In only a very few cases have they abandoned these trappings of status so as to be able to work more effectively. During the rainy season their visits to the farm families come almost to a complete stop. Insects afflict the social workers wearing halter tops, and mud dirties their expensive shoes. Motor vehicles are unable to function away from the main highway, and walking through the mud is inconceivable.

Civil servants have another way in which they unconsciously emphasize their status. Walking is avoided; they ride everywhere in their government-issued vehicles, even for distances of only one block. Whether this is done in an effort to avoid the dirt, as an expression of physical separation from the local persons, or merely as an unconscious way of emphasizing their higher status, is hard to determine. Rarely are the farmers given rides in these vehicles. More often than not, farmers have to pay for crowded and sporadic rides in micro-buses. The numerous vehicles of the government agencies are restricted either by law, or by individual preferences, to civil service functions. Since the farmers often see these young technicians driving into town at high speeds, they conclude that these youngsters are but a band of *moleques*,[3] an expression that might reflect the resentment many farmers feel.

Since many of the farmers do not accept or utilize the advice of inexperienced extensionists, they feel the latter's high salaries are a waste of public funds that might be better administered if given directly to the farmer. It should be noted that all these behaviors are not meant to irritate the settlers. Rather, they are part of the cultural make-up of young urban Brazilians. These behaviors constitute an expression of the moral order of Brazilian society. This order dictates the rules of day-to-day interaction, is highly redundant about social hierarchy, and is more deeply ingrained than newly legislated ideas about the order of the world. Both the farmer and the civil servant act according to the assumptions of a hierarchical order (Mendonça 1979).

Social Interaction: Context and Conflict

Unconscious cultural behavior on the part of both farmers and government administrators has led to a lack of understanding on both sides. The farmer views the actions of civil servants as conscious efforts to undermine his own efforts. The local government employees view the deferential behavior of many farmers as indicative of social awkwardness, illiteracy, and dependence. Each one plays his role well and fails to communicate effectively with the other. The day-to-day behavior of the civil servants is appropriate for an urban area, but not for a rural one. The behavior of the farmer is "correct" if he were approaching a traditional rural patron, but inappropriate given the unusual attitude of the civil servants.

Unlike upper classes elsewhere in Brazil, government employees do not wish to get involved in patron-client relationships in the Transamazon. They do not see themselves as belonging to the social order in the Transamazon and have no intention of staying permanently. Whenever a colonist seeks a favor, civil servants generally refuse personal involvement with the potential client. This is confusing to farmers who culturally have grown accustomed to seeking protection, credit, and favors (*jeitinhos*) from persons in high social positions. The client interprets this refusal as an expression of bad will towards the colonists on the part of the civil servants, not as a sign of noninvolvement in local affairs, which is the usual intent. For instance, it is often rumored among the colonists that government employees are sons of fazendeiros and have a vested interest in seeing the colonization efforts fail so that they may come in and buy off the land.

The conflicts between farmers and civil servants also result from their differential perceptions of the priorities in agricultural development. A colleague applied a paired comparison questionnaire to five colonists and five agronomists, in which each person was asked to choose which of a pair of factors was most important in limiting agricultural production in the area (see Table 9.2). Rarely do the priorities match. The colonists envisioned poor health and exploitation by others as the most serious obstacles, whereas agronomists gave technical factors, such as transportation and prices, the highest ratings. These differences mean that the policy priorities most likely reflect administrators' rather than farmers' perceived needs.

By far the most significant institution with which the farmers interact in the Transamazon is the Colonization Agency (INCRA). When the highway project was conceived, INCRA was charged with the execution of the concomitant colonization along its margins. During the first two years practically everything was handled by INCRA: credit, salaries, food subsidies, sale of tools, provision for seeds, medical treatment, and education. Over time, INCRA has been delegating many of the above functions to other institutions, which are more specialized in these given areas. The Bank of Brazil, in conjunction with the extension service, now handles credit. Medical treatment is provided by a number of agencies. Education is now governed by the Ministry of Education in both planned villages and towns. Minimum salaries and seeds are still handled by INCRA, but now are distributed through the village mayor's office rather than by the central office. The coordinating body of INCRA now keeps track of lot

TABLE 9.2
CONTRAST BETWEEN COLONISTS' AND AGRONOMISTS' PRIORITIES

Which of the following pair of factors do you believe is the most important in limiting your present agricultural production?

	RANKINGS*	
	COLONO	TECHNICIAN
1. Poor state of health	1	6
2. Exploitation by other people	2	11
3. Lack of technical help, seed, and fertilizers	3	4
4. Poor roads and deficient transportation	4	1
5. Low prices for my products	5	2
6. Diseases of animals and plants	5	3
7. Lack of credit	6	10
8. Lack of machinery and equipment	6	6
9. Bad luck	7	12
10. Too much water	8	9
11. Lack of adequate feed for animals	9	10
12. Shortage of labor	10	7
13. Too many weeds	11	5
14. Poor soil	12	8

* Rank order of most important to least important factors is based on average number of times one factor was chosen over another. Five colonos and five engineers answered the questionnaire.
SOURCE: Bradfield 1974:21

assignments and topographic measurements, and receives visitors and newcomers.

Dealing with INCRA is not a simple affair for the farmer. As the bureaucratic delegation of authority is fairly inflexible, if a department head is out, those in lower positions are unable to make decisions, sign papers, or even speak for him. The result is that when the farmer goes to seek information or a signature on a piece of paper, he often finds the needed official is absent, and no one in the office can guarantee when he will return, or act in his name. Several trips may be necessary before the farmer can reach the person he needs. To take advantage of INCRA resources, whether financial or administrative, a person almost needs his own vehicle so as to frequent the agency's headquarters and learn their erratic schedules. The farmer without such transportation has to weigh carefully how many days and cruzeiros he can afford to lose in order to seek INCRA assistance. Many prefer to do without this assistance, so as to avoid the irritation of waiting in offices and losing work.

In part, these problems lie in the long-standing lack of coordination among government agencies in Brazil, resulting from the sectoral structure of the rural development effort (see discussion in note 14, Chapter 7).

One might expect that, even if there is such poor delegation of office authority, at least the farmer could leave his document in the office and return assured that it would be signed and processed in a reasonable period. Or perhaps the extension service could deliver the documents to the farmers instead and take the opportunity to carry out some of their own interview work. That is, however, not the case.

Mutual suspicion and a lack of cooperation are the distinguishing features which mark the interrelations of the public agencies, as may be seen in the relations between the Bank of Brazil and INCRA. The President of the Republic charged the Bank with providing credit to farmers at the subsidized annual interest rate of 7 percent, using the land title as collateral. Since the Bank of Brazil is a commercial bank and not a credit agency, the extension service (ACAR-Pará) was given the job of supervising credit, making the plans, and approving payments.

Credit Obtention and the Impact of Roads

The process of obtaining credit in itself turned out to be a time-consuming process that became a serious constraint on a farmer's production costs. In May or June, colonists made a loan request by indicating the acreage they planned to clear and plant in the three major food crops or in such permanent crops as black pepper, *guaraná*, cacao, and others.[4] Making out the initial credit plan is a relatively simple step, but even so it entails one to three trips to the planned town of Brasil Novo.

TABLE 9.3
COSTS INVOLVED IN SECURING CREDIT*

	MAN-DAYS	COST (IN CR$)
Making the plan	1 to 3	15 to 45
Confirmation of approval	3 to 5	45 to 75
Reception of six payments	12 to 20	180 to 300
Transportation costs	—	340 to 600
Pay interest on loan	1 to 2	15 to 30
Total	17 to 30	595 to 1050

* Based on a 50% sample of Vila Roxa Residents.

After credit is approved, it is the responsibility of the extension agency to approve each of the six payments (*parcelas*), which are to be doled out with the completion of each step of land preparation. For instance, the agent is supposed to inspect the underclearing before money is released for tree felling, and so on. Rarely does the extensionist visit farmers. Nevertheless, the requirements that the farmer seek a "release of credit funds" from the extensionist remain. Accordingly, the farmer must find the extension agent of his area and obtain the authorization for each parcela. This could take anywhere from one to as many as four or five trips.

Once the authorization is obtained, the farmer has to make his way to Altamira and seek release of the funds by the bank. The bank functions only between 8:00 A.M. and noon, Monday through Friday. If the transaction with the extension agent can be completed before 10:00 A.M., the farmer has a small chance of getting to Altamira before the bank closes. With the system of transportation as it is, this is very unlikely. Under the best conditions, a farmer loses two work days and pays at least Cr$40 in transportation for each parcela. If one adds the cost of the farmer's labor per day, each parcela costs a farmer a minimum of Cr$70. Frequently, this figure may be two or three times higher.

After the harvest, the farmer must go into town once again to pay the interest on the normal three-year loans. One-year loans, on the other hand, are simply discounted from whatever of the annual production is sold to COBAL-CIBRAZEM. Sometimes the annual loans are paid in cash after selling all of the produce to a private dealer. While the time lost for this process differed from farmer to farmer, during the time of my fieldwork there were no cases where less than seventeen man-days (equivalent to Cr$255) and Cr$340 for transportation were expended.

The minimum cost of obtaining a loan is Cr$595. Adding the charge of 7 percent interest, say Cr$168, on the most commonly requested loan of Cr$2,400, the total cost of a loan rises to Cr$763. This is a minimal figure since, as previously indicated, a farmer may need to make a great number of trips to obtain his payments. Bunker (1978), in a study that replicated my credit obtention research, came up with similar figures and noted that there were cases wherein the costs of getting credit exceeded the loan amount. In addition, the time lost in the obtainment of credit falls exactly in the periods of most intensive agricultural labor. Between the costs of interest rates, transportation, and work-days lost, a farmer may spend from one-third to one-half of his loan simply to obtain credit. This is likened to his paying, not 7 percent, but 33 to 50 percent interest on his bank loan, and in the end having only one-half of his loan available for farm purposes. It is no wonder that farmers have had little to show for the amount of credit they have received from the bank.

Credit obtention proved to be one of the most serious constraints to agricultural production, despite its availability. More time is lost in seeking credit than in illness (see next chapter). Repaying bank loans was particularly difficult for those whose farms lacked good roads. Access to the farmers' land was severely hampered by the decision to give greater priority to the speedy completion of the main highway rather than to the systematic completion of all service roads connecting farms to markets. In 1972 alone 612 kilometers of service roads were not built as planned, and promised, due to underbidding by construction companies. Most farm lots in the Altamira Project are not along the main highway, but may be situated as far back as 20 kilometers from it. Since the colonists expected these side roads to be constructed, many planted sizable crop areas, with the expectation of a large marketable surplus. When harvest time came and no access road had been built, much of this production was left stacked in the fields and was destroyed by pests and rotted by humidity.

Farming decisions which were based on the assumption of a passable road eventually led to the inability of many farmers to pay back their bank loans, and as a result they lost their bank credit in the following years. It seems unjust to criticize the poor technology and productive capacity of the Transamazon pioneers under these circumstances. By 1974, the national and international news media voicing the attitude of the Geisel Administration criticized the Transamazon Project, expressing disappointment at its low agricultural yields. While some critics mentioned the lack of roads and other transportation difficulties, the direct connection between poor transportation and farmer productivity was rarely made. As of 1974, the road system served only a minority of the region's producers. The lack of passable side roads affects not only the transportation of agricultural goods, but also the extension services, the development of agrovilas on side roads, and the provision of health care. In short, the general well-being of farmers is dependent on this most basic facility. If both national and local economic goals are ever to be met, construction and maintenance of side roads should be accorded comparable importance to that of the main highway. There are numerous cases throughout Latin America where maintenance of project roads is inadequate despite high public investment. With the lush plant growth and heavy rains of the humid tropics, a feeder road will be impassable in one or two years if it is neglected (Nelson 1973:204).

Availability of credit and expectations of passable roads influence farm management strategies. If a farmer knows he has access to credit and a good road, he is likely to clear a larger area than he might otherwise. He may invest a large proportion of savings into underclearing in the expectation of getting his money back when the first installment of the loan comes in. However, if the bank money is released too late, the appointed time for tree felling may have arrived without any sign of incoming funds. The farmer may again dip into his own savings or borrow locally, but may not have enough money to completely clear the total area he started. In some cases the farmer may let part of the large undercleared area go to secondary growth. If so, he has lost his scarce savings and will have to pay back the loan from the limited area which was cleared and planted.

If the fields produce, but the harvesting funds are late, he may even lose a sizable portion of his production in the fields due to insufficient funds to pay harvesters. In either case, the poor timing of credit release is a serious obstacle to increasing farm production.

Besides timing, the credit institutions did not whole-heartedly share the President's commitment to small farming development. Bank personnel dealt as little as possible with the small farmer, restricting their role to paying loans on the approval of the extension agency. Bank employees never thought of visiting agrovilas or of offering short courses or lectures on how to make the most of one's bank credit and how to decipher the official credit papers which are received by all colonists. Since only 20 percent of the farmers had had previous bank credit experience, they were unfamiliar with the process and would have benefited from such short courses. Most farmers seeking regular credit from the bank find their applications rejected, except for a small number of aggressive entrepreneurs who deal directly with the bank manager on a first-name basis. The bank manager in turn shows preference for these entrepreneurs, whose interest in cattle production is attractive to the bank. Normally, farmers receive only short-term loans to finance cereal crop production.

Persons who seek financial aid to establish small commercial operations of, say, manioc, tobacco, and other regional cash crops are also rejected. No effort was made during the study period to inform farmers of how they could develop a plan which might be attractive and profitable to the bank. Cattle enterprises, on the other hand, are readily welcomed. If the farmer can demonstrate that he has a reasonably good pasture and corral, money for barbed wire, fencing, and purchase of more cattle is not hard to come by. Whether this is due to the bank's perception of the low production potential of the Amazon, or whether it reflects the generally accepted belief that cattle production is always profitable, is hard to establish. The effective result is that farmers find few alternatives to develop their capital resources, even in a frontier area, due to the limited set of options acceptable to credit institutions.

Health and Educational Facilities

Health can also be a serious constraint to agricultural production in the Transamazon region, or any regions where infectious disease has not been brought under control (see next chapter for a detailed discussion of health status). Vila Roxa residents enjoy relatively good health.[5] The government provides health resources through the Public Health Service (SESP), the Malaria Service (SUCAM), and mobile units that visit roadside villages once a week. Two private doctors and two dentists attend the town of

Altamira as well. Five pharmacies serve the Altamira area, although their supplies run low in the rainy season. The pharmacists are reluctant to import medications by boat due to high losses from breakage. Because of the numerous patients that SESP has to handle, government doctors treat patients curtly to avoid lengthy conversations. As a result, patients feel their illness is sloppily diagnosed and that the prescribed cure will probably be ineffective. Many colonists have limited their visits to government doctors for this reason, and have turned to home remedies as an alternative solution to their ailments.

In Vila Roxa, for example, even the nurse's aide at the local health post has little rapport with the village residents. Most of her family and friends are in Altamira, and girlfriends come out occasionally to Vila Roxa to stay with her. Normally the nurse's aide administers first aid treatment and vaccines, and keeps a record of the diagnoses and treatment prescribed during the weekly visits of the mobile doctor. When pharmaceuticals are not available from the post's supply, she sometimes refers patients to other colonists, who can supply them with herbal cures. Those living deep in the side roads rather than in planned villages also find it difficult to travel the long distances if they are already weakened by disease. Choice of location, again, determines one's access to a resource which can have major significance in one's adaptation and survival in the area.

Vila Roxa has a two-room primary school, which is staffed by four teachers. The teachers are not outsiders, but are family members of Vila Roxa farmers. The school is a rich source of information, since it gathers together a large number of children who are important disseminators of knowledge about plants, animals, and other families in the area. The school day is split into two sessions: the first two grades meet in the morning, and the third and fourth grades meet in the afternoon. It is interesting to note that the textbooks selected for the school teach a great deal of the folklore of the Amazon, especially caboclo myths about the forest. The children memorize such myths as part of their school experience. Whether or not such myths will become truly integrated into their knowledge as they grow up in the Amazon remains to be seen.

Those who complete the four years of primary school can then go on to ginásio (junior high) in Altamira. The factors which limit the use of further educational resources are distance and money. The micro-bus that makes the trip to the school each evening travels only along the main highway artery, and does not even pull into the village. The only ginásio operating in town is a Catholic school. Therefore, for each student an annual tuition fee of about US$15 is paid, uniforms have to be sewn, and transportation must be arranged (US$15 per month per person), a cost prohibitive to most families. Only families in which the teenagers pay their own way can afford such expenses. Despite the abundance of government vehicles in the area, none has been made available to increase the number of agricultural area youths who have the opportunity to get a secondary education in Altamira.

A public junior high school has existed in Altamira since 1973, but the classroom furniture has not arrived from the manufacturer in South Brazil. It is possible that use of this school may reduce the costs somewhat, but it is still the high cost of transportation which most limits the colonists' access to educational resources beyond primary levels. Ten teenagers in Vila Roxa made the daily trip to Altamira in 1974, and two more were attending in 1975. It is interesting to note that half of the students are Pentecostal Protestants who value their education enough to overcome their religious resistance to attending the Catholic school.

For those with fewer financial resources, short courses taught locally are available. Courses in electrical training, in handicrafts, in raising fruit trees, in cattle and swine husbandry, and in permanent crop cultivation are taught in Vila Roxa and in a school four kilometers away from the village. The exploitation of educational opportunities is limited only by its physical unavailability, or cost. A number of families choose to live in the village, rather than on distant lots, because they wish their children to have access to education. This positive choice for education has a negative effect, in that it reduces the availability of family labor at the farm site. Completion of junior high school is an important avenue for social mobility, since it opens opportunities in well-paying jobs in the government bureaucracy, and is required for entering technical schools (*curso técnico*) or teacher training (*pedagógico*).

Educational levels among the adults were supposed to be indicators of likely success, according to government plans. The Northerner and Northeasterner were pictured as "illiterates" and, by extension, the Southern and Central-West inhabitants were said to have had more access to education and to have made good use of this opportunity. Tabular data on education as it relates to agricultural productivity and income can be found in Moran (1975; 1979c). While Northerners (41 percent) and Northeasterners (28 percent) did account for a major portion of the illiterate population in the Transamazon in 1973–74, the same groups also accounted for the greatest portion of the most fully educated. Forty percent of those farmers who completed primary school were from the North, and 30 percent were from the Northeast. This points to the variability among persons within these two regional groups. The other two groups have a more even distribution of persons in the various educational categories. While it may be true that educational facilities have been less available in the North and the Northeast, those who could take advantage of such an opportunity were more likely to complete their schooling than those from the South and Central-West regions.

It has often been assumed that education, or lack thereof, acts as a serious constraint or limiting factor to agricultural development (Schultz 1964:174–84). Nelson (1973:73) has suggested that in the pioneering stages of new land development, education may not be critical to farming success. Education can actually become a deterrent to the hard work required in clearing a jungle area and establishing it in crops. In areas of the world where education is not universal and is not taken for granted, those with a higher education often take on a higher status that culturally inhibits their performance of manual tasks. The educational level of Transamazon settlers is generally low, but some have completed primary school.

While income does not automatically go up with increased education, an educated farmer's income does have a tendency to go up over time— as the region moves from a "pioneering stage" to a "consolidation stage" (Nelson 1973:73). However, it should be noted that the illiterate group is able to provide a more stable source of income to their families than those in the other groups. Those with more education do relatively better in earning wages to supplement farm income. They also improve quickly over time. For 1973–74, their gross income was over Cr$17,000, which strongly contrasts with the Cr$10,655 of those with incomplete primary school; Cr$6,335 earned by those who could read and write; and Cr$8,968 for illiterate farmers. Note too, that even after three years, literacy in itself is no guarantee of better living standards. A number of the illiterate colonists have managed to hold jobs as foremen that give them valuable experience without the prerequisite of schooling.

The presence of government agencies also makes a considerable economic contribution to many family budgets in the Vila Roxa area. Although they import most of their technical personnel, the government opens its lower-level jobs to local people. These are sometimes filled by farmers' children who, in this way, earn sufficient wages to help their families and advance their own educations. This is especially the case with the agronomic experimental station near Vila Roxa, which employs up to twenty teenagers and young adults as secretaries, field workers, and mechanics. Without this input of salaries, Vila Roxa would be much poorer and its population less optimistic about the future.

From Individuals to Community

The earliest social bonds among the immigrants were those created by families which traveled together to the Transamazon. These families continue to visit each other regularly. The men engage in labor exchange and share farming information. The women discuss gardening, children, home remedies, and the problems of home economics. The few extended kin groups which came, arrived together, so that these multi-head families had both kin ties and companionship as bases for visiting one another.[6] Visiting is used to maintain social bonds, to offer articles for sale, to exchange food, and to find out about wage labor opportunities in the area.

Lacking extended family networks, extensive compadrio ties,[7] and a traditional village environment with drinking establishments, tiny market stands, and other places for popular gathering, the pioneers have utilized more basic relationships to provide a degree of social cohesion. Since the colonists were brought in groups from their home states, friendships were formed in transit, and the families helped each other adjust during the first difficult months. Many of the men of these groups chose their lots together on the same side road and now walk to their fields joking and discussing farm plans and local gossip.

It took more than three years for some farmers to seek broader social networks than those of their original immigrant group. Few of the farm families knew each other before beginning the trip, but their joint experiences and shared expectations of success in the Amazon have created lasting bonds and solidarity among them. Facing an unknown environment, the farmers clung to each other for a certain measure of security and common experience. Common region of origin has provided some sense of social cohesion. Fearnside (1978) has noted that in an area west of Vila Roxa a heavy concentration of Northeasterners took residence. A concentration of German-descent gaúchos is located 80 to 110 kilometers west of Altamira. Amazonian caboclos are concentrated in the first thirty kilometers west of Altamira.

The central meeting place in Vila Roxa is the village's general store. Since soft drinks and beer are sold, the store is used by teenagers as a meeting place, by the men as a bar, and by the women as a visitation center. There are times of the day during which each of these groups dominates. Women and little children are there during most of the morning and early afternoon hours. Teenagers and young unmarried adults come after work during the late afternoon and dominate the premises on Sunday mornings and afternoons. The men stop by early in the morning on their way to the fields, or late at night. The local football game on Sunday serves as the social divider. As the young men leave the store on Sunday to go to the game, the married Protestants take over the store. The Catholic adult men also go to watch the game, and in a few cases to participate.

The store is a source of informal credit. As a gathering place, it also serves as a "clearing house" for arranging seasonal wage labor, buying-and-selling, or learning of the latest events in Altamira or Brasil Novo, where government offices have been centralized since mid-1973. The store's radio provides a means of contact with the outside world and noise to drown the pervasive quiet of life in the village. In more than one way, the radio's music and news minimize the isolation of rural life in the

Amazon. The store owners have an optimistic outlook on life in the region, and their encouragement has helped to cool the hot tempers of many.

One of the houses nearest the highway in Vila Roxa serves as the village mayor's office. This small office acts as a post office, a central distributing point for government-selected seeds, and a local contact with an INCRA official, the mayor, who is chosen by INCRA and is an employee of that agency. Although complaints are frequently heard in other planned villages about their mayors, Vila Roxa residents appreciate theirs. The mayor makes sure that the central area is kept reasonably cleared of vegetation and has arranged, on occasion, for a small rice and castor bean crop that is left for residents to pick. Vila Roxa residents regard their village as the most attractive planned village in the region, and give the credit to the mayor.

Also unusual is the fact that the mayor takes trips deep into the side roads to check on the farming progress of colonists. According to colonization plans, extension agents and village mayors are supposed to carefully scrutinize the settlers' performances. Vila Roxa's mayor is one of the few who ventures into the side roads to perform this function. Though his reports are not always favorable, he has gained the colonists' respect as a result of his "courage." The mayor bought a relatively large tract of land (3,000 hectares) at the end of the side roads in an area which has been set aside for cattle ranching. He has already indicated his interest in hiring some of the nearby settlers for labor. He has even extended some informal credit. Therefore, his trips have a mixed purpose, and he may be laying the necessary groundwork towards becoming a patron to a group of eager clients in the side roads near his land.

The mayor is in his Vila Roxa office only a few hours a day. However, the office is open during working hours and is run by the daughter of a Vila Roxa farmer, employed by INCRA as a secretary. She has excellent rapport with the mayor. The selection of this secretary may have been based partly on the fact that she came from the same state as the mayor himself. She has a third-year ginásio education and is capable of handling the office's business. She knows where everyone lives, what they plant, how they are doing, and the current operating policies of the colonization agency. Therefore she is in a position to be helpful to farmers seeking information. Being a colonist's daughter, she does not maintain the type of social distance characteristic of other government representatives. Her information is given in terms that the farmer can understand, and they feel free to ask further questions if they have not understood. While she does, indeed, aspire to a better government job and to acceptance among the urban government agents, she shares too deeply the farmer's plight to be able to ignore it as do other government agents, and so serves her informational functions well. The mayor knows this, and lets her handle practically all office business.

The mayor's office is also used to sell the seeds selected and distributed by the government. Here the colonists obtain the mayor's signature so that they can claim their minimum salaries, which are paid by the Altamira branch of the Bank of Brazil. This gives the mayor one further opportunity to keep in contact with the village population.

Some of the social gatherings in Vila Roxa have a recreational, as well as an informational role. The general store, home visiting, and school serve this double function. However, many group activities are directed by government employees. Two such activities organized by the ACAR social workers are the 4-S Club[8] and the Mothers' Club. Catholic youth participate in the 4-S meetings, as do a number of Protestant teenagers, despite their parents' disapproval of such "frivolous" activities. The youth hold evening meetings once a week in the interdenominational church building to talk, play games, and plan dances. The club provides a chance for village youth to gather, and is an excellent opportunity to develop their leadership and cooperation skills. However, as the ACAR social workers are present at every regular meeting, the youngsters often defer to their authority, and effectively let them take over the meetings. The first president of the club was the previously mentioned mayor's secretary, who was well known to both the social workers and the teenagers. There were no complaints heard from the boys during her period of leadership despite her relative youth (fifteen years old) and sex. She was more self-assured and interested in social events than were the boys. But within three years the boys have gained enough self-confidence to take over the leadership, thereby replicating the normal pattern of male-dominated social leadership common throughout Brazil.

The club, unlike its United States prototype, has minimal agricultural objectives, despite idealistic goals in the by-laws of the organization. A small fruit garden (*horta*) and a black pepper stand belong to the club as educational and money-making projects. However, it was nearly impossible to get the group to volunteer to work in them. A short newsletter was published by the social workers twice during our stay in the village. It was largely the work of the club president and the social workers, and included songs, gossip about people, and reports on the various social events in the area during the previous period. Such a situation leads to complaints about the paper's contents every time a new issue appears.

The 4-S Club has organized a more or less autonomous soccer team which practices often and plays against a similar team made up of the young men who work at the agricultural station. While the experimental station workers also belong to the 4-S Club, there are enough young men to make two ample teams. The overlapping social groups keep the rivalry on a friendly basis rather than a serious one. The mayor and some of the younger colonists even play on the 4-S team.

The Mothers' Club was organized by the social workers to teach women about hygiene, vegetable gardening, nutrition, and baking, and to develop their community awareness. It serves as a chance for the women to get out of the house and gather socially. Like the 4-S Club, the Mothers' Club is mainly frequented by the Catholics of the village. No handicrafts or other items are made for money-raising projects, as occurs in other areas of Brazil. The club owns an oven, and women take the opportunity to make their cakes in it. As in the 4-S Club, the social workers try to cajole the club members into speaking up and taking initiative in the club activities. All this is to no avail. The membership is erratic; many colonist women feel that they do not gain anything new from the simplistic lectures, and that the "socializing" is worthless. In the two years of its existence, the club has never had enough cohesion to elect officers. Meetings are not called unless the social workers arrange for them. Most of the regularly attending members are women who either have few children or have responsible older children who can care for the house in their absence. These women do not make many trips to their lots. Therefore, they have more time to attend the meetings and engage in crocheting and the other handicrafts that are taught.

Another important source of information are the infrequent public meetings held by the social workers and extension agents. Every few months the INCRA or ACAR social workers call general meetings to inform families of recent government rules that affect them. For example, one meeting was intended to force final decisions by farmers on whether they were going to buy the Vila Roxa houses or move permanently to their lots. Such meetings are not effective in bringing about a dialogue between government institutions and the farmer. But insofar as they gather the farmers together, they serve the broader purpose of informal information exchange after the meeting is over. Farmers feel that the social workers are not really interested in their welfare, and note that the agents rarely visit them at home.

The extensionists also give short courses on various aspects of crop production and animal husbandry. However, these classes are more academic than practical. The information comes from the extensionists' own training and has not been adapted to local conditions. For example, a great deal of time is devoted to discussing feed rations in the animal husbandry course. It is usually advocated that the farmer use commercially prepared rations that are suggested in the texts, when no supply of such feeds exists locally. The cost would be prohibitive if they were imported, yet no suggestions are offered as to what combination of local grains and tubers would make a viable substitute. The courses are usually attended only by the teenagers of the 4-S Club, who view this merely as an opportunity for a change of scene and possible recreation.

Social workers run Vila Roxa's social life according to either urban or textbook premises, especially in the field of entertainment. The passive reaction of the farmers to such an approach is seen by the social workers to confirm their belief that rural people are socially backward or awkward. Thus, much of the social life is artificially induced. Activities are planned and imposed by social workers and circuit missionaries, rather than being initiated by the people themselves.

The earliest community-initiated social events were the soccer games, and occasional bingos or raffles, all of which generally occur on Sundays. The games of chance are used to raise money for a variety of purposes, such as buying new uniforms for the football team, buying school equipment, and collecting funds for the patron-saint feast. They are useful both as money-raising events and as events which give the settlers confidence in their organizational capabilities. The bingo games are well attended and generate interest among all segments of the Catholic population. School-age children are sent around selling the tickets, and each week's prizes are the topic of conversation several days before and after the event. Bingo games were initiated by Catholic Northeasterners who had some urban background and fell under the "broker" category.

One important source of social cohesion is common religious affiliation. This source of cohesion was especially important among the Pentecostal Protestant sects (*crentes*). Two groups predominate, the Assembly of God (*Assambléia de Deus*) and the Brazilian Christian Congregation (*Congregação Cristã no Brasil*). Both are made up mainly of migrants from Paraná, and together comprise one-fourth of the Vila Roxa residents. Pentecostal sects tend to attract low education, low success farm workers who find comfort in the emotionalism and hope provided by the services (Willems 1967:189). Many of the crentes who came to the Transamazon were somehow influenced by the church communication network. Not uncommonly, one member of a Pentecostal sect came to the Transamazon and wrote of his initial experiences to the pastor back home, encouraging other congregation members to come. In this way, the news of available land was spread, and fears were calmed about the dangers to life in the Amazon. In one case the crentes of one town in the state of Paraná migrated together and eventually colonized a side road along the Transamazon. It is possible to find a planned village, not far from Vila Roxa, wherein more than half of its population belongs to one Pentecostal sect. The religious unity of the Pentecostals made them receptive to the notion of agricultural cooperatives promoted by INCRA. For most of them a cooperative offered the prospects of additional credit, better prices, and government assurance. Few brokers ever joined in the planning sessions for a local cooperative, pointing out that they didn't need such dubious support. Historically, leaders of cooperatives are highly suspect because of the frequency with which funds disappear. Two cooperatives were started in the Altamira colonization area, and both collapsed due to financial and leadership problems. The more successful farmers refused to support the cooperative, because the leadership was in the hands of unsuccessful farmers. In at least one of the two, cash funds were mismanaged by a Pentecostal-affiliated cooperative president. Smith reports that an effort to initiate a cooperative in the Marabá colonization area failed when the president allegedly fled with the cooperative's funds (1976a:154).

The Pentecostals, in addition to their evangelical zeal, forgo the "worldly pleasures" of smoking, dancing, drinking, wearing "extravagant" clothes, and participating in sports. This tends to set them apart from their Catholic neighbors. Protestants generally do not join in the 4-S Club or the Mothers' Club, perhaps because the meetings are held in the interdenominational church building. To them it is the "Catholic Church," and in the words of one Protestant lady, the building represents "the gates of Hell." In school, conflict occurs when the Catholic catechist comes to teach religious songs to all the children, and when teachers encourage the children to dance and sing at recess, which is not approved of by the Pentecostal parents. Neither are the Protestants involved in the formation of compadrio or fictive kin ties, a primary bonding mechanism throughout Latin America. Unflattering stereotypes also add to the schism. Protestants view Catholics as people with little "religion," who are frequently drunk, beat their wives, and squander their money on loose women, smoking, and gambling. Catholics, on the other hand, see crentes as illiterate Bible-mongers, and they quickly tire of the crentes' holier-than-thou attitude.

Such feelings of antagonism are openly expressed, but as one group feels "sorry" for the other, little hostility arises to provoke a community rift along religious lines. Such feelings do, however, serve to unite the respective groups in their opposition to each other. The crentes hold weekly prayer meetings in their own homes and refuse to use the "interdenominational" church building in the center of Vila Roxa. Ecumenism, or dialogue among churches, is viewed as a "papist plot" to undermine the faith of those outside the Roman Catholic Church, according to a numbers of crentes. They distribute a number of pamphlets provided by their churches exposing this plot. They also form work parties to help each other in the fields, and they are currently active in organizing a farmers' cooperative.

As yet the Catholics are lacking in comparable religious unity. Rural Brazilian Catholicism is made up of a number of varieties, and each region varies significantly in its ritual practices, patron-saints, and festivals. In Vila Roxa one finds a blending of many such traditions from the North, Northeast, and South, but none has clearly dominated. There is not yet a traditional *rezador* or *beata* (lay religious leaders). An Austrian priest comes once a month to say Mass. On the other Sundays, simple prayer services are led by a catechist, who has been appointed by the priest. The choice of the catechist was not very fortuitous, since the man does not live within the village. Therefore, he lacks influence in the social life of the community.

Neither of the two Catholic religious leaders encourages the selection of patron-saints, nor the creation of a lay brotherhood (*irmandades*). After three years, during a family baptism celebration, a small group of Northeastern Catholics decided that it was high time to choose a patron-saint, to have an auction (*leilão*) in his honor, and to celebrate his feast day. Until this time no one had even held a traditional post-baptism party, much less given any serious thought to the choice of a patron-saint.

Emergence of Community Leadership

The Northeasterners involved in the baptism celebration had come from the state of Rio Grande do Norte. After the baptism of their two new relatives, they went to the general store owned by a Rio Grande do Norte entrepreneur to drink beer and soft drinks. The bill was paid by one of the godparents, an entrepreneur who owns another general store down the road, and who is emerging as the most upwardly mobile colonist in the area. The men stood or sat in the back room near the refrigerator, while the women and children stayed in the front room drinking soft drinks. The women shared stories about children, while the men in the back recalled how much partying had followed baptisms at home. Conversation quickly turned to the lack of social life in Vila Roxa and in the Transamazon in general. The men understood that no one was in any kind of economic condition to engage in such luxuries as partying and drinking. While no one at the party admitted having been economically successful in the last three years, they noted that they thought perhaps by now "other" local residents had earned enough (*tem condições*) to be able to start a patron-saint feast. While even the entrepreneurs could not yet afford to give cattle as a contribution to the festivities, they thought several people in the area could donate a goat, a sheep, chickens, or pigs to be auctioned in honor of the saint. Such auctions are frequently opportunities for conspicuous spending (Harris 1956:231–33; Wagley 1953: 195) and several of the party-goers said that they would pay whatever they had to just to keep their own animals. All in all, the cost did not matter, they said, since the money would help to beautify the church for the saint.

The favorite saints of their home region were considered as possible choices for the Vila Roxa patron, but none of their feast days fell within a convenient time in the agricultural calendar. They agreed that the feast must be in October, a month of relative inactivity, while farmers are waiting to burn their fields and when people have available cash after selling their harvest of rice and beans. The instigators also felt that, since this was a farming community, it would be preferable to choose a male saint, especially one that was legendary as "a worker." No one knew who the patron-saint of Altamira was, so this was immediately eliminated as a possible choice. They finally hit upon St. Francis, a choice which was facilitated by already having an image of this saint in the village.[9] They all drank to having made the choice and left the party enthusiastic at the prospect of a festival that would unite the Catholic community.

This reunion was socially significant in that it crystalized the incipient social organization of Vila Roxa. It involved two important local entrepreneurs, both owners of general stores, and two of the most successful independent farmers in Vila Roxa. Three out of the four owned over ten head of cattle apiece. Two cattle owners were related by affinal ties, and the third was emerging as the most aggressive patron-entrepreneur in the Vila Roxa area. No Southerners were involved, but a Central-West female, the daughter of an independent farmer and also the mayor's secretary, acted as godmother for one of the baptized children. The compadrio thus established at the baptisms served to link two of the most successful independent farmers with the high income earners in the area. This will facilitate receiving personal credit in the future. What is of particular interest is that the bonds of this group run through two sets of female relatives. An enterprising caboclo independent farmer married into one group, and a Central-West family joined through the bonds of coparenthood. The caboclo who married into this network is very successful and is driven forward by his wife, the sister of the successful patron already mentioned. His small family enjoys a fairly high standard of living for the area. What he lacks in a large cattle herd (only four), he makes up by selling manioc flour, tobacco, and other products, which give him the highest net return for farm produce in the community. His wife also earns a teacher's salary.

Unlike the traditional Amazonian residents, colonists do not yet seek to improve their economic status through fictive kinship ties with the authorities who make up the upper class in the region. Several factors account for this. First, farmers have little day-to-day interaction with government officials. Second, the officials refuse to get personally involved in the lives of the settlers, and often spend only a short time in the area themselves. Upper and lower classes in the Transamazon have no personal socio-economic links. However, those among the settlers who have achieved a modicum of success are guaranteeing this position by associating with each other. In due time, I expect clients will seek the help and protection of these patrons.

The Catholic entrepreneurs are essentially following a traditional elitist pattern by reinforcing their position through fictive kin ties with socio-economic equals (Harris 1956:153). Among Vila Roxa's brokers, compadrio ties have begun to be used to reinforce kinship bonds when they exist or to solidify *conterráneo*, that is, region-of-origin friendships. While entrepreneurs also began with this latter pattern they have now begun to strengthen their economic links with other successful independent farmers regardless of their state of origin. This broker group is not rich, but in the short period of three years they have achieved a certain measure of success. Each one has cleared well over twenty-five hectares, each owns some cattle, each has several hectares in pasture, and the two entrepreneurs own general stores that do brisk business. All have numerous pigs and poultry, one owns a pick-up truck, and another is a cooperative vice president. Some already own gas stoves, gas lamps, and sewing machines, although they give greater priority to investment than to consumption. All the women in the families are literate and either manage the stores or are integral parts of the farm production effort, depending on whether they belong to entrepreneurs' or independent farmers' families.

Such economic well-being has led this small group of three or four men to become informal leaders among the less successful farmers. The impersonal dealings with federal agencies have been unsatisfactory to the majority of Transamazon farmers, who are accustomed to personal relationships with their superiors. A well-known Brazilian anthropologist, Diégues Jr. (1973:151–64) has pointed out that most rural Brazilians have learned their behavior in a fazenda environment, and that the absence of such an environment leads to disassociation and isolation. The social structure of rural Brazil is characterized by a great socio-economic distance between the owner of the land and the laborer. So ingrained is this system that, despite its time-honored exploitation of laborers, it has persisted and even made its way into the new society of the Transamazon agrovilas.

To deal successfully with the governmental institutions, a farmer needs to be on a socio-behavioral level comparable to that of the bureaucratic personnel. Those farmers who are accustomed to giving deferential treatment to the upper class in rural environments are virtually ignored when they behave this way with busy urban bureaucrats. Such behavior gains them little, and even leads to a sense of powerlessness and to ineffective use of institutional resources. Faced with powerlessness, these persons seek the protection and security of a personal patron with whom they can engage in balanced reciprocity (Sahlins 1972:188–200; Johnson 1971:115). This is not to say that the exchange is equal, but there is an effort on both sides to return services rendered. The entrepreneurs who own general stores are able to extend informal credit to Vila Roxa residents. Although they originally had little intention of doing so, their client neighbors were so insistent in their pleas that the entrepreneurs gave in (cf. Adams 1975: 47–48). This extension of credit is not without its benefits to the store owner. Before such indebtedness, he was faced with a very mobile and uncommitted clientele. After extending credit, clients purchased only in his store, even though prices were not necessarily the most advantageous. The entrepreneurs deal with bureaucratic officials, not with deference, but with aggressive confidence, and this attitude proves highly successful.

The entrepreneur with motorized transportation will also carry other colonists to the hospital in cases of emergency. A number of times they were noted to take a personal interest and made sure that their client, or members of his family, was well attended at the hospital. This sort of intervention is important to persons who often cowered before the physicians and nurses. Gratitude for such "protection" in time of need is usually repaid by buying at the entrepreneur's store and working on his land to pay back debts or to earn wages. This may mean that the client accepts a lower wage than he might get elsewhere, but with his "patron" he knows he has a degree of protection during crises.

The leadership which stems from the entrepreneur's economic status also extends into the social and religious realm. While dances are organized by the 4-S Club, and women meet socially in the Mothers' Club, the general store is the real community gathering place. The only area of leadership not preempted by social workers or the priest, the organization of a patron-saint festival, was taken up by the entrepreneurs. They assumed the role of sponsoring the celebration and organizing the people for the event. The celebration was successfully carried out in October 1974, and the Bishop came from Altamira to say Mass. Several auctions and dances had been initiated to collect money to beautify the church. It was truly the first party to be organized without the guidance of a social worker, and was the liveliest held in the community's short history.

Economic success, then, seems to precede the assumption of social and religious leadership in incipient communities. Before a certain level of economic well-being had come about, no one seriously sought to fill the available positions for leadership in the community. The social workers undisputedly ran the parties, club meetings, and even the farmer meetings, but with a minimum of success. The entrepreneurs have begun to fill these gaps and will undoubtedly assume the leadership roles now held by social workers. The patron responsibilities to provide credit, wages, and protection; to act as spokesman; and to provide socioreligious leadership have all been assumed by entrepreneurs. This situation is now becoming apparent as many clients refer to their new leaders as *patrão*. Linguistically, the status positions are being marked to express the realities of the social environment.

This emergence of a patrão class serves to fill a growing gap in local authority. The Colonization Agency (INCRA) is moving part of its personnel to areas further along the highway to administer new regions being opened. The entrepreneurs now provide the services expected of a patron. As outsiders who never identified themselves with the local immigrant population, the government administrators were beyond the informal social controls of compadrio, credit indebtedness, and neighborliness.

The churches, the general store, the medical post, household visiting, the mayor's office, and club meetings provided a physical setting for day-to-day socio-economic behavior such as labor exchange and credit giving. The colonists found out from each other who needed wage laborers, what the going price was for produce, and who was open to extending credit either locally or in Altamira. The social linkages which are shown in daily behavior took shape in such social situations. In time, one might predict that these locally-generated patrons may be elected to local political offices and play a growing role in local affairs.

As we see, social strategies vary with groups of differing origins, economic classes, and religions. Utilization of the resources of government institutions calls for knowledge that is learned either in cities or in managerial positions. Entrepreneurs are, therefore, most successful in dealings with formal institutions, followed by artisans who provide needed skilled labor to government agencies. Laborer-farmers have been unsuccessful in dealings with institutions and have begun to depend on the entrepreneurs to plead their cases. Independent farmers may deal directly with institutions or use the services of the entrepreneur. The latter does not imply the same degree of dependence, since independent farmers tend to be in fairly stable economic condition and own considerable assets. This frees them from debt obligations that also entail control over their economic activities. Independent farmers, too, have overcome some of the bureaucratic bottlenecks by asking for long-term credit rather than short-term credit, and by using the loans for technological innovations such as powersaws. This has effectively lowered their costs in obtaining credit and allowed them control over a desired service for which they can charge profitable fees. Since this group is the most agriculturally productive, it is important that such costs be reduced so that more government funds are used for productive purposes.

Health, Diet, and Disease

10

The Amazon region has long been heir to a reputation for unhealthfulness matched by few other areas in the world. Malaria, yellow fever, Chagas' disease, leishmaniasis, arboviruses, snake bite, and numerous other problems have been noted to make human adjustment to the region difficult, if not impossible. Moreover, the dominance of starchy root crops such as manioc, sweet potatoes, and taro in the native agricultural systems has been said to increase the susceptibility of populations to disease agents due to protein undernutrition. In examining the health problems of this Amazon population, morbidity and mortality rates are considered as they affect different age-sex groupings, the spatial and seasonal distribution of diseases, the manner of treating them, and the impact of illnesses upon work productivity. The diet of the population, as it is tied to management of health and disease, is also discussed. It will become evident that the seriousness of the disease and its impact upon the productivity of adults engaged in farm labor determine whether the illness is treated primarily through the folk medical system or through access to the public health service.

Cultural Interpretations

Rural Brazilians share a set of pre-modern explanations of disease and its treatment based upon classical Greco-Roman theories.[1] These conceptions regulate proper meal patterns and food preferences, and govern routine activities such as infant care, personal hygiene, and daily chores. In short, they form a mode of structuring everyday patterns of subsistence and survival. This folk medical system reflects the worldview of the population and their knowledge of resources. As new cures are tried, and proven successful, they are categorized and labeled to fit the rest of the conceptual system (Foster 1958:18; Erasmus 1952:422–23; Redfield 1941:41; Alland 1970:40).

183

The folk beliefs about health, diet, and disease of the Transamazon population generally center on natural explanations. This naturalistic view of epidemiology means that the colonists emphasize the physical individual in their cures, rather than more ephemeral qualities such as sinfulness, "spirits," or the breakage of social taboos characteristic of illnesses considered to be "supernaturally caused." During my fieldwork, I rarely noted even instances of *promessas* (vows to make personal sacrifices or a donation to a favorite Catholic saint); such vows are common in rural Brazil (Araújo 1959:91; Wagley 1953:220–24).

As in other folk medical systems, the Brazilian system proposes that there must be an internal factor interacting with an external factor in order to produce a disease.[2] Table 10.1 summarizes disease agents and cures. Rural Brazilians take several natural conditions to be "weakening agents." These deprive the body of its natural resistance to external agents of illness. Basically, by Brazilian standards, one must somehow be weakened (internal factor) before one can succumb to a disease (external agent). Such a view differs from that of other cultures, which may seek intrusive foreign objects or "trapped airs" as internal factors related to illness (Wagley 1977).

Several weakening factors are recognized in lowering the body's resistance to disease: previous illness, poor diet, negligence, and hot/cold imbalance. First is the situation where a patient has already been ill and through lack of proper care has become weakened and subject to more serious complications. Second, it is believed that if one's diet has been inadequate over an extended period of time, one's blood is weakened and the subject vulnerable to serious illness. This is especially true during periods of intense activity or attacks of intestinal worms. In the folk view of the circulatory system, the food one eats is transformed by the stomach into elements which make up the blood (cf. Kiev 1968:43; Adams 1953: 15). Since the blood is believed to serve both as nourishment to the parts of the body and as a general transport system, its make-up and consistency are very important. In the folk view, if the blood is weakened from an inadequate diet, the blood thins, and does not have enough substance to flow forcefully through the body. Not only does this thinning seem to reduce the quantity of blood and its normal forceful flow, it is also believed that an actual loss of blood from something such as hemorrhaging or intestinal parasites also weakens the remaining supply. A person with weak blood is conceived to have little energy, low "blood pressure," and a tendency to chronic illness.

Ethnomedical Classifications

The Transamazon colonists classified illnesses, foods, medicines, states of their bodies, and other features of the environment according to a conceptual scheme based on hot/cold opposition. This conceptual system was brought to Brazil by the Portuguese, who in turn had obtained and perpetuated this heritage from Greek, Roman, Arab, and Jewish medical writers (Foster 1953:203; Buarque de Holanda 1962:145–60; Oliveira-Marques 1971:151–52). In medieval times this system was taught in the medical schools and was based on the humoral doctrines of Hippocrates and Galen. The humoral theory states that a balance between the four humors (blood, phlegm, yellow bile, and black bile) and their aspects (hot/cold, wet/dry) must be maintained to keep the body in good health (Temkin 1973:87–88). Hippocrates established the practice of studying physical symptoms to determine which particular humors were out of balance and treating symptoms with foods and medicines of the opposite nature. In Brazil, the imbalance of heat is more prevalent in folk definitions of disease than is the problem of excessive cold.[3] Likewise, blood became the humor of central interest. The body becomes hot through ingestion of an excess of conceptually hot foods; exposure to a hot climate; and activities such as cooking, ironing, and sexual relations. When the natural harmony of the body is upset, the body is vulnerable to injury from sudden cold shock. This occurs in varied ways through the introduction of a conceptually cold item in the environment (see Table 10.2). Severe cold shock can lead to the stopping of all body flows, including blood, urine, fecal matter, and air. A strong emetic must be applied to purge the body quickly of the offending food.

The hot/cold dichotomy in Brazil also stipulates that certain periods of the life cycle are times of hot/cold imbalance. These include infancy, the menstrual cycle, and postpartum periods—all of which are considered as hot. Persons in these stages are believed to be highly prone to hot/ cold shock, and great care is exercised to avoid foods, medicines, or activities likely to increase the already hot condition of the body (Fleming-Moran 1975).

Another factor which tends to weaken the body is negligence in treating blood that is considered to be contaminated. Blood that remains contaminated over any length of time is believed to gradually weaken and eventually behave like blood which has been improperly nourished. It is thought that one's blood can become contaminated for a variety of reasons. Conceptually, toxic elements include an excess of insect bites and strong pharmaceuticals, or foods which are supposed to "agitate" the blood. Other circumstances contaminate the blood by "dirtying" it, such as having a venereal disease, by missing a menstrual period, or by accumulating impurities by avoiding purifying sweaty work. Finally, an excess of conceptually dangerous food, such as game meat, also tends to dirty one's blood. (Table 10.3 summarizes the factors that weaken and dirty the blood, and forms of strengthening/cleaning it.)

TABLE 10.1

EXAMPLES OF DISEASE AGENTS AND RESULTING CURES

DISEASE	INTERNAL AGENT	EXTERNAL AGENT	SYMPTOMS	CURE
1. Malaria	—Weak blood (poorly fed)	—"Hot" stagnant water —Mosquito bite transmits "hot" water	—Violent, recurrent fever, chills, nausea (hot) —Liver pain —Contaminated, weak blood	Antimalarials (bitter, hot) "Liver medicine" (cool?) Vitamins (cool)
2. Measles (*sarampo*)	—Children are naturally weak —Weak blood	—"Hot *bafo*" (breath) —"Catch another's fever" —"Catch it from the air"	—Malaise, fever, red rash (hot) —Cough, congestion (hot) —Nausea, diarrhea (hot)	*Sabougeiro* (hot) *Espriteira* (cool?) *Hortelã miúdo* (cool) *Capim Santo* (cool) or Guava leaf (cool)
3. Intestinal parasites (*vermes*, or *lombrigas*)	—Weak blood (poorly fed)	—Eating with dirty hands —Eating raw vegetables —Walking barefoot —Newly opened ground	—Thin, pallid, "lack of blood" —Cranky, nervous (hot) —Worms in feces, stomach ache	Iron tonics (?) Vitamins (cool) *Capim Santo* (cool) *Poejo* (hot-cool) *Batata de purga* (cool) *Hortelã grande* (hot/cool) *Mastruz* (cool?)

Disease	Internal Agent	External Agent	Symptoms	Cure
4. Stopped or scanty menstrual flow (*sangue preso/regra não quer descer*)	—Body "hot" from period	—"Cold" food —Exposure to cold	—Abdominal pain, headache, nausea, nervousness (hot) —Scanty menstrual flow (cold ?)	*Poejo* (hot/cool) *Hortela miudo* (cool) *Canela* (hot-cool) *Elevante* (hot/cool) *Hortela grande* (hot/cool) *Arruda* (bitter-hot) *Cena* (bitter-hot) *Quina* (bitter-hot) *Alfazema* (bitter-hot) *Mostarda* (bitter-hot) *Ortemisa* (bitter-hot)
5. Excessive menstrual flow (*hemorragia*)	—*Sangue remoso* (contaminated) —Body "hot" from period	—An excess of "hot" foods	—Menstrual flow is heavy, dark, clotted, strong odor (hot)	*Maravilha* (cool) *Rosa branca* (cool) *Batata de purga* (cool) *Pega pinto* (cool) *Fedegoso* (cool ?) *Arruda* (hot)
6. Open, inflamed wound (*ferida inflamada*)	—Contaminated blood	—Previously closed wound is opened —Lack of care —"Hot" foods	—Becomes larger, pus, weeping, inflamed, sore (hot)	Mercurochrome Iodine (hot ?) Alcohol (hot ?) Absorbent powders (*pô secante*) *Agua oxigenada* (?) Vitamins (cool) *Batata de purga* (cool)

Source: Fleming-Moran 1975: 43–45

TABLE 10.2
PROBLEMS CAUSED BY HOT-COLD SHOCK:
EXAMPLES GIVEN BY VILA ROXA RESIDENTS

OVERHEATED STATE	PLUS COLD SHOCK	RESULT
1. Menstruating woman	—Eats "cold" lemons —Drinks "cold" soft drink —Walks in rain	Flow of menses is stopped (*sangue preso*)
2. Feverish child	—Eats "cold" papaya —Gets a cool bath	Fever is trapped inside body (*recaida de febre*)
3. Eating a large meal of heavy or "hot" foods	—Drink cold water —Take a bath in a stream —Eat several cold fruits	*Constipação* (fatal if not purged)
4. High fever of malaria	—Drink sugar cane juice (*garapa de cana*)	Instant death
5. Drink coffee	—Drink cool water	Teeth have tendency to decay
6. "Hot" infant in the teething process	—Use of a cool herbal medicine in excess —Mix his formula with cold water	Teeth do not erupt properly
7. Mother who is "hot" in postpartum	—Eats "cold" acid fruits given at hospital	Death
8. Menstruating girl	—Eats a mango	Death
9. Feverish condition	—Exposed to mist or dew (*sereno*)	Worsens to pneumonia
10. Walk in hot sun to the health post	—Get a cool shot	Illness?
11. Physical exertion (woman)	—Caught in cool rain	Menstrual period becomes irregular
12. Wash dishes in hot water	—Rinse them in cold	Pain and swelling
13. Wash clothes in hot sun	—Wash water is spilled on one's head	Chest congestion
14. Newborn baby with unhealed navel	—Given cool herbal remedy	Navel will not heal

SOURCE: Fleming-Moran 1975:48–49

TABLE 10.3
CONDITIONS OF THE BLOOD

DEBILITATING FACTORS	HEALTHY BLOOD	IMPROVING FACTORS
—Previously ill —Lack of adequate diet or lack of "non-fortifying status foods" —Action of intestinal parasites who "drink blood" —Actual loss of large quantity of blood (*hemorragia*)	—*Sangue fraca* (weak blood) → —Blood continues to weaken, becomes "thin," does not flow forcefully through the body; impurities begin to build up and raise body heat	—Better diet, vitamin shots, iron tonics rebuild blood
OR: CONTAMINATED BY OUTSIDE SOURCES —*Sangue agitada*: from "heat" produced by hot weather, excess of insect bites —*Sangue intoxicada*: from allergic reaction to certain "strong" foods, drugs —*Sangue suja*: from history of venereal disease, a sedentary life, lack of sweat —*Sangue remosa* (dangerous blood): includes the above plus blood contaminated by "reabsorbed menses," of too many "hot" foods	—Blood becomes contaminated from build-up of impurities and excess body "heat"; blood becomes "thick" (*sangue grossa*) resulting in high blood pressure, nervousness, as thick blood pushes against the veins and tries to release the impurities →	—Take a "cooling" blood purifier
	—Blood remains contaminated over a long period (impurities do not escape or are never purified); this begins to destroy the blood itself; becomes gradually *sangue fraca*; leads to *doencas feias*	—"Pushes" out heat and impurities in the forms of fever, inflammation, eruptions, pus —Blood is "cleaned," cooled by purgatives

SOURCE: Fleming-Moran 1975:40

Such contaminated blood is considered to be too thick (*grossa*), a condition which is conceptually opposed to weak, thin blood. In this thickened state, the blood does not circulate as it should, and the colonists believe such phenomena as nervousness and high blood pressure result from thick blood that is trying to "push out." Thick, contaminated blood acts like a seething volcano. If a person is already sick, his condition will worsen and take a long time to heal. If there is a relatively minor surface abrasion, the contaminants will erupt in any number of rashes, boils, and inflammations. If, on the other hand, this circulating mass of impurities and excess heat is denied an exit, the blood itself will pay the price. It will become as weak and thin as the blood which, by folk standards, has suffered from an inadequate food supply. Thus it closes the circle by becoming a weakening factor which lowers the body's internal defenses to disease.

The similarity between these folk concepts and Western concepts is sometimes striking. Poor nutrition does make one more prone to infection and prolonged illness. Nutrients from one's food do make up the blood cells and affect the blood's capacity to carry other nutrients. Fever does help to kill infectious microorganisms. Finally, inflammation and pus do in fact occur when the body is pushing out offending organisms and toxins (Alland 1970:81; Williams 1973:11–155, 332–42). In discussing the various illnesses that affected the people of Vila Roxa in 1972–74 we will return to these concepts whenever they influenced the population's response to the disease.

Potential Problems Resident in the Forest Environment

A number of the diseases which are most feared by outsiders rarely affected the Transamazon settlers. *Sylvan yellow fever*, potentially fatal to humans, for instance, rarely affects the settlers, since transmission occurs mainly in the top of the forest canopy. No cases were reported in the period 1971 to 1974 despite widespread clearing of forest and the presence of many unvaccinated settlers. Smith (1976a:198) believes this lack of a problem is due to the absence of the urban vector for yellow fever, *Aedes aegypti*, and the characteristic population cycle of the sylvan vectors.[4] Other arboviruses are probably present in the forest, but they have no significance for the migrants.[5] Chagas' disease has also been detected in wild animals along the Transamazon, but no cases have been reported among the immigrants. The disease is caused by the protozoan *Trypanosoma cruzi* and is maintained in a forest cycle by reduviid bugs serving as vectors, and armadillos and rodents acting as principal hosts. Given the animal feeding habits of the forest vectors, the likelihood of infection is reduced, but the spread of domestic vectors of the disease is likely to increase with time.

Leishmaniasis is endemic to the Amazon and pathogenic to humans. It causes large, ulcerous sores particularly in the infant to nine-year-old age group, among which occur 81 percent of the cases (Lacaz et al. 1972: 279). In the Amazon, rodents are the principal reservoirs, and several species of sand flies act as vectors for the protozoan. Although very few cases of the disease have been reported, the man-biting habits of at least one of the vectors, *Psycholopygus wellcomei*, increase the probability that people engaged in hunting or gathering in the forest will suffer from it in time.

Among the other potential health problems in the area are: onchocerciasis, Bancroft's filiarisis, and schistosomiasis. Onchocerciasis, or African river blindness, was unknown in South America until cases were documented among Waica Indians in the Northwest Amazon (Morães et al. 1973), though the disease has been known in Mexico for at least thirty years. Since at least one of the vectors identified in the Northwest region is also present in the Altamira/Xingú region, the danger exists that infected travelers may bring the disease (Rassi et al. 1975). As there is no chemo-prophylaxis at present against the parasite, onchocerciasis could prove a severe health hazard in the future.

Bancroft's filiarisis, caused by another tissue-inhabiting nematode, *Wucheria bancrofti*, could also become a problem since the vector is well established in the Transamazon. *Culex pipiens fatigans*, the principal Brazilian vector, breeds year-round in man-made pools along the road and in the vicinity of settlers' homes. Pathological effects vary, but in the advanced states (i.e., elephantiasis) it seriously restricts mobility.

Schistosomiasis is a serious problem affecting an estimated 200 million people world-wide. It is caused by *Schistosoma* spp., which lodges in the intestinal wall. Northeast migrants have spread the disease to southern Brazil, and their movement into the Amazon could have similar consequences.[6] Although the disease usually takes several years before serious pathological effects are evident, it causes lesions and fibrosis in organs such as the liver and lungs, and reduces work capacity and resistance to diseases (WHO 1966; Weisbord et al. 1973). Since the intermediate host, *Biophalaria straminea*, has been found in streams draining the Altamira region (Morães 1972; Pinheiro et al. 1974a), and the host, the black rat (*Rattus rattus*), is present in farmers' homes, a potential threat exists.

The health problems that most seriously plagued the colonists of Vila Roxa were the same as those found throughout the colonization areas of Marabá and Altamira: accidental trauma, malaria, gastro-enteritis, problems with the reproductive system, childhood diseases, helminthiasis, and skin lesions (Smith 1976a). Table 10.4 presents the number of cases admitted into the local hospital between 1971 and 1973. It should be noted that the hospital data do not portray true disease rates. In fact, they only give a "tip of the iceberg" indication of the health problems. Despite this

TABLE 10.4

MORBIDITY AND MORTALITY AT ALTAMIRA HOSPITAL

DISEASE	1971			1972			1973		
	CASES	% ADMITTED	DEATHS	CASES	% ADMITTED	DEATHS	CASES	% ADMITTED	DEATHS
Malaria	158	48.6	4	188	21.4	2	501	36.7	17
Trauma	49	15.1	1	110	12.6	4	139	10.2	5
Gastro-intestinal	29	8.9	2	154	17.5	16	132	9.7	26
Respiratory	26	8.0	1	104	11.8	7	103	7.5	9
Helminths	10	3.1	–	41	4.6	–	84	6.1	–
Simulid bites	1	0.3	–	25	2.8	–	52	3.8	2
Snake/scorpion bites	11	3.3	–	26	2.9	–	27	1.9	–
Population	5,741			9,600			11,740		

SOURCE: SESP Hospital in Altamira. Data collected by, and courtesy of, Nigel Smith, 1976a.

drawback, they do reveal the most critical health problems along the highway area. A stratified random sample of households (N=101) that I
conducted in Altamira highway communities indicated that colonists lost
an average of 11.5 days per year due to illness or injury. The most frequent culprit was malaria, but the most incapacitating was accidental
trauma. In these cases it was not uncommon to find persons who had lost
from 90 to 108 days from work.

Malaria

Malaria is the most serious health problem throughout the Amazon,
and the Transamazon area is no exception.[7] It accounts for 44 percent of
hospital admissions, and in 1973 11.4 percent of the highway population
within a 250-kilometer radius of Altamira had contracted the disease
(Smith 1976a:210). Of these, 1.5 percent had to be hospitalized. In the
first couple of years of settlement, malaria in Vila Roxa was limited to
men who lived on their lots during the week. Their families, who remained
in the agrovila during the week, were not exposed to the mosquitoes. Now
that families are moving to the lots, the incidence of malaria is rising
among women and children. During the 1973–74 study period, 20 percent
of the Vila Roxa families had at least one member who had contracted
malaria.

Malaria now afflicts all age and sex groups with an approximately equal
probability. It is contracted while sleeping at home or while living in the
forest. Malaria morbidity varies considerably along the Transamazon (see
Figure 10.1 and Table 10.5). In the Marabá area the rate of infection
was nearly twice as high as that in the Altamira area (18.0 versus 9.7

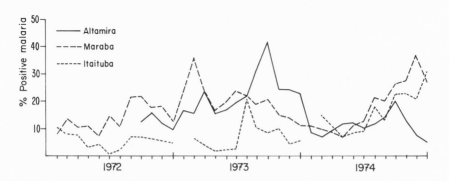

Fig. 10.1 Variability in Malaria Incidence along the
Transamazon Highway
Source: SESP Hospitals in Altamira, Marabá,
and Itaituba; courtesy of Smith 1976a:221

TABLE 10.5

MALARIA INCIDENCE ALONG DIFFERENT STRETCHES OF THE TRANSAMAZON HIGHWAY, 1971–1974

STRETCH	KM	1971			1972			1973			1974		
		SLIDES EXAM.	NO. POS.	% POS.	SLIDES EXAM.	NO. POS.	% POS.	SLIDES EXAM.	NO. POS.	% POS.	SLIDES EXAM.	NO. POS.	% POS.
Pará Norte-Marabá	150	483	30	6.2	3,664	422	11.5	3,422	450	13.1	7,699	1,408	18.3
Marabá-Jatobal	120	222	19	8.6	3,541	288	8.1	2,674	485	18.1	3,124	164	5.2
Jatobal-Altamira	380	1,006	281	28.0	1,085	139	12.8	7,284	2,159	29.6	4,913	636	12.9
Altamira-Itaituba	500	724	20	2.8	5,024	147	2.9	6,939	417	6.0	3,944	168	4.2
Total	1,150	2,436	350	14.4	13,314	996	7.5	20,319	3,511	17.3	19,680	2,376	12.1

NOTE: Pará Norte is on the west bank of the Araguaia River.
SOURCE: SUCAM, Belem; Smith 1976a:220

percent). The reasons for the great variation are not fully understood, but it is believed that low-lying, riverine areas such as that of Marabá are more ideal breeding grounds for the malaria vectors. The peak of malaria transmission occurs in the early part of the rainy season, probably due to the increase in breeding loci. This peak coincides with the critical time of planting, which cannot be delayed without consequent poor crop development. Another minor peak occurs at the end of the rainy season, when labor is again needed for harvesting and marketing of cereal crops (see Figure 10.2). The impact of malaria on work capacity and agricultural

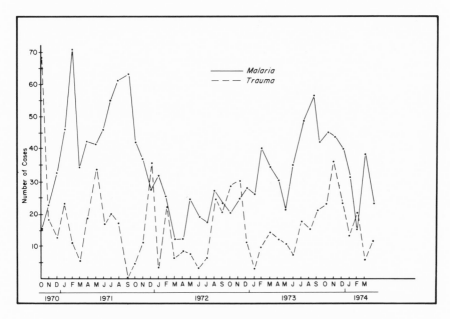

Fig. 10.2 Seasonal Fluctuations in the Incidence of Malaria and Trauma

productivity is significant, therefore, not only in terms of total days lost due to illness but also due to the timing of such occurrences. Smith (1976a: 226) estimated an average work loss of approximately fourteen days in the Marabá area in 1974, while in a stratified random sample (N=101) in the Altamira region, I found the average loss to be eight work days per occurrence. Thus, the Marabá area is affected not only by twice the rate of infection, but also by twice the work loss among those infected.

Smith (1976a:227) found a total of eight species of Anopheline larvae in roadside ponds. Of these, four have been incriminated as vectors for human malaria in South America. These roadside ponds are close to homes of settlers and are probably implicated in infection. The male population is also bitten while bathing in ponds and streams at sunset after the completion of farm work.[8] Although mosquito nets placed over beds or hammocks would deter malarial vectors, few settlers employ them. Not only are they relatively expensive (US$10 each in Altamira), but only a few of the colonists believe that mosquitoes are malaria transmitters.

Cultural explanations for malaria vary. Many colonists mentioned that in order to catch malaria one had to have "weak blood."[9] Secondly, malaria is believed to be externally induced by having walked in, being exposed to, or having drunk "hot" water (i.e., stagnant water). Some residents added that stagnant pools are full of rotting material, and that mosquitoes are found in such water. The bite of the mosquitoes transfers some of this hot, rotted material into the bloodstream, causes the blood to heat up, and brings on violent fevers. This fever is distinguished from others because it does not go away with mild remedies such as aspirin (Fleming-Moran 1975:58).

As malaria symptoms are severe and highly debilitating, Vila Roxa residents waste no time in getting a blood test and taking the antimalarial pills supplied by the Public Health Service. Most colonists do not attempt to cure malaria with home remedies when cloroquine is available.[10] However, since the folk system of judging illnesses dictates that one has a "disease" only when there are symptoms present, people tend to stop taking the medication as soon as the violent fevers and chills stop—but before the plasmodium has been controlled. In time, the fevers return again. Following the end of the fevers, the colonist returns to work but takes vitamin shots or "liver medicine" (conceptually "cool") since the antimalarial pills (conceptually "hot") are said to cause liver inflammation.

Trauma

Accidental trauma is mostly incurred by men in the twenty- to fifty-year-old age bracket while they are engaged in clearing their fields and other agriculture-related tasks. As the injury is generally severe and the man is the principal breadwinner of the family, the injured person is rushed to the hospital rather than being treated at home. Because of their seriousness, the impact of these injuries on working capacity is significant. Of the four major causes of hospitalization, trauma cases take more time for recuperation than malaria cases, with an average stay in the hospital of 6.2 days (Smith 1976a:237).[11]

After release from the hospital, most trauma cases cannot immediately return to strenuous physical activity. The one man in Vila Roxa who was known to be hospitalized from trauma in 1972 had not recovered after more than one year, and his wife had to take over the financial support of the family. When the injury occurs in field preparation, the family may have to find its income in nonfarm activities. According to doctors interviewed by Smith (1976a), road accidents also represent a significant proportion of the injury cases at both Altamira and Marabá Hospitals. Trauma is likely to remain a perennial problem in the Transamazon region.

Gastro-Intestinal Problems

Although less than 1 percent of the Altamira population was hospitalized due to gastro-intestinal problems, gastro-enteritis was the chief cause of death among the population. The problem was particularly severe during 1971 when the migrants were housed in overcrowded quarters with inadequate facilities. Gastro-enteritis and dehydration were the principal cause of infant mortality between 1970 and 1974, accounting for 48 percent of deaths in the infant to four-year-old age group (Smith 1976a:241). There appears to be no noticeable seasonal pattern to the incidence of the disease.

Contaminated drinking water is a major cause of gastro-intestinal disease along the Transamazon. As of late 1974, only four of the twenty-six agrovilas were equipped with a piped water system. Most of the people get their water from streams and ponds, which also serve as washing, bathing, and defecating facilities. Amoebic dysentery (*Entomoeba histolytica*), giardiasis (*Giardia lambilia*), and bacteria such as *Shigella dysenteriae* are leading causes of gastro-intestinal disease in this region (see Table 10.6). Only ten of the twenty-six agrovilas are equipped with privies, and none have toilets. Most colonists, therefore, defecate within a short distance of their houses, usually under cover of a banana or maize patch. Even when privies are available they are not always used with regularity. The unpleasant odors resulting from improper maintenance and the presence of spiders and other arthropods discourage the use of these facilities.

Unhygienic methods of garbage disposal and food storage are another major source of gastro-intestinal disease. Wasted food is discarded in backyards, where it attracts flies. The flies in turn feed on fecal matter and contaminate unguarded food with pathogenic bacteria and amoebas. Cockroaches, also abundant in the houses despite DDT sprayings, feed avidly on unguarded food, especially at night. Cockroaches (*Blattaria* spp.) are vectors for at least forty-four species of pathogenic bacteria, as well as for amoebic dysentery. Black rats (*Rattus rattus*) feed and defecate on foodstuffs and are implicated in gastro-intestinal disease along the highway. The colonists' custom of storing produce at home facilitates this form of transmission.

Lack of hygiene is largely the result of low living standards and cannot be expected to change until economic conditions improve. The colonists do

TABLE 10.6

PERCENT OF TRANSAMAZON POPULATION WITH GASTRO-INTESTINAL
INFECTIONS CAUSED BY PATHOGENIC PROTOZOA

REGION	YEAR	SLIDES EXAMINED	% POSITIVE ENTAMOEBA HISTOLYTICA	% POSITIVE GIARDIA LAMBILIA	% POSITIVE BALANTIDIUM COLI
Altamira	1971	1,050	23.4	22.6	0.6
	1972	6,601	8.1	15.3	0.2
	1973	8,067	3.0	7.1	0.1
	1974	5,120	5.7	13.2	0.1
Marabá	1971	362	43.6	23.2	0.5
	1972	4,750	5.1	24.8	–
	1973	5,161	12.4	27.9	0.1
	1974	4,779	11.6	23.8	–

NOTE: The sampled population includes recently arrived settlers who must undergo an examination for parasites in order to secure a health card, as well as patients referred to SUCAM by public health doctors.
SOURCE: SUCAM, Belém; Smith 1976a:244

a remarkably good job of keeping their homes clean given the constraints they work under, since provision of insect- and rat-proof containers, pure water, and adequate disposal facilities is costly and time consuming. It is notable, for example, that the higher incidence of gastro-intestinal diseases in the Marabá region is associated with that area's lower land productivity.

Helminthiasis Problems

Intestinal worms are a significant public health problem along the highway, although they seldom cause hospitalization. In 1973, 65 percent of the colonists tested were infected with at least one species of helminth.[12] While a light worm burden of a single species may not significantly affect the working capacity of a well-nourished adult, polyparasitism accompanied by heavy loads of parasites can impair the health of children and adults alike. Roundworms (*Ascaris lumbricoides*) were found in 68 percent of the highway population sampled. Roundworms are known to interfere with the digestion and absorption of proteins and fat (Venkatachalan and Patwardhan 1953). In severe cases the roundworms can block the entrance to the small intestine, considerably reducing food absorption and resulting in bloated stomachs. Considering the high rates of infestation,

Ascaris undoubtedly reduces the stamina of highway settlers. Roundworm eggs are highly resistant to dessication and can remain viable for months. Given the frequent practice of defecation near houses, and the absence of coprophagous beetles, the acquisition of ova by children playing in the yards is frequent. House flies, improperly washed vegetables, and drinking water are also implicated in the epidemiology of *Ascaris*.

Whipworm (*Trichuris trichuria*) occurs in 42 percent of the highway population sampled (Smith 1976a:250). A large concentration of the worms can result in chronic diarrhea, dehydration, and anemia in children. The epidemiology is related to the sanitary conditions discussed for roundworms.

Hookworm (*Necator americanus*) is present in 43 percent of the population. Large burdens result in anemia, since the parasite ingests blood from the interior surface of the small intestine and causes local hemmorrhaging. After hookworm eggs have passed onto the ground in feces, the larvae eventually hatch and enter the human host through the skin, usually in the region of the feet. Given the high prices for shoes in the region and the prevalent economic conditions, improvements in sanitary practices will follow betterment in income.

Respiratory Problems and Childhood Diseases

Respiratory infections are particularly severe among young children. In 1971–74 they were the second most important cause of infant mortality in the hospitals, accounting for 25 percent of deaths in the infant to four-year-old age group (see Table 10.6). Adults suffer only mild respiratory infections, and this problem does not seriously affect the productivity of farmers.

It is in relation to childhood diseases that the folk view of causation in disease plays a most important role. Parents believe that children are "weak" in infancy and early childhood. Because the symptoms usually begin with fever, runny nose, cough, and skin eruptions, many mothers lump the various illnesses under the category of little children's fevers (*febrezinhas de criança*). The child's weak blood is believed to accumulate impurities after exposure to contagion. These impurities disrupt the regular flow of blood, and fever accumulates in the blood. When the fever pushes the impurities out, it leaves the impurities on the surface in the form of a rash. During this critical stage, the child must be protected from contact with anything which is conceptually "cold," as this will lead to the fever being trapped in the body, leading to pneumonia, severe diarrhea, and even death.

Childhood diseases are thought to begin with a little cold (*gripezinha*), or runny nose and malaise. Then the child gets the fever, and in some cases the eruptive rash, which reclassifies the disease as one of the child-hood fevers. If the fever reenters, it weakens the blood and the patient contracts an "ugly disease" (*doença feia*). This is a general euphemism for diseases with severe symptoms such as pneumonia, croup, wild cough, and even tuberculosis (Fleming-Moran 1975:62).

After a child has begun to recuperate, the treatment is completed by helping rebuild the child's weak blood through the use of vitamins and cool blood purifiers. If the symptoms appear suddenly and fail to respond to treatment, a mother may infer that her child has contracted the "evil eye." At this point she may seek a blesser to cure the disease. The blesser in Vila Roxa generally attributed the "evil eye" to an outsider who had envied the child, or to the child's parents if they had experienced anger or resentment towards the child. In Brazilian terms, both are unacceptable social behavior. Four cases were treated in Vila Roxa to the best of my knowledge during the 1973–74 period. All cases involved infants of Northeastern parents.

Problems of the Reproductive Tract

One-third of the herbal plants used in the community were associated with these problems—the majority of which were used for symptoms linked to the menstrual cycle. A menstruating woman is conceptually "hot," as is her menstrual flow. She is therefore weakened internally from this heat and an easy prey to hot-cold shock. If a woman in this "hot" condition is exposed to a cold situation, it is believed that her menstrual flow will stop and become trapped in her body. To counteract this cold shock, conceptually "hot" remedies are given so that the menses are re-leased. Among such hot herbs are cinnamon, senna, and rue. However, the symptoms created by the trapped menses lead to overheating, and to relieve these hot symptoms a cooling remedy is called for. This poses a dilemma. To get the flow started a hot remedy is called for; to get relief from the symptoms a cool one is indicated. Most of the hot herbs such as rue, fedegoso (*Cassia occidentalis*), senna (*Cassia acutifolia*), and quina (*Quassia amara*) are recognized by the women as potential abortives. Generally, the "hot" remedy is taken first. If the symptoms persist, the cooling herb is taken.

When a woman wishes to become pregnant, she may try to facilitate conception by taking a blood purifier such as *pega pinto* (*Boheraavia hirsuta*), castor oil, or *batata de purga* (*Colvolvulus operculatus*). These cleanse the womb and keep the blood from overheating. According to local beliefs about pregnancy, the woman continues to menstruate during the nine-month gestation period, but the menses are not allowed to escape.

This extra blood is recycled in the system and makes the blood too thick to flow properly. Cooling blood purifiers help thin the blood.

The postpartum period is one of the most intense times of personal hygiene and diet regulation in a woman's life. The new mother is seen as extremely vulnerable, as her body is believed to be open. The windows of her room are kept closed to avoid drafts. She spends two to three days in bed, lying on her side with her legs drawn together. She takes cool foods—usually light colored and bland (*papa*). These include specially bought cookies, crackers, oatmeal, teas, and marmalades. She will either hire help or have the help of a female relative in keeping house for her. The length of this period varies from thirty to forty days and is known as *resguardo*. Ironing and cooking are particularly avoided during resguardo, as they may cause heat to enter the womb and cause inflammation. Those foods avoided during menstruation are avoided even more strictly at this time.

Skin Problems and Bites from Insects

Bites inflicted by female black flies (*Simulium* spp.) present a significant public health problem, especially in the Altamira region. Although in most cases the reaction to simulid bites is limited to localized temporary edema, in some victims disseminated mucocutaneous hemorrhaging occurs, particularly among children. The etiological agent involved in the acute clinical manifestations of the disease, called the "hemorrhagic syndrome of Altamira" (Pinheiro et al. 1974b), has not been fully established, but is attributed to hypersensitivity or to a response to a toxin in the saliva of the black flies. Black fly biting becomes so intense during the rainy season that some families abandon their lots and seek respite in the roadside agrovilas or in Altamira.[13] The major peak of simulid feeding coincides with the rice harvest in May, and settlers in some areas experience difficulty in contracting harvest labor because of the flies.

At least three species of flies are known to bite man in the Altamira region (*Simulium amazonicum*, *S. incrustatum*, and *S. pintoi*), and elimination of their breeding grounds is unlikely given the presence of streams throughout the region. Smith (1976a:280) estimated that a family of six would spend US$192 on commercial insect repellents during the course of the six-month rainy season—an amount equal to the expected income from the sale of about one hectare of rice. Most colonists, as a result, resort to covering much of their body surface with clothing—including long-sleeved shirts and pants tied with rope at the ends to prevent insect penetration. While this strategy keeps the insects out, it also reduces the cooling effect of perspiration and reduces stamina and comfort.

More significantly, the bites itch intensely at night and are vigorously scratched, thereby opening the way for secondary infection. Given the sanitary conditions in the area, skin ailments are relatively frequent. Colonists use sensation, contagion, secretions, and size to diagnose the different kinds of skin lesions commonly found. Table 10.7 schematizes the distinctive features of skin ailments.

Treatment depends on the size and nature of the problem. Closed surface ailments are treated with cool remedies such as ointments. When the first break in the skin's surface appears, it is assumed that the impurities will escape through this opening. Colonists feel that skin lesions are very likely to turn into large ones unless steps are taken. Small open wounds are treated with liberal application of antiseptics, hydrogen peroxide, and powders. When the small surface wounds (*perebas*) have turned into larger and more infected ones, the patient may decide to take something to help his blood. These cures include herbal purifiers such as *batata de purga* (*Convolvulus operculatus*), *carua* (unidentified), *mastruz* (*Chenopodium anthelminthicum*), or vitamins and antibiotics. Since skin problems of this type are common and do not interfere with daily responsibilities, they are not considered serious. Only when they become persistent and unsightly do people worry that there may be something wrong internally. Many residents are ashamed to bear large ulcerated wounds, as these are conceptually linked to syphilis.

Avoidance of foods becomes more important as the seriousness of the skin problem increases. Foods eaten conform to the notion of light, snacking fare also used to feed infants and small children. The foods must be light in color and bland in flavor. A majority of the allowed fruits and vegetables are of European origin, while those avoided are of African or New World origin. The high cost of such foods raises them in the estimation of the colonists. Lean meat is preferred, thereby avoiding hard-to-digest fats, such as those found in large game animals or fish. Some foods are avoided if they have strange physical characteristics, such as a slimy secretion or a rough surface (e.g., spiny maxixe (*Cucumis anguria*) or okra). See Table 10.8 for the food classification system employed by the population.

Food Consumption in Vila Roxa

No extensive food consumption survey has been carried out among the colonist population that came to the Transamazon Highway. Because the collection of food consumption data is helpful in assessing the health status of a population, a limited survey among Vila Roxa households was carried out by Millicent Fleming-Moran and myself. Numerous methods of collecting the data are possible, each of them presenting some limitation

TABLE 10.7

Diagnosing and Naming Skin Ailments: A Decision Model

SKIN SURFACE BROKEN?	ANY SENSATION?	SELF-CONTAINED?	CONTAGIOUS TO OTHERS	BLISTERS/SECRETIONS?	MAGICAL CAUSE?	SIZE DISTINCTION?
YES	pain/irritation	yes	no	no	no	small (*pereba*) large (*ferida*)
	no	no	yes	yes	no	large, spreading (*ferida brava* or *leshe*)
	soreness	yes (*queimadura*) no (*tumor*)				
	itching	yes	yes	yes (*sarna*) no (*empinge*)		
			no (*picada*)			
		no	no	yes	yes (*cobreiro*) no (*bolinha*)	
				no (*coceira*)		
No	no	no		yes (*pano branco*)		
				no (*pano vermelho* or *pano preto*)		

TABLE 10.8

The Hot-Cold Gradient as Seen in Foods

	Unacceptable Foods during illness	Occasionally acceptable	Acceptable Foods during illness
Very hot	*Anta* (tapir) *Jabuti* (land turtle) *Guariba* (howler monkey) *Porco do mato* (peccary) *Paca vermelha* (paca) *Cutia vermelha* (cutia) *Tatu* (armadillo) Duck Turkey *Galinha preta* (black chicken) *Galinha de Angola* (guinea hen) *Veado* (deer)		
Hot	Uncastrated mature steer (beef) *Dourado* (oily fish) Sardines (oil pack, dried) Black beans Domestic pork Roasted ears of corn *Couve* (cabbage family) Cabbage Eggs*	*Paca branca* (paca) *Cutia branca* (cutia) *Veado* (deer) Domestic pork *Dorado* (fish) *Farinha puba* Brazil nuts Condensed milk	Castrated/immature beef *Maizena* (cornstarch) Fresh corn products Butter Coffee Condensed milk Garlic Kid Red beans Powdered milk

TABLE 10.8 (Continued)

	UNACCEPTABLE FOODS DURING ILLNESS	OCCASIONALLY ACCEPTABLE	ACCEPTABLE FOODS DURING ILLNESS
Temperate			Boiled fresh milk Young/immature chicken Broths, soups Cheese *Farinha branca* "Mulato" beans White beans "Jaula" beans Onion *Traira* (fish)
Cool	*Batata doce* (Sweet potato) Papaya Bananas (*São Tome, comprida, perua*) *Nhame* *Taioba* (taro) *Favas* (fava beans) Raw milk "Milk pumpkin" Okra *Chuchu* (chayote)	*Pescada* (fish, usually dried) *Batata doce* (sweet potato) *Laranja* (orange) Papaya *Banana maçã* (small)	Rice Breads, cakes Macaroni, noodles Crackers *Batatinha* (Irish potato) Sweet manioc tubers Apples Pears Carrots Green pepper *Mingaus* (paps/pudding) Lettuce "Caboclo" pumpkin Domestic tomatoes

TABLE 10.8 (Continued)

	UNACCEPTABLE FOODS DURING ILLNESS	OCCASIONALLY ACCEPTABLE	ACCEPTABLE FOODS DURING ILLNESS
Cold	Other fish		
	Shell fish		
	Crab		
	Shrimp		
	Pineapple		
	Coalhada (yogurt)		
	Vinegar		
	Lemons		
	Jilo (Solanum gilo)		
	Maxixe		
	Cucumber		
	Mango		
	Wild fruits		
	Wild tomatoes		
	Guava		
	Watermelon		
	Jack fruit		

* Classification uncertain
SOURCE: Fleming-Moran 1975:82–84

in accuracy, representativeness, time cost, or replicability. In this survey I used as a unit the farm household, probably the most common unit in food consumption surveys because it is both an economic and a dietary unit (Pekkarinen 1970:147). As a method of collecting household data I chose "food accounts in families" over the weighing method,[14] food sampling for chemical analysis, national food balance sheets, daily diaries, or weekly recall (Pekkarinen 1970:148–63 evaluates the merits of each method). In the family account, I interviewed the male and female heads of a household and recorded food consumed over the previous four-week period. Amounts were noted by weight; by whether the food was produced by the household, purchased, or received from others; and by seasonality variations. A complete list of all foods available in the region was used in interviews to reduce memory omissions.

The level of protein consumption is highly variable among human populations (Masek 1959). This is also true within a population—particularly in stratified societies. Despite the alleged scarcity of animal protein in tropical rain forests, no survey has ever noted signs of protein deficiency among autochthonous South Americans in their native habitats.[15] Silva et al. (1959) calculated that game meat was the chief provider of animal protein among the population of thirty-six riverine Amazon towns, supplying seventy-one grams per person per day. No cases of protein deficiency were noted in any of these interior communities, in contrast to urban areas of the Amazon.[16] No signs of protein malnutrition were noted among the adult population of the Transamazon agrovilas near Altamira. Cases of child malnutrition were recorded in Altamira hospital, but this probably resulted from a folk tendency to restrict a child's diet to starchy (and classificatorily "cool") foods during diarrhea episodes.

Smith (1976a:165) noted that children between the ages of zero and three were particularly prone to malnutrition in the three agrovilas he studied. Weaning begins before the first year, in strong contrast to the aboriginal practice of prolonged lactation. Breastfeeding was not highly regarded among many mothers, who turned to a combination of formula, powdered milk, and banana, and maize or manioc porridge (*papas*). Because of the frontier conditions, sterilization of baby bottles was seldom or inadequately practiced, facilitating the occurrence of gastro-intestinal disease among infants. Because of the high cost of powdered milk, many mothers are forced during periods of low cash flow to dilute the formulas to the point that little nutrition is provided to the child.

The mean daily per capita intake of animal protein was 40.6 grams. This figure does not reflect the significant differentials between colonists in purchasing power or hunting ability; seasonality in availability of game; nor is it normalized for age and sex. Since 70 percent of the Vila Roxa population is under the age of twenty, the intake for working adults is considerably higher than the above mean figure, particularly among males—who receive the most generous portion of meat served at each meal. Animal protein intakes varied even more between caboclos and newcomers in the community. As noted earlier, caboclos hunt a mean of 36 kilograms per month, a figure twice the mean for the whole population. In contrast, some of the clients who neglected hunting were able to get only one-half of the mean. They met their dietary needs by spending their agricultural loans on food purchases, chiefly in the form of salted fish from Altamira. The 40.6 grams of animal protein are supplemented by a mean intake of vegetable protein of 27.1 grams per person per day, which, together, places the people of the agrovila well above the minimum requirements.[17]

The greater portion of calories in the Vila Roxa diet in 1972–74 came from carbohydrates (54 percent). Fat intakes are 35 percent of total calories, a figure well above the recommended intake of the Food and Nutrition Board of the National Research Council (Williams 1973:29). The proximity of the community to markets in Altamira and Brasil Novo turned many farmers into intensive gardeners. Weekly, several of them took lettuce, tomatoes, cabbage, onions, and other herbs to market and sold them at considerable benefit. Moreover, most of them overproduced, and their families and friends benefited from this relatively unusual supply of greens in the rural Brazilian diet (Castro 1967). Rather than decrease over the next few years, one can expect the amount of game meat hunted to increase. There were very few farmers who hunted in the community with any regularity between 1972 and 1974, but more were learning to lose their fear of the forest and venturing with others in search of desirable animals. Eventually, however, the increase in the number of hunters can be expected to bring about a rapid decline in available game, and the population will have to turn to beef, pork, and poultry production to supply the necessary protein.

A detailed nutritional survey using the weighing method of chemical analysis of food would be required to accurately assess the vitamin adequacy of the diets of Vila Roxa farmers. Given the substantial intakes of papayas, mangoes, and parsley (coentro) in the diet, levels of Vitamin A are probably adequate. Tomatoes, pumpkins, and peppers frequently added to the daily plate of beans, and wild fruits such as the palm fruits of buriti and açai, also contribute to Vitamin A adequacy. The consumption of legumes and meats probably puts the population within the adequate levels of Thiamine, Niacin, and Riboflavin intake.[18] Only a few citrus fruit trees have begun production in the area, but the availability of wild fruits rich in Vitamin C provides an important dietary contribution that needs to be assessed. The consumption of tomatoes and other vegetables made possible by the community vegetable gardeners provides a supplement not traditionally available in rural Brazil (Interdepartmental Committee 1965).

TABLE 10.9
FOOD CONSUMPTION OF VILA ROXA COLONISTS*

	KILOCALORIES	PROTEIN (G)	FAT (G)	CARBOHYDRATE (G)
Manioc flour	56,800	568	280	10,000
Manioc tuber	26,400	264	140	5,000
Rice	56,800	568	280	10,000
Sweet potato	23,400	340	140	5,000
Taro	9,900	190	20	2,370
Beans	23,600	1,560	100	4,280
Corn	9,600	350	320	2,210
Bread	5,380	720	640	10,800
Sugar	38,000	–	–	1,990
Liquor	10,000	–	–	traces
Milk	2,510	1,320	1,375	1,910
Oil	35,360	–	4,000	–
Butter	7,160	3	810	40
Game meat	72,000	2,520	5,400	–
Beef	16,000	680	1,200	–
Pork	18,880	448	1,880	–
Fish	7,800	1,740	28	–
Canned meat	16,000	680	1,200	–
Eggs	6,520	520	460	–
Squashes	4,600	246	24	1,008
Bananas	6,800	88	16	1,888
Papayas	7,600	240	40	4,000
Pineapple	4,160	32	16	1,100
Sugar cane	4,100	–	–	960
Lemons	270	11	3	3
Tomatoes	440	22	4	98
Garlic	1,370	62	2	308
Onions	360	15	2	82
Lettuce	140	12	2	25
Wild fruits**				
Total	471,950	13,199	18,384	63,072
Per capita per day	2,420 kcals	68 g	94 g	323 g

* Based on a 50-percent sample of Vila Roxa, using food account method. Data are per household (6.5 members) per four-week period. Conversions from weight-based data to calorie-protein-fat and carbohydrate equivalents made by use of Watt and Merrill (1963).
** Omitted too often by farmers to permit a reliable estimate.

In a nutritional survey of Northeast Brazil, researchers associated the plantation system prevalent on the coastal zone with the marginal undernutrition they found, as 38 percent of the food calories produced in the zone were export crops—chiefly sugar and cocoa (Interdepartmental Committee 1965). The introduction of large-scale mining, ranching, and cash crop projects into the Amazon must be monitored carefully with an eye to both social equity and nutritional consequences. Under a small-farm system, both traditionally and at present, the Amazonian population achieved satisfactory levels of nutrition. It would be unfortunate if the national effort to develop the Amazon results in the introduction of malnutrition into Amazonian rural areas.[19]

The generally favorable dietary status of the Vila Roxa population, even during the difficult period of adjustment to a generally unfamiliar environment, reflects a number of favorable economic and locational factors. Vila Roxa's location within twenty-three kilometers of Altamira, and a comparable distance to Brasil Novo, means that the population can find seasonal employment to supplement declines in the productivity of hunting or farming. Smith (1976a) and I (Moran 1975) noted the difference between the physical appearance of colonists in side road agrovilas and those along the Transamazon Highway. As indicated in Chapter 6, the availability of services in the former was inferior to those in the latter. The location of Vila Roxa on a relatively high point of land, the availability of latrines, and a water tower made health conditions significantly better in Vila Roxa than in more isolated agrovilas. Even the less productive laborer-farmers were able to achieve satisfactory diets through wage labor and the application of government loans for food consumption.

Managing Health

The Transamazon colonists brought a folk medicine system from their areas of origin, which had deep roots in the Western concepts of health. In several ways their experiences replicated the colonial experience of the Portuguese. Just as the Jesuits had adopted the new plants encountered within the conceptualizations of the humoral doctrine, so did the immigrants experiment and adjust their knowledge of the environment as it changed from the familiar one of their areas of origin to that of the Amazon frontier. However, like the Portuguese before them, they preferred to import their herbal remedies rather than adopting those of the native population.

The herbalists in the agrovila are women of about thirty-five years of age, who have raised several healthy children, and who brought medicinal plants to the frontier area. Herbs imported from the various regions of Brazil are slowly being introduced to new users, as herbalists substitute plants from their regions in the absence of the one requested. The most commonly used herbs are those of Old World origin, are not region-specific, and are planted in the immediate vicinity of the house. Most New World plants of strict medicinal usage are planted away from the houses on the farm lots. These plants are usually those with strong purgative or emetic action. Medicinal herbs that were once wild plants to their Portuguese ancestors are still treated with respect. Plants familiar to the local caboclo population are generally feared and avoided by the new-comers. There has been very little dissemination of herbal information from the caboclo to the immigrant population (Fleming-Moran 1975:36).

In addition to the herbalists in the region, the public health service is available to serve the population. In some of the communities a health post with a nurse's aide exists and is visited once a week by a physician and supporting personnel. The nurse's aide does home visitations, pre-natal check-ups, immunizations, and provides first aid. Medical supplies available at the health post are limited to gauze, mercurochrome, Jensen's violet, and tetanus vaccines. The weekly visit is used to examine persistent maladies, to collect fecal and urine samples, to take blood tests, and to prescribe medication. Most prescriptions are filled in the town of Alta-mira, twenty-three kilometers away, where the only hospital in the region and several pharmacies are located. Two private general practitioners and two dentists also operate in Altamira for those who can afford to pay for private consultations (SESI 1974). In addition, faith healers and Afro-Brazilian possession cults exist in town to help those with diseases believed to have supernatural causes.

Alterations brought about by road construction crews and colonists have changed the character of both pathogens and vectors. These changes re-quire solutions specific to the area's environmental problems. Parasites which normally are cycled in animals turn on man when the destruction of the forest eliminates or reduces the animal fauna. The increase in the density of the human population enhances the virulence of a disease that may have remained largely isolated within a small group in the past. In the undisturbed habitat, mosquito vectors of malaria and yellow fever and the sand fly vectors of leishmaniasis are confined to the canopy, but forest clearance brings them to ground level, where they bite man. The reduction in forest may also involve a loss of animal protein sources and a reduction in both nutrition and health status. Vickers (1976) has noted a 40 percent reduction in hunting yields at a new site within the first year. More research that includes epidemiological, nutritional, and agri-cultural factors in assessing the impact of human occupation of tropical forest ecosystems is needed (cf. review of state-of-knowledge in UNESCO 1978).

The evidence presented in this chapter suggests that farm productivity was not seriously affected by disease or poor diet, except for a minuscule portion of the population. A wide range of diseases affected the popula-tion, but many of the most feared have not yet materialized for the colonists—among them Chagas' disease, onchocerciasis, Bancroft's filiarisis, schistosomiasis, yellow fever, and leishmaniasis. Malaria remains the most serious problem, but is rarely fatal to adults, and work loss from malaria has not been significant. Cultural and ecological factors are implicated in its persistence. The construction of roads, the clearing of forest, and the stopping of medication before the plasmodium has been effectively suppressed are all involved. Trauma is the most serious factor in reducing productivity, but it affects only a small portion of the population. The other problems are chronic but only rarely keep the population from working, although work capacity may be reduced. Research on diet and disease as they affect work capacity in the Amazon is badly needed.

The most serious adult illnesses, in terms of rates both of morbidity and of mortality, were commonly referred to Western medical practitioners from the public health service. Those illnesses which are chronic but less serious insofar as day-to-day performance of work, are primarily treated with herbal remedies, careful attention to dietary taboos, and care in personal hygiene. For less serious health problems folk remedies are reasonably effective, are low in cost, are easily accessible, and provide the patient with a greater sense of control over the disease because of the personal attention provided by neighbors and folk healers. Reductions in morbidity rates for most of these chronic problems will come naturally with improvements in income. The rates for malaria, trauma, gastrointestinal, and respiratory ailments, on the other hand, may not necessarily be reduced thereby, and may severely impair the productivity of adults and the lives of children. Efforts at improving the health status of the population should concentrate in the areas wherein dependence on modern medicine already exists due to the seriousness of the ailments and the inefficacy of traditional herbal cures.

Levels of Analysis in Amazon Research: Theory, Method, and Policy Implications

The preceding chapters have raised a number of recurrent dilemmas present in Amazonian studies: is the Amazon fragile or not? Are its soils fertile or sterile? Can societies in the region advance beyond the level of tropical forest cultures without destroying the habitat? Was Transamazon Highway colonization a failure or a success? What will the future hold for the region? These questions are not simply provocative speculations. Despite a not insignificant volume of research on each of these topics, there is evidence to support positions on both sides of these questions. After examining the available research, it is my contention that some of the heated debates about the Amazon's habitability and potential reflect a tendency to generalize about processes in one level of analysis from data and research carried out at another level. In this chapter I explore the implications of this tendency for understanding human ecological interactions in the Amazon Basin generally, and Transamazon colonization in particular.

The great bulk of Amazonian research, whether anthropological, agronomic, or ecological, has been highly site specific. There is an absence of systematic coverage of habitat types, of the impact of various types of technologies per habitat type, and of representative aggregate data for major social, ecological, and economic indicators. Perhaps the most systematic sampling carried out in the Amazon has been by agronomists (Sombroeck 1966; Falesi 1972; IPEAN 1974). But even these surveys restricted themselves to sites within close proximity of the Amazon River and the Transamazon Highway respectively, thereby leaving out many habitat types. The heated debate in anthropology over the availability of animal protein in the Amazon and its social and cultural consequences is based chiefly on data from three sites (Chagnon 1968; Holmberg 1969; Siskind 1973), none of which had hunting as the main focus of their research design. As evidence has accumulated in this past decade contrary views have emerged, but all studies, again, have been site specific and do not permit aggregation, since systematic sampling of habitat types has not yet taken place. Despite the lack of systematic sampling applied to soils of the Amazon and to animal biomass productivity per habitat type, there has been no lack of theorizing about the role of proteins in tropical forest societies or about the consequences of poor soils on aboriginal societies or others to follow. Are these debates based on an appropriate sampling procedure capable of addressing the macro-level questions that were posed at the beginning of this chapter?

Much of the available data is simply not comparable but, rather, distinct to particular habitats and levels of technology. Whereas it is normal to seek to understand one level in terms of the other, such a task may not be appropriate. The question before us is, can site-specific studies (micro-level) be the basis of region-wide statements and analyses (macro-level)? A moment's reflection will tell us that extrapolations from one level to another cannot work. In sociology this sliding between levels is known as the "ecological fallacy," wherein statements about individuals are derived from aggregate data (Robinson 1950). It is generally understood that micro- and macro-levels of analysis have distinct goals and answer different questions. Economics long ago recognized this fact formally by distinguishing between macro- and micro-economics. Macro-level studies rely on aggregate data from a broad and representative sample of the universe in question. Micro-level studies rely on careful observation of individuals in a population in order to understand the internal dynamics of the population.

Each level possesses a specificity that is remarkably unique to it, and each level permits the investigator to focus on different types of questions. Questions concerned with *how* certain processes take place are best handled by micro-level studies. Questions which, on the other hand, ask *why* things happen in a given manner call for consideration of external relations and structural constraints. How people are organized into production units calls for site-specific methods. Why they are organized into individual households rather than communal ones for producing goods can only be tackled by a comparative approach heavily reliant on historical, economic, and political analyses of a large and representative sample of data. The macro-study is not only bigger than the sum of the micro-studies, it is structurally different.

Geographers have been particularly aware of the scale problem in reference to trying to comprehend a large region while only studying small areas within it. McCarthy et al. (1956:16) noted that "every change in scale will bring about the statement of a new problem and there is no basis for assuming that associations existing at one scale will also exist at another." The caveats of the 1950s have given way to calls for integration of the macro- and micro-levels of analysis (Beer 1968; Dogan and Rokkam 1969), but the dilemma of bringing together what are different processes remains unresolved.

This concern is part of the larger question of how scientists can delimit their field of study, and what the implications of setting those particular bounds are to the relevance or completeness of the analysis. That the bounds that one sets to one's investigation define the scope and relevance of one's conclusions has long been recognized. What is less frequently noted is that the conclusions at each of these levels are distinct and, at the same time, each one is relevant to a complete understanding of human behavior. The results of a community study may not be generalized to a whole society, but the internal structure of a community is relevant to understanding how a community is affected by larger external forces (Epstein 1964:102). At a level of analysis broader than the community it might appear that the larger external forces shape the life of local communities in relatively homogeneous ways (Watson 1964:155; Blok 1974; Schneider and Schneider 1976). The focus on the community, on the other hand, shows individuals responding positively to actually change the external forces themselves (Bennett 1967), so that communities also affect external forces. Only limited explicit attention has been given to this issue of level shifting (Hagget 1965).

A system under study must be bounded. The thorny issue of how one area of social life within a larger whole can be isolated in order to permit systematic study has been discussed at great length in a volume edited by Gluckman (1964). The authors in that volume concluded that the chief concern was how to bound the system without omitting anything relevant or important. They concluded that a social anthropologist is justified, and can be most productive, if he/she restricts the scope to what they call micro-sociology and leaves aggregate phenomena to macro-sociologists, economists, and political scientists. While such an allocation of research interests has been productive for all the disciplines involved, it has not facilitated study of how local and larger social units dynamically relate to each other. I believe that by thinking about levels of analysis along disciplinary lines it has been possible to ignore some important questions: What is the relationship between types of data and a given level of analysis? and What does one learn about human adaptation from each level of analysis?

It has not been sufficiently recognized that each level's scope obscures relationships observable at other levels, particularly as one moves from local research to regional or national levels (Devons and Gluckman 1964: 211). The greater the scope of the level, the less are details of group and individual behavior and ideology analytically recognized. There are, for example, significant differences in the mean demographic behavior of small and large populations because of greater variation in the former. The scale of the researched area also affects the analytic results in significant ways. The Amazon is a perfect case in point. Confusion over the area in question is common. Some writers, as we have here, use the term to refer to the Amazon Basin, the drainage area of the Amazon River and its tributaries. Others use the legal definition used in Brazil for development planning (*Amazonia legal*), which includes large areas of savannas in the central plateau. Others define it by rainfall parameters. Since population distribution is usually uneven, small areal units have a wider range and variance of population distribution than larger units such as countries or large regions like the Amazon. Likewise, since mobility occurs mainly over short distances, small areal units are critical to micro-demographics but appear as insignificant in aggregated data as compared to natural changes in population (J. Clarke 1976). Thus the relative significance of migration and natural change depends more on the size of the area studied (level of analysis) than on real demographic differences. The relationship of the particular to the general is a scale-linkage problem that remains incompletely resolved (cf. Hagget 1967).

This lack of recognition is evident in the frequency with which analysts use micro-level data to address regional or national issues and the even more frequent use of aggregate data to design programs to be implemented at the local level. What has been missing from both research and policy-making is the conscious acknowledgement that each level addresses very different kinds of processes and that generalizations should confine themselves to the level in which the research took place.

Ellen considers the issue of "analytical closure or boundedness" as central to both social and ecological studies. He argues that the most important consideration in bounding a system at either the local or the regional level is whether or not the system is able to reproduce itself within that unit (1979:10). The elegant notion of "system" or "ecosystem" that has gained popularity since the 1960s tends to cloud over the difficulty of bounding an analytical unit. Anyone familiar with the ecosystem concept will readily recognize that the ecosystem is a flexible unit which is bounded by the needs of the researcher. It seldom, if ever, has characteristics which facilitate replicability, nor is it obvious on reading a study what the breadth of the study was—Was it an intensive study of a household, a village, a valley, a geoeconomic region, a nation, or a biome? The positive uses of the ecosystem concept are many and I, in no way, wish to denigrate the many ways that this concept serves to emphasize the interconnectedness of the living and nonliving components of the biosphere. What I wish to point out, however, is that reference to the ecosystem as one's unit of analysis has produced results that address important human ecological relations within a single level—not to the whole of the human adjustments.

Geertz was the first anthropologist to argue for the usefulness of the ecosystem as a unit of analysis in social cultural anthropology. In *Agricultural Involution* (1963) he tested Steward's emphasis on subsistence and found it wanting. He showed by a broad use of historical records that

Indonesia's agricultural patterns could be understood only in terms of the economic restrictions of the Dutch colonial authorities. In fact, Geertz used the *region* of Indonesia as his ecosystem unit. He identified two contrasting agricultural systems and discovered their roots in the historical development of Indonesia's colonial economy.

In contrast, Rappaport's study of ritual and ecology in the New Guinea Highlands (1968) defined the ecosystem unit in terms of the material exchanges of a *local population*. This difference is not surprising given the flexibility of the ecosystem concept in biology. But how can one compare studies which deal with ecosystemic interactions at different levels? In the last chapter of *Pigs for the Ancestors* (1968) Rappaport acknowledged that a local population engages in material and nonmaterial exchanges with *other local populations* which, in the aggregate, can be called "regional populations." These, he suggests, are likely to be more appropriate units of analysis for long-range evolutionary studies, given the ephemeral quality of local populations (1968:226). Unfortunately, other anthropologists did not follow up on this insight into the differences between relatively synchronic micro-level studies and diachronic macro-level approaches.

From study of the varied uses of the ecosystem unit by Rappaport and Geertz, and from the examination of debates surrounding the human occupation of the Amazon Basin, I began to pursue the possible association between levels of analysis and major points of disagreement in Amazonian studies. Anthropologists have long used local communities as their fundamental units of study wherein a cultural or ethnographic method could be applied (Steward 1950:21). Most scholars have been quite aware that individual communities are part of larger wholes, but such functional interdependencies have seldom become a part of the analysis itself.

It has been common in ecological anthropology to carry out studies in local communities in order to facilitate the quantification of variables or to study populations before the full impact of the modern world reaches them (Rappaport 1968; Nietschmann 1973; Waddell 1972; Moran 1975; Baker and Little 1976). While all these researchers recognize the value of addressing larger population and ecological units, they have chosen to limit the scope of the investigation for the sake of precise data gathering. In such studies, the community is seen as a closed system for the purposes of analysis. While such a device has undoubtedly provided great insight into internal functional patterns, it has tended to neglect the relations of the community to the outside world and the impact of the outside world upon the community's structure and function. Localized studies provide insight into family structure, subsistence strategies, labor inputs, health and nutritional status, flow of energy, socialization, and cultural institutions. Studies at this level cannot address issues of social evolution, explain changes in the economic structure of society, patterns of economic development, or political economy. These issues can be addressed only with a different type of research method which emphasizes historical, geographical, economic, and political change over time.

Ecological anthropological studies will always require investigation of the way local populations interact with other components in the local ecosystem. The case for an emphasis on micro-level study in ecology has been convincingly argued by Brookfield (1970:20), who pointed out that an adaptive system can best be studied at this level because such a system model "acquires the closest orthomorphism with empirical fact." Nevertheless, regional analyses add a very different and much needed insight into the processes of human adaptation. A regional study emphasizes historical and economic factors and considers many local-level phenomena as secondary to the historical forces at play (cf. Braudel 1973; Smith, Thomas 1959; Bloch 1966). It is notable that the regional analyses of both Geertz (1963) and Bennett (1969) predominantly use historical factors in explanation. Bennett defined the region of the North American Northern Plains in terms of its historical unity (1969:26). He was able to explain the adaptive strategies of four distinct ethnic groups in terms of differential access to resources, differential access to power loci, and social/cultural differences. Thus, while he was able to flesh out the social/cultural details of the population through local interviews and by studying ethnic interactions, an understanding of the operative historical and economic forces required aggregate data from social and economic history. Such a choice of level can come only from a recognition of the appropriate level at which certain questions can be addressed. Julian Steward's difficulties in achieving his goals in his Puerto Rico study can be traced to a failure to shift from his micro-level analysis of a group's "culture core" to macro-level analysis of the Puerto Rican political economy. Steward's earlier micro-level studies had successfully generated sophisticated analyses of the internal structure of patrilineal bands and their articulation with selected habitat features. The Puerto Rico study, however, needed to move beyond the study of specific human/habitat interactions and move towards a dynamic model of structural transformations and relate the articulation of Puerto Rican communities to the World System through which many community features could be understood through time.

The relevance of the above considerations about levels of analysis and the scale of sampling appropriate to answering given questions helps shed light on some of the major questions asked about human occupation of the Amazon. An examination of the levels at which generalizations have been made will serve both to suggest the articulation between levels and to identify some of the major gaps in our current knowledge about the area. Of special interest will be the results from studies of soils, use of other environmental resources, healthfulness of the region, provision of agricultural inputs to colonization, and the analysis of the constraints to development.

Levels of Analysis and Amazonian Soils

The problem of scale emerges at the outset as one of the fundamental problems in the ability to differentiate between Amazonian soils. Most maps available are at a scale of from 1:100,000 to 1:500,000. These macro-scale maps show the soils of the Amazon to be primarily oxisols (latosols), with a small area of inceptisols (alluvial soils) along the flood plain (National Academy of Science 1972). If a connection is attempted between these soils and the human use of them, as is often the case, discussions will emphasize that these soils are problematic; their utilization is restricted to long fallow swidden agriculture with shifting of fields every two to three years due to rapid declines in fertility caused by the loss of the limited nutrients made available after the burn. A great deal of the prevalent pessimism about the potential of the Amazon as a settlement area is based on this level of analysis.

But how representative is the available data? Does it provide an adequate enough representative sample of the whole basin to permit macro-level generalizations about the region's potential? Reliance, until recently, on the simple dichotomy between the flood plain (2 percent) and the terra firme (98 percent) is at a level of generality not likely to generate systematic scaling of the Amazonian regional system, and suggests that the two areas are more similar than is likely to be the case. Given the difficulties of approaching the problem of local and regional variation, some researchers have suggested the use of "nested sampling" (Hagget 1967:175). Such an approach serves to sample a region in a systematic manner by sampling a number of units at different scale levels: region, sub-region, district, sub-district, and localities. Studies done elsewhere have noted that variability increases with movement down to the micro-scale units in the sampling process. For the Amazon there is no available soil mapping at a scale that permits observation of specific soils, except for a few isolated localities (Furley 1979; Ranzani 1978). Is the absence of such detailed micro-scaled maps critical?

When one changes the scale from the Amazon as a whole to specific sub-regions, the homogeneity evident at the regional level yields to increased variability. Instead of two soil types, three to five become common. Not only is there increased detail in visible soil types, but even the areal extent of soil types may be misjudged (Ranzani 1978). A technologically sophisticated aerial survey of the Amazon using sideways-looking radar (RADAM 1974) at a scale of 1:100,000 observed that the dominant soil type in the sub-region of Marabá was that of ultisols. A localized study by Ranzani in Marabá (1978), at a scale of 1:10,000, concluded that oxisols constituted 65 percent, entisols 22 percent, and ultisols *only* 13 percent of the soils in the area in question. Scale is important when variability is present.

Whereas maps at a scale of 1:100,000 to 1:500,000 may be useful in matters of geologic history and geomorphology and answering general questions about the relationship between soils and biotic productivity, speciation, and climate, they are of little use in addressing questions about the human use of resources, the social organization and structure of human communities, and their adaptive strategies. The general unavailability of micro-scale mapping has been a major obstacle to the study of human ecological processes in the Amazon and may explain the use of macro-scale maps by investigators. Nevertheless, the difficulties resulting from generalizations based on macro-scale maps need to be recognized.

The problem lies in the different amounts of information that can be included in a soil map. Maps in orders of 1:20,000 and up are not useful for land management. A planner or a researcher using such a map will assume that all the soils labeled with a particular name will have the same characteristics, as does a "typical profile." Yet, soils within the same order, say oxisols, and within close proximity to each other, may still differ significantly in effective cation exchange capacity, in exchangeable aluminum, in pH, in water retention capacity, and in nutrient levels in different horizons (Buol and Couto 1978:71). A macro-scale map might suggest that soil users can move from place to place with a uniform land management approach and can expect similar results everywhere. This has been, in fact, a dominant viewpoint in anthropological writings about the Amazon tropical rain forest peoples. Given the lack of micro-scale studies of a sufficient number of areas by systematic sampling, it has been easy for investigators to dismiss variations as "non-representative" and to accept the macro-scale data. Such a decision is incorrect from the point of view of geographical sampling (Duncan, Cuzzort, and Duncan 1961) and its analytical implications.

From the point of view of policy, reliance on macro-scale maps has had serious consequences. The decision to focus colonization along the Transamazon Highway in Altamira was based on the identification of medium to high fertility alfisols, which appeared to dominate in the region cut by the road. Colonists were placed on all available lots as they arrived, since soils appeared homogeneously good, and the same crops were promoted. It was not until the colonists were settled on their land that micro-level soil sampling was carried out by Moran (1975a), Smith (1976a), and Fearnside (1978) in the Altamira area, and by Ranzani (1978) and Smith (1976a) in the Marabá region. These investigators discovered that the soils of the area are a patchwork, with radical differences in nearly every kilometer. Thus, the soils of Altamira were highly variable, with the medium to high fertility alfisols making up only 8 percent of the total soils and being scattered in small patches.

The recognition that land use planning can only take place at the micro-level could have led to a different pattern of occupation, a less homogeneous effort at agricultural extension, reduced likelihood of loan defaults due merely to location on soils too poor for farming, and reduction of many other problems that affected the performance of farmers in the Transamazon and which were discussed earlier in this book. Macro-level land planning led to the promotion of three cereal crops throughout the region and later to cattle or plantation crops.

Not only was planning affected by the inappropriate macro-perspective to land planning, but so was the evaluation of farmer performance. Whereas some farmers familiar with Amazonian micro-variability refused to go along with the practices promoted by the government and obtained good yields from their diversified agricultural operations, the use of aggregate production data, rather than farm management surveys, hid the differential performance of farmers and led to a reduction of support to the whole small-farming population. Instead of identifying the strategies that worked, as a good farm management survey would have done, the aggregate analysis provided no details about what management practices worked, but only stated that the output did not meet expectations set before the project began. At the evaluation stage, the agencies involved used inappropriate quantitative tools to measure farmers' productivity, to identify limiting factors, and to correct actions. All that the aggregate analysis measured was the output of the sector in response to inputs provided. The analysis did not show, *and could not show*, that the inputs were not timed to the needs of farmers, that institutional performance was a constraint in itself, and that the technological inputs were in part responsible for the low yields in two out of the three years measured. The micro-level analysis of Vila Roxa farming carried out earlier in this book brought out the variability in farmers' responses to available soils and natural resources. I have shown here and elsewhere (Moran 1979b) that the caboclo population had precise knowledge of forest resources and soil types, and that they got better results than did farmers following practices promoted by the planners. Their use of the region's resources is more complete, more rational, and more efficient than that of outsiders.

Levels of Analysis and the Amazon's Healthfulness

Most ecological studies which address problems of populations in the humid tropics inevitably cite poor health conditions and health status as serious constraints on the well-being of these populations. Indeed, a number of potential health problems are present in the tropics, and without adequate control they can become serious obstacles to human adaptability. However, my micro-level analysis has shown that farmers lost fewer working days due to illness than they lost in the process of obtaining credit and other dealings with government institutions. In fact, they lost no more days due to illness (11.5 days) than the standard number of "sick days" currently allotted to American (U.S.) state government employees (12 days per year).

Several of the most common health problems in Vila Roxa and elsewhere in the Transamazon resulted from the low economic status of the population, and are traditionally reduced with an increase in purchasing power. The most severe problems required some modification in cultural understanding: better knowledge of how vegetation falls when cut (trauma) and better knowledge of how the malarial plasmodium behaves in the body (to reduce the incidence of insufficient dosages of medication). Health problems, then, were not a significant deterrent to productivity, although they can be if the income of the population declines and nutritional intake is reduced. The difficulties in farm productivity, as we have seen, are in no small part a result of the mismatch between macro-level policy and evaluation and the micro-level realities of farm households managing very diverse production factors, which are unrecognized by those providing the inputs.

Levels of Analysis and the Provision of Inputs

Macro-level analyses had often cited that in the Amazon and elsewhere the lack of sufficient credit was a major obstacle to increases in food production. In the Amazon Basin, analysts have added that the archaic system of aviamento, wherein traders controlled the supply of goods to the Amazon interior and long-term credit was extended at exorbitant rates, was fundamental to the permanence of the region in a state of underdevelopment. The macro-level solution to this situation was to provide credit at favorable rates through the normal channels of the Bank of Brazil. In making such a policy decision, planners failed to take into consideration: (a) the structure of social relations, (b) the costs of monitoring the credit worthiness of a population in a rain forest region, (c) the differential experience of farmers with bank credit, and (d) the traditional forms of allocating cash inputs—all micro-level constraints on the use of capital resources. Nor did the planning process allow for the imperfections in the administration of inputs by government agencies at the local level. Credit institutions were unable to release funds in accordance with the agricultural schedule of the specific areas in question. Extension agents were unable to monitor the progress of farm work, yet continued to require elaborate procedures designed to monitor credit worthiness. The aggregated data showed a high rate of credit default; however, the reasons for such defaults could only come from farm management surveys—micro-level studies at the level of the individual farm, which were not part of the monitoring process in the colonization scheme.

Micro-level analysis of the cost of credit has shown earlier that costs have been unreasonably high. Cost of loans was not the 7 percent per annum face cost, but was 50 percent due to lost labor time in obtaining release of funds. Moreover, lack of previous experience in using agricultural credit led to misallocation. Clientilistic farmers tended to consume their loans rather than apply them to the intensive use of limited areas, as did brokers. Micro-level analyses might have led to the creation of education programs geared at improved management of capital resources.

The credit structure created reflected stereotypes about "modernization" and the realities of the Brazilian economic system. Manioc and other root crops were associated with the Northeast and the Amazon Basin, both viewed in Brasilia as economically-backward areas. In order to modernize, planners saw the change of crops as a vehicle to socio-economic change. In addition, the growing urban populations of Brazil consume large amounts of rice, corn, and beans. By giving credit for the cultivation of these three crops they expected that they would not only be modernizing Amazonian agriculture, but also be providing a product with high demand in national markets. Although such a view reflects considerable naiveté about how to get agriculture moving, it does not really tell us why the credit schemes failed.

The problem can also be understood if one analyzes the influence of external bureaucratic factors within the micro-context. Before the creation of a small farm sector in the Amazon, the banks had preferred to give large loans to ranchers. The shift in policy in 1970 was forced upon the banks from above. This formal change in policy, however, could not legislate the informal behavior of credit personnel. Bank managers did not treat all farmers equally, as the presidential fiat might suggest and as planning might have it. Rather, they gave better credit deals to farmers capable of interactive behavior which they recognized as equal to theirs (e.g., entrepreneurial farmers, "having a future"), and those who had cattle ranching as an objective. The administrative costs of establishing a few cattle enterprises is less for the bank and the government than are the costs of providing numerous small loans (Katzman 1976). Schemes to produce manioc flour on a commercial scale did not receive much attention, despite the scarcity of manioc flour in the region and evidence in local markets that its price per kilo was four times that of rice.

Credit institutions were also not attuned to the agronomic constraints to cereal production in some parts of the Amazon Basin. While cereals can be grown in the Amazon Basin, they are more susceptible to pests and diseases, and require soils of higher initial fertility than do root crops.

Though cereals could be grown well on alfisols, they would not fare so well on oxisols and ultisols. They also usually require substantial fertilizer inputs after the first or second year of cultivation, but levels of fertilizer input for tropical soils have as yet to be worked out per crop and per soil type (Tropical Soils Research Program 1976:137).

The aggregated data from the banks and the government food wholesaler, CIBRAZEM, showed that low amounts of rice, corn, and beans had been marketed by Transamazon farmers. These low production levels were attributed to the low level of technology in use and the lack of entrepreneurial spirit among the farmers. It was a case, as Wood and Schmink (1979) have reminded us, of blaming the victim. The negative evaluation of farmer performance comes as no surprise when one considers the inappropriateness of the data. Input/output data for a sector created a mere three years before could have hardly yielded results capable of explaining poor performance. Only micro-level farm management investigations could have gotten to those factors.

Macro- and Micro-Approaches to Development

Cardoso and Müller (1977), Bunker (1978:23), and Wood and Schmink (1979) attribute the shift in policy from small farming to large-scale development in 1974 to contradictions in the Brazilian authoritarian system. On the one hand, the regime seeks legitimation through the execution of socially-beneficial schemes, and on the other hand, yields to pressures from the dominant capitalist sector, which supports its continued existence. These internal contradictions reflect the ambivalence of a regime seeking permanence but aware that its benefits are inequitably distributed. These contradictions, in turn, negate possible benefits that might be derived from the socially-oriented projects undertaken. The lack of institutional cooperation, the high cost of access to government services, and the imposition of unfamiliar regulations and inappropriate crop priorities have directly contributed to the low levels of performance by farmers, which has justified the reduction of incentives to the small farm sector. This conclusion is entirely justified.

However, such an analysis addresses only macro-level structural constraints and neglects other considerations of, at least, comparable significance in understanding the process. While I will not deny the structural contradictions in the process of Transamazon colonization, I have shown in this book that nearly 40 percent of the small farmers in a micro-level study had achieved broker or rural manager status and respectable levels of income and productivity; had assumed religious and economic leadership in their communities; and are expanding their landholdings, cattle herds, and productive capacities. Emphasis on the exploitation of rural labor by external capitalism homogenizes the colonist population into an undifferentiated peasantry. In fact, some of these same farmers became, not just tools of capitalism, but capitalists themselves.

Emphasis on the macro-level would deny that 40 percent of the Vila Roxa population their real accomplishments in the face of the multilevel constraints posed by institutions, interest groups in the authoritarian state, and the complex ecological variability from place to place in the Amazon. It is often forgotten that most farmers are still on their land (80 percent), that new ones arrive each day from throughout Brazil to claim tracts, and that levels of production have increased more often than they have decreased.

It is all too common when discussing development or human adaptation from a macro-perspective to forget that at that level it is the population which "develops" or "adapts," not the individuals. While it may be true that the human species has shown remarkable adaptability to the varied environments of the earth, this is not equivalent to saying that local populations or individuals show comparable adaptability. Indeed, the concept of adaptation should always specify "adaptive for whom?" since what is adaptive to an individual may spell ruin for the group and yet benefit the biotic environment due to reduced pressure (Ellen 1979). Rappaport, in the final chapter of *Pigs for the Ancestors* (1968), noted that local populations were highly ephemeral, which is not to say that the species is maladaptive. I have shown elsewhere (Moran 1975) that local populations hold on to familiar strategies of resource use even in radically different environments, sometimes with disastrous consequences (cf. Laughlin and Brady 1978). New ecological and economic structures allow some individuals to develop appropriate strategies, while others will continue to rely on familiar strategies that satisfy minimum survival requirements. Some individuals and groups in a local population will adapt more than others to changing environments. While no one has yet dared to quantify such a proposition, I dare say that there are probably more failures than successes in the process of human adaptation to new environmental settings. While such a prospect appears gloomy, it also represents the necessary process of adaptation—in which individuals possessing a variable set of qualities and resources are differentially capable of responding to changes in their environment. The alternative to this process would be to have a homogeneous population whose inventory of strategies might lack solutions to as yet unforeseen circumstances.

Human adaptation and social differentiation do not occur in a vacuum. This process of social reproduction reflects the adaptation of the Transamazon population to local habitat (micro), to the economic and structural realities of the Brazilian nation, and to the ability to function within the social field provided by a colonization setting and a rain forest environment (macro). About 40 percent of the population of Vila Roxa suc-

ceeded by making these and other appropriate adjustments to both micro-
and macro-level constraints. This 40 percent has differentiated itself from
the other 60 percent by assuming the status of rural managers, a status
that was neither inherited nor achieved by inhumane exploitation of the
60 percent majority. In fact, it was the 60 percent which began to refer
to the other 40 percent as "patron" and to reestablish the hierarchical
order to which they were adapted in dependency-breeding plantations.
That as many as 40 percent of the population have been able to adjust
despite relatively lowly beginnings is a remarkable achievement for any
population. For instance, only about 18 percent were able to achieve
comparable control over their economic activities in Marabá (Velho 1976:
208). These differences may be due to ecological constraints, greater structural conflicts between colonists and large-scale developers, and differences
in the make-up of the population itself (Velho 1972; Smith 1976a; Gall
1978; Fearnside 1978; Wood and Schmink 1979).

The development of the Amazon is constrained by a centralized approach to planning and implementation. This approach did not begin in
1964, but has deep historical roots (Roett 1972). The priorities set for
the development of the Amazon were aggregate in character: to improve
Brazil's foreign exchange balance, to promote national integration, and
to reduce social tensions in the Northeast. In none of the planning
documents is there mention of the project in terms of micro-level processes. The performance of Brazil's agricultural sector has kept up with the
rapid increase in population and its demand for food only through the
opening up of new lands (Schuh 1970), not through improved performance of the sector. To some degree this is the result of the economics of
frontier agriculture vis-à-vis post-frontier intensification (Margolis 1979).
It is also a result of the patrimonial or authoritarian structure of Brazil's
bureaucracy, which has been incapable of using anything other than aggregate inputs for policy-making.

The choice made in 1974 to turn to large-scale development took place
because of the structure of the Brazilian bureaucracy and the aggregate
inputs that serve to formulate its policies. Hirschman has pointed out that
planners tend to be biased against programs that involve technological un-
certainties and prefer to avoid projects that involve dealing with large
numbers of people (1967:39–44). The problem is, thus, general to all
bureaucratic structures. In Brazil's case that structure is also remarkably
centralized (i.e., authoritarian), which makes the structure of decision-
making even less amenable to inputs from micro-level studies. The more
centralized the structure of decision-making, the less able it is to process
complex information incorporating the variability present in any areally
extensive system. The result is a structure of decision-making which is
insensitive to micro-level variability and has a tendency to homogenization
of both environmental and social variables. Economists have noted that

the result of economic policies in Brazil since 1964 has been to increase the gap between income groups, to a more evident distinction between haves and have-nots. Ecologists have also noted a tendency to treat the Amazon as a forest which can be cleared with equivalent results anywhere. The question which is central to the future of the Amazon region is whether or not the structure of the Brazilian bureaucracy is capable of adjusting its policies to include inputs from specific sites to optimize productivity and conservation per site. The implications of such a structural change will be explored in a future publication (Moran n.d.).

Articulating Levels of Analysis

The analytical articulation of micro- with macro-levels of analysis is still in a conceptual and methodological developmental stage. Responsible for the current state of ambiguity are the disciplinary lines followed by most investigators and a tendency to work within a given level, to the exclusion of the other. Nevertheless, scientists are often expected to address questions and make generalizations that reach beyond the bounds of the level at which they work. It is in overextending the natural limits of a given level that problems have arisen in the interpretation of processes such as the potential of the Amazon, the productivity and management of the soils, the obstacles to colonization, and the balance between conservation and productivity.

For the purposes of field research, it is seldom practical to try to investigate more than one level. But as the debates that have been reviewed earlier would suggest, to mix levels leads to unproductive debates, which obscure the complex processes studied. Levels are hierarchically structured and exhibit both vertical and horizontal interactions. Most research has focused upon horizontal interactions within a given level. Vertical hierarchical organization has received much less attention and remains problematic both theoretically and methodologically.

Minimally, the first requirement to overcome the current dilemma is the recognition of the distinctiveness of levels of analysis. Once they are recognized, the differences between levels pose little difficulty for specific empirical studies with limited and clear objectives. A study of a sample of groups in a rural community makes it possible to generalize about group structure, although not about the structure of peasantries. To arrive at the latter type of generalization requires systematic comparisons of a fair number of different groups in different rural areas—ideally, a representative sample of them. In short, the research design must be adapted to the level of organization to be explained, and explanations must be confined to that level. Each explanation nests within the other level and operates within the general constraints set by the other level. Thus, while each hypothesis is restricted to a particular level of analysis, structural and functional aspects of ecosystems are affected by processes at other levels. Each hierarchical level adds a layer to our understanding of the total human adaptational situation. Levels, while distinct, are continuous and not dichotomous (Goldscheider 1971:39–44). What this distinction implies is that we must confront this methodological and sampling problem in the hopes of clarifying explanations of the human adaptive process. While we should all aspire to integrate macro- and micro-level explanations, this integration cannot be achieved by mixing levels between the data-gathering and the interpretational stages. Synthesis can only result from preliminary separation of micro- and macro-analyses. Only after the level-specific processes have been interpreted can we hope for a reintegration of the levels.

Amazonian studies stand to benefit a great deal from the clear separation between levels of analysis. The micro-level adjustments studied by ecologically-oriented social scientists need to be clarified in light of the modifications of these adjustments resulting from macro-level processes, such as the capitalization of the countryside, the creation of dependence on formal organizations, and the extraction of surplus to fuel the Brazilian and international urban-industrial complex. Most anthropological studies see the impact of these macro-level processes upon local communities as a serious loss. Indeed, viewing local communities as affected by and affecting regional, national, and international processes changes many of the considerations that individuals must evaluate in making decisions, and the potential for individual loss is probably increased. It is highly doubtful that local communities, even in "isolated areas of the Amazon," have ever been truly "closed" and therefore naturally bounded as units of analysis. The bounding is a product of the types of questions being asked by the investigator. Amazonian community studies have yielded useful analyses about social organization, cultural values, and subsistence systems in specific human communities. Less successful have been efforts to connect these micro-level studies to regional-level questions. Regional-level approaches have successfully addressed questions about the conflict between the goals of national and international entities and local populations, between production and conservation, and between development at a regional scale and decreases in living standards by individuals.

Amazonian Potential

The next decade will further clarify the question of the potential of the Amazon. There is increased recognition that the region is very heterogeneous and probably varies a great deal in fragility and/or resiliency from place to place. We already know that white-sand/black-water river watersheds are particularly susceptible to desertification. The soils are extremely variable throughout the basin and demand site-specific strategies of utilization. Clearly, areas with low initial soil fertility should be protected from predatory forms of exploitation, and reserves should be created to prevent a breakdown in the closed nutrient cycle of the forest. Macro-level approaches, whether through region-wide colonization or the promotion of development poles (e.g., Polamazonia), are too macro- to permit the development of the necessary site-specific strategies of resource use. What is needed is a nested approach to resource use, as discussed earlier: building up systematic sampling of sub-regions, districts, and localities so that information flows from specific sites through each level of the hierarchy in order to permit adjustment to variation. Continued study of human communities under a variety of conditions and levels of integration to the regional, national, and international community is needed to better understand the balance between social development and environmental conservation in the Amazon.

The current state of knowledge is too fragmentary and the forms of exploitation too insensitive to micro-level variation to assert that the limiting factor to Amazonian development is everywhere environmental, rather than structural and resulting from inappropriate macro-level policies. The success of Transamazon colonization was mixed. Using government projections as a standard against which to measure success, the colonization proved a failure. Such projections, however, were optimistic in the extreme and failed to take into consideration the common obstacles faced by a population adjusting to an unfamiliar habitat, the difficulty of delivering inputs according to a site-specific agricultural schedule, and the insensitivity of the planning policies in addressing local needs. At the local level it is possible to see numerous success stories of individuals who, with limited means, achieved remarkable results, and who provide insight into the strategies that may work in creating productive agricultural systems.

Predicting the future of the Amazon does not seem a profitable exercise. The danger of continued deforestation without adequate knowledge of its consequences to specific areas is real and worrisome. On the other hand, the pace of research has quickened and useful results have in some cases been incorporated into conservation plans. The continued decimation of aboriginal peoples is a loss of major consequence, but efforts to guarantee them rights to land will probably meet with increased success as the international community pressures Brazil into obeying its own Constitution. The Amazon will continue to be exploited, sometimes poorly, sometimes disastrously, and in time, perhaps, wisely. The monolithic developmental strategies used until now may give way to the needed flexible strategies capable of incorporating diversity of local conditions into the execution of projects designed to exploit the land, provide jobs and income, and achieve the multiple goals pursued by citizens and nation alike. These multiple goals will not be achieved easily. They can be made a part of policy only when there is change in the bureaucratic structures around which Brazil is organized as a nation, when micro-level information can be processed by those same structures, and when decisions reflect the existence of many Amazons, not just of a homogeneous one.

Appendix: Soil Analyses

SOILS UNDER FOREST

	pH[a]	P[b] (PPM)	K[c]	Ca+Mg[d]	SUM OF EX-CHANGEABLE BASES	EXCHANGE-ABLE[e] ALUMINUM	EFFECTIVE CEC	C[f] (%)	N[g] (%)	O.M.[h] (%)	C/N RATIO	SOIL COLOR[i] (WET)
					(IN MILLIEQUIVALENTS PER 100 GRAMS)							
	4.9	1	0.08	0.05	0.58	0.4	0.98	0.53	0.05	0.91	11	10 YR 4/4
	5.7	1	0.35	5.4	5.75	Traces	5.75	1.58	0.16	2.71	10	5 YR 3/4.5
	4.1	4	0.04	0.1	0.14	1.0	1.14	0.68	0.06	1.17	11	10 YR 4/4
	5.8	1	0.18	7.2	7.38	Traces	7.38	1.29	0.23	2.23	6	10 R 2/3
	4.0	1	0.09	0.3	0.39	2.5	2.89	1.11	0.12	1.90	9	10 YR 4/4.5
Average	4.9	1.6	0.15	2.7	2.85	0.78	3.68	1.04	0.12	1.78	9.2	
Range	4.0–5.8	1–4	0.04–0.35	0.03–7.2	0.14–5.75	Traces–2.5	0.98–7.38	0.53–1.58	0.05–0.23	0.91–2.71	6–11	

[a] Determined potentiometrically in water using a glass electrode.
[b] Extracted by use of 0.025 NH_2SO_4 solution and determined colorimetrically in acid solution of Ammonium molybdate.
[c] Extracted by use of 0.025 NH_2SO_4 solution and determined with a flame photometer.
[d] Extracted by using a 1.00 N solution of KCl and determined with 0.025 N of EDTA.
[e] Extracted using a 1.00 N Solution of KCl and determined with 0.025 N or N_2OH.
[f] Determined by use of 0.4 N solution of Potassium dichromate.
[g] Determined by use of Kjaldahl digestion flask and 0.02 NHCl solution.
[h] Calculated according to the formula O.M. % = % C = % C × 1.72 (where 1.72 is k factor used to convert C to O.M.).
[i] Determined by use of color chips in M. Oyama and H. Takehara, Revised Standard Soil Color Charts, 1967.

SOILS IN NEWLY BURNED FIELDS

pH	P (PPM)	K	CA+MG	SUM OF EX-CHANGEABLE BASES	EXCHANGE-ABLE ALUMINUM	EFFECTIVE CEC	C (%)	N (%)	O.M. (%)	C/N RATIO	SOIL COLOR (WET)
		(IN MILLIEQUIVALENTS PER 100 GRAMS)									
7.2	32	0.79	7.9	8.69	Traces	8.69	1.58	0.22	2.71	7	10 R 3/6
5.2	6	0.55	6.5	7.05	0.1	7.15	1.36	0.19	2.34	7	5 YR 4/4
5.0	5	0.33	3.7	4.03	0.2	4.23	1.63	0.19	2.80	9	5 YR 6/6
4.7	5	0.11	1.9	2.01	0.9	2.91	1.96	0.19	3.37	10	7.5 YR 4/3.5
Average 5.5	12	0.44	5.0	5.44	0.3	5.44	1.63	0.20	2.80	8	
Range 4.7–7.2	5–32	0.11–0.79	1.9–7.9	2.01–8.69	Traces–0.9	2.91–8.69	1.36–1.96	0.19–0.22	2.34–3.37	7–10	

Soils in First Year of Cultivation

pH	P (PPM)	K	Ca+Mg	Sum of Exchangeable Bases	Exchangeable Aluminum	Effective CEC	C (%)	N (%)	O.M. (%)	C/N Ratio	Soil Color (Wet)
			(In milliequivalents per 100 grams)								
4.1	2	0.20	1.3	1.50	5.9	7.4	1.83	0.26	3.15	7	7.5 YR 4/3.5
5.6	35	0.24	4.5	4.74	0.2	4.94	1.33	0.17	2.29	8	5 YR 3/3.5
4.3	4	0.16	0.5	0.66	5.0	5.66	3.20	0.24	5.51	13	7.5 YR 3/3
4.5	3	0.04	0.6	0.64	0.7	0.8	0.85	0.06	1.47	14	10 YR 4/3.5
4.5	1	0.04	0.6	0.64	1.0	1.64	0.81	0.08	1.39	10	10 YR 2/3
5.8	6	0.09	3.6	3.69	Traces	3.69	0.79	0.07	1.36	11	10 YR 4/4.5
4.7	3	0.05	1.2	1.25	0.8	2.05	1.01	0.09	1.74	11	10 YR 4/4.5
6.2	13	0.12	2.9	3.02	Traces	3.02	0.60	0.08	1.03	8	10 YR 3/3
5.2	1	0.09	5.4	5.49	Traces	5.49	1.11	0.16	1.90	7	5 YR 3/4
4.5	1	0.25	1.5	1.75	5.6	7.35	1.78	0.22	3.06	8	7.5 YR 4/5.6
4.5	5	0.22	0.1	0.32	5.6	5.92	5.69	0.38	9.78	15	5 YR 2/1.5
4.2	1	0.05	0.2	0.25	1.0	1.25	0.79	0.06	1.35	13	10 YR 4/4
4.1	2	0.05	0.1	0.15	1.2	1.35	1.14	0.08	1.95	14	10 YR 4/4
6.2	26	0.85	12.4	13.25	Traces	13.25	2.67	0.43	4.60	6	7.5 YR 3/1.5
Average 4.9	7.4	0.175	2.5	2.67	1.9	4.56	2.04	0.17	2.90	10	
Range 4.1–6.2	1–35	0.04–0.85	0.1–12.4	0.25–13.25	Traces–5.9	0.8–13.25	0.60–5.69	0.06–0.43	1.03–9.78	6–15	

SOILS IN SECOND YEAR OF CULTIVATION

pH	P (PPM)	K	CA+MG	SUM OF EX-CHANGEABLE BASES	EXCHANGE-ABLE ALUMINUM	EFFECTIVE CEC	C (%)	N (%)	O.M. (%)	C/N RATIO	SOIL COLOR (WET)
			(IN MILLIEQUIVALENTS PER 100 GRAMS)								
5.4	6	0.17	1.8	1.97	0.2	2.17	0.58	0.05	1.00	12	7.5 YR 4/6
4.8	1	0.13	1.5	1.63	1.8	3.43	0.99	0.09	1.70	11	10 YR 4/6
5.0	5	0.12	2.4	2.52	0.4	2.92	1.16	0.09	2.00	13	10 YR 3/2.5
5.2	3	0.59	0.7	1.29	1.9	3.19	1.27	0.12	2.19	11	10 YR 3/4
4.7	1	0.04	0.3	0.34	1.4	1.74	0.55	0.05	0.95	11	10 YR 5/4.5
4.6	2	0.19	0.7	0.89	5.6	6.49	3.82	0.22	6.58	17	7.5 YR 2/2.5
6.9	35	0.15	5.5	5.65	Traces	5.65	0.83	0.11	1.42	8	7.5 YR 3/4
5.0	3	0.05	0.9	0.95	Traces	0.95	0.36	0.04	0.62	9	10 YR 4/4.5
6.3	14	0.25	3.3	3.55	Traces	3.55	0.68	0.07	1.17	10	10 YR 3/3.5
5.2	6	0.25	6.1	6.35	Traces	6.35	1.92	0.18	3.29	11	7.5 YR 4/3.5
4.4	1	0.06	0.8	0.86	1.8	2.66	0.74	0.08	1.27	9	10 YR 5/6
5.9	5	0.32	6.4	6.72	Traces	6.72	1.08	0.15	1.85	7	10 YR 4/4.5
Average 5.3	6.8	0.19	2.5	2.73	1.8	3.82	1.16	0.10	2.0	11	
Range 4.4–6.9	1–35	0.05–0.59	0.3–6.4	0.34–6.72	Traces–5.6	0.95–6.72	0.36–3.82	0.04–0.22	0.62–6.58	7–17	

SOILS IN THIRD YEAR OF CULTIVATION

	pH	P (PPM)	K	CA+MG	SUM OF EX-CHANGEABLE BASES	EXCHANGE-ABLE ALUMINUM	EFFECTIVE CEC	C (%)	N (%)	O.M. (%)	C/N RATIO	SOIL COLOR (WET)
			(IN MILLIEQUIVALENTS PER 100 GRAMS)									
Average	4.5	1	0.07	0.3	0.37	3.8	4.17	1.75	0.14	3.01	13	7.5 YR 2.5/1
	6.3	20	0.05	3.3	3.35	Traces	3.35	0.57	0.05	0.99	11	10 YR 3/4
	5.4	10	0.06	1.8	1.86	1.9	3.76	0.88	0.10	2.00	12	
Range	4.5– 6.3	1–20	0.05– 0.07	0.3– 3.3	0.37– 3.35	Traces– 3.8	3.35– 4.17	0.57– 1.75	0.05– 0.14	0.99– 3.01	11–13	

Soils under Secondary Growth

pH	P (PPM)	K	CA+MG	SUM OF EX-CHANGEABLE BASES	EXCHANGE-ABLE ALUMINUM	EFFECTIVE CEC	C (%)	N (%)	O.M. (%)	C/N RATIO	SOIL COLOR (WET)
			(IN MILLIEQUIVALENTS PER 100 GRAMS)								
4.8	1	0.05	1.5	1.55	1.7	3.25	1.01	0.13	1.74	8	2.5 YR 3/4
4.8	1	0.13	0.2	0.33	4.6	4.93	0.61	0.07	1.05	9	7.5 YR 5/4
4.9	1	0.11	0.4	0.51	1.3	1.81	0.28	0.03	0.42	9	5 YR 4/6
5.1	1	0.05	0.6	0.65	0.4	1.05	0.47	0.04	0.81	12	7.5 YR 5/4
4.1	1	0.12	0.1	0.22	1.9	2.12	1.14	0.08	1.97	14	7.5 YR 4/4
Average 4.7	1.0	0.09	0.6	0.652	1.98	2.99	0.70	0.07	1.20	10	
Range 4.1–5.1		0.05–0.13	0.1–1.5	0.22–1.55	0.4–4.6	1.05–4.93	0.28–1.14	0.03–0.13	0.42–1.97	8–14	

Notes

1. The Amazon Basin

1. More than 400 large-scale ranching projects have been approved by the Amazon Development Agency (SUDAM); thousands of families have begun farming; and numerous mining and lumber projects are, or will soon be, operating.

2. It remains to be seen whether or not an economic reorientation will occur. The companies exploiting iron ore at Serra dos Carajás will be able to ship the ore by railroad to São Luis and directly to export markets. The bauxite mines in the flood plain will be able to export by way of the rivers, as in the past.

3. Brazil planned to export its industrial goods to Peru and elsewhere, but Peru decided not to link up the Transamazon with the Peruvian jungle roads in order to prevent the flooding of its markets.

4. This gap was only officially recognized in 1978, when the outgoing President Ernesto Geisel announced that 1979 would be "the year of the Amazon" and called upon Brazilians to help formulate a new policy for the Amazon.

5. Large-scale deforestation is potentially dangerous due to greater erosion potential, separation of the deforested areas from seed sources, and more rapid destruction of the protective root mat.

6. Note particularly the articles by N. Smith, P. Fearnside, and the author. Their work is highly complementary and *in toto* gives a comprehensive view of the landscape changes, economic activities, and carrying capacity.

7. These reasons were used to justify a turnabout in policy, which redirected government policy in 1974. In that year the government announced that it would reduce its support of colonization and promote Amazonian development by favoring large-scale developers (PID 1975).

8. The Guiana and Brazilian shields are large stable blocks of igneous and metamorphic rock dating from the carboniferous period. The old sedimentary plain, laid down since Paleozoic times, is known as the Amazonian Plain (Sternberg 1975:9–10). Rivers rising from these areas carry few inorganic sediments. Rivers like the Xingú have little sediment to deposit when they enter the Amazon mainstream (Sternberg 1975:14).

9. Other tributaries of the Amazon, such as the Rio Negro, are classified as "black-water rivers," are "inky" in appearance, carry little sediment, but have a high content of dissolved organic substances such as pigments from plant materials, and a low level of biological productivity (Sternberg 1975:37–40).

They are said to arise in the highly leached areas of white sand and podzolic soils.

10. Várzeas make up 1 to 2 percent of the Amazon Basin—some 64 to 70,000 square kilometers (Falesi 1974).

11. Many Indians, however, retreated to the relative safety above the fall zone, to the broad upland river network of the upper Xingú. Trade and communication between these groups led to the emergence of the Xingú aboriginal culture group, the remainder of which is now entrenched in the Xingú Reserve Park (Sternberg 1975:29).

12. In the mid-eighteenth century they were responsible for 69 percent of cacao exports and 98 percent of the clove and sarsaparilla from the eastern Amazon (Alden 1974:53). In part their success is responsible for their conflicts with civilian settlements and their eventual elimination as a religious order in 1755 (Azevedo 1930).

13. It is questionable if such small areas are effective floral or faunal refuges. The lack of personnel at the IBDF (Forest Protection Service) made policing of the vast area impractical.

14. This life history material will be used in a future publication to explore the social context of development in the Amazon.

2. TROPICAL RAIN FOREST ECOSYSTEMS

1. The best overall source concerning tropical forests is still P. W. Richard's book *Tropical Rain Forests* (1952). Useful, too, is the edited volume comparing African and South American forests (Meggers et al. 1973). The synthesis volume from UNESCO (1978) is a fine reference book and updates the above items.

2. Throughout I will use the term *tropical rain forests* interchangeably with *humid tropics* (Fosberg et al. 1961).

3. Biomass measurements are still relatively scarce and have been conducted in areas of less than 0.25 hectares. Since biomass measurements are strongly correlated with uncorrected volumes, biomass variability is great. At this time one can cite only biomass for specific areas with any confidence as to its general representativeness (UNESCO 1978:128).

4. May (1975) has questioned whether there is a positive relationship between diversity and stability. He argues that communities with complex webs of interaction are more fragile. May's argument is a theoretical one which remains to be tested in the field and in different types of rain forests.

5. In a radioactive isotope study, 99.9 percent of the phosphorus and calcium moved from leaves to roots without contacting the mineral soil (Stark and Jordan 1978).

6. This resulted from a confusion between *latosols*, a soil type characterized by high levels of secondary oxides and low silica, and *laterite*, a material capable of hardening immediately upon exposure to air. This confusion was made popular after a publication by McNeil (1964).

7. In addition to certain species being represented by a large number of individuals, there exist numerous species represented by a very small number, not infrequently only one specimen (UNESCO 1978:93). The heterogeneity of rain forests has been explained as resulting from herbivore pressure. The seeds, fruits, and seedlings of trees form the major food sources for many host-specific animals. The pressure is greatest close to the parent trees since the predator population concentrates its numbers near it. With distance, the

number of herbivores decreases, and thus the likelihood of a seedling surviving is greater the farther one goes from the parent tree (Richards 1973). Hubbel (1979) has recently argued that tree distribution is clumped, not maximally dispersed.

8. The composition of rain forest trees is also characterized by the absence of dominant species.

9. The three layers are said to form an upper story of solitary giants, a middle story of umbrella-shaped trees of relatively uniform height, and a lower canopy of mosses, ferns, palms, and epiphytes that receive little light.

10. There are two noticeable peaks in flowering–at the beginnings of the wet and the dry seasons (UNESCO 1978:614).

11. Herbert Baker (1970) reviews the theories that attempt to explain evolutionary rates.

12. Vickers (1979) evaluated the concept of tropical forest culture and critiqued reductionist analyses.

3. ABORIGINAL USE OF AMAZONIAN RESOURCES

1. Chagnon explains village fissioning in terms of tribal politics (1968). However, he provides evidence that proximity between settlements is associated with increased levels of warfare (1973).

2. Wagley (1969), in a classic article, showed the differential impact of permissive and restrictive population policies under conditions of social change. With the introduction of European diseases the less adjusted Tenetehara were better able to maintain their numbers than the more restrictive Tapirapé.

3. As an adaptive strategy it is more effective than abortion or contraception. The latter, until the invention of the condom, was seldom effective. Abortion could be effective, but it had the undesirable effect of killing mothers only slightly less frequently than killing the embryo (Harris 1974b).

4. It is not clear whether these differences in animal biomass reflect natural versus exploited yields or differences in forest productivity (oligotrophic versus eutrophic environments).

5. Hunters follow a variety of hunting goals, which reflect adjustments to resources. Some hunts occur in daytime only and may involve the hunter alone. Out of this type of hunting may emerge a group effort if one hunter identifies the presence of a band of, say, peccaries. Perhaps most common of all are group hunts that involve two or three hunters who carry out this work as part of their kinship obligations to provide for their families.

6. One exception appears to be the Amahuaca of the Peruvian Amazon (Carneiro 1970b). It is very telling that the Amahuaca appear to exhaust the game in their territory within five years.

7. Although Heider notes that among the Dani of Western Irian there was very little interest in sex and no apparent tension resulting therefrom (1970).

8. More research is needed to establish whether the use of insects and small game is an adjustment to the economy of hunting or results from game depletion.

9. It should be noted that all three populations cited are in upland forest areas, where bird fauna is more available, but where other game is scarce.

10. Indeed, a persistent problem in the ethnography of the Amazon has always been the numerous taboos on large game—found most frequently in

flood plain populations. Ross (1978) interprets the taboo in the light of cost efficiency: taboos served to maintain an aquatic orientation, which yields more per unit of labor than hunting in riverine settings.

11. One exception to this rule are rituals associated with the collection of turtle eggs (Vickers 1976:123). Smith (1974a:91) notes that the Tumpassa of the Beni believe that a huge spirit turtle protects the species, especially during the egg-laying period.

12. Most common piscicidal plants are the roots of *Derris* spp. and *Tephrosia* spp.; the calix of *Paullinia* spp. and *Serjania* spp. and the seeds of *Jacquinia* spp. The most common active element in them is Rotenone (Gottlieb and Mors 1978).

13. The abundance of turtles and their eggs continued well into the nineteenth century, when Bates (1962) noted that at least 48 million eggs were crushed yearly to make oil for trade with the Portuguese. *Podocnemis* is today dangerously close to extinction due to uncontrolled predation, disturbance of the egg-laying process because of motorized river traffic in beach areas, and wasteful resource management.

14. More detailed discussion of swidden agriculture can be found in Chapter 8 and in the classic studies of Conklin (1957), Geertz (1963), and Spencer (1966).

15. Where forest clearings are very large, the hydrological cycle is significantly modified, rapid runoff could lead to severe erosion and more destructive flood levels, and soils might dry more rapidly. The effect of large-scale deforestation on micro-climate is unknown, but micro-climates would obviously be changed—particularly with increased surface temperatures and changes in local precipitation.

16. Horticultural Efficiency = Kilocalories produced/Kilocalories spent on production = 17,556,680/337,206 = 52:1.

4. THE IMPACT OF COLONIALISM AND AN EXTRACTIVE ECONOMY

1. The Amazonian economy went from a "traditional" or domestic mode of production (cf. Sahlins 1972) to one of dependence on the emergent world capitalist system (Wallerstein 1974). In this new structural position the Amazonian population produced raw materials for export in exchange for manufactured goods that contributed to a decline in domestic production. The profits were controlled by elites allied politically, at first, and later economically, to external capital entrepreneurs. This process has been studied in Sicily by Blok (1974) and by Schneider and Schneider (1976).

2. Between 1850 and 1900, for instance, the population of the Amazon doubled as a result of the rubber boom and a Northeastern drought. During that period the inhabitants were dependent on imports for their basic needs. Efforts at creating agricultural settlements were partially successful, but rarely due to the government's colonization policies.

3. The Gaiosos' more lasting influence came from their introduction of cattle into the area.

4. Arlene Kelly's historical research in the Altamira area documents the role of the rubber baron José Porfirio in the development of settlement (Kelly 1975).

5. MIGRATION TO THE AMAZON

1. The no-growth experience of most Amazonian settlements during the colonial period elicited in the national period conscious efforts to promote the development of immigration and agricultural settlement. A Land Law was passed in 1850 in an effort to regularize titles and provide more security to potential settlers. However, the law failed to affect the practices in the Amazon due to inadequate compliance in the distant areas of the Amazon. Another law, in 1895, sought to improve land registration, but it became more concerned with the legitimation of large land claims than with smallholder claims.

2. Japanese migrants were not allowed into Brazil until the 1920s, for racist reasons.

3. Two recent dissertations study the impact of Northeastern droughts on out-migration (Brooks 1972 and Cuniff 1970).

4. An excellent historical analysis of colonization policies in the state of Pará between 1750 and 1930 has been written by Anderson (1976).

5. "The high rate of decline and disappearance of colonies was as much due to the erratic governmental attention paid to them as to the destruction of the land on which they were situated" (Anderson 1976:178).

6. *Amazonia legal* is a unit for regional planning. It includes the entire states of Pará, Amazonas, and Acre; parts of Mato Grosso, Goiás, and Maranhão; and the federal territories of Amapá, Roraima, and Rondônia. It covers 5 million square kilometers, or about 60 percent of the Brazilian territory.

7. The *Boletim do Museu Paraense Emilio Goeldi* publishes articles in the fields of anthropology, botany, and zoology. Monographs regularly appear in the museum "Publicações Avulsas" series. The library is the best single repository of Amazonian studies. The 1966 Conference on the Amazonian biota met at the museum.

8. Reserves of an estimated 18,000 million tons with an iron content of 66 to 69 percent have been discovered at the Serra dos Carajás site, south of Marabá on the Tocantins River. Great bauxite and manganese reserves have also been discovered near the Serra dos Carajás Mountains. Other bauxite sites: near Paragominas on the Belem-Brasilia highway, in the municipality of Oriximiná on the Trombetas River, and on the Jarilandia holdings. The largest, at Trombetas, holds an estimated 500 million tons. Port facilities are now being built, and much of the ore (an estimated 3.5 million tons/annum) will be exported (Kleinpenning 1978:31).

9. Following the Northeastern experience of the 1960s economists realized that purely industrial development without agricultural development can lead to effects which mitigate against overall development.

10. Two recent publications alerting readers to the invasion of the Amazon by multinationals give the impression that every inch of the basin is being actively exploited (Davis 1977). While the potential is clearly there, most firms find the costs of operating in the basin too high, and their operations exist only on paper as a means of reducing their tax liability.

11. The Ministry of Agriculture (Ministério da Agricultura 1972a:197) set the following estimates of production: rice (1,500 kg/ha), beans (800 kg/ha), corn (1,500 kg/ha), manioc (20,000 kg/ha), cotton (1,200 kg/ha), cacao (600 kg/ha). While these are not bumper crop levels, no allowance was made for differences in soil and terrain, nor for correctives to overcome limiting factors. Net profit on 11 hectares was estimated at Cr$6,571 annually.

12. INCRA was created in 1970 to replace the former Institute of Agrarian

Reform (IBRA). IBRA was created after 1964 to encourage colonization, but in five years only 1,458 families had homesteaded on IBRA project areas. IBRA concentrated on zoning, surveying, and tax collecting (Gomes da Silva 1971:227, 185).

13. See Chapter 8 for an analysis of the productivity of farmers from different regions. The Southerners who came did not exhibit greater "progressiveness" than settlers from other regions.

14. The colonization agency used the following values in estimating the available labor force: adult males $= 1.0$; adult females $= 0.75$; teenage boys $= 0.50$; and teenage girls $= 0.35$. Selection preference was given to families with a labor force of 2.5 and up.

15. The applicant was not supposed to own land at the time of application. Any properties they held at the time of application were often placed in the care of a nearby relative. The latter would generally deposit a good portion of the enterprise's profits as liquifiable insurance for the colonists in the Transamazon.

16. The other two integrated colonization projects (PIC's) being located near Marabá on the Tocantins River and Itaituba on the Tapajós River. Smith (1976a) studied an agrovila near Marabá, and Poats (1975) the dispersed roadside colonization in Itaituba.

6. TYPES OF SETTLEMENTS AND TYPES OF MIGRANTS

1. About 100 meters above sea level, or 20 meters above Altamira.

2. Only one case of snakebite was recorded in the local study area; this took place in the uncut brush between Vila Roxa and a temporary shelter down the road.

3. Social class as a distinctive unit was not appropriate given the apparent equality among colonists: all were "landless" in regions of origin; all received homesteads of equal size and equal access to inputs.

4. Compadrio ties are usually established during ritual occasions such as weddings, baptisms, and graduations.

5. This is a role similar to Wolf's *cultural broker*, an "individual who is able to operate both in terms of community-orientation and national-oriented expectations" (1956:1072). These brokers are quite distinct from the "broker capitalists" which Schneider and Schneider (1976) define in terms of their alliance to extra-regional economic interests and disinterest in local development. The commercial entrepreneurs in Altamira are closer to the description of the broker capitalist.

6. Indeed, the background of some colonists was so diverse that in some cases the assignment of one to a category was a difficult exercise. In those cases I went by the predominant background items.

7. THE USE OF FOREST RESOURCES IN THE TRANSAMAZON

1. Although it is true that a great deal of individual variability is present in all cultures (Pelto and Pelto 1975), traditional cultures tend to be far less pluralistic than modern societies (White 1949).

2. Billington (1967:16) has suggested in his studies of the frontier situation

that simplification of a pioneer's cultural baggage is a process that often occurs in migration to frontier areas.

3. Caboclo resource use is based largely on aboriginal practices. However, it is less complex since households live in an isolated state along river banks, and work cooperation between households was sporadic.

4. Because the colonist communities created by the government were built away from the river, fishing is of minor importance in the diet of the farmers. Some salted fish is bought on the weekly trips to market and, more rarely, a few small fish are obtained by teenagers in the small streams cutting through farmland. Most of these are under one kilogram each—chiefly *traira* (*Hoplias malabaricus*) and varieties of small catfish. A number of stream-ponds were created by road crews when highway fill dammed up small streams. Smith (1976a:185) estimated that there may be as many as 1,000 such artificially created ponds along the highway, ranging in size between 0.5 and 10 hectares each. He believes that they could be stocked with native species and thereby add to the protein resources available in the area, especially as game yields decline. Aqua-culture integrated with pig raising could produce a high yielding system for the farmers (Smith 1976a:188). It could also help control the spread of malarial mosquitoes. Turtle farming was common in the nineteenth century in backyard ponds in the Brazilian Amazon and provided an important dietary supply in the rainy season, when fish are harder to catch and hunting is unpleasant (Smith 1974a). Since turtles are herbivorous, they would not compete with man for the fish, and the feces from the pigs could supply a rich nutrient to the environment, stimulating productivity of aquatic vegetation.

5. The rituals to get rid of panema serve to reestablish an attitude of care and respect in the hunting behavior of the hunter.

6. The Brazilian Institute of Forestry Development will prosecute a man who sells animal pelts and see that he and his family are expelled from the colonization area for such violations. Game hunting is allowed only for consumption purposes.

7. The giant armadillo (*Priodontes giganteus*) is rarely hunted, since it is relatively scarce, although cases were mentioned by hunters.

8. Large bands of forty or more howler monkeys (*Alouatta belzebub*) roam the area. Capuchins (especially *Cebus apella*) are the monkeys which are most often killed for food. Also found in the area are *sauim* or squirrel monkeys (*Saimiri sciureus*), *macaco barrigudo* (*Lagotrix* spp.), *zogue-zogue* (*Callicebus* spp.), owl monkeys (*Aotus trivirgatus*), and other unidentified species such as *mão de ouro, cara branco, quatro olhos,* and *cuambá.*

9. Among the bird species in the area are *Ortalis* spp., *Penelope* spp., *Crax* spp., *Psophia* spp., *Dendrocygna* spp., *Leocopternis* spp., *Anodorhuchus hyacinthinus, Ara* spp., *Ramphastos* spp., *Tangara* spp., *Nasica* spp., and *Monassa* spp.

10. Research has been carried on by Nigel Smith on the impact of colonization on game species (1976a, 1977).

11. The Altamira region is relatively poor in forest fruits. Among the notable absences are: *araçá* (*Psidium araca*), *buriti* (*Mauritia vinifera*), *bacuri* (*Platonia insignis* Mart.), *biribá* (*Rollinia orthopetala*), *ingá* (*Inga* spp.), *jenipapo* (*Genipa americana*), *murici* (*Byrsonima crassifolia*), *miriti* (*Mauritia flexuosa*), and *pupunha* (*Guilielma speciosa*).

12. This is the amino acid sorely lacking in the make-up of manioc protein. This lack has been used to condemn manioc as a quality carbohydrate

food (Rogers and Milner 1965; Moran 1973:35–36). Brazil nuts are also a rich source of high-quality protein and vitamins (Williams 1973).

13. Protein and vitamin intake among rural Brazilians is usually considered to be low. Açaí is consumed in enormous amounts in the Amazon whenever available. It is Pará state's favorite fruit, as indicated by their saying: "Quem para em Pará para, se toma açaí, fica" ("Whoever stops in Pará, stops. If he drinks açai, he stays") (Castro 1967:57). Pupunha is comparable to carrots (8,900 micrograms per 100 grams), burití and tucumã are many times richer (30,000 and 31,000 micrograms per 100 grams, respectively). Pupunha is also rich in fats (Chavez et al. 1949).

14. The failure to recognize the major and real beneficiaries of the colonization program partly resulted from the sectoral structure of the Brazilian bureaucracy. In conventional sectoral structure, a department is given responsibility over a particular function. That unit then deals only with its special functions and remains effectively isolated from other sectors of the rural development effort. The result is not only isolation, but also lack of communication and even a degree of jealousy/competition among the functional sectors. In protecting their sectoral turf, the whole effort at regional development is choked by lack of information.

15. A total of 240 soil samples were taken in the Altamira area. Samples included both fertility cores (0- to 10-centimeters depth) and complete soil profiles (0- to 180-centimeters depth). Samples were collected and brought back to Vila Roxa, where a careful description of the soil was done, and soil color was assessed with the aid of soil color charts (Oyama and Takehara 1967). They were then labeled and taken weekly to the local experimental station. The samples regularly went by mail pouch to the Institute of Agronomic Research in Belem (IPEAN-EMBRAPA). There the samples were submitted to chemical analysis. A detailed description of these methods may be found in Moran (1975).

8. Agriculture in the Transamazon

1. Some of the other terms that refer to this widespread agricultural system are "fire agriculture," swidden, *milpa*, *kaingin*, *chena*, *citemene*, and *ladang* (Popenoe 1960:4; Conklin 1963; Spencer 1966).

2. Carbon is lost when the litter layer is destroyed by burning, and the soil is exposed to the action of water and sun. Humus decomposition increases as a result of aeration, and surface conditions can deteriorate rapidly unless a crop quick to provide soil cover has been planted. The growth of crops and the development of secondary succession hold this process in check.

3. This assumes paying the unusually high salaries of the Transamazon region (Cr$15 per day).

4. These figures are very high due to the denseness of flood plain vegetation and the heavy labor requirements to carry out ring-barking of the larger trees in the area studied by Rodrigues Lima (1956).

5. The tarefa varies from place to place in Brazil. See Smith (1972) for various equivalents of this unit.

6. The Altamira price of the powersaw itself was approximately Cr$5,000 (US$710) in 1974, and most farmers needed bank financing for its purchase. The cost of chains was also high. A number of powersaw users still preferred to use scaffolds because the cutting was faster above the buttresses.

7. US$50 per hectare are provided by the Bank of Brazil for clearing forest and planting cereals. No credit is provided for hiring labor or purchasing agricultural inputs if a colonist wishes to keep a field in constant cereal or root crop production. Such credit is given only for permanent crops such as cocoa, rubber, and black pepper.

8. Other problem areas are the high labor costs of weeding and the difficulties of pest control.

9. Fearnside's data from another colonization area of Altamira suggests that weed invasion leads to rapid declines in the quality of pastures and potential cattle yields (1979a). Falesi (1976) is more optimistic based on some longitudinal field studies in Paragominas, Pará.

10. Colonists noted that weeds were not a nuisance at first, but that as more land was cleared, more aggressive "volunteers" invaded fields—particularly grasses of African origin.

11. On the positive side, weeds are a vital component of the Amazon ecosystem. They check soil erosion, restore nitrogen and organic matter, and begin the process of succession required in the maintenance of a stable forest ecosystem. While continuous cultivation is possible in the alfisols, the cost of agricultural inputs to bring the other soils into continuous production is at present prohibitive and unwarranted—given the current market structure and the density of population.

12. Birds cause greater damage in other tropical areas, e.g., dickcissels (*Spiza americana*) cause serious damage in rice and sorghum in Central America (Woronecki et al. 1974).

13. The fresh corn pudding forms included *canjica*, a sweet dessert made from the fresh kernel pulp, which has been strained to remove the kernel skins. This is cooked down with sugar and cinnamon to form a sliceable paste. Angú is made with similar ingredients, except that the kernel skins are left in and the mixture has more of a pudding consistency. The *tamal* form called *pamonha* is made with salt instead of sugar, and is boiled in a corn husk wrapper.

14. Beetle damage to stored beans has also been noted in Zaïre's rain forest areas (Jurion and Henry 1969:247). Up to 93 percent of the beans were destroyed within twelve months.

15. Smith (1976a:145) notes that yields were 443 kilograms per hectare in 1972, but that they declined due to a fungus disease thereafter.

16. A similar description of fungal damage to *Phaseolus* is given by Carter in his study of a lowland Guatemala farming community (1969:9). This may be a biome-level constraint, rather than a localized phenomenon.

17. The latter is also true of manioc, sweet potatoes, and certain varieties of dry or upland rice—all of which are native to tropical environments (Sanchez and Buol 1975:602). Sugar cane and pineapples also appear to thrive in the hot/humid conditions and soil conditions (Marzola and Bartholomew 1979).

18. Sutmoller et al. (1966) have pointed out that serious malnutrition has been found in Amazon valley livestock. Mineral deficiencies have been noted that caused spontaneous fractures in the hind legs. Instances of potassium and manganese are low, and serious deficiencies of phosphorus, sodium, copper, and cobalt keep reproductive levels and carcass weights low.

19. This is a traditional arrangement found in Brazil; Riviére (1972) discusses its practice in Roraima, in the northern Amazon.

20. Among the toxic weeds of importance in the area are *salsa* (*Ipomoea asarifolia*), *samambaia* (*Pteridium aquilinum*), *maniva de veado* (*Manihot*

quinquepartita), *canudo* (*Ipomoea fistulosa*), *erva* (*Ipomoea tiliaceae* and *Tragia bahiensis*), *erva roxa* (*Cephaelis colorata*) (IPEAN 1973b).

21. Current laws consider the cutting of the native forests to be "an improvement" to the land. An established pasture adds to that value even further. This ancient law conflicts with more recent conservationist laws. It is not difficult to see why colonists often clear an area larger than they can effectively manage. In case a buyer appears, the greater the area "improved" (i.e., deforested), the higher will be the sale price.

22. SUDAM has helped subsidize large livestock projects. Over US$1 billion were spent on SUDAM-approved projects between 1965 and 1979. Goodland (1980) considers large-scale livestock as the worst use of Amazonian resources. Hecht (forthcoming) reports that 85 percent of the cattle ranches near Paragominas had gone out of business by 1977. The area began to be occupied around 1965.

23. The one exception is the vaqueiros of Marajó Island, whose cattle-raising tradition goes back to the Jesuit mission before 1750. Goodland (1980) believes that large-scale cattle raising should be confined to Marajó, the flood plain, and the cerrado.

9. SOCIAL AND INSTITUTIONAL LIFE

1. This view has been most consistently held by British social anthropologists who focus on social systems as fields of tensions, "full of imbalance, of cooperation and contrasting struggle" (Gluckman 1954:21; 1955). These emphases are also evident in Fortes' emphasis on the tug between centripetal and centrifugal tendencies in social systems (1945) and in studies of village fissioning counteracted by cross-cutting alliances based on marriage (Colson 1953; Turner 1957).

2. Both administrators and technicians are usually agronomists with the equivalent of a bachelor's degree.

3. The term *moleque* commonly means urchin or black urchin. However, its usage by farmers in referring to government agents had the connotation of "spoiled children."

4. The obtention of large loans to establish permanent crops was contingent upon possession of a definitive title to the homestead. Only 58 percent of farmers had been able to get them. The rest, who received merely a permit of occupation, could only obtain short-term loans for rice-corn-bean production. However, only the permanent crops provide high enough returns to absorb the fixed costs of rural credit (Bunker 1978:31).

5. During our one-year residence in Vila Roxa, only two children died, due to croup and asthma. Twenty percent of the households had at least one person who suffered from malaria. Two persons suffered from trauma, and their agricultural labor was much impaired.

6. Since Vila Roxa was one of the first agrovilas built and occupied, INCRA was more successful in scattering the population, and the early immigrants tended to represent larger kin groups. Poats (1979, personal communication) has noted that in the Itaituba roadside colonization, sizable extended kin groups are present, and they chose land next to each other.

7. Compadrio refers to fictive kin ties which are established during such ritual occasions as baptisms, weddings, and graduations. As noted in Chapter 9, these are just now being established among brokers. During 1973–74 there

were five elopements associated with marriages. They were the result of severe parent-child tensions. The tension resulted from the elopement of a son who, thereby, deprived his father of his labor—as the son usually claimed a separate homestead. This is a stress common in colonization areas, where land is readily available. Effective parental control over the children well into adulthood is common only in land-scarce, highly populated areas.

8. Similar to the 4-H Clubs in the United States.

9. An employee of the colonization agency, who drove the ambulance in the area, had a serious car accident. He made a *promessa* that if he got well he would buy an image of St. Francis for the Church. He did recover, and he bought the image, but the little saint remained in his house since the Vila Roxa Church could not adequately house the saint. This man also happened to be a native of Rio Grande do Norte.

10. HEALTH, DIET, AND DISEASE

1. This discussion is based on an analysis of folk medical practices by Fleming-Moran (1975) in the same region of the Transamazon.

2. This dual factor system reinforces the idea that disease results from interaction between people and their physical and spiritual world (Lynch 1969:209; Opler 1963:33; Santos Filho 1966:15; Kiev 1968:43; Adams 1953:17). In fact, this dual system may be a simplification of the Hippocratic notion of *ketasis*, wherein factors of one's environment and one's own susceptibility must be calculated in determining the course of the disease (Galdston 1954:13–20).

3. Emphasis on cold imbalance is found in other areas of Latin America (Foster 1953; Simmons, O. 1955; Currier 1969).

4. Canopy vector populations are believed to increase during the rainy season but to decline rapidly during the dry season—precisely the time when settlers clear forest and may expose themselves to the sylvan vectors of yellow fever.

5. Woodall (1967) identified a total of sixty arboviruses in the Brazilian Amazon, of which sixteen were found among humans. Only one of these has affected tested Transamazon settlers.

6. As of May 1974 a total of 222 cases had been identified during routine medical examination given arriving colonists. They were treated with Entrenol, which is 80 percent effective on first dose. No follow-up took place.

7. The strains *Plasmodium falciparum*, *P. vivax*, and *P. malariae* are all found in the Transamazon region. Resistance of *P. falciparum* to cloroquine treatment was first noted for the Brazilian Amazon in 1948 (Mein and Rosado 1948).

8. Women bathe in the morning while doing the wash in the river.

9. Resulting from poor diet, neglect of contaminated blood, or previous bouts with illness.

10. In cases when it was unavailable, the native caboclo population was able to identify the bark of "quina" (*Quassia amara*) and make an effective tea that reduced malaria fever.

11. Respiratory, gastro-intestinal, and malaria cases averaged 4.5 to 4.9 days.

12. These rates compare favorably with poor urban districts, where 80 to 99 percent of the children are infected (Azevedo and Maroja 1956; Causey

et al. 1947; Lowenstein 1963; Costa et al. 1965).

13. Pinheiro et al. (1974b) noted as many as 250 black fly bites per man per hour in the Altamira region during the rainy season.

14. The weighing method was used briefly but abandoned due to the time that it took, the notable change in customary cooking practices that resulted, and the lack of representativeness possible (cf. Reh 1962).

15. The absence of protein deficiency may be due to the low densities of population and the riverine orientation of many autochthonous groups.

16. Kwashiorkor was more prevalent among children ages zero to three and of the lower socio-economic class in Belem (Santos 1955). They had been weaned in 92 percent of the cases, and received a diet of carbohydrates.

17. The normal range of adult body weight was 43 to 50 kilograms. Given that the minimum daily protein requirement is 1.0 to 0.8 grams per kilogram of body weight, the population is well above that. Seasonal deficiencies may occur, but the data does not permit any remarks on seasonal distribution.

18. Vitamin B deficiencies, such as beri-beri, afflicted Amazonian populations in past times when the traditional system of agricultural production was disrupted by extractivism. Castro (1967:74) estimated that 50 percent of the rubber collectors during the Rubber Era were afflicted by this nutritional disease. With the decline in rubber prices in the 1920s, beri-beri virtually disappeared from the basin (Castro, p. 76).

19. The diets of pregnant women need particular attention given the serious consequences for both mother and child of undernourishment (Frisancho 1979:184–90). Low weight neonates experience a greater incidence of inadequate respiratory function; metabolic disturbances; poor resistance to infection; anemia; and inadequate renal function.

Bibliography

Adams, Richard N.
   1953   Un Análisis de las creencias y prácticas médicas en un pueblo indígena de Guatemala. Guatemala: Instituto Indigenista Nacional.
   1975   Energy and Structure. Austin: University of Texas Press.

Albuquerque, M. de
   1969   A Mandioca na Amazônia. Belem: SUDAM.
   1973   Cultura da Mandioca. Circular no. 16. Belem: IPEAN.

Alden, Dauril
   1974   O Significado da Produção de Cacau na Região Amazônica. Belem: NAEA/UFPa.

Alland, Alexander
   1970   Adaptation in Cultural Evolution: An Approach to Medical Anthropology. New York: Columbia University Press.
   1975   Adaptation. Annual Review of Anthropology 4:59–73.

Alvim, P. de T.
   1977   The Balance Between Conservation and Utilization in the Humid Tropics. In Prance, G. and T. Elias, eds. Extinction is Forever. New York: N.Y. Botanical Garden.
   1978   Perspectivas de Produção Agrícola na Região Amazônica. Interciencia 3(4):243–49.

Alvim, P. de T., and F. P. Cabala
   1974   Un novo sistema de representação gráfica da fertilidade do solos para cacau. Cacau Atualidades 11(1):2–6.

Anderson, Robin
   1976   Following Curupira: Colonization and Migration in Pará (1758–1930). Ph.D. dissertation, University of California (Davis), Department of History.

Araújo, A. M.
   1959   Medicina Rústica. São Paulo: Companhía Editôra Nacional.

Arensberg, C., and S. Kimball
   1965   Culture and Community. New York: Harcourt, Brace and World.
   1968   Family and Community in Ireland. 2d ed. Cambridge, Mass.: Harvard University Press.

250

Arrúe, María del Carmen
1976   Folk Medicine on the Transamazon Highway in Brazil: A Case
       Study. B.A. Honors thesis, Department of Anthropology, Univer-
       sity of Florida.

Azevedo, João Lúcio de
1930   Os Jesuítas no Grão Pará. Coimbra: n.p.

Azevedo, M., and R. Maroja
1956   Inquérito Parasitológico entre Crianças, Realizado nos Municípios
       de Ponta de Pedras e Souré, Pará. Revista do SESP 8(2):469–78.

Bailey, F. G.
1964   Two Villages in Orissa (India). *In* Closed Systems and Open
       Minds, edited by M. Gluckman. Chicago: Aldine.

Baker, Herbert
1970   Evolution in the Tropics. Biotropica 2(2):101–11.

Baker, Paul T.
1966   Ecological and Physiological Adaptations in Indigenous South
       Americans. *In* The Biology of Human Adaptability, edited by
       Paul T. Baker and J. S. Weiner. Oxford: Clarendon Press.

Baker, Paul T., and M. Little, eds.
1976   Man in the Andes. US/IBP Synthesis Series no. 1. Stroudsburg,
       Pa.: Dowden, Hutchinson and Ross.

Baker, Randall
1979   The Administrative Trap. Paper presented at the African Studies
       Seminar, April 24. Indiana University.

Baldanzi, Giampiero
1959   Efeitos da Queimada Sobre A Fertilidade do Solo. Pelotas, Rio
       Grande do Sul: Instituto Agronómico do Sul.

Baldus, H.
1970   Os Tapirapé: Tribo Tupí no Brasil Central. São Paulo: Editôra
       da Universidade de São Paulo.

Bartholomew, W. V. et al.
1953   Mineral Nutrient Immobilization Under Forest and Grass Fallow
       in the Yangambi Region. INEAC Serie Scientifique 57:1–27.

Baruzzi, R. G. et al.
1977   The Kren-Akorore: A Recently Contacted Indigenous Tribe.
       Health and Disease in Tribal Societies. Amsterdam: Elsevier-
       Holland.

BASA (Banco da Amazônia, S.A.)
1971   Programa Especial de Crédito Rural. Belem, Pará: BASA.

Bates, Henry W.
1962   The Naturalist on the River Amazons. Berkeley: University of
       California Press.

Bates, Marston
1952   Where Winter Never Comes. New York: Scribners.
1960   The Forest and the Sea. New York: Vintage Books.

Beckerman, S.
    1979   The Abundance of Protein in Amazonia: A Reply to Gross.
            American Anthropologist 81(3):533–60.
    1980   Fishing and Hunting by the Barí of Colombia. *In* Studies in Hunt-
            ing and Fishing in the Neotropics, edited by R. Hames. Benning-
            ton, Vt.: Bennington College.

Beer, Stafford
    1968   Management Science. Garden City, N.Y.: Doubleday.

Benchimol, Samuel
    1966   Estrutura Geo-Social e Econômica da Amazônia. Vol. 2. Manaus:
            Edições do Govêrno do Estado de Amazonas.

Bennett, John
    1967   Microcosm-Macrocosm Relationships in North American Agrarian
            Society. American Anthropologist 69:441–54.
    1969   Northern Plainsmen. Chicago: Aldine.
    1972   The Significance of the Concept of Adaptation for Contemporary
            Socio-Cultural Anthropology. *In* Proceedings of the 8th Congress
            of Anthropological and Ethnological Sciences S-7:237–41.
    1976   The Ecological Transition. London: Pergamon Press.

Bigarella, J. J., and G. G. Andrade
    1965   Contribution to the Study of the Brazilian Quaternary. Geological
            Society of America, Special Paper 84:433–51.

Billington, Ray Allen
    1967   The American Frontier. *In* Beyond the Frontier, edited by Paul
            Bohannan and Fred Plog. Garden City, N.Y.: The Natural His-
            tory Press.

Bittencourt, Luis Carlos
    1974   Polamazônia: Empresários e Não Colonos. Comércio e Mercados
            8:34–35.

Bloch, M.
    1966   French Rural History. Berkeley: University of California Press.
            Originally published in 1931.

Blok, Anton
    1974   The Mafia of a Sicilian Village, 1860–1960: A Study of Violent
            Peasant Entrepreneurs. New York: Harper and Row.

Boserup, Ester
    1965   The Conditions of Agricultural Growth. Chicago: Aldine.

Bourne, Richard
    1978   Assault on the Amazon. London: Victor Gollancz.

Bradfield, Stillman
    1974   An Agrovila of the Transamazonica Highway in Brazil. Report of
            a Visit to Vila Roxa. Cali, Colombia: CIAT, Small Farm Systems
            Program.

Braudel, Fernand
    1973   The Mediterranean and the Mediterranean World in the Age of
            Philip II. 2 vols. New York: Harper and Row.

Briquet de Lemos, A. A.
  1976   Cerrado: Bibliografia Analítica. Brasilia: EMBRAPA.

Bromley, Ray
  1979   The Colonization of Humid Tropical Areas in Ecuador. Paper presented at the University of Cambridge Conference on Colonization in Amazonia.

Brookfield, H. C.
  1970   Dualism and the Geography of Developing Countries. Presidential address at the Australian and New Zealand Association for the Advancement of Science.

Brooks, Reuben
  1972   Flight from Disaster: Drought Perception as a Force in Migration from Ceará, Brazil. Ph.D. dissertation, University of Colorado, Department of Geography.

Brown, K., and O. Sexton
  1973   Stimulation of Reproductive Activity of Female *Anolis sagrei* by Moisture. Physiological Zoology 46:168–72.

Brush, Stephen
  1979   An Anthropological Appraisal of Latin American Farming Systems. Studies in Third World Societies 7:107–16.

Bruzzi, P.
  1962   A Civilização Indígena do Vaupés. São Paulo: Linográfica.

Buarque de Holanda, S.
  1962   História Geral da Civilização Brasileira. Vol. 2. São Paulo: Difusão Européia do Livro.

Buckman, Harry, and N. Brady
  1969   The Nature and Properties of Soils. 7th ed. New York: Macmillan.

Bunker, S.
  1978   Institutional Interdependence and the Failure of Rural Development Programs in Pará, Brazil. Paper delivered at annual meeting of the American Sociological Association. San Francisco, Sept. 4–8.

Buol, S. W., and W. Couto
  1978   Fertility Management Interpretations and Soil Surveys of the Tropics. Diversity of Soils in the Tropics. Madison, Wis.: ASA and SSSA.

Burkhalter, Steve
  1975   Vila do Xingú, An Amazon Community. M.A. thesis, University of Florida, Department of Anthropology.

Cain, Stanley, and G. M. de Oliveira Castro
  1959   Manual of Vegetation Analysis. New York: Hafner Publishing Company.

Camargo, José G. de Cunha
  1973   Urbanismo Rural. Brasília D. F.: INCRA.

Camargo, M., and I. C. Falesi
  1975   Soils of the Central Plateau and Transamazon Highway of Brazil.

In Soil Management in Tropical America, edited by E. Bornemisza and A. Alvarado. Raleigh, N.C.: Soil Science Department, North Carolina State University.

Cancian, Frank
1976 Social Stratification. Annual Review of Anthropology 5:227–48.

Cardoso, F. H.
1975 Autoritarismo e Democratização. Rio de Janeiro: Paz e Terra.

Cardoso, F. H., and G. Müller
1977 Amazônia: Expansão do Capitalismo. São Paulo: Brasiliense.

Carneiro, Robert L.
1957 Subsistence and Social Structure: An Ecological Study of the Kuikuru. Ph.D. dissertation, University of Michigan, Department of Anthropology.
1961 Slash-Burn Agriculture: A Closer Look at Its Implications for Settlement Patterns. *In* Man and Culture, edited by Anthony F. Wallace. Fifth International Congress of Anthropological and Ethnological Sciences.
1970a The Transition from Hunting to Horticulture in the Amazon Basin. Eighth Congress of Anthropological and Ethnological Sciences 3:243–51.
1970b Hunting and Hunting Magic Among the Amahuaca of the Peruvian Montaña. Ethnology 9(4):331–41.
1974 Slash-and-Burn Cultivation Among the Kuikuru and its Implications for Cultural Development in the Amazon Basin. *In* Native South Americans, edited by Patricia Lyon. Boston: Little, Brown and Company.

Caron, R.
1971 Curé d'Indiens. Paris: Union Généróle d'Editions.

Carter, William E.
1969 New Lands and Old Traditions. Gainesville, Fla.: University of Florida Press.

Carvalho, J. C.
1951 Relações Entre os Indios do Alto Xingú e a Fauna Regional. Rio de Janeiro: Museu Nacional.

Casagrande, J., S. Thompson, and P. Young
1964 Colonization as a Research Frontier: The Ecuadorian Case. *In* Process and Pattern in Culture, edited by R. Manners. Chicago: Aldine.

Castro, Josué de
1967 Geografia da Fome. 10a edição. São Paulo: Editôra Brasiliense.

Causey, O. R., and C. E. Causey
1974 Transmissible Disease in the Brazilian Amazon. *In* Man in the Amazon, edited by Charles Wagley. Gainesville, Fla.: University of Florida Press.

Causey, O. R. et al.
1967 Incidencia de Parasitos Intestinais do Homem em Belem, Pará e Visinhanças. Revista do SESP 1(2):221–33.

Cavalcante, P.
1972   Frutas Comestíveis da Amazônia. Vol. 1. Belem: Publicações Avulsas do Museu Goeldi.
1974   Frutas Comestíveis da Amazônia. Vol. 2. Belem: Publicações Avulsas do Museu Goeldi.

Cavalcanti, Mario de Barros
1967   Da SPVEA à SUDAM. Belem: Universidade Federal do Pará.

Chagnon, Napoleon
1968   Yanomano: The Fierce People. New York: Holt, Rinehart and Winston.
1973   The Cultural Ecology of Shifting Cultivation Among the Yano-mano Indians. Peoples and Cultures of Native South America, edited by D. Gross. Garden City, N.Y.: Doubleday.

Chagnon, N., and R. Hames
1979   Protein Deficiency and Tribal Warfare in Amazonia: New Data. Science 203:910–13.

Chavez, J. M., E. Pechnik, and I. V. Mattoso
1949   Estudo da Constitução Química e do Valor Alimentício da Pupun-ha (*Guilielma speciosa*, Mart.). Arquivos Brasilienses de Nutrição 6(3):185–92.

Chorley, R. J.
1973   Geography as Human Ecology. *In* Directions in Geography, edited by R. J. Chorley. London: Methuen.

Clarke, J.
1976   Population and Scale: Some General Considerations. *In* Popula-tion at Microscale, edited by Leszek Kosinski and John Webb. New Zealand: Commission on Population Geography.

Clarke, William
1966   From Extensive to Intensive Shifting Cultivation: A Succession from New Guinea. Ethnology 5:347–59.
1971   Place and People. Berkeley: University of California Press.
1976   Maintenance of Agriculture and Human Habitats within the Trop-ical Forest Ecosystem. Human Ecology 4(3):247–59.

Coleman, N. T., S. B. Weed, and R. J. McCraken
1959   Cation Exchange Capacity and Exchangeable Cations in Piedmont Soils of North Carolina. Proceedings of the Soil Science Society of America 23:146–49.

Collier, Richard
1968   The River that God Forgot. New York: Dutton.

Colson, Elizabeth
1953   Social Control and Vengeance in Plateau Tonga Society. Africa 23:199–212.
1971   The Social Consequences of Resettlement. London: Manchester University Press.

Colwell, R.
1973   Competition and Coexistence in a Simple Tropical Community. American Naturalist 107:737–60.

Conklin, Harold C.
1957 Hanunóo Agriculture: A Report on an Integral System of Shifting Cultivation in the Philippines. Forestry Development Paper no. 12. Rome: Food and Agriculture Organization of the United Nations.
1963 The Study of Shifting Cultivation. Washington, D.C.: Panamerican Union.

Contini, E.
1976 A Colonização na Transamazonica. M.A. thesis, Fundação Getúlio Vargas, Rio de Janeiro, Brazil.

Costa, O. R. et al.
1955 Inquérito Parasitológico entre Crianças Realizado em Seis Municípios da Zona Bragantina, Estado do Pará, em 1950. Revista do SESP 8(1):231–56.

Coudreau, Henri
1897 Voyage au Xingú. Paris: A. Lahure.

Couto e Silva, Golberry do
1957 Aspectos Geopolíticos do Brasil. Rio de Janeiro: Biblioteca do Exército.

Crist, R., and C. Nissly, eds.
1973 East from the Andes. Gainesville, Fla.: University of Florida Press.

Cruls, Gastão
1939 Impressões de uma Visita à Companhia Ford Industrial do Brasil (Estado do Pará). Revista Brasileira de Geografía 1(4):1–25.

Culbert, T. P., P. C. Magers, and M. L. Spencer
1978 Regional Variability in Maya Lowland Agriculture. In Pre-hispanic Maya Agriculture, edited by P. D. Harrison and B. L. Turner. Albuquerque: University of New Mexico Press.

Cunha, Euclides da
1913 À Margem da História. 2d ed. Pôrto, Portugal: Livraría Chardron.

Cunniff, Roger
1970 The Great Drought: Northeast Brazil 1877–1880. Ph.D. dissertation, University of Texas (Austin), Department of History.

Currier, R.
1969 The Hot-Cold Syndrome and Symbolic Balance in Mexican-American Folk Medicine. In The Cross-Cultural Approach to Health Behavior, edited by R. L. Lynch. Madison, N.J.: Fairleigh Dickinson University Press.

Damon, A., ed.
1974 Physiological Anthropology. New York: Oxford.

Davis, Shelton
1977 Victims of the Miracle. New York: Cambridge University Press.
1980 Mining Projects Endanger Amazon's Yanomamo Tribe. Multinational Monitor 2/80:20–21, 78.

Davis, S., and D. Mathews
1976 The Geological Imperative. Cambridge, Mass.: Anthropology Resource Center.

Denevan, William
1966a A Cultural Ecological View of the Former Aboriginal Settlement in the Amazon Basin. The Professional Geographer 18:346–51.
1966b The Aboriginal Cultural Geography of the Llanos de Mojos de Bolivia. Berkeley: University of California Publications.
1971 Campa Subsistence in the Gran Pajonal, Eastern Perú. Geographical Review 61:496–518.
1973 Development and the Imminent Demise of the Amazon Rain Forest. Professional Geographer 25(2):130–35.

Denevan, William, ed.
1976 The Native Population of the Americas in 1492. Madison: University of Wisconsin Press.

Devons, E., and M. Gluckman
1964 Conclusion: Modes and Consequences of Limiting a Field of Study. In Closed Systems and Open Minds, edited by M. Gluckman. Chicago: Aldine.

Dickinson, Joshua C.
1972 Alternatives to Monoculture in the Humid Tropics of Latin America. The Professional Geographer 24(3):217–22.

Diégues Júnior, Manuel
1973 Populações Rurais Brasileiras. In Vida Rural e Mudança Social, edited by Tamas Szmecsanyi and O. Queda. São Paulo: Companhía Editôra Nacional.

Dobyns, Henry
1966 Estimating Aboriginal American Population. Current Anthropology 7:395–416.

Dogan, M., and S. Rokkan, eds.
1969 Social Ecology. Cambridge, Mass.: M.I.T. Press.

Doughty, Paul, Henry Dobyns, and A. Holmberg
1966 Measurement of Peace Corps Program Impact in the Peruvian Andes: Final Report. Washington, D.C.: The Peace Corps.

Dozier, Craig
1969 Land Development and Colonization in Latin America. New York: Praeger.

Dreyfus, S.
1963 Les Kayapó du Nord. The Hague: Mouton.

Duncan, O., R. P. Cuzzort, and B. Duncan
1961 Statistical Geography: Problems in Analyzing Areal Data. Glencoe, Ill.: Free Press.

Durham, William
1976 The Adaptive Significance of Cultural Behavior. Human Ecology 4(2):89–121.

1979   Scarcity and Survival in Central America. Stanford: Stanford University Press.

Eden, Michael
1978   Ecology and Land Development: The Case of Amazonian Rainforest. Transactions of the Institute of British Geographers (new series) 3(4):444–63.

Eder, James
1977   Agricultural Intensification and the Returns to Labour in the Philippine Swidden System. Pacific Viewpoint 19:1–21.

Eisenberg, J., and R. Thorington
1973   A Preliminary Analysis of a Neotropical Mammal Fauna. Biotropica 5(3):150–61.

Ellen, Roy
1978   Problems and Progress in the Ethnographic Analysis of Small-Scale Human Ecosystems. Man 13(2):290–303.
1979   Introduction: Anthropology, the Environment and Ecological Systems. In Social and Ecological Systems, edited by P. Burnham and R. Ellen. London: Academic Press. A.S.A. Monograph 18.

Epstein, A. L.
1964   Urban Communities in Africa. In Closed Systems and Open Minds, edited by M. Gluckman. Chicago: Aldine.

Erasmus, C.
1952   Changing Folk Beliefs: The Relativity of Empirical Knowledge. Southwestern Journal of Anthropology 8:411–28.

Evans, C., and B. Meggers
1968   Archeological Investigations on the Rio Napo, Eastern Ecuador. Contributions to Anthropology no. 6. Washington, D.C.: Smithsonian Institution.

Falesi, Ítalo Claudio
1972   Solos da Rodovía Transamazônica. Boletim técnico no. 55. Belem, Pará: IPEAN.
1974   Soils of the Brazilian Amazon. In Man in the Amazon, edited by Charles Wagley. Gainesville, Fla.: University of Florida Press.
1976   Ecosistema de Pastagem Cultivada na Amazônia Brasileira. Boletim tecnico do Centro de Pesquisa Agropecuária do Trópico Umido no. 1. Belem, Pará: CPATU.

Farnworth, Edward, and Frank Golley, eds.
1974   Fragile Ecosystems: Evaluation of Research and Applications in the Neotropics. New York: Springer-Verlag.

Fearnside, Philip
1978   Estimation of Carrying Capacity for Human Populations in a Part of the Transamazon Highway Colonization Area of Brazil. Ph.D. dissertation, University of Michigan, Department of Biological Sciences.
1979a   Cattle Yield Prediction for the Transamazon Highway of Brazil. Interciencia 4(4):220–25.

1979b The Development of the Amazon Rain Forest: Priority Problems for the Formulation of Guidelines. Interciencia 4(6):338–42.

1979c Land Use Allocation of the Transamazon Highway Colonists of Brazil and Its Relation to Human Carrying Capacity. Paper presented at the University of Cambridge Conference on Colonization in Amazonia.

Federov, A. A.
1966 The Structure of the Tropical Rain Forest and Speciation in the Humid Tropics. Journal of Ecology 54:1–11.

Ferri, M. G., ed.
1963 Simpósio sobre o Cerrado. São Paulo: Editôra da Universidade de São Paulo.
1971 III Simpósio sobre o Cerrado. São Paulo: Editôra da Universidade de São Paulo e Editôra Blücher.
1976 IV Simpósio sobre o Cerrado. São Paulo: Editôra da Universidade de São Paulo e Editôra Itatiaia.

Fittkau, E. J.
1968 The Fauna of South America. *In* Biogeography and Ecology in South America, edited by E. J. Fittkau et al. Vol. 2. The Hague: Junk.

Fittkau, E. J., and H. Klinge
1973 On Biomass and Trophic Structure of the Central Amazonian Rain Forest Ecosystem. Biotropica 5(1):2–14.

Fittkau, E. J. et al., eds.
1968 Biogeography and Ecology in South America. The Hague: Junk.

Fleming-Moran, Millicent
1975 The Folk View of Natural Causation and Disease in Brazil and Its Relation to Traditional Curing Practices. M.A. thesis, University of Florida, Department of Anthropology.

Fleming-Moran, M., and E. F. Moran
1978 O Surgimento de Classes Sociais numa Comunidade planejada para ser Igualitária. Boletim do Museu Paraense Emilio Goeldi. Nova Serie. Antropologia 69:1–38.

Forde, C. Darryl
1934 Habitat, Economy and Society. New York: Dutton.

Forman, S.
1975 The Brazilian Peasantry. New York: Columbia University Press.

Fortes, Meyer
1945 The Dynamics of Clanship Among the Tallensi. London: Oxford University Press.
1970 Time and Social Structure and Other Essays. London: Athlone Press.

Fosberg, F. R.
1973 Temperate Zone Influence on Tropical Forest Land Use: A Plea for Sanity. *In* Tropical Forest Ecosystems in Africa and South

America, edited by B. Meggers et al. Washington, D.C.: Smithsonian.

Fosberg, F. R. et al.
1961 Delimitation of the Humid Tropics. The Geographical Review 51(3):333–47.

Foster, G.
1953 Relationships Between Spanish and Spanish-American Folk Medicine. Journal of American Folklore 66:201–19.
1958 Problems in Intercultural Health Programs. New York: Social Science Research Council.

Foster, George M., and John H. Rowe
1951 Suggestions for the Field Recording of Information on the Hippocratic Classification of Disease and Remedies. Kroeber Anthropological Society Papers 5:1–5.

Frikel, P.
1959 Agricultura dos Indios Mundurucú. Boletim do Museu Paraense Emilio Goeldi. N. S. Antropologia 4:1–35.
1968 Os Xikrín. Publicações Avulsas no. 7. Belem: Museu Goeldi.

Frisancho, A.
1979 Human Adaptation. St. Louis: C. V. Mosby.

Frisch, Rose, and J. McArthur
1974 Menstrual Cycles: Fatness as a Determinant of Minimum Weight Necessary for their Maintenance or Onset. Science 185:949–51.

Furley, Peter
1979 Development Planning in Rondonia based on Naturally Renewable Resource Surveys. Paper presented at the University of Cambridge Conference on Colonization in Amazonia.

Galdston, I., ed.
1954 Beyond the Germ Theory. New York: Health Education Council.

Galey, John
1979 Industrialist in the Wilderness: Henry Ford's Amazon Venture. Journal of Interamerican Studies and World Affairs 21(2):261–89.

Gall, Norman
1978 Letter from Rondonia. American Universities Field Staff Reports no. 9–13/South America.

Galvão, Eduardo
1951 Panema: Uma Crença do Caboclo Amazónico. Revista do Museu Paulista 5:221–25.
1955 Santos e Visagems: Um Estudo da Vida Religiosa de Itá. São Paulo: Companhía Editôra Nacional.
1963 Elementos Básicos da Horticultura de Subsistencia Indígena. Revista do Museu Paulista 14:120–44.

Gates, Paul W.
1960 The Farmer's Age: Agriculture 1815–1860. New York: Harper and Row.

Geertz, Clifford
1963   Agricultural Involution. Berkeley: University of California Press.

Glick, Curtis
1975   The Cultural Impact of the Transamazon Highway on a Traditional Community. M.A. thesis, University of Florida, Center for Latin American Studies.

Gluckman, M.
1954   Rituals of Rebellion in South-East Africa. Manchester: Manchester University Press.
1955   Custom and Conflict in Africa. Oxford: Blackwell.

Gluckman, Max, ed.
1964   Closed Systems and Open Minds: The Limits of Naivety in Social Anthropology. Chicago: Aldine.

Goldenweiser, Alexander
1937   Anthropology. New York: F. S. Crofts and Company.

Goldscheider, C.
1971   Population, Modernization, and Social Structure. Boston: Little, Brown.

Gomes da Silva, José
1971   A Reforma Agrária no Brasil. Rio de Janeiro: Zahar Editores.

Gómez-Pompa, A., et al.
1972   The Tropical Rain Forest: A Non-Renewable Resource. Science 177:762–65.

Goodland, Robert
1980   Environmental Ranking of Amazonian Development Projects in Brazil. Environmental Conservation 7(1):9–26.

Goodland, R., and M. G. Ferri
1979   Ecologia do Cerrado. São Paulo: Editôra da Universidade de São Paulo e Livraria Itatiaia.

Goodland, R. J., and H. S. Irwin
1975   Amazon Jungle: Green Hell to Red Desert? Amsterdam: Elsevier.

Gottlieb, O., and W. Mors
1978   Fitoquímica Amazónica: Uma Apreciação em Perspectiva. Interciencia 3(4):252–63.

Gourou, Pierre
1966   The Tropical World. 4th ed. New York: Wiley.

Greenland, D. J., and J. Kowal
1960.   Nutrient Content of a Moist Tropical Forest of Ghana. Plant and Soil 12:154–74.

Gross, Daniel
1975   Protein Capture and Cultural Development in the Amazon Basin. American Anthropologist 77(3):526–49.

Gross, Daniel, ed.
1973   Peoples and Cultures of Aboriginal South America. New York: Natural History Press.

Gross, D. et al.
 1979 Ecology and Acculturation Among Native Peoples of Central Brazil. Science 206:1043–50.

Gudeman, S.
 1978 Anthropological Economics. Annual Review of Anthropology 7: 347–77.

Haffer, J.
 1969 Speciation in Amazonian Forest Birds. Science 165:131–37.

Haggett, P.
 1965 Scale Components in Geographical Problems. *In* Frontiers in Geographical Teaching, edited by R. J. Chorley and P. Haggett. London: Methuen.

Hames, Raymond
 1979 A Comparison of the Efficiencies of the Shotgun and the Bow in Neotropical Forest Hunting. Human Ecology 7(3):219–52.

Hames, Raymond, ed.
 1980 Studies in Hunting and Fishing in the Neotropics. Working Papers on South American Indians no. 2. Bennington, Vt.: Bennington College.

Hammel, E. A.
 1969 Power in Ica: The Structural History of a Peruvian Community. Boston: Little, Brown.

Hanna, J. M., and P. T. Baker
 1974 Comparative Heat Tolerance of Shipibo Indians and Peruvian Mestizos. Human Biology 46:69–80.

Hanson, E. P.
 1965 New Conquistadors in the Amazon Jungle. Americas 17(9):1–8.

Harris, Marvin
 1956 Town and Country in Brazil. New York: Norton.
 1968 The Rise of Anthropological Theory. New York: Crowell.
 1974a Why a Perfect Knowledge of all the Rules One Must Know to Act Like a Native Cannot Lead to the Knowledge of How Natives Act. Journal of Anthropological Research 30(4):242–51.
 1974b Cows, Pigs, Wars and Witches. New York: Vintage Press.
 1977 Cannibals and Kings. New York: Random House.

Harrison, P., and B. Turner, eds.
 1978 Pre-Hispanic Maya Agriculture. Albuquerque: University of New Mexico Press.

Hasek, V. C.
 1971 Casa Tropical de Madeira: um Modelo de Habitação Rural para a Amazônia. Belem, Pará: SUDAM.

Hawley, Amos
 1973 Ecology and Population. Science 179:1196–1201.

Hecht, Susan
 forthcoming Some Environmental Consequences of Conversion of

Forest to Pasture in Eastern Amazonia. Ph.D. dissertation, University of California at Berkeley, Department of Geography.

Hegen, E. E.
1966 Highways into the Upper Amazon. Gainesville: University of Florida Press.

Heider, Karl
1970 The Dugum Dani. Chicago: Aldine.
1972 Environment, Subsistence and Society. Annual Review of Anthropology 1:207–26.

Helm, June
1962 The Ecological Approach in Anthropology. American Journal of Sociology 67:630–39.

Hemming, John
1978 Red Gold: The Conquest of the Brazilian Indians. Cambridge, Mass.: Harvard University Press.

Herrera, R.
1979 Nutrient Distribution and Cycling in an Amazon Caatinga Forest on Spodosols in Southern Venezuela. Ph.D. thesis, University of Reading, England.

Herrera, R., C. Jordan, H. Klinge, and E. Medina
1978 Amazon Ecosystems: Their Structure and Functioning with Particular Emphasis on Nutrients. Interciencia 3(4):223–31.

Hirschman, A. O.
1967 Development Projects Observed. Washington, D.C.: Brookings Institution.

Holdridge, L. R.
1967 Life Zone Ecology. Rev. ed. San José, Costa Rica: Tropical Science Center.

Holmberg, Allan
1969 Nomads of the Long Bow. New York: Natural History Press.

Honda, E. M. S.
1972 Peixes Encontrados nos Mercados de Manaus. Acta Amazonica 2:97–98.

Hubbell, Stephen
1979 Tree Dispersion, Abundance, and Diversity in a Tropical Dry Forest. Science 203:1299–1309.

Humboldt, Alejandro de
1942 Viaje a las Regiones Equinocciales del Nuevo Continente. 5 vols. Caracas: Biblioteca Venezolana de Cultura. Originally published in 1852.

Hutchinson, Harry
1957 Village and Plantation Life in Northeastern Brazil. Seattle: University of Washington Press.

IBGE (Instituto Brasileiro de Geografia e Estatística)
  1970 Sinopse Preliminar do Censo Demográfico da Região Norte. Rio
        de Janeiro: IBGE.
  1972 Estatísticas do Município de Altamira. Mimeographed.

IBRD (International Bank for Reconstruction and Development)
  1973 Country Report: Brazil. Washington, D.C.: IBRD.

Idrobo, J. M., ed.
  1969 II Simposio y Foro de Biologia Tropical Amazonica. Bogotá,
        Col.: Editorial Pax.

INCRA (Instituto Nacional de Colonização e Reforma Agraria)
  1975 Secretaría de Planejamento, letter of 6 February.

Interdepartmental Committee on Nutrition for National Development
  1965 Northeast Brazil: Nutrition Survey (March–May 1963). Wash-
        ington, D.C.: Office of the Assistant Secretary of Defense.

IPEAN (Instituto de Pesquisa e Experimentação Agropecuaria do Norte)
  1967   Contribuição ao Estudo dos Solos de Altamira. Circular no. 10.
         Belem, Pará: IPEAN.
  1973a Relatório Anual (1972–73) da Estação Experimental da Trans-
         amazônica. Belem, Pará: IPEAN.
  1973b Programa Integrado de Expansão da Pesquisa Agropecuaria na
         Amazônia. Belem, Pará: IPEAN.
  1973c Relatório de Atividades (1972–73). Belem, Pará: IPEAN.
  1974   Solos da Rodovía Transamazônica: Trecho Itaituba–Rio Branco.
         Belem, Pará: IPEAN.

IRRI (International Rice Research Institute)
  1973 Annual Report. Los Baños, Philippines. Mimeographed.

Janzen, Daniel
  1967 Synchronization of Sexual Reproduction of Trees within the
        Dry Season in Central America. Evolution 21:620–37.
  1970 Herbivores and the Number of Tree Species in Tropical Forests.
        American Naturalist 104:501–28.
  1975 Tropical Agroecosystems. In Food: Politics, Economics, Nutrition
        and Research, edited by Philip Abelson. Washington, D.C.: Ameri-
        can Association for the Advancement of Science.

Johnson, Allen
  1971 Sharecroppers of the Sertão. Stanford, Calif.: Stanford Univer-
        sity Press.
  1974 Ethnoecology and Planting Practices in a Swidden Agricultural
        System. American Ethnologist 1:87–101.
  1977 The Energy Costs of Technology in a Changing Environment: A
        Machiguenga Case. In Material Culture. Proceedings of the
        American Ethnological Society. St. Paul, Minn.: West Publishing
        Company.

Jones, William
  1959 Manioc in Africa. Stanford, Calif.: Food Research Institute.

Jordan, C. F.
  1971 Productivity of a Tropical Forest and its Relation to a World
        Pattern of Energy Storage. Journal of Ecology 59:127–42.

1979   Composition, Structure, and Regeneration of a Tierra Firme Forest of the Amazon Basin of Venezuela. Annual Report of the Institute of Ecology: Project on Nutrient Dynamics of a Tropical Rain Forest Ecosystem. Athens: University of Georgia.

Jordan, C. F., and E. Medina
1978   Ecosystem Research in the Tropics. Annals of the Missouri Botanical Garden 64(4):737–45.

Jordan, C. F., and C. Uhl
1978   Biomass of a "Tierra Firme" Forest of the Amazon Basin. Oecologia Plantarum 13:387–400.

Jordan, C. F. et al.
1979   Nutrient Scavenging of Rainfall by the Canopy of an Amazonian Rainforest. Biotropica, in press.

Jornal da Transamazônica
1972   A População de Amazônia. P. 2.

Junk, W. J.
1975   Aquatic Wildlife of Fisheries. *In* The Use of Ecological Guidelines for Development in the American Tropics. Morges, Switzerland: International Union for Conservation of Nature and Natural Resources.

Jurion, F., and J. Henry
1969   Can Primitive Farming Be Modernized? London: Agra-Europe.

Katzman, M. T.
1976   Paradoxes of Amazonian Development in a "Resource-Starved" World. Journal of Developing Areas 10(4):445–60.

Kelly, Arlene
1975   The Xingú and José Porfírio. M.A. thesis, University of Florida, Department of History.

Kiev, Ari
1968   Curanderismo: Mexican-American Folk Psychiatry. New York: The Free Press.

King, J. A.
1973   The Ecology of Aggressive Behavior. Annual Review of Ecology and Systematics 4:117–38.

Kleinpenning, J. M. G.
1975   The Integration and Colonization of the Brazilian Portion of the Amazon Basin. Nijmegen, Holland: Institute of Geography and Planning.
1978   A Further Evaluation of the Policy for the Integration of the Amazon Region (1974–76). Journal of Economic and Social Geography 69:78–85.

Klinge, H.
1978   Studies on the Ecology of Amazon Caatinga Forest in Southern Venezuela: Biomass Dominance of Selected Tree Species in the Amazon Caatinga near San Carlos de Rio Negro. Acta Cientifica Venezolana 29:258–62.

Klinge, Hans, and William Rodrigues
1968 Litter Production in an Area of Amazonian Terra Firme Forest. Amazoniana 1:287–310.

Klinge, H. et al.
1975 Biomass and Structure in a Central Amazonian Rain Forest. *In* Tropical Ecological Systems, edited by Frank B. Golley and E. Medina. New York: Springer-Verlag.

Lacaz, C. et al.
1972 Introdução à Geografía Médica do Brasil. São Paulo: Editôra Blücher.

Ladell, W. S. S.
1964 Terrestrial Animals in Humid Heat: Man. *In* Handbook of Physiology: Adaptation to the Environment, edited by D. B. Dill et al. Washington, D.C.: American Physiological Society.

Laraia, R. de B., and R. da Matta
1967 Indios e Castanheiros. Rio de Janeiro: Difusão Européia do Livro.

Lathrap, D.
1968 Aboriginal Occupation and Changes in River Channel on the Central Ucayali, Peru. American Antiquity 33:62–79.
1970 The Upper Amazon. London: Thames and Hudson.
1976 Our Father the Cayman, Our Mother the Gourd. *In* Origins of Agriculture, edited by C. A. Reed. The Hague: Mouton.

Laughlin, C., and I. Brady, eds.
1978 Extinction and Survival in Human Populations. New York: Columbia University Press.

Leach, E. R.
1954 Political Systems of Highland Burma. London: Athlone Press.

Leacock, S.
1964 Economic Life of the Maué Indians. Boletim do Museu Paraense Emilio Goeldi. N. S. Antropologia 19:1–30.

LeCointe, P.
1947 Arvores e Plantas Úteis da Amazônia Brasileira. São Paulo: Companhía Editôra Nacional.

Lee, Richard B.
1968 What Hunters Do for a Living, or How to Make Out on Scarce Resources. *In* Man, the Hunter, edited by Richard B. Lee and I. DeVore. Chicago: Aldine.
1972 Population Growth and the Beginnings of Sedentary Life Among the !Kung Bushmen. *In* Population Growth: Anthropological Implications, edited by B. Spooner. Cambridge, Mass.: MIT Press.

Leigh, Egbert Giles, Jr.
1975 Structure and Climate in Tropical Rain Forest. Annual Review of Ecology and Systematics 6:67–86.

Lent, H., ed.
1967 Atas do Simpósio sobre a Biota Amazônica. 7 vols. Rio de Janeiro: Conselho Nacional de Pesquisas.

Leung, W. W.
 1961 Food Composition Tables for Use in Latin America. Bethesda,
    Maryland: Interdepartmental Committee on Nutrition for Na-
    tional Defense.

Lévi-Strauss, C.
 1948 Tribes of the Upper Xingú River. *In* Handbook of South Ameri-
    can Indians, edited by J. Steward, vol. 3.

Linares, Olga
 1976 Garden Hunting in the American Tropics. Human Ecology 4(4):
    331–49.

Livingstone, F. B.
 1968 The Effects of Warfare on the Biology of the Human Species. *In*
    War: The Anthropology of Armed Conflict, edited by Morton
    Fried et al. New York: Doubleday.

Lizot, J.
 1978 Population, Resources and Warfare Among the Yanomami. Man
    12(4):497–517.
 1979 L'Economie Primitive. Libre 4:69–113.

Longman, K. A., and J. Jenik
 1974 Tropical Forest and its Environment. London: Longman.

Lowenstein, F. W.
 1963 Nutrition and Health in School Children in a Brazilian Amazon
    Town. J. Trop. Ped. Afric. Child Health 8(4):88–96.

Lowenstein, Frank
 1968 Some Aspects of Human Ecology in South America. *In* Bio-
    geography and Ecology in South America, edited by E. J. Fittkau
    et al. The Hague: Junk.
 1973 Some Considerations of Biological Adaptation by Aboriginal Man.
    In Tropical Forest Ecosystems in Africa and South America,
    edited by Betty Meggers et al. Washington, D.C.: Smithsonian In-
    stitution Press.

Lowie, R.
 1917 Culture and Ethnology. New York: D. C. McMurtrie.

Lynch, R. L., ed.
 1969 The Cross-Cultural Approach to Health Behavior. Madison, Wis.:
    Fairleigh Dickinson University Press.

Lyon, Patricia, ed.
 1974 Native South Americans. Boston: Little, Brown and Company.

Mahar, Dennis
 1976a Fiscal Incentives for Regional Development: A Case Study of
    the Western Amazon Basin. Journal of Interamerican Studies and
    World Affairs 18(3):357–76.
 1976b Fiscal Incentives and the Economic Development of Western
    Amazonia. Brazilian Economic Studies (IPEA) 2:147–74.
 1979 Frontier Development Policy in Brazil: A Study of Amazonia.
    New York: Praeger.

Margolis, Maxine
  1973 The Moving Frontier. Gainesville: University of Florida Press.
  1979 Seduced and Abandoned: Agricultural Frontiers in Brazil and the United States. *In* Brazil: Anthropological Perspectives, edited by M. Margolis and W. Carter. New York: Columbia University Press.

Marzola, D. L., and D. P. Bartholomew
  1979 Photosynthetic Pathway and Biomass Energy Production. Science 205:555–59.

Masek, Joseph
  1959 Recommended Nutrient Allowances. World Review of Nutrition and Dietetics 3:153–93.

Massing, A.
  1979 Economic Development and its Effect on Traditional Land Use Systems in the Tropical Forests of West Africa. Studies in Third World Societies 8:73–95.

May, R. M.
  1975 Diversity, Stability and Maturity in Natural Ecosystems, with Particular Reference to the Tropical Moist Forests. Rome: FAO. Mimeographed.

Maybury-Lewis, David
  1956 Diet and Health in an Acculturated Tribe. Proceedings of the 32d International Congress of Americanists. Copenhagen.
  1967 Akwẽ-Shavante Society. Oxford: Clarendon Press.

Mayer, John
  1970 The Brazilian Household: Size and Composition. Ph.D. dissertation, University of Florida, Department of Sociology.

McArthur, R., and E. O. Wilson
  1967 The Theory of Island Biogeography. Princeton: Princeton University Press.

McCarthy, H. H., J. C. Hook, and D. S. Knos
  1956 The Measurement of Association in Industrial Geography. Department of Geography, University of Iowa.

McNeil, M.
  1964 Lateritic Soils. Scientific American 211(5):86–102.

Meggers, Betty
  1954 Environmental Limitations on the Development of Culture. American Anthropologist 56:801–24.
  1957 Environment and Culture in the Amazon Basin: An Appraisal of the Theory of Environmental Determinism. *In* Studies in Human Ecology. Washington, D.C.: Anthropological Society of Washington/Organization of American States.
  1971 Amazonia: Man and Culture in a Counterfeit Paradise. Chicago: Aldine.
  1972 Prehistoric America. Chicago: Aldine.
  1974 Environment and Culture in Amazonia. *In* Man in the Amazon,

edited by Charles Wagley. Gainesville, Fla.: University of Florida Press.
1975 Application of the Biological Model of Diversification to Cultural Distributions in Tropical Lowland South America. Biotropica 7(3):141–61.

Meggers, Betty, and C. Evans
1957 Archeological Investigations at the Mouth of the Amazon. Bureau of American Ethnology Bulletin no. 167. Washington, D.C.: Smithsonian Institution.

Meggers, Betty, E. S. Ayensu, and W. D. Ducksworth, eds.
1973 Tropical Forest Ecosystems in Africa and South America. Washington, D.C.: Smithsonian Institution Press.

Mein, R., and P. Rosado
1948 Experiencia com Novos Medicamentos contra a Malaria no Programa da Amazônia. Revista do SESP 1(4):1059–1091.

Melby, John
1966 Rubber River: An Account of the Rise and Collapse of the Amazon Boom. *In* Readings in Latin American History, edited by Lewis Hanke, vol. 2. New York: Crowell.

Mendonça, Eugene
1979 Agricultural Development: When Cooperation Fails. Royal Anthropological Institute News 31:4–5.

Metráux, A.
1948 Tribes of the Juruá-Purús Basins. *In* Handbook of South American Indians, edited by J. Steward, vol. 3.

Miller, Darrel
1975 Amazon Town: 1948–1974. M.A. thesis, University of Florida, Department of Anthropology.

Ministério da Agricultura
1972a Altamira 1. Brasília D.F.: INCRA.
1972b Amazônia: Uma Alternativa para os Problemas Agrários Brasileiros. Mimeographed.

Mittermeier, R.
1975 A Turtle in Every Pot. Animal Kingdom, April/May, pp. 9–14.

Morães, M.
1972 A Esquistosomose na Amazônia. Revista da Universidade Federal do Pará 2(2):197–219.

Morães, M. et al.
1973 Onchocerciasis in Brazil. Bulletin of the Pan American Health Organization 7(4):50–56.

Moran, Emilio F.
1973 Energy Flow Analysis and *Manihot esculenta* Crantz. Acta Amazonica 3(3):28–39.
1974 The Adaptive System of the Amazonian Caboclo. *In* Man in the

Amazon, edited by C. Wagley. Gainesville: University of Florida Press.

1975 Pioneer Farmers of the Transamazon Highway: Adaptation and Agricultural Production in the Lowland Tropics. Ph.D. dissertation, University of Florida.

1976a Agricultural Development in the Transamazon Highway. Latin American Studies Working Papers. Bloomington: Indiana University.

1976b Manioc Deserves more Recognition in Tropical Farming. World Crops 28(4):184–88.

1977 Estratégias de Sobrevivência: O Uso de Recursos ao Longo da Rodovia Transamazonica. Acta Amazonica 7(3):363–79.

1979a Human Adaptability: An Introduction to Ecological Anthropology. N. Scituate: Duxbury Press.

1979b Strategies for Survival: Resource Use Along the Transamazon Highway. Studies in Third World Societies 7:49–75.

1979c Criteria for Choosing Homesteaders in Brazil. Research in Economic Anthropology 2:339–59.

1979d Mobility and Resource Use in Amazonia. Paper presented at University of Cambridge Conference on Colonization in Amazonia.

n.d. Amazonian Development: Structural and Interactional Constraints. Manuscript in preparation.

Moreau, R.
1948 Ecological Isolation in a Rich Tropical Avifauna. Journal of Animal Ecology 17:113–26.

Mors, W., and C. Rizzini
1966 Useful Plants of Brazil. San Francisco, Calif.: Holden-Day.

Mott, G. O., and H. L. Popenoe
1975 Ecophysiology of Tropical Grasslands. Unpublished manuscript.

Murphy, R.
1958 Mundurucú Religion. Berkeley: University of California Press.

Murphy, R., and Y. Murphy
1974 Women of the Forest. New York: Columbia University Press.

Murphy, R., and B. Quain
1955 The Trumaí Indians of Central Brazil. Seattle: American Ethnological Society Monographs.

Myers, T.
1973 Toward the Reconstruction of Prehistoric Community Patterns in the Amazon Basin. In Variation in Anthropology, edited by D. Lathrap and J. Douglas. Urbana, Ill.: Illinois Archeological Survey.

National Academy of Science
1972 Soils of the Humid Tropics. Washington, D.C.: National Academy of Science.

Nelson, Michael
1973 The Development of Tropical Lands: Policy Issues in Latin America. Baltimore, Md.: The Johns Hopkins University Press.

Netting, Robert
1968   Hill Farmers of Nigeria. Seattle: Washington University Press.

Newman, Russell
1975   Human Adaptation to Heat. *In* Physiological Anthropology, edited by Albert Damon. New York: Oxford University Press.

Nietschmann, Bernard
1972   Hunting and Fishing Focus among the Miskito Indians, Eastern Nicaragua. Human Ecology 1(1):41–67.
1973   Between Land and Water. New York: Seminar Press.

Nimuendajú, C.
1939   The Apinayé. Washington, D.C.: Catholic University Press.
1948a Tribes of the Lower and Middle Xingú River. *In* Handbook of South American Indians, edited by J. Steward, vol. 3.
1948b The Mawé and the Arapium. *In* Handbook of South American Indians, edited by J. Steward, vol. 3.
1948c The Mura and the Piranha. *In* Handbook of South American Indians, edited by J. Steward, vol. 3.
1952   The Tukuna. Berkeley: University of California Press.

Nye, P. H., and D. J. Greenland
1960   The Soil under Shifting Cultivation. Technical Communication no. 51. Harpenden, U.K.: Commonwealth Bureau of Soils.

Oberg, K.
1953   Indian Tribes of Northern Mato Grosso. Washington, D.C.: Smithsonian Institution.

Odum, Eugene
1969   The Strategy of Ecosystem Development. Science 164:262–70.

Odum, Howard T.
1971   Environment, Power and Society. New York: Wiley Inter-Science.

Odum, Howard, and F. Pigeon, eds.
1970   A Tropical Rain Forest. Springfield, Va.: U.S. Department of Commerce/Atomic Energy Commission.

Oliveira-Marques, A. H. de
1971   Daily Life in Portugal in the Late Middle Ages. Madison: University of Wisconsin Press.

Opler, M.
1963   The Cultural Definitions of Illness in Village India. Human Organization 22:32–35.

Oyama, M., and H. Takehara
1967   Revised Standard Soil Color Charts. Tokyo, Japan: International Soil Science Society.

Pechnick, E., and J. M. Chaves
1945   O Açaí, um dos Alimentos Básicos da Amazônia. Anais da Associação Química Brasileira 4:169.

Pekkarinen, Maija
1970   Methodology in the Collection of Food Consumption Data. World Review of Nutrition and Dietetics 12:145–71.

Pinheiro, F. et al.
1974a Infectious Diseases along Brazil's Transamazon Highway. Bulletin of the Pan American Health Organization 8(2):111–21.
1974b Hemorrhagic Syndrome of Altamira. The Lancet 1(7859):639–42.

Pires, J. M.
1978 The Forest Ecosystems of the Brazilian Amazon: Description, Functioning and Research Needs. *In* Tropical Forest Ecosystems. Paris: UNESCO.

Poats, Susan
1975 Kilometer 42: A Transamazon Highway Community. M.A. thesis, Department of Anthropology, University of Florida.

Popenoe, Hugh
1960 Effects of Shifting Cultivation on Natural Soil Constituents in Central America. Ph.D. dissertation, University of Florida, IFAS.

Prance, G. T.
1973 Phytogeographic Support for the Theory of Pleistocene Forest Refuges in the Amazon Basin, Based on Evidence from *Dischapetalaceae* and *Lecythidaceae*. Acta Amazonica 3(3):5–28.
1978 The Origin and Evolution of the Amazon Flora. Interciencia 3(4): 207–22.

Preto-Rodas, Richard
1974 Amazonia in Literature: Themes and Changing Perspectives. *In* Man in the Amazon, edited by C. Wagley. Gainesville: University of Florida Press.

Price, A. Grenfell
1939 White Settlers in the Tropics. New York: American Geographical Society.

Price, P. D.
1977 Acculturation, Social Assistance, and Political Context: The Nambiquara of Brazil. Proceedings of the XLII Congress of Americanists, Paris. Pp. 603–609.

PRONAPA
1970 Brazilian Archeology in 1968. American Antiquity 35(1):1–23.

RADAM (Radar da Amazonia)
1974 Levantamento de Recursos Naturais. Vol. 5. Rio de Janeiro: Ministério de Minas e Energía.

Radcliffe-Brown, A. R.
1940 On Social Structure. Presidential address to the Royal Anthropological Institute. J.R.A.I. 70.

Ranzani, G.
1978 Alguns Solos da Transamazonica na Região de Marabá. Acta Amazonica 8(3):333–55.

Rappaport, Roy
1968 Pigs for the Ancestors. New Haven, Conn.: Yale University Press.
1971a The Flow of Energy in an Agricultural Society. Scientific American 224(3):116–32.

1971b The Sacred in Human Evolution. Annual Review of Ecology and Systematics 2:23–44.
1977 Ecology, Adaptation and the Ills of Functionalism. Michigan Discussions in Anthropology 2:138–90.

Rassi, E. et al.
1975 Preliminary Report of a New Vector of Onchocerciasis in the Americas. Bulletin of the Pan American Health Organization 9(1):10–12.

Redfield, Robert
1941 The Folk Culture of Yucatan. Chicago: University of Chicago Press.

Reh, Emma
1962 Manual on Household Food Consumption Surveys. Rome: FAO.

Reichel-Dolmatoff, G.
1971 Amazonian Cosmos. Chicago: University of Chicago Press.
1976 Cosmology as Ecological Analysis: A View from the Rain Forest. Man 11:307–18.

Reina, Ruben
1967 Milpas and Milperos: Implications for Prehistoric Times. American Anthropologist 69:1–20.

Reis, Arthur Cézar Ferreira
1942 Síntese de História do Pará. Belem, Pará: n.p.
1968 A Amazônia e a Cobiça Internacional. 3d ed. Rio de Janeiro: Gráfica Record Editôra.

Resende, Eliseu
1973 As Rodovías e o Desenvolvimento do Brasil. Rio de Janeiro: Ministério de Transportes.

Ribeiro, Darcy
1970 Os Indios e a Civilização. Rio de Janeiro: Editôra Civilização Brasileira.

Richards, Paul W.
1952 The Tropical Rain Forest. Cambridge: University Press.
1969 Speciation in the Tropical Rain Forest and the Concept of the Niche. Biological Journal of the Linnean Society 1:149–53.
1973 The Tropical Rain Forest. Scientific American 229:58–67.

Richerson, Peter
1977 Ecology and Human Ecology: A Comparison of Theories in the Biological and Social Sciences. American Ethnologist 4(1):1–26.

Riviére, P.
1972 The Forgotten Frontier. New York: Holt, Rinehart and Winston.

Robinson, W. S.
1950 Ecological Correlations and the Behavior of Individuals. American Sociological Review 15:351–57.

Rocha Penteado, Antônio
1967 Problemas de Colonização e de Uso da Terra na Regiáo Bragan-

tina do Estado do Pará. 2 vols. Belem, Pará: Universidade Federal do Pará.
1978   Condições Geo-ecológicas da Amazônia Brasileira. Revista do Museu Paulista 21:1–17.

Rodrigues Lima, Rubens
1956   A Agricultura nas Várzeas do Estuário do Amazonas. Belem, Pará: Instituto Agronómico do Norte.

Roett, Riordan
1972   Brazil: Politics in a Patrimonial Society. Boston: Little, Brown.

Rogers, D., and M. Milner
1965   Amino Acid Profile of Manioc Leaf Protein in Relation to Nutritive Value. Economic Botany 17:211–16.

Rosenblat, Angel
1954   La Población Indígena y el Mestizaje en America. 2 vols. Buenos Aires: Editorial Nova.

Ross, Eric B.
1978   Food Taboos, Diet, and Hunting Strategy: The Adaptation to Animals in Amazon Cultural Ecology. Current Anthropology 19: 1–36.

Ruddle, K.
1970   The Hunting Technology of the Maracá Indians. Antropológica 25:21–63.
1973   The Human Use of Insects: Examples from the Yukpa. Biotropica 5(2):94–101.
1974   The Yukpa Cultivation System. Ibero-Americana 52:1–197.

Russell, Joseph
1942   Fordlandia and Belterra Rubber Plantations on the Tapajós River, Brazil. Economic Geography 18:125–45.

Ryden, S.
1950   A Study of South American Indian Hunting Traps. Revista do Museu Paulista 4:247–352.

Sahlins, M.
1972   Stone Age Economics. Chicago: Aldine.

Sahlins, M., and E. Service
1960   Evolution and Culture. Ann Arbor: University of Michigan Press.

Sanchez, Pedro
1976   Properties and Management of Soils in the Tropics. New York: Wiley-Interscience.
1977   Advances in the Management of Oxisols and Ultisols in Tropical South America. Proceedings of Seminar on Soil Environment and Fertility Management in Intensive Agriculture. Tokyo, Japan.

Sanchez, Pedro, and S. W. Buol
1975   Soils of the Tropics and the World Food Crisis. Science 188: 598–603.

Sanchez, Pedro et al.
1972 A Review of Soils Research in Tropical Latin America. Technical Bulletin 219. Raleigh: North Carolina Agricultural Experiment Station.
1974 Investigaciones en Manejo de Suelos Tropicales en Yurimagüas, Selva Baja del Perú. Paper presented at Seminarío de Sistemas de Agricultura Tropical (Lima, Peru, 1–8 June 1974).

Santos, Abelardo
1955 Kwashiorkor: Alguns Aspectos Estudados em Belem do Pará. Belem: Gráfica da Revista de Veterinaria.

Santos, Roberto
1968 O Equilíbrio da Firma Aviadora e a Significação Econômica. Pará Desenvolvimento 3:7–30.

Santos Filho, L.
1966 Pequena História da Medicina Brasileira. São Paulo: São Paulo Editôra.

Sargent, Frederick, ed.
1974 Human Ecology. Amsterdam: North Holland Publishing Company.

Scazzocchio, Françoise, ed.
in press Land, People, and Planning in Contemporary Amazonia. Cambridge (UK): Centre of Latin American Studies, University of Cambridge.

Schneider, J., and R. Schneider
1976 Culture and Political Economy in Western Sicily. New York: Academic Press.

Schuh, G. Edward
1970 The Agricultural Development of Brazil. New York: Praeger.

Schultes, R. E.
1960 Native Narcotics of the New World. Pharmacological Sciences.

Schultz, Theodore
1964 Transforming Traditional Agriculture. New Haven, Conn.: Yale University Press.

Schurz, William
1925 Rubber Production in the Amazon Valley. Washington, D.C.: Government Printing Office.

Schwaner, T. D., and C. F. Dixon
1974 Helminthiasis as a Measure of Cultural Change in the Amazon Basin. Biotropica 6(1):32–37.

SESI (Serviço Social da Indústria)
1974 SESI em Ação na Transamazônica: Altamira. Industria e Produtividade, June, pp. 76–80.

Silva, W. et al.
1959 Inquérito sobre Consumo de Alimentos e Nutrimentos: Avaliação

do Estado Nutritivo e Situação Econômica da População da Amazônia. Boletim da Comissão Nacional de Alimentação 9(2):1–60.

Simmons, I. G.
1974 The Ecology of Natural Resources. New York: Wiley (Halsted Press).

Simmons, O.
1955 Popular and Modern Medicine in Mestizo Communities of Coastal Peru and Chile. Journal of American Folklore 68:57–71.

Sioli, Harald
1951 Alguns Resultados e Problemas da Limnología Amazônica. Boletim Técnico do Instituto Agronómico do Norte no. 24. Belém, Pará: IAN.
1973 Recent Human Activities in the Brazilian Amazon Region and their Ecological Effects. *In* Tropical Forest Ecosystems in Africa and South America, edited by Betty Meggers et al. Washington, D.C.: Smithsonian Institution.

Siskind, Janet
1973 To Hunt in the Morning. New York: Oxford University Press.

Slovic, P., H. Kunreuther, and G. White
1974 Decision Processes, Rationality and Adjustment to Natural Hazards. *In* Natural Hazards, edited by Gilbert White. New York: Oxford University Press.

Smith, Nigel
1974a Destructive Exploitation of the South American River Turtle. Yearbook of the Association of American Geographers 36:85–102.
1974b Agouti and Babaçú. Oryx 12(5):581–82.
1976a Transamazon Highway: A Cultural Ecological Analysis of Settlement in the Lowland Tropics. Ph.D. dissertation, University of California, Berkeley, Department of Geography.
1976b Utilization of Game Along Brazil's Transamazon Highway. Acta Amazonica 6(4):455–66.
1976c Spotted Cats and the Amazon Skin Trade. Oryx 13(4):362–71.
1977 Influencias Culturais e Ecológicas na Produtividade Agrícola ao longo da Transamazônica. Acta Amazonica 7:23–28.
1978 Agricultural Productivity Along Brazil's Transamazon Highway. Agro-ecosystems 4:415–32.
1979 Aquatic Turtles of Amazonia: An Endangered Resource. Biological Conservation 16(3):165–76.

Smith, T. Lynn
1969 Studies of Colonization and Settlement. Latin American Research Review 4:93–123.
1972 Brazil: People and Institutions. Baton Rouge: Louisiana State University Press.

Smith, Thomas
1959 The Agrarian Origins of Modern Japan. Stanford: Stanford University Press.

Snyder, David
1967   The Carretera Marginal de la Selva: A Geographical Review and Appraisal. Revista Geografica 67:87–100.

Sombroek, W. G.
1966   Amazon Soils. Wageningen: Centre for Agricultural Publications and Documentation.

Spencer, Joseph E.
1966   Shifting Cultivation in Southeast Asia. Berkeley, Calif.: University of California Press.

Sponsel, Leslie
n.d.   The Hunter and the Hunted in the Amazon. Ph.D. dissertation, Department of Anthropology, Cornell University, in progress.

Sprout, H., and M. Sprout
1965   The Ecological Perspective on Human Affairs. Princeton, N.J.: Princeton University Press.

SPVEA (Superintendencia para a Valorização Economica da Amazonia)
1960   Política de Desenvolvimento da Amazônia (1954–60). Belem: SPVEA.

Stark, L. and T. McDonald, eds.
forthcoming   Amazonia: Extinction or Survival? Madison: University of Wisconsin Press.

Stark, N.
1969   Direct Nutrient Cycling in the Amazon Basin. *In* II Simposio y Foro de Biología Tropical Amazónica. Bogotá: Editorial Pax.
1970   The Nutrient Content of Plants and Soils from Brazil and Surinam. Biotropica 2:51–60.
1971a Nutrient Cycling: Nutrient Distribution in Some Amazonian Soils. Tropical Ecology 12:24–50.
1971b Nutrient Cycling II: Nutrient Distribution in Amazonian Vegetation. Tropical Ecology 12:177–201.
1972   Nutrient Cycling Pathways and Litter Fungi. Bioscience 22:355–60.

Stark, N., and C. F. Jordan
1978   Nutrient Retention by the Root Mat of an Amazonian Rain Forest. Ecology 59:434–37.

Stark, N., and M. Spratt
1977   Root Biomass and Nutrient Storage in Rain Forest Oxisols near San Carlos de Rio Negro. Tropical Ecology 18:1–19.

Steila, Donald
1976   The Geography of Soils. Englewood Cliffs, N.J.: Prentice-Hall.

Sternberg, Hilgard O'Reilly
1956   A Agua e o Homem na Várzea do Carreiro. 2 vols. Rio de Janeiro: Universidade do Brasil.
1973   Development and Conservation. Erkunde 27:253–65.
1975   The Amazon River of Brazil. Wiesbaden: F. Steiner Verlag.

Steward, Julian
    1950   Area Research: Theory and Practice. New York: Social Science Research Council.
    1955   Theory of Culture Change. Urbana, Ill.: University of Illinois Press.

Steward, Julian, ed.
    1939-1946   Handbook of South American Indians. 7 vols. Washington, D.C.: Bureau of American Ethnology.
    1956   The People of Puerto Rico. Urbana, Ill.: University of Illinois Press.

Steward, Julian, and L. Faron
    1959   Native Peoples of South America. New York: McGraw-Hill.

Stewart, Norman
    1968   Some Problems in the Development of Agricultural Colonization in the Andean Oriente. Professional Geographer 20(1):33–38.

SUDAM (Superintendência do Desenvolvimento da Amazônia)
    1971a   Subsídios ao Plano Regional de Desenvolvimento (1972–74). Belem: SUDAM.
    1971b   Relatório de Marabá e Altamira. Mimeographed.
    1972   Relatório Geral. Belem, Pará: SUDAM.
    1974   Estudos Básicos para uma Política de Desenvolvimento dos Recursos Florestais na Amazônia. Belem, Pará: SUDAM.
    1975   II Plano de Desenvolvimento da Amazônia (1975–79). Belem: SUDAM/BASA.
    1976   Polamazônia: Síntese. Belem: SUDAM.

Sutmoller, P., A. Vahia de Abreu, J. van der Grift, and W. G. Sombroeck
    1966   Mineral Imbalances in Cattle in the Amazon Valley. Communication no. 53. Amsterdam: Royal Tropical Institute.

Sweet, David
    1974   A Realm of Nature Destroyed. Ph.D. dissertation, University of Wisconsin, Madison, Department of History.

Swift, Jeremy
    1977   Sahelian Pastoralists: Underdevelopment, Desertification, and Famine. Annual Review of Anthropology 6:457–78.

Tambs, Lewis
    1974   Geopolitics of the Amazon. In Man in the Amazon, edited by C. Wagley. Gainesville, Fla.: University of Florida Press.

Taylor, Griffith
    1951   Geography in the 20th Century. London: Methuen.

Taylor, K.
    1974   Sanumá Fauna Prohibitions and Classifications. Caracas, Venezuela: Fundación LaSalle de Ciencias Naturales.

Temkin, O.
    1973   Galenism: Rise and Decline of a Medical Philosophy. Ithaca: Cornell University Press.

Théry, H., and H. R. d'Arc
    1979   State and Entrepreneurs in the Development of Amazonia. Paper
            presented at the University of Cambridge Conference on Coloni-
            zation in Amazonia.

Thomas, Franklin
    1925   The Environmental Basis of Society. New York: The Century
            Company.

Thomas, R. B.
    1973   Human Adaptation to a High Andean Energy Flow System. De-
            partment of Anthropology Occasional Papers. University Park:
            Pennsylvania State University.

Tropical Soils Research Program
    1976   Annual Report 1975. Raleigh, N.C.: Soil Science Department,
            North Carolina State University.

Turner, F. J.
    1920   The Frontier in American History. New York: Henry Holt.

Turner, V. W.
    1957   Schism and Continuity in an African Society. Manchester: Man-
            chester University Press.

Uhl, Christopher
    1980   Studies of Forest, Agricultural, and Successional Environments
            in the Upper Rio Negro Region of the Amazon Basin. Ph.D. dis-
            sertation, Department of Botany, Michigan State University.

UNESCO (United Nations Educational, Scientific and Cultural Organization)
    1978   Tropical Forest Ecosystems: A State-of-Knowledge Report. Paris:
            UNESCO.

USDA (United States Department of Agriculture)
    1970   Economic Progress of Agriculture in Developing Nations (1950–
            1968). Foreign Agricultural Economic Report no. 59. Washington,
            D.C.: USDA.

Valverde, Orlando, and C. V. Dias
    1967   A Rodovia Belém-Brasília. Rio de Janeiro: IBGE.

Van der Hammen, T.
    1977   Changes in Vegetation and Climate in the Amazon Basin and
            Surrounding Areas during the Pleistocene. Geol. Mijnb. 51:641–
            43.

van Heerden, Pieter
    1968   The Foundation of Empirical Knowledge. Wassenaar, Holland:
            N. V. Vitgeverij Wistik.

Vanzolini, G.
    1970   Zoología Sistemática, Geografía e a Origem das Especies. São
            Paulo: Instituto de Geografía.

Vayda, A. P.
    1968   Hypotheses About Functions of War. *In* War: The Anthropology

of Armed Conflict and Aggression, edited by M. Fried et al. New York: Natural History Press.

Vayda, A. P., and Roy Rappaport
1976   Ecology, Cultural and Noncultural. *In* Human Ecology, edited by P. Richerson and J. McEvoy. North Scituate, Mass.: Duxbury Press.

Velho, Otávio Guilherme
1972   Frentes de Expansão e Estrutura Agrária. Rio de Janeiro: Zahar Editores.
1976   Capitalismo Autoritario e Campesinato. São Paulo: Difel.

Venkatachalan, P., and V. Patwardhan
1953   The Rule of *Ascaris lumbricoides* in the Nutrition of the Host. Trans. Roy. Soc. Trop. Med. and Hyg. 47(2):169–75.

Vergolino e Silva, Anaíza
1971   O Negro no Pará. *In* Antologia da Cultura Amazonica, edited by Carlos Rocque, vol. 6. São Paulo: Amazônia Edições Culturais.

Veríssimo, José
1970   A Pesca na Amazônia. Belem, Pará: Universidade Federal do Pará.

Vickers, William
1975   Meat is Meat: The Siona-Secoya and the Hunting-Prowess-Sexual Reward Hypothesis. Latin Americanist 11(1):1–5.
1976   Cultural Adaptation to Amazonian Habitats: The Siona-Secoya of Eastern Ecuador. Ph.D. dissertation, University of Florida, Department of Anthropology.
1979   Native Amazonian Subsistence in Diverse Habitats: The Siona-Secoya of Ecuador. Studies in Third World Societies 7:6–36.
1980   An Analysis of Amazonian Hunting Yields as a Function of Settlement Age. *In* Studies in Hunting and Fishing in the Neotropics, edited by R. Hames. Bennington, Vt.: Bennington College.

Waddell, Eric
1972   The Mound-Builders. Seattle: University of Washington Press.

Wagley, Charles
1948   Regionalism and Cultural Unity in Brazil. Social Forces 26:457–64.
1951   The Brazilian Amazon: The Case of an Underdeveloped Area. *In* Four Papers Presented in the Institute for Brazilian Studies. Nashville, Tenn.: Vanderbilt University Press.
1952   The Folk Culture of the Brazilian Amazon. Proceedings of the 29th Congress of Americanists. Chicago: University of Chicago Press.
1953   Amazon Town. New York: Macmillan.
1968   The Latin American Tradition. New York: Columbia University Press.
1969   Cultural Influences on Population: A Comparison of 2 Tupi Tribes. *In* Environment and Cultural Behavior, edited by Andrew P. Vayda. New York: Natural History Press.

1971   An Introduction to Brazil. Rev. ed. New York: Columbia University Press.

1974   Introduction. *In* Man in the Amazon, edited by C. Wagley. Gainesville: University of Florida Press.

1977   Welcome of Tears: The Tapirape Indians of Central Brazil. New York: Oxford.

Wagley, Charles, ed.
1974   Man in the Amazon. Gainesville, Fla.: University of Florida Press.

Wallace, Alfred Russell
1895   Travels on the Amazon and Rio Negro. 5th ed. London.

Wallerstein, I.
1974   The Modern World-System: Capitalist Agriculture and the Origins of the European World-Economy in the 16th Century. New York: Academic Press.

Wambeke, A. van
1978   Properties and Potentials of Soils in the Amazon Basin. Interciencia 3(4):233–42.

Watson, W.
1964   Social Mobility and Social Class in Industrial Communities. *In* Closed Systems and Open Minds, edited by M. Gluckman. Chicago: Aldine.

Watt, B. K., and A. L. Merrill.
1963   Composition of Foods: Raw, Processed, Prepared. Agriculture Handbook no. 8. Washington, D.C.: USDA.

Watters, R. F.
1971   Shifting Cultivation in Latin America. Rome: FAO.

Weisbord, B. et al.
1973   Disease and Economic Development. Madison: University of Wisconsin Press.

Werner, D. et al.
1979   Subsistence Productivity and Hunting Effort in Native South America. Human Ecology 7(4):303–15.

Wesche, Rolf J.
1967   The Settler Wedge of the Upper Putumayo River. Ph.D. dissertation, University of Florida, Department of Geography.

White, Leslie
1949   The Science of Culture. New York: Grove Press.

Whitmore, T. C.
1975   Tropical Rain Forests of the Far East. Oxford: Clarendon.

Whittaker, R. H.
1970   Communities and Ecosystems. New York: Macmillan.

Whitten, Richard
1979   Comments on the Theory of Holocene Refugia in the Culture History of Amazonia. American Antiquity 44(2):238–51.

WHO (World Health Organization)
　　1966　Measurement of the Public Health Importance of Bilharziasis. WHO Technical Report 349:1–93.

Wilbert, J
　　1974　Yukpa Folktales. Los Angeles, Calif.: University of California Latin American Studies Center.

Willems, Emilio
　　1967　Followers of the New Faith: Culture Change and the Rise of Protestantism in Brazil and Chile. Nashville, Tenn.: Vanderbilt University Press.

Williams, Sue Rodwell
　　1973　Nutrition and Diet Therapy. 2d ed. St. Louis: C. V. Mosby.

Wissler, Clark
　　1917　The American Indian. New York.
　　1926　The Relation of Nature to Man in Aboriginal America. New York: Oxford University Press.

Wolf, Eric
　　1955　Types of Latin American Peasantry. American Anthropologist 57:452–71.
　　1956　Aspects of Group Relations in a Complex Society. American Anthropologist 58:1065–1078.

Wood, C., and M. Schmink
　　1979　Blaming the Victim: Small Farmer Production in an Amazon Colonization Project. Studies in Third World Societies 7:77–93.

Woodall, J.
　　1967　Virus Research in Amazonia. Atas do Simpósio sobre a Biota Amazonica 6:31–63.

Woronecki, P. et al.
　　1974　Vertebrate Damage Control Research in Agriculture. Annual Report, Instituto Colombiano Agropecuário. Cali, Colombia.

Yang, W. Y.
　　1965　Methods of Farm Management Investigations. Rev. ed. Rome: Food and Agriculture Organization of the United Nations.

Zerries, O.
　　1954　Wild und Buschgeister in Südamerika. Wiesbaden: Steiner.

Index

ACAR-Pará (*Associação Brasileira de Crédito e Assistencia Rural do Pará*): duties of, 81–82, 165–66; salary of workers, 161 (table); activities organized by, 174–75; extension agents employed by, 173, 222

Achipayas Indians, 11

Achuara Indians, 49

Acre: established, 71; included in *Amazonia legal*, 242n6

African rain forests: size of, 3; trees in, 28; physiological adjustment to, 31; agriculture in, 43, 115–16; population densities in, 51

agricultural cooperatives, 176–77

agriculture, in Amazon Basin: evaluation of, 5, 6, 219–26, 229; effect of temperature on, 35–36; traditional association between fishing and, 51; among aborigines, 53–56; colonial sugar plantations, 58; extractivism hindrance to, 59–63, 66, 69; steps of Brazilian government to forward, 68–84 *passim*; self-sufficient, 94, 95; practiced by caboclos, 99; selection of soil for, 105–12; effective methods of, 114–18; land preparation techniques for, 118–24; changes in soil due to, 124–27; planting practices, 127–36; schedule of tasks in, 133 (table); harvesting and marketing, 136–41; financing of, 138, 152–55 *passim*, 165–68, 180–81, 222–24; success at, among different segments of population, 141–43, 146–50; cattle raising part of, 143–45; mixed, 145–46; economic strategies among practioners of, 150–57; health problems as constraint to, 163, 164 (table), 168, 183, 193, 195, 196, 211–12, 222; importance of education to, 170–71, 175; success in, as criterion

of social standing, 180. *See also* slash-and-burn agriculture

agropolis: description of, 15; as center for administrative functions, 17; Brasil Novo as, near Vila Roxa, 85. *See also* Brasil Novo

agrovilas: description of, 15, 16, 17; importance of good situation for, 18, 85; lack of conformity in side-road, 87; transportaion among, 88; preference for living on land or in, 89; characterized by social distinctions, 180; health conditions in, 193, 197, 210. *See also* Vila Roxa

Alcoa, 76

alfisols: nutrient rich, 25; prominent soil type in tropics, 27; a major soil type in Altamira area, 39, 40, 220, 221; as preventer of erosion at Vila Roxa, 125; corn yields from, 139; growth of cereals on, 224; continuous cultivation possible on, 246n11

Altamira: history of, 8, 11–12, 65, 66; location of, 8, 13; population of, 13 (table); economy of, 13–14, 94; changed by coming of Transamazon Highway, 13–14; as supply center for Transamazon planned communities, 14–15, 16, 90; climate of, 35–38; physical features of, 38–40, 220–21; medical facilities in, 71, 82, 88, 168–69, 211; schools in, 71, 83–84, 169–70; as center for farm colonization, 77, 83 (table); government agents in, 81, 160; SESI services in, 84; location of Vila Roxa in relation to, 85, 210; transportation to and from, 88; migration of Transamazon caboclos to, 100; presence of capybara near, 103; interaction between caboclos and colonization administration in, 105, 108; soil

283

Mundurucu Indians, 47, 56
Mura Indians, 47, 53
Museu Paraense Emilio Goeldi, 72, 242n7

Nambiquara Indians, 42
New Guinea, 43, 217
Northeast Brazil: plantation system in, 65; drought in, 69, 241n2; planting of cowpeas in, 134; *vaqueiros* from, 144; religious traditions from, 177; malnutrition in, 209–10; need to reduce social tensions in, 226; association of root crops with, 223; unequal development of economic sectors of, 242n9
Northeasterners: came as rubber collectors to Amazon, 65; fled drought into Amazon, 69, 70, 71; brought by Transamazon Highway into Amazon, 75; planned to be large percentage of Transamazon settlers, 77, 99, 108, 146; feared migration to Amazon, 78; percent of settlers at Vila Roxa, 89, 90 (table), 172; stereotype of, 146, compared to other Transamazon settlers, 147–50; education among, 170; chose patron-saint for Vila Roxa, 178–79; carriers of disease, 191, 200
Northern Brazil: provided settlers for Vila Roxa, 90 (table); religious traditions from, 177
Northerners: agricultural performance in Transamazon, 147–49 *passim*; education among, 170
Nucleo Colonial do Guama, 72

onchocerciasis, 191, 212
"Operation Amazonia," 73
Orinoco Basin, 24
Orinoco River tribes, 53
Oriximiná (on Trombetas River), 242n8
oxisols: effect of, on structure and function of rain forests, 25; a major soil type in tropics, 27; a major soil type in Altamira area, 39, 40; hindrance to erosion in Vila Roxa area, 235; manioc yields from, 139; on macro-scale maps of Amazon, 219, 220; suitability for growing of cereals, 224

panema, 101, 244n5
Pará: obtained rights to Vitória port, 12; contribution of cocoa to export revenues of, 59; cattle raising in, 75, 76, 145; migrants to Transamazon from, 81; number of Vila Roxa residents

from, 90 (table); *caboclos* from, 100, 108; soil devoted to pasture grass in, 143; included in *Amazonia legal*, 242n6
Paragominas (Pará): site of bauxite holdings, 242n8; weed invasion in pastures, 246n9; failure of cattle ranches in, 247n22
Parakana Indians, 42
Paraná: coffee growing in, 70, 81; number of Vila Roxa residents from, 90 (table); type of Transamazon settlers from, 147, 176
patron-client relationships: in rubber trade, 65; in Transamazon, 93, 95, 163; in Vila Roxa, 173, 179, 180–82, 226
Paumari Indians, 53
Penas Indians, 11
Pentecostals (*crentes*), 88, 170, 176-77
Perimeter Road, 1
Pernambuco, state, 58, 90 (table), 137
Piauí, 90 (table)
PIN (Program of National Integration), 73, 75
planned colonization, problems of, 8
plinthite, 26, 27
podzols, 25, 34, 40
Pombal, Marquis of, 60
Porfirio, José, 11–12, 65
Portugal: occupation of Xingú by, 10–11; demand for turtles, 53, 56, 62; impact on Amazon Basin of conquest by, 58–67; herbal remedies of, 210–11; medical theory brought to Brazil from, 185
Presbyterians, 88
Priestley, Joseph, 63
Protestants, 88, 170, 172, 174, 176-77

Quaternary, 35

rats, 87, 138, 139, 191, 197
religion: provision for, in Transamazon settlements, 17; "interdenominational" church in Vila Roxa, 17, 88, 174; church as developer of social bonds, 159, 182. *See also* Catholics; Protestants
reproductive system problems, 191, 200–201
rice: in economy of Altamira, 13; planting of, 55, 127, 133 (table), 135; growing of, in missions, 60; production of, during Rubber Era, 70; government plan for Transamazon production of, 77; bank financing of, 79,